A CULTURAL HISTORY OF THE SEA

VOLUME 1

A Cultural History of the Sea
General Editor: Margaret Cohen

Volume 1
A Cultural History of the Sea in Antiquity
Edited by Marie-Claire Beaulieu

Volume 2
A Cultural History of the Sea in the Medieval Age
Edited by Elizabeth Lambourn

Volume 3
A Cultural History of the Sea in the Early Modern Age
Edited by Steve Mentz

Volume 4
A Cultural History of the Sea in the Age of Enlightenment
Edited by Jonathan Lamb

Volume 5
A Cultural History of the Sea in the Age of Empire
Edited by Margaret Cohen

Volume 6
A Cultural History of the Sea in the Global Age
Edited by Franziska Torma

A CULTURAL HISTORY OF THE SEA

IN ANTIQUITY
VOLUME 1

Edited by Marie-Claire Beaulieu

BLOOMSBURY ACADEMIC
LONDON • NEW YORK • OXFORD • NEW DELHI • SYDNEY

BLOOMSBURY ACADEMIC
Bloomsbury Publishing Plc
50 Bedford Square, London, WC1B 3DP, UK
1385 Broadway, New York, NY 10018, USA

BLOOMSBURY, BLOOMSBURY ACADEMIC and the Diana logo are
trademarks of Bloomsbury Publishing Plc

First published in Great Britain 2021
This edition published in Great Britain 2024

Copyright © Bloomsbury Publishing, 2021

Marie-Claire Beaulieu has asserted her right under the Copyright, Designs and
Patents Act, 1988, to be identified as Editor of this work.

Cover image © Exekias, "Dionysos Crossing the Sea with Dolphins"
500 B.C.E. Attic eye cup on ceramic in Staatliche Antikensammlungen, Munich

All rights reserved. No part of this publication may be reproduced or
transmitted in any form or by any means, electronic or mechanical, including
photocopying, recording, or any information storage or retrieval system,
without prior permission in writing from the publishers.

Bloomsbury Publishing Plc does not have any control over, or responsibility for,
any third-party websites referred to or in this book. All internet addresses given
in this book were correct at the time of going to press. The author and publisher
regret any inconvenience caused if addresses have changed or sites have
ceased to exist, but can accept no responsibility for any such changes.

Every effort has been made to trace copyright holders and to obtain their
permissions for the use of copyright material. The publisher apologizes for any
errors or omissions and would be grateful if notified of any corrections that
should be incorporated in future reprints or editions of this book.

A catalogue record for this book is available from the British Library.

A catalog record for this book is available from the Library of Congress.

ISBN: HB: 978-1-4742-9901-5
Set: 978-1-4742-9910-7
PB: 978-1-3504-5097-4
Set: 978-1-3504-5130-8

Series: The Cultural Histories Series

Typeset by Integra Software Services Pvt. Ltd.
Printed and bound in Great Britain

To find out more about our authors and books visit www.bloomsbury.com
and sign up for our newsletters.

CONTENTS

LIST OF ILLUSTRATIONS vii
ABBREVIATIONS xi
GENERAL EDITOR'S PREFACE xv
Margaret Cohen

Introduction 1
Marie-Claire Beaulieu

1 Knowledges 19
 Georgia L. Irby

2 Practices 43
 Mirella Romero Recio

3 Networks 59
 Zaraza Friedman

4 Conflicts 79
 Jorit Wintjes

5 Islands and Shores 109
 Gabriela Cursaru

6 Travelers 129
 Raimund Schulz

7 Representations 153
 Valérie Toillon

8	Imaginary Worlds *Iris Sulimani*	173

NOTES	193
BIBLIOGRAPHY	209
NOTES ON CONTRIBUTORS	231
INDEX	234

ILLUSTRATIONS

0.1	Pottery, red-figured Calyx-Krater (bowl for mixing wine and water): the sun and the stars	4
0.2	Mermaid at Clonfert Cathedral	11
0.3	Heracles roasts sacrificial meat. Athenian white-ground lekythos, *c.* 500 BCE	15
0.4	A view from Glastonbury Tor in 2014	18
1.1	The shield of Achilles by Angelo Monticelli	22
1.2	Theoretical reconstruction of Anaximander's map	24
1.3	The diurnal tidal cycle according to Poseidonius	32
1.4	Fresco of dolphins in a seascape in the Megaron of the Queen, Knossos, Crete	37
1.5	Fresco of Minoan fisherman with tuna and mackerel, Akrotiri, *c.* 1600 BCE	38
1.6	Fresco from the Tomb of the Diver, Paestum, *c.* 470 BCE	39
2.1	The sacred promontory between Cape Saint Vincent and Sagres (Portugal) with the lighthouse at present	47
2.2	The kothon at Motya (Sicily). The sacred pool of Baal 'Addir/Poseidon	48

2.3	Anchor discovered at Cape Palos (Murcia, Spain) with inscriptions to Zeus Casio and Aphrodite *Sozousa*. In Laymond and Jiménez de Cisneros y Hervás (1906)	50
2.4	Lead anchor stock	50
2.5	The strait of Messina from Torre Faro (Sicily)	53
3.1	Map of trading goods in the second century BCE	61
3.2	Timber transport by sea; Sargon's II palace at Khorsabad	63
3.3	Weighing lead or gold ingots by the shore	66
3.4	Lead ingots from Caesarea Maritima, Israel	67
3.5	Tabularius recording of a cargo of bag-shape jars; Piazzale delle Corporazioni, Ostia, Italy	73
3.6	*Kyrenia Liberty* at sea trial, Cyprus	76
4.1	Early amphibious operations, twenty-third century BCE	88
4.2	The battle in the Delta. *(a)* Egyptian ship turning over a ship full of enemy warriors (detail from Medinet Habu reliefs); *(b)* Egyptian sailor using a rope or a grappling hook to overturn an enemy vessel	91
4.3	The eastern Mediterranean, 490 to 413 BCE	95
4.4	Important battles, 540 to 201 BCE	100
4.5	Major naval operations in northwestern Europe, 55 BCE to 357/358 CE	103
4.6	The Mediterranean, 31 BCE to 533 CE	105
4.7	Graffito from the Roman fort at Vechten, possibly depicting a Roman warship	106
4.8	Graffito from the Roman harbor of Berenike (Egypt), possibly depicting a trading vessel on the Indian route, *c.* 25 to 50 CE	107
5.1	Poseidon holding a trident, with the island Nisyros on his shoulder, battling a Giant (probably Polybotes)	112
5.2	The map of the Cyclades. Compiled by the Danish cartographer Johann Lauremberg (1590–1658)	113

ILLUSTRATIONS   ix

5.3 Mosaic of Haidra (Tunisia) representing cities and islands of the
     Mediterranean, *c*. the end of the third or the beginning of the
     fourth century   117

6.1 Model of a penteconter ("fifty-oared"), the standard galley of
     colonization and sea battle in the archaic period   134

6.2 Phoenician and Greek colonization in the Archaic period
     (*c*. 800–550 BCE)   135

6.3 Statue of Pytheas outside the Palais de la Bourse, Marseille   140

6.4 The so-called Lenormant Relief, *c*. 410 BCE, from the Athenian
     Acropolis, showing the rowers of an Athenian trireme ("with
     three banks of oars")   143

6.5 The connections between the Mediterranean and the
     Far East (China) in the first century CE over land and sea   148

7.1 Terracotta stirrup jar with octopus, 1200–1100 BCE   155

7.2 Shipwreck crater, 760–700 BCE. Ischia sp. 1/1.
     Based on Boardman 1998: fig. 161   157

7.3 Kylix (cup) black- and red-figure, 510–500 BCE. London,
     British Museum E2   160

7.4 Terracotta vase in the form of a ketos, *c*. 650–600 BCE   162

7.5 Altar of Domitius Ahenobarbus. The wedding of
     Poseidon and Amphitrite, end of second century BCE.
     Munich, Glyptothek inv. 239   167

7.6 Detail from a mosaic with the God Oceanus and the triumph
     of Neptune and Amphitrite, from Utica, Tunisia, second to third
     century CE. Tunis, Musée National Du Bardo   169

7.7 Odysseus's ships destroyed by the giant Laestrygonians
     Scene from the Odyssey. Wall painting from a private
     house on the Esquiline Hill, Rome, mid to first century BCE   170

7.8 Thalassa. Personification of the sea. Mosaic from the
     Church of the Apostle, Madaba (Jordan), *c*. 568 CE   171

8.1 Imaginary islands   176

8.2 The voyage of Euhemerus   181

8.3	The journey of Zeus	182
8.4	The journey of Iambulus	184
8.5	The journey of Sesostris	192

ABBREVIATIONS

A. *Suppl.*	Aeschylus, *Suppliant Women*
[Aeschylus] *Ag.*; *Eum.*	Aeschylus, *Agamemnon*; *Eumenides*
Acts	Acts of the Apostles
Aelian, *On Animals*	Aelian, *On the Nature of Animals*
Alc.	Alciphron, *Letters*
Ant. Lib., *Met.*	Antoninus Liberalis, *Metamorphoses*
Anth. Pal.	*Palatine Anthology*
Ap. Rhod.	Apollonius Rhodius, *Argonautica*
Apollod.	Apollodorus, *Library*
Apollod. *Epit.*	Apollodorus, *Epitome*
Apollonius, *Arg.*	Apollonius Rhodius, *Argonautica*
App., *B C iv.*	Appian, *Civil War*
Apul., *Met.*	Apuleius, *Metamorphoses*
Arat. *Phaen.*	Aratus, *Phaenomena*
Arist., *Met.*	Aristotle, *Meteorologica*
Arr., *Per.*	Arrian, *Periplus*
Artem., *Onir.*	Artemidorus, *The Interpretation of Dreams*
Athenaeus	Athenaeus, *The Deipnosophists*
Avienus	Avienus, *Ora Maritima*
Bacchyl.	Bacchylides, *Odes*
Becker, *Anecd.*	Immanuel Becker, *Anecdota Graeca* (Berlin 1814)
Caes., *BG*	Caesar, *Gallic Wars*
Call. *HDelos*	Callimachus, *Hymn to Delos*
Cassiod., *Var.*	Cassiodorus, *Variae epistolae*
Cassius Dio	Cassius Dio, *Roman History*

Cic. *de nat. deor.*	Cicero, *De natura deorum*
Cic., *Fam.*	Cicero, *Epistulae ad familares*
CIL	*Corpus Inscriptionum Latinarum*
D.C.	Cassius Dio, *Roman History*
D.H.	Dionysius of Halicarnassus, *Roman Antiquities*
De Principis Instructione	Gerald of Wales, *De Principis Instructione*
Dio Chrys., *Or.*	Dio Chrysostom, *Orations*
Diod. Sic.	Diodorus Siculus, *Bibliotheca Historica*
D.L.	Diogenus Laertius, *Lives and Opinions of Eminent Philosophers*
Dion. Hal.	Dionysius of Halicarnassus, *Roman Antiquities*
Eur., *Andr.*; *Cyc.*; *Hel.*; *Her.*; *Hipp.*; *Hec.*; *IA.*; *Ion*; *Phoen.*; *Thes.*	Euripides, *Andromache*; *Cyclops*; *Helen*; *Heracles*; *Hippolytus*; *Hecabe*; *Iphigenia at Aulis*; *Ion*; *Phoenician Women*; *Theseus (fragments)*
Eust., *Od.*	Eustathius, *Commentary on the Odyssey*
FrGrHist	Felix Jacoby, *Fragmente der Grieschichen Historiker* (Berlin 1923–)
Frontin., *Aq.*	Frontinus, *The Aqueducts of Rome*
Hdt.	Herodotus, *Histories*
Hes., *Cat.*	Hesiod, *Catalog of Women*
Hes., *Op.*	Hesiod, *Works and Days*
Hes., *Theog.*	Hesiod, *Theogony*
Hes., *Frg.*	Hesiod, Fragments
h.Hel.	*Homeric Hymn to Helios*
h.Merc.	*Homeric Hymn to Hermes*
h.Sel.	*Homeric Hymn to Selene*
h.Ap.	*Homeric Hymn to Apollo*
h.Dem.	*Homeric Hymn to Demeter*
h.Dion.	*Homeric Hymn to Dionysus*
h.Diosc.	*Homeric Hymn to the Dioscuri*
Himer., *Or.*	Himerus, *Orations*
Hist. Aug. Gall.	*Historia Augusta, Gallienus*
Hom., *Il.*; *Od.*	Homer, *Iliad*; *Odyssey*
Hor., *Ars P.*; *Epod.*	Horace, *Ars Poetica*; *Epodes*
Hyg., *Fab.*	Hyginus, *Fabulae*
IG	*Inscriptiones Graecae*
Joseph., *Vit.*	Josephus, *The Life*
Juv.	Juvenal, *Satires*
LIMC	*Lexicon Iconographicum Mythologiae Classicae*
Livy	Livy, *Ab Urbe Condita*
Lucan	Lucan, *Pharsalia*
Luc. *VH, Ddeor.*	Lucian, *True History, Dialogues of the Gods*

[Lucian] *DMar.*	Lucian, *True History, Dialogues of the Sea Gods*
Lyc. *Alex.*	Lycophron, *Alexandra*
Lyc. *Al. Schol.*	Lycophron, *Scholia ad Alexandram*
Mart., *Epigr.*	Martial, *Epigrams*
Mela	Pomponius Mela, *Geography*
Mimn.	Mimnermus, *Elegies*
NA	Aelian, *On the Nature of Animals*
Navigatio	*Navigatio Sancti Brendani Abbatis*
Ora	Avienus, *Ora Maritima*
Orph. Arg.	*Orphica Argonautica*
Ov., *Am.*; *Fasti*; *ex Ponto*; *Ibis.*; *Met.*; *Trist.*	Ovid, *Amores*; *Fasti*; *Epistulae ex Ponto*; *Ibis*; *Metamorphoses*; *Tristia*
P. Oxy., P.Teb.	Papyri of Oxyrhynchus, of Tebtynis
Paus.	Pausanius, *Description of Greece*
Pers., *Sat.*	Persius, *Satires*
Phaedr., *Fab.*	Phaedrus, *Fabulae*
Pherec.	Pherecydes
Philostr., *Her.*	Philostratus, *Heroicus*
Phot.	Photius, *Lexicon*
Pind., *Nem.*; *Ol.*; *Pyth.*	Pindar, *Nemean Odes*; *Olympian Odes*; *Pythian Odes*
Isthm., *HZeus*; *Paeans*	*Isthmian Odes, Hymn to Zeus*; *Paeans*
Pl., *Cri.*; *Phaed.*; *Phdr.*; *Ti.*; *Resp.*	Plato, *Critias*; *Phaedo*; *Phaedrus*; *Timaeus*; *Republic*
Plb.	Polybius, *Histories*
Plin., *NH*	Pliny the Elder, *Natural History*
Plut., *Mor.*; *Vit. Thes.*; *Sert.*; *De Is. et Os.*	Plutarch, *Moralia*; *Theseus*; *Sertorius*; *Isis and Osiris*
PMG	Denys Page, *Poetae Melici Graeci* (Oxford, 1962)
Praep. evang.	Eusebius, *Praeparatio evangelica*
Procop., *Vand.*	Procopius, *The Vandal War*
ps.-Arist. *Mir. ausc.*	Pseudo-Aristotle, *Mirabilia Auscultationes*
Pseud. Scyl.	Pseudo-Scylax, *Periplus*
Ptol., *Geog.*	Ptolemy, *Geography*
Q.S.	Quintus Smyrnaeus, *Posthomerica*
Pet. *Satyricon*	Petronius, *Satyricon*
Schol. Ap. Rhod.	Scholia to Apollonius Rhodius, *Argonautica*
Schol. *Od.*	Scholia to the *Odyssey*
Sen., *HF*; *Oed.*	Seneca the Younger, *Hercules Furens*; *Oedipus*
Sen., *Quaest. Nat.*	Seneca the Elder, *Quaestiones Naturales*
Serv., *ad Aen.*	Servius, *Commentary to Vergil's Aeneid*
SIG	*Sylloge Inscriptionum Graecarum*

Solin.	Solinus, *The Wonders of the World*
Soph., *Aj.*; *Phil.*; *Trach.*	Sophocles, *Ajax*; *Philoctetes*; *Women of Trachis*
Stesich.	Stesichorus, *Odes*
Stob.	Stobaeus, *Anthology*
Str.	Strabo, *Geography*
Suet., *Aug.*; *Iul.*; *Tib.*	Suetonius, *Life of Augustus*; *Life of Caesar*; *Life of Tiberius*
Tac., *Ann.*	Tacitus, *Annals*
TEGP	Daniel Graham, *The Texts of Early Greek Philosophy* (2010)
Theoc., *Id.*	Theocritus, *Idylls*
Theophr.	Theophrastus, *Historia Plantarum*
Thuc.	Thucydides, *The Peloponnesian War*
Tzetz., *ad Lyc. Al.*	Johannes Tzetzes, *Commentary to Lycophon, Alexandra*
Val. Max.	Valerius Maximus, *Memorable Deeds and Sayings*
Vell.	Velleius Paterculus, *Roman History*
Verg., *Aen.*; *G.*	Vergil, *Aeneid*; *Georgics*
Xen., *An.*	Xenophon, *Anabasis*

GENERAL EDITOR'S PREFACE

MARGARET COHEN

Over the past thirty years, oceanic studies has emerged in the humanities as a leading interdisciplinary field. It owes its importance to its capacity to give an account of globalization spanning millenia that is robustly cross-cultural. As this new field has taken shape, it has both incorporated and revised an earlier generation of scholarship, which attended to maritime transport, naval warfare, and global exploration, often within a framework of national history. Contributions of oceanic studies range across scales: from showing how maritime transport and marine resources join separated lands into water-based regions to resurrecting how a meeting on a beach between societies never before in contact could create intractable structures of domination to revealing the impact of a single photograph from outer space of the earth as a blue planet. Today, oceanic studies aims to tell the stories of all who have traveled the seas: professionals, adventurers, passengers, forced migrants—and animals.

Further, this emerging field recognizes that the seas are a rich realm for the imagination, all the more so given the paradoxical tension between their remoteness for many people and yet their life-sustaining importance. It is telling that a poet, the Nobel prize-winning Derek Walcott, has penned the memorable phrase, "The Sea is History." At the same time, the imagination of the seas is not purely fanciful but rather takes shape in relation to located marine environments and how humans practice them, leading humanists to engage the reality of the physical world. When modern oceanography and marine biology took shape in the nineteenth century, these sciences established the oceans as a nonhuman natural realms, despite their prehistory in mixed, practical knowledge conjoining environmental curiosity with the pursuit of power, or wealth. Since this disciplinary cleavage, the sea has time and time again shown us the need to recognize its existence for and with humans, as well as in itself.

In the twenty-first century, the importance of the sea in world-defining developments, including second-wave globalization, postcolonial conflict and climate change, has become so evident that its social and cultural reality cannot be ignored. In the words of Franziska Torma, volume editor of *The Global Age*, such developments have "forced us to 'think science and humanities' together, because science provides data and humanities 'translate' them into social and academic interpretation; this opens up historical perspectives on the oceans from antiquity to the present" (Franziska Torma, personal communication, May 2020). Whether drawing on nautical archaeology resurrecting sunken cities and shipwrecks, or using scientific research about the impact of climate change on coastal communities, oceanic studies is taking the lead among humanities fields in pursuing this urgent, if vexed, disciplinary crossing.

In editing *A Cultural History of the Sea*, I have been fortunate to work with volume editors who have made major contributions to setting the agenda of oceanic studies in its twenty-first-century form. Taken together, their expertise encompasses the oceans of the globe, notably the Mediterranean, the Indian Ocean, the Atlantic, and the Pacific and includes the history of science and the environment as well. We have launched our project from our institutional homes in transatlantic universities, even as we mark our starting point at once to acknowledge and brush against the grain of Western-oriented perspectives. Further, readers will see that the abstraction Western itself fractures when subjected to the pressure of water-based movement and seafaring practices. Thus, maritime travel creates far-flung contact zones across thousands of kilometers, which cannot be reduced to the orientation of the West, even if Western Europe may have been a point of departure. These contact zones are characterized by extreme social complexity, which modify those whom they involve, and the importance of the physical environment in such contact zones creates yet another set of considerations. The demands of a sea-oriented life, moreover, unmoor those who work on ships to the point where they may be a culture unto themselves, unnervingly apart from their societies, due to such factors as the rigors of shipboard living and the multicultural *habitus* even on vessels enforcing the routes of empire.

Our interest in conveying the heterogeneous histories that meet on the sea extends to the themes we have chosen for our series' organization. A unique feature of the Bloomsbury *Cultural History* series is to devise eight chapter headings for each volume that can run from antiquity to the present. These headings address culture understood in its expansive, anthropological sense: as designating the diverse realms of practices organizing the structures of a society. In the case of the seas, important aspects include but are not limited to war, technology, and trade at sea, scientific knowledge, as well as myth and imagination. We defined our themes in a fashion that would enable contributors to present a democratic history. Thus, for example, we framed histories of "War and Empire," at sea as "Conflicts," to take account of the many scales of violent struggles at sea, including frames of state-supported navies, non-state actors, and the violence of shipboard life, ranging from mutinies to treatment of passengers and transport of the enslaved. Or thus, we reframed the theme "Science and Technology," as "Knowledges," to provide an opportunity to include knowledge beyond the strict boundary of science. Such knowledge ranges from philosophical speculation in classical antiquity to sea knowledge and practice outside Western paradigms.

In organizing the chapters, we have respected conventional Western historical periodization, which has been shaped by events on land. At the same time, readers will find within the volumes chapters that take up the question of whether such periodization stops at the shore, due to the previously mentioned pressures of a sea perspective on concepts whose operations are focused toward the land. Thus, the history of Egyptian seafaring and contacts with other cultures of the Mediterranean basin traverses the land-based periodization of this particular culture, traditionally understood in terms of its ruling dynasties, from Greek prehistory through the classical period and into Roman times, roughly the second millennium BCE to the first century CE. Within the modern era, to take the example of a single technology, the years from 1769 to 1989 form one period in the history of navigation, although this epoch runs across three volumes in the series. In 1769, British engineer John Harrison perfected a chronometer that would keep accurate time over a long traverse. With the ability to compare noon during a ship's traverse and noon at an arbitrarily defined starting point— it became the Greenwich Meridian by convention—navigators could finally establish their longitude while a ship was sailing, a development that would vastly improve safety at sea, even if it took decades to expand beyond naval circles. Celestial navigation would remain the best practice for establishing a ship's location until the invention of the global positioning system (GPS) in the third quarter of the twentieth century, which could be dated to 1989, when the US Department of Defense launched a satellite system that would become GPS, replacing with the touch of a few buttons the arduous calculations needed for celestial navigation.

Another dimension to the specificity of sea-based periodization is the timescale of the oceans as a physical environment. For eons marine history moved at a geological pace, but in the age of the Anthropocene we are learning about the human impact on a realm of the planet long considered an inexhaustible resource and a vast power beyond human reach. Such an impact can occur within a person's lifetime, as is the case, for example, with melting ice caps at the poles, which have drastically diminished in satellite visualizations, dating back to 1979 (Starr 2016).[1] This impact in turn is affecting societies, from Indigenous inhabitants of the Arctic to farmers around the world, who depend on weather patterns disrupted by global warming. Yet further entangling human and geological timescales at sea, melting ice caps open up new shipping routes through the Arctic, which present potential for a greater human footprint there.

The global consequences of polar ice melt exemplify how a sea perspective reorients terrestrial units of geographical analysis, which is the case not only for the oceans as an environment but also for the oceans as an arena of human practice. Chapters across the series reveal how state-drawn borders may be less important for cultures at sea than fluid spaces defined by natural features, and how islands or coasts eccentric from the perspective of land-based history may play an outsized, formative role in a nation's oceanic ambitions. Further, sea transport produces states that are at once joined under the same flag yet are also territorially disconnected, with unique and uniquely difficult administrative features. Yet another challenge, at the lexical level, is that when we try to express oceanic phenomena with language from the land, we reach to unsatisfactory imagery that impedes understanding. A good example today is the great "garbage patch" of pollution in the Pacific Ocean. The figure of a "patch" misleadingly limits its reach and does not capture the microscopic pervasion of plastic in sea water.

The seas are vast expanses, whose study drives home the point that any research is necessarily fragmentary and located. Contributors to these volumes include established and emerging voices, who have written chapters that are original research around our central themes rather than summaries of secondary literature. Volume editors have encouraged their contributors to present their insights in whatever way they thought would best bring out the originality of their topic and suit their disciplinary expertise. Some have used the narrative of a survey. Others have taken a single event as their canvas, whether the event is exemplary or tellingly anomalous. Yet others have spun out their questions at the scale of one marine environment.

Such flexibility is also important because "the sea" of our series' title is not one thing. Rather, the saltwater element is culturally constructed and imagined in widely different ways, depending on who is engaging with it and to what ends. This range is evident as well in the rich imagery accompanying the chapters, which is another feature of the *Cultural History* series. Thus, readers will see how in antiquity, the sea was never represented directly but rather suggested metonymically on frescoes and vases, with depictions of fish, ships, or mythological sea creatures. Grand seascapes, exhibiting the ocean as a theatre of awe, in contrast, compelled transatlantic audiences in the Enlightenment and Romantic eras. One constant across centuries are practical charts, which have used a variety of methods, shaped by different epistemes and environments, to find and mark paths across the waters, all nonetheless sharing an aim of safety. To draw a parallel between navigating vast, and in many cases, untracked waters and emergent areas of scholarship: as readers constellate the diverse subjects and approaches collected in this series, I hope they will gain a better understanding of the abiding, pervasive human interface with the seas as well as recognize new and future directions for oceanic studies.

Introduction

The Real and the Imaginary Sea and the Legacy of Antiquity

MARIE-CLAIRE BEAULIEU

In book 11 of the *Odyssey*, Odysseus sails westward to the Ocean to visit the seer Tiresias in Hades. This mythical river encircles the world: it lies beyond the saltwater sea and the lands of men. Visiting the kingdom of the dead by sailing to the Ocean is the only way for Odysseus to learn the way back home to Ithaca.

It may seem curious that Odysseus enters the world below by sailing to the furthest reaches of the sea. However, in the Greek worldview, the horizon, where Odysseus stands, is the place where the earth, the sea, and the sky meet. Euripides (*Hippolytus* 742–50) calls the Ocean σεμνὸν τέρμονα οὐρανοῦ, "the holy boundary of the sky." He says that this area, beyond the Pillars of Heracles (Gibraltar) is forbidden to sailors: it is the territory of the gods (Nesselrath 2005; Segal 1965). It is where Zeus's palace is and where the Hesperides guard the fruit of immortality. According to Hesiod, it is also where the chasm of Tartarus opens, the deepest part of the Underworld:

ἔνθα δὲ γῆς δνοφερῆς καὶ Ταρτάρου ἠερόεντος
πόντου τ' ἀτρυγέτοιο καὶ οὐρανοῦ ἀστερόεντος
ἑξείης πάντων πηγαὶ καὶ πείρατ' ἔασιν

[This is where, in order, are the sources and ends of the dark earth, misty Tartarus, the barren sea and the starry sky.]

(*Theogony* 736–8)

The Ocean is therefore a point of contact between different planes of existence, namely the mortal realm, the Underworld, or Hades, and the world of the gods, Olympus. Hesiod explains that all these realms are connected through the hydrological network. The Ocean is the father of all rivers, chiefest of whom is Styx, the river of the Underworld (*Theogony* 337–70).

In this way, the Ocean connects the different parts of the world in a physical manner. However, the Ocean also connects the world in a spiritual manner. Hesychius, commenting on line 292 of the *Theogony*, writes that the Ocean is the "air in which the souls of the dead leave." In this view, the Ocean is the path to the afterlife. And indeed, line 292 of the *Theogony* describes Heracles' "crossing of the path of Ocean" (διαβὰς πόρον Ὠκεανοῖο) during the labors that eventually earn his immortality.

Not only is the Ocean thought to be a path. The word *pontos* "sea," derives from the Proto-Indo-European (PIE) root *pent-, which refers to a passageway from one shore to another, especially one that is difficult to cross (Chantraine 1968: *s.v.* "Pontus").[1] Indo-Iranian cognates of the word, for instance Sanskrit *pántāḥ*, designate a path strewn with obstacles. The same PIE root also yields Greek πατεῖν "to walk," Latin *pons* "bridge," and English *path*, all of which relate to the idea of crossing a distance or, as in the case of *pons*, an obstacle (Householder and Nagy 1972: 767–8).[2] Accordingly, the sea is often metaphorically represented as a path or road, as in ὑγρὰ κέλευθα "the watery ways" (e.g. *Od*. 3.71); ἰχθυόεντα κέλευθα "the fish-filled ways" (e.g. *Od*. 3.177); ἠερόεντα κέλευθα "the misty ways" (*Od*. 20.64); εὐρώεντα κέλευθα "the dank ways" (*Od*. 24.10); πόρους ἁλός "the paths of the sea" (e.g. *Od*. 12.259); and θαλάσσης εὐρυπόροιο "of the broad-wayed sea" (e.g. *Il*. 15.381). In the *Odyssey*, 9.260, Odysseus gives an account of his labors on the paths of the sea: παντοίοις ἀνέμοισιν ὑπὲρ μέγα λαῖτμα θαλάσσης, οἴκαδε ἱέμενοι, ἄλλην ὁδὸν ἄλλα κέλευθα ἤλθομεν, "we [were driven] by all sorts of winds over the great chasm of the sea, wishing for home, and we went on this and that road." In this way, the sea is a connector, a point of contact between various areas and peoples of the world; by the same token, the sea, in its mythological idealization as the Ocean, is a point of connection with the spiritual world, the residences of the dead and the gods.

The ambiguity of the sea as both a physical and a spiritual reality is expressed in its Homeric epithets. The sea bears the curious epithet *pontos atrugetos*, "the barren sea," and is also paradoxically called *pontos ichtuoentos*, "the fish-filled sea" (e.g. *Od*. 14.135–6). The "barren sea" evokes the fruitlessness of saltwater, its complete sterility, whereas the "fish-filled sea" seems to evoke nourishment. But perhaps the two are not so antithetical. While it is undeniable that the ancients consumed fish, in particular the wealthier classes of society, the epithet may actually evoke a darker aspect of the sea, namely the fish devouring the bodies of shipwrecked sailors, as famously represented on the Pithekoussai krater (see Valérie Toillon's contribution in this volume, Figure 7.2. See Mirella Romero Recio, this volume, for the religious implications of death at sea. See also Sacks 1989; Savoldi 1996).

The "barren sea," upon further examination, also points to the ambiguous nature of the sea in ancient thought. The ancients used water widely for purification rituals (Ginouvès 1962; Parker 1983). They had specific rules about using fresh water from an underground source (usually a spring or well) instead of surface run-off for ritual purposes. However, in some cases, purification rituals could require saltwater, for instance a fourth-century BCE regulation from Ceos, which prescribed the use of saltwater to purify the houses of the recently deceased (*IG* XII.5 593 = *LSCG* 97, A.14–17. See Parker 1983: 38; Beaulieu 2018). This kind of purification is dramatized in Euripides' *Hecuba* (609–14), where the queen gives a funeral bath to her daughter Polyxena using saltwater, stressing the young woman's eternal sterility as she becomes the Bride of Hades, a common tragic trope for women who die before marriage (Rehm 1994). Saltwater is in fact such a powerful agent of purification that it can serve functions beyond the mortal realm, and purify the gods. Every year, the Athenians washed the statue of Athena in the saltwater of the harbor at the festival of the Plynteria (Sourvinou-Inwood 2011), while hymns speak of celestial bodies such as the moon and stars renewing their brightness daily in the waters of the Ocean (*Il.* 18.483–9; *Od.* 23.347; Mimn. 11.4 (West) 2; *h.Sel.* 7–8; *h.Merc.* 68–9; *h.Hel.* 15–16; Stesich. 8, 1–3 (*PMG*); Hes., *Op.* 566). A krater in the British Museum shows this scene, where the stars, personified as young men, dive in the water of the Ocean under the eyes of the retreating Night and oncoming Day (Figure 0.1).

This volume will explore the tension between the realities of the sea-oriented lifestyle of the ancient Greeks and Romans and the worldview attached to this lifestyle, as expressed in religious and artistic practices. Indeed, the ancients focused their lifestyle heavily upon the Mediterranean, which connected the Greek world to its neighbors as early as the second millennium BCE, and which the Romans came to call *mare nostrum*, "our sea." The Mediterranean was thus a vector of growth in all aspects of ancient life, conveying ideas, beliefs, and knowledge as well as commercial goods and the means for warfare. Many broad-ranging studies in the field of Classics address the connectedness afforded by the Mediterranean, as will be found in the extensive bibliography included in this volume.

However, the ancient world was connected far beyond the reaches of the Mediterranean. The Near East, Northern Europe, India, Western Africa, and even China all appeared on ancient itineraries at one time or another. As connections with distant lands were forged and lost, so the ancient cultures and practices of seafaring evolved to serve different needs. Interestingly, new knowledge about distant places only seemed to make the world larger, as the

FIGURE 0.1 Pottery, red-figured Calyx-Krater (bowl for mixing wine and water): the sun and the stars. © The Trustees of the British Museum.

ancients kept imagining farther and farther lands to project their imagination (see the contributions by Raimund Schulz and Iris Sulimani in this volume). In this way, the knowledge and practices of seafaring went hand in hand with imagination, both shaping and shaped by the ancient worldview.

The chapters in this volume address the multilayered and often, to a modern mind, contradictory meanings of the sea in antiquity. One such apparent contradiction is the distinction between the sea, which usually meant the Mediterranean, and the Ocean, a mythical concept. One may think that growing scientific observations and increased oceanic travel through the centuries may have dispelled mythical thinking about the Ocean. However, Georgia L. Irby's paper on Knowledges of the Sea explains that investigations and scientific observations about the Ocean influenced cartography and geography, but only in a limited way. Indeed, these disciplines were mostly concerned with the practicalities of sailing from one point to another, but the Ocean was a cosmological concept that bounded the world. Thinkers from the end of the archaic period down to Roman times grappled with theories about the shape of the world and its composition, in which Ocean played a major role as an organizing principle. In this way, as Irby demonstrates, maritime exploration and observations on tides, currents, and other oceanic phenomena contributed, rather than detracted from, the speculation about the nature of the mythical Ocean.

With the Ocean and, by extension, the sea, taking such an important role as a vector of mythical and religious thought, we may wonder how communication with the divine functioned in this context. Mirella Romero Recio examines religious practices at sea, founded upon the universal fears experienced by sailors, chiefly shipwreck. Out of this specific community of worshippers arose particular forms of communication with the divine that sought to obtain protection from the innumerable dangers of the sea. Sailors feared that their bodies would be lost at sea in case of shipwreck, thus preventing the administration of funeral rites and entrance into the afterlife. Perhaps unsurprisingly, sailors created their own places of worship, often in the open air and near the coasts, on promontories and capes visible from the sea. Their dedications often included the tools of their trade, such as anchors and votive vessels. Through careful examination of these sacred places and offerings, as well as the texts detailing the religious practices that animated this worship, Romero Recio shows that the religion of mariners had important cross-cultural commonalities all around the ancient Mediterranean.

The fears experienced by sailors were motivated by frequent shipwrecks, which, paradoxically, are today a boon for the fast-developing field of underwater archaeology. From these sunken ships, Zaraza Friedman gathers information on the types of merchantmen that plied the Mediterranean. Using further evidence from mosaics, graffiti, murals, and literary sources, she paints a vivid picture of the commercial activity that flourished in the ancient world, focusing particularly on the span of time between the Hellenistic age and the early Byzantine period, unraveling the complex trade networks that criss-crossed the Mediterranean. The types of cargo transported by these merchantmen is interesting and often surprising, ranging from fine foods to silk and precious metals, as well as staples such as olive oil. The question of how the cargo was arranged is also important, since a poorly balanced load could lead to shipwreck.

However, shipwreck was not always accidental, and conflict at sea was common. These conflicts were grounded in commercial and political interests, which were usually so entangled as to be quite indistinguishable from one another. In addition, piracy and private actions were quite common. For this reason, unlike most scholars of ancient naval warfare, Jorit Wintjes shies away from organizing his paper based on the distinction between state actors and non-state actors. Indeed, important state resources could be mobilized by states against non-state actors, such as Pompey's campaign against the Cilician pirates in 67 BCE. Moreover, this distinction is quickly eroding in light of the recognition of vast gray areas, such as the extant use of privateers by state navies up to the 1856 Declaration of Paris, which was also the case in antiquity. Instead, Wintjes proposes a thorough review of the practices of ancient sea warfare while paying attention to the theoretical boundaries of the topic as well as the limitations imposed by the sources: while warfare that was considered a state action may be rather well documented, there are rarely reliable traces of private actors engaged in such warfare, yet the two are deeply interconnected. Wintjes thus examines the history of conflict at sea from Egyptian and Akkadian campaigns near the end of the third century BCE down to the early sixth century CE. He provides an overview of the development of naval and in particular amphibious operations, giving special attention to the design and technology of naval warfare.

Beyond the technology and practicalities of seafaring, the topology of the sea is meaningful in the ancient experience. As seafaring often involved a series of landings on islands, bits of terra firma isolated in the immensity of the sea, the ancients thought of islands as a liminal location where important moments of passage can occur, such as coming of age rituals for men and women, and religious experiences such as epiphanies. In fact, the formation process of islands is often narrated as the gradual fixation of a floating disc of land, indicating the mutable nature of islands and their remote character in the Greek worldview. For this reason, as Gabriela Cursaru shows, islands are often the home of exiles and pariahs, or the place where children whose legitimacy is in question grow up before reclaiming their rights, such as Perseus. Similarly, the seashore on the continent is viewed as a space *betwitxt and between*, that mediates between the unbounded, moving sea and the fixed and regulated inhabited land. In this way, the representation of shores and islands in ancient literature brings to the fore the ancient conception of the sea as a point of connection between the sensible world and what lies beyond.

The practical counterpoint of this conceptual vision of islands is that island-hopping was a common way to cover great distances at sea, starting in the second millennium BCE. As time went by, more daring itineraries were devised and exploration reached ever further, connecting the Mediterranean to the distant civilizations in the Western, Eastern, and Southern oceans. Raimund Schulz discusses the travel networks of antiquity. He shows that exploration and travel were usually motivated by commercial or expansionist objectives. Yet exploration also had a powerful impact on culture, because it moved ideas, technologies, goods, and people around the world. Schulz concludes his chapter on the intriguing question of a planned voyage from Spain across the Atlantic in the beginning of the first millennium CE, and discusses the reasons why this final dream of antiquity never materialized.

Given the rich symbolism of the sea and the large place it took in the ancients' lives, one would expect an equally rich iconography of seascapes in ancient art. Yet Valérie Toillon's chapter on the representation of the sea makes the rather surprising observation that, while the ancients lived by the sea and largely derived their livelihood from the sea, their art practically never depicted seascapes. They mostly represented the sea by metonymy, using fish and other marine animals as a representation of the maritime space. Often, these representations of the sea served as a political symbol to promote the power and wealth of nations. In addition, the conception of the sea as a gateway to the world beyond gave rise to a host of representations including monsters and mythical creatures, which often took on the role of eschatological symbols.

The sea was the locus where the ancients projected their worldview and much of their imagination. As an unbounded and undefined space, it could easily take on the color of any dream or utopia, with islands, unattached to any continent, as the support of paradisiacal worlds. Iris Sulimani shows, in the final chapter of the volume, that the sea was the locus where the ancients projected a better human world, free from the hardships of mortal existence. Sulimani explains that these imaginary worlds were pictured on islands, either in the Mediterranean or in the Ocean, at the four cardinal points. The development of these utopian alternate worlds coincided with opposite changes in the real world, in particular the Roman Civil War. Intellectuals projected their desire for a peaceful society onto far-flung locations which elaborated upon the mythical islands of the Blessed. However, rather than remaining purely imaginary, these islands were thought to be real, and voyages were made to them, stressing once again the continual overlap between the mythical conception of the sea and its realities in antiquity.

THE LEGACY OF ANTIQUITY: THE BRENDAN STORY

This conception of the sea in antiquity is perhaps even more clearly seen when looking through the lens of later centuries, which blended a rich classical heritage with the native cultures of Europe and emerging Christianity. Even in this new context, the powerful symbolism of the sea and its attendant myths conveyed much the same message as in antiquity: the sea is a physical reality that leads to a spiritual one, far beyond the reach of mortals.

The sea plays a very important role in the immensely popular *Navigatio Sancti Brendani Abbatis*, the Navigation of Saint Brendan the Abbott. The sources of the work are complex, blending a strong influence from classical works such as the *Odyssey* with Irish folklore and Christian monastic ideals. The story stems from the life of Brendan, a historical fifth-century abbott of Clonfert in Ireland. Brendan undertook a journey on the North Atlantic with a group of his monks, where they visited many islands. These voyages are attested in various early medieval texts (Barron and Burgess 2002: 15–16). However, the story of Saint Brendan quickly became legendary throughout Europe, with Brendan and the monks setting out to find the *Terra Repromissionis Sanctorum*, the Promised

Land of the Saints, and encountering a host of monsters, mythological figures, and biblical sights along the way.

This story was first written in the tenth century in a culturally neutral dialect of Latin, yet perhaps influenced by the Irish language (Barron and Burgess 2002: 15). Already at that point, the narrative included many aspects of Irish folklore, biblical episodes, and classical legacies. Many have noted the similarities between Brendan's journey and the Irish legends known as *immrama* and *echtrae* (Egeler 2017: 25–64; Tracy 1996). Immrama are set in a Christian perspective (the story of Brendan belongs to this genre), whereas echtrae are properly Irish. However, both genres feature a voyage across numerous islands where the hero, after many adventures, enters the Otherworld. In echtrae, the hero usually encounters magicians and fairies. While the heroes of immrama also encounter supernatural or monstrous beings, usually it is in the context of testing their Christian faith.

By the fifteenth century, the text and narrative of the *Navigatio* had been adapted and translated into virtually every European language. It is even said that Columbus carried a copy on his transatlantic voyage, yet another instance where a real oceanic voyage takes on the color of a mythical journey.

Like Columbus, many still believe that Brendan sailed as far as America. This belief prompted Tim Severin and his crew to reconstruct Brendan's boat, sailing from Ireland through the British Isles, the Faroes, and Iceland in 1976, and then to Greenland and finally Newfoundland in 1977. The boat was a traditional Irish open boat known as a *curragh* with a wooden frame over which animal skins are stretched (Severin 1978). This vessel is described in some detail in the *Navigatio* (*Navigatio* 4),[3] and Severin reproduced it faithfully with materials and techniques that would have been available in the time of Brendan. The crossing was difficult, and consequently makes for an engrossing tale of adventure, just like Brendan's original *Navigatio*. This adventure also proved that such a journey could have been made in a leather boat in the fifth century, long before Columbus or even the Vikings made the journey.

Beyond the history and technology of navigation, why take such pains to reconstruct a legendary voyage? Charting the geography of mythical journeys is nothing new, and in fact already in antiquity, travelers sought out the location of Odysseus's stops in his adventures and pointed out features of the landscape that had changed after Heracles' passage, such as the rocks of Gibraltar, known then as the Pillars of Heracles (Diod. Sic. 4.18, see Pocock 1962; Allen 1976). Roller observes that indeed, "all remote places came to be connected with [Heracles]" (2006: xv). In Brendan's case, the efforts at reconstituting his journey are many, and take him in widely different directions. While Severin argued for the "stepping stone" route through the North Atlantic, others have him take a southerly route to visit Madeira, the Sargasso Sea, the Azores, perhaps even Jamaica, or the coast of the Carolinas! (see Creston 1957: 230–40). This southerly route seems to be warranted by some versions of the Brendan text, which have him seek Paradise "just under Mount Atlas," which is usually placed in North Africa (Babcock 1919). This southerly route is also made more credible by the trade winds and currents of the mid-Atlantic, which would have helped a small boat considerably. How to reconcile such different views? Could this geographical uncertainty point to the spiritual nature of the voyage? Perhaps the journey cannot be charted in geographical terms because it took place in the spiritual realm.

All versions of the *Navigatio*, starting with the earliest tenth-century Latin version, explain that Brendan and his monks embarked on their voyage for spiritual reasons. The monks receive the visit of Barrind (also named Barinthus), an abbott whose son Mernoc heads a community of monks on an island in the sea. Barrind tells Brendan and his monks that, on a visit to Mernoc, he was taken by his son to an island nearby, which was full of fruit, grassy, and filled with precious stones. In the middle of the island flows a river, and when they tried to cross it, a young man appeared, who forbade them to go any further. The young man revealed that the island is the Promised Land of the Saints, where it is never night, because the light of Christ shines on it. With this story, Brendan becomes eager to see the Promised Land of the Saints. Not long after, he sets out from Ireland with fourteen monks (*Navigatio* 1–2).

The voyage thus has an eschatological purpose: to see what lies beyond the reach of human life, the afterlife. In antiquity too, the sea serves as a looking glass into the future: not the future within our lifetime but rather after its end, in the afterlife. The sea god Proteus, captured by Menelaus (*Od.* 4.333–570; Détienne [1967] 1996: 53–67) reveals the way back to Sparta as the lost hero requests. More importantly, Proteus tells Menelaus that after his death, he will live in the Islands of the Blessed, where no toil, disease, or strife will disturb the perfect peace and banqueting of the inhabitants (see Sulimani in this volume). Similarly, another sea god, Nereus, reveals to Heracles the location of the island of the Hesperides, where the apples of immortality are guarded by the Nymphs (Apollod. 2.114). These gods, known to the Greeks as *Halios Geron* (the Old Man of the Sea), embody the sea's function as a pathway between life and afterlife. They can see beyond the reach of mortality. So does Brendan: at the outset of the journey, Brendan foretells the fate of two of the monks (*Navigatio* 5), predicting that they are going to betray the group, a prophecy which is eventually accomplished in the course of the voyage. Brendan prophesizes not only the physical end of his treacherous monks but also the monks' spiritual end. He says "Vobis [Deus] preparabit tetterrimum iudicium" (God will provide a most horrible judgment for you). In this way, the voyage can be seen as the spiritual journey of the faithful through the trials of life, which ends in paradise for those who remain true (Bernard 2007; Iannello 2010).

In some versions of the story, such as the late fourteenth-century Dutch version and the early fifteenth-century German version, Brendan's journey is motivated by a pressing spiritual need. In this version, Brendan once found a book detailing the marvels of God's creation, such as the two paradises above the earth, huge islands in the Ocean, and fish with forests on their backs (Barron and Burgess 2002: 107). In disbelief, Brendan burns the book, incurring the wrath of God. As penance, Brendan is ordered to sail and see marvels in order to write a new book in which he will recount all that he has seen. Brendan's faith itself is at stake, which of course threatens his ultimate destiny in the afterlife. Accordingly, at the end of the tale, once Brendan has dutifully fulfilled his mission, an angel announces that Brendan is ready to die and go to heaven, whereupon the saint dies immediately.

The spiritual nature of Brendan's journey is apparent throughout the narrative in all versions of the story. As Brendan and his monks sail, they encounter a series of monsters and marvels, such as an island with enormous sheep (*Navigatio* 9, the Island of Sheep, often identified with the Shetland Islands or the Faroes) or a place where the sea is clear as crystal, enabling the monks to see all the fish and monsters on the bottom (*Navigatio* 21). Beyond the entertaining storytelling, which no doubt is part of the intent of the narrative, most of these episodes carry a moral or religious lesson. In the case of the Clear Sea episode, the monks are very scared of the fish and ask Brendan to say Mass in hushed tones. However, Brendan celebrates Mass as loudly as he can, and says to his monks that Christ is the lord of all things and of the fish as well. The fish indeed circle around him throughout the ceremony, and then disperse in the sea without harming the monks.

In another place, according to the Dutch and German versions, Brendan and the monks encounter a mermaid:

> When all this was over at last, they resumed their journey and once more got into great difficulties, because they saw a beast coming towards them with a human body and face, but from the waist downwards it was fish. It is called a siren, a very lovely creature with a beautiful human shape; it sings so well and its voice is so sweet that whoever hears it cannot resist sleep and does not know what he is doing. When this sea monster approached them, the shipmen fell asleep and let the ship drift: the monks too forgot themselves completely because of its voice and did not know where they were.
>
> (Barron and Burgess 2002: 141)

This episode recalls a well-known Odyssean episode, where unlike Odysseus's comrades, the monks fall prey to the siren's voice. As for Brendan, in the Dutch version at least, he prays to God to be protected from the creature, perhaps a reminiscence of Odysseus's precautions when he is about to sail past the sirens' island. Indeed, both Brendan and Odysseus make sure they remain aware so as to hear the siren's song without suffering its harmful effects. However, all the monks fall asleep and the ship drifts to an island inhabited by demons, which Brendan has to fend off.

This episode, or one similar to it, may be illustrated in the twelfth-century Clonfert Cathedral, built on the remains of the sixth-century church founded by Brendan. The chancel arch shows a mermaid (Figure 0.2) holding a comb and a mirror. Interestingly, the mermaid episode seems to bear no moral lesson in the text. Yet, the mermaid is the only female figure encountered by Brendan and the monks and therefore may represent their renunciation of women. The

FIGURE 0.2 Mermaid at Clonfert Cathedral. © Wikimedia Commons (public domain).

comb and mirror of the Clonfert mermaid may hint at this, as objects associated with female beauty and sexuality.

Other episodes place Brendan and his monks face to face with biblical stories and with the best and the worst of religious experiences. Their first adventure after leaving Clonfert has them put on to an island with a marvelous castle filled with precious items such as jewels and pieces of armor. While no one seems to inhabit the castle, Brendan and his monks are nonetheless magically fed and they settle in for the night. When all have fallen asleep, Brendan witnesses the devil, in the guise of an "Ethiopian boy," tempting one of the brothers to steal a precious bridle from the house. The brother is the same one, in fact, whose demise Brendan prophesized upon their departure. Brendan prays over him and expels the devil, and the brother dies and goes to heaven, while his body is buried on the spot (*Navigatio* 6–7).

The monks embark again and, not long after this distressing episode, find themselves on an island that is stony and without grass. They settle there and start a cooking fire when the mountain starts shaking. Puzzled, the monks turn to Brendan, who reveals that the island is none other than Jasconius, the largest fish in the Ocean, and the monks promptly depart (*Navigatio* 10). The story vaguely recalls Jonah's encounter with the whale, and seems to signal that the monks have entered a world where the legends of the Bible come to life, and where their faith will be tested, just like Jonah's. Nonetheless, the monks return to Jasconius every year thereafter during their quest, to celebrate Easter on the whale's back (*Navigatio* 15), perhaps to mean that they are at peace with their spiritual mission on the Ocean.

A myriad of such biblical episodes that compare and contrast different experiences of faith populate the *Navigatio*, bringing home the point again and again that the Ocean is the locus of the monks' spiritual experience and contact with God. In the Paradise of Birds, the souls of the angels who fell at the time of Lucifer's destruction are allowed to appear on holy days and Sundays in the forms of white birds, singing God's praises (*Navigatio* 11). On another island, Brendan and his monks spend time in the pious community of Ailbe, where the monks live off miraculous food and do not age (*Navigatio* 12), an interesting reminiscence of the ancient Islands of the Blessed, or perhaps the perfect life of the Hyperboreans (see Romm 1992). Not far from there, however, Brendan and his monks encounter the Island of Smiths (*Navigatio* 23), where the earth puffs up in smoke and ashes. Brendan warns his monks against this place, because it is hell (a forge, with its fire and heat, was a common metaphor for hell in the Middle Ages). However, the episode does not end in biblical fashion: in a scene that is reminiscent of the Cyclops episode in the *Odyssey*, the monks are driven away by an aggressive smith who throws a ball of slag at them and almost capsizes their boat.

Their final encounters in this spiritual journey are two sharply contrasting figures, namely Judas and Paul the Hermit. Judas, the traitor who sold Christ for money, is found by the monks sitting on a rock in the middle of the Ocean, covered only by a small mantle. Judas explains that this is a place of rest for him, and he is allowed to visit it on Sundays and holy days. As demons arrive to bring him back to hell, Brendan intercedes and obtains a promise that Judas will not return to hell until the next morning (*Navigatio* 25). As for Paul the Hermit, after leaving the monastery of Saint Patrick in a self-steering boat, he came to a rock in the Ocean where he lived for thirty years on food provided by an otter. After that, he lived for sixty years on the magical water of a well on his island. He tells Brendan that he is in fact 140 years old, and he is clothed in nothing but the white hair that grows on his body. Paul concludes their interview by telling Brendan that after spending Easter with Jasconius, he will find the objective of his quest, namely the Promised Land of the Saints (*Navigatio* 26). The episode recalls the Old Man of the Sea of antiquity, as Paul prophesizes Brendan's success, which also leads to the saint's death.

This voyage between the different extremes of good and evil and the marvelous diversity of the world brings Brendan and his monks to the end of their quest, the actual barrier between the visible and the invisible worlds. This barrier takes the shape of a dense fog, after which the monks put to shore in a bright light (*Navigatio* 28). The metaphor is manifest: after the darkness of mortality and death comes the light of the afterlife (Beaulieu 2015). Guided by the steward, who lives on an island close by and supplies them with food and drink, they set foot on a land that bears wonderful fruit without the need for agriculture, is full of jewels, and is fanned by a soft ocean breeze, exactly like the ancient paradise of the Islands of the Blessed. As they explore the island, they discover that it is split in two by a river. But when they attempt to cross this river, a young man appears and announces that it is not yet time for Brendan to die. However, strong with the vision of the afterlife finally afforded to them by this initiatory sea voyage, Brendan and his monks return to Clonfert where they spread the story and where Brendan dies shortly after his return.

In most versions, the entire voyage lasts seven years, a highly significant number given the biblical overtones of the story. Seven represents perfection and the completion of God's work, as for instance in the story of Genesis. Interestingly, in the Dutch version of the *Navigatio*, in which Brendan has burned the Book of Creation, the journey lasts nine years. Nine represents a full cycle that brings a change, both in the Bible and in classical antiquity. For instance, Jesus dies at the ninth hour of the day and in the *Iliad* the siege of Troy lasts nine years. In this way, both these versions of the *Navigatio* signal that Brendan and his monks have completed their spiritual achievement.

LIGHT AND DARK: CLASSICAL MYTHOLOGY IN THE BRENDAN STORY

The story of Brendan is imbued with classical myths, in particular the *Odyssey*, whose plot revolves around Odysseus's passage between life and death, and back to Ithaca. This transition is represented as light and darkness, which alternate throughout the *Odyssey* (Marinatos 2010). When the narrative starts, Odysseus is presumed dead, and his son Telemachus goes in search of news, saying that his father is ἄϊστος ἄπυστος, "unheard of and invisible" (*Od.* 1.241–243). And in fact, Odysseus can be said to be traveling in the invisible world, the divine world, where he encounters goddesses such as Circe and Calypso and the monstrous Cyclops Polyphemus. However, turning his back on the immortal life that is offered to him by Calypso, Odysseus chooses to return home. To do so, he must actually visit Hades to question the dead seer Tiresias on the way home. Odysseus finds him on the advice of Circe, sailing to the Ocean, past the country of the Cimmerians, which is shrouded in "fog and clouds" (ἠέρι καὶ νεφέλῃ κεκαλυμμένοι, *Od.* 11.14–19). Much like the Old Man of the Sea, Tiresias prophesizes the trials Odysseus will face upon his return to Ithaca, but, more importantly, he speaks of Odysseus's death: "Death will come to you far away from the sea, a gentle death, when you are worn out by wealthy old age; your people will be happy around you. I say this infallibly" (134–7). The word used by Tiresias to describe the truth of his prophecy is *nemertes*, a characteristic of the prophecies of the Old Man of the Sea (Détienne [1967] 1996: 53–67), indicating that the knowledge that comes from this god is *absolute* truth.

And indeed, at the end of his journey, Odysseus manages to *come out* of the fog: when he enters the harbor of Ithaca, he leaves the mist and enters the bright sun (Bierl 2004). The island of Ithaca, his home, is called "far-seen Ithaca" throughout the *Odyssey* (*Od.* 2.167, 9.21, 13.325, etc.). Incidentally, Odysseus reaches his home through the harbor, which is sacred to Phorcys, another deity that bore the name of Old Man of the Sea (*Od.* 13.96). Odysseus, much like his later counterpart Brendan, has thus acquired the knowledge that resides beyond the sea and attained a higher level of consciousness (Duchêne 1992; Moreau 1994; Scarpi 1988).

Many have seen Gilgamesh as a precursor to Odysseus in his quest for the afterlife (Burgess 1999). Among many adventures, this hero, king of Uruk in the third millennium BCE, attempts to obtain immortality. To do so, he journeys in the dark for twelve days, and then past the Waters of Death to meet Utnapishtim, the sole survivor of the great Flood, who was granted immortality by the gods. However, Gilgamesh fails in both the ways Utnapishtim suggests to obtain immortality. First, he fails to defy sleep and sleeps continuously for seven days. Second, he obtains a rejuvenating plant but loses it to a snake. Gilgamesh must go home empty handed after getting a glimpse of the world beyond.

Perhaps the most compelling ancient precursor to the Brendan story is Heracles. The hero, like Brendan and his monks, must battle his own demons in a series of tasks to move past mortality and earn a paradise that lies beyond the darkness of death. Heracles toils through impossible tasks to redeem the murder of his wife and children, caused by a fit of madness sent over him by Hera. He vanquishes a variety of monsters, such as the Nemean lion and the Lernaean Hydra, in a civilizing journey through Greece where he cleanses the country of the beasts and brigands that plague it. The four last labors, however, are of a different kind. Heracles must navigate to the Ocean, where he will finally earn immortality. These labors include the Cattle of Geryon, the Apples of the Hesperides, Cerberus, and the encounter with Geras. To accomplish these tasks, Heracles must leave the ordinary mortal world and cross beyond the boundary of Night and Day, over the Ocean. He manages this extraordinary journey by borrowing or stealing the solar cup of Helios, the sun god who travels around the world every day, and thus effects the cosmic transition between light and darkness.

The imagery of light and dark that was prevalent in the stories of Odysseus, Gilgamesh, and Brendan is seen again here. The boundary between life and death is a passage between clarity and darkness, or between Day and Night, and this passage also leads down into to the Underworld, or up into Olympus (Chazalon 1995; Ferrari-Pinney and Ridgway 1981). A lekythos (oil flask) in the Metropolitan Museum of Art shows precisely this moment in Heracles' journey. As Heracles prepares to fetch Cerberus from Hades, the misty figures of the Dawn and Night cross paths above the head of Helios (Figure 0.3).

FIGURE 0.3 Heracles roasts sacrificial meat. Athenian white-ground lekythos, *c.* 500 BCE. © Metropolitan Museum of Art, New York, 41.162.29 (public domain).

Further elements of Heracles' last few tasks stress that he is crossing the boundary between light and dark, or between life and death. The island of Geryon, the three-bodied cowherd, is called Erytheia, "The Red Island," or sunset island, thought to be located just outside the Pillars of Heracles, in the entrance to the Atlantic but also near the mythical Ocean. Geryon's dog Orthrys is Cerberus's brother, and also three bodied. They share this unusual feature with only one other mythological figure, the goddess Hecate, a night goddess, patron of magicians, who reigns over crossroads where ghosts wander and frequently visits the Underworld.

Moving on from Erytheia after sacrificing the cattle of Geryon, a task which Diodorus says was the actual token of Heracles' immortality (Diod. Sic. 4.23.2, see Jourdain-Annequin 1989: 520–37), Heracles reaches the island of the Hesperides, the Nymphs of the sunset (*hespera* means "evening" in Greek). There, he wins the golden apples of immortality. However, instead of immediately ascending to Olympus, this complex myth overdetermines Heracles' victory over death, showing him next fetching Cerberus from Hades and finally crushing Geras, the personification of Old Age.[4] These two tasks show the hero returning from the Underworld, a mark that he is impervious to death, and defeating old age, which no mortal can usually escape. After having conquered humanity's worst fear, and its most inevitable destiny, Heracles finally ascends to Olympus where he is reconciled with Hera and marries her daughter Hebe, the goddess of youth, once again stressing that the hero has overcome the limitations of mortality (Holt 1992; Laurens 1996; Winiarczyk 2000).

PUTTING BRENDAN ON THE MAP

Just like Heracles and Odysseus, who both left their mark on Greek geography, the Brendan story is imagined to unfold in real places. Long before Tim Severin undertook to reenact Brendan's crossing of the Atlantic in a leather boat, medieval mapmakers included the Promised Land of the Saints in their charts, conflating them with the ancient Islands of the Blessed, known as *Insulae Fortunatae* in Latin. The Hereford map (*c.* 1300) depicts six Islands of the Blessed in the Western Ocean near which a legend reads: "Fortunatae insulee sex sunt insule Sancti Brendani" (The six Fortunate islands are the islands of Saint Brendan) (Westrem 2001: 389, no. 987). Similarly, the contemporary Ebstorf Map reads: "Insula Perdita. Hanc invenit Scs. Brandanus, a qua cum navigasset, a nullo hominum postea est inventa" (The Lost Island. Saint Brendan discovered it, and after he sailed away from it, no one ever found it again) (Kugler 2007: map 59/10).[5]

Despite the obviously mythical nature of the islands, sailors in the age of discovery attempted to find them, looking in the Canaries, where some ancient authorities placed the Islands of the Blessed (see Sulimani in this volume). The Canaries, so called after the ancient name of one of the Fortunate Islands, Canaria, the Island of Dogs, were explored starting in 1312. When the Canaries did not show any sign of being the wonderful, lush islands filled with precious stones described in the *Navigatio*, sailors looked further. In the sixteenth century, the Portuguese pilot Pedro Vello claimed that he landed on the island of Saint Brendan (Viera y Clavijo [1772] 1991: 45–6). However, a hurricane cut short his exploration of the island and he had to sail away quickly. Later, as he attempted to find the Island of Saint Brendan again, Vello could never return to it, thus apparently confirming the legend on the Ebstorf Map. Similarly, when a Franciscan friar thought he had seen the Island of Saint Brendan from a telescope set up on Tenerife in the Canaries, a dark cloud obscured the horizon and the island was never seen again (45–6). The episode recalls the deep fog that encircles the Promised Land of the Saints and through which Brendan is allowed to sail after his spiritual journey on the Atlantic.

CONCLUSION

The superimposed meanings of the sea in antiquity as both a physical and a spiritual reality have traversed the centuries and blended with evolving cultural and societal beliefs and customs. In this way, the story of Brendan bears remarkable similarities with the paradisiacal island of Avalon, which in Welsh means "the island of fruit." This island was identified as early as the twelfth century as the "island" of Glastonbury (Figure 0.4), which at the time was a low hill surrounded by a vast marshland, nowadays drained. According to Gerald of Wales (*De Principis Instructione* 1.20, fo.107r), the monks who lived in the abbey claimed to have found the bones of Arthur and Guinevere there, thus connecting a place of Christian worship with old Celtic tales. In the *Vita Merlini* (908–940), Barrind (or Barinthus), the same who originally encourages Brendan and his monks to sail for the Promised Land of the Saints in the *Navigatio*,[6] leads Arthur to Avalon after the disastrous battle of Camlann where Arthur and his enemy Mordred give one another a deadly blow. In Avalon, Arthur recovers and it is said that he will one day return to claim his kingdom.

Similarly, the lost world of Atlantis, first described by Plato in *Timaeus* and *Critias*, was a society of wonderful power located on islands in the Ocean, past the Pillars of Heracles, but eventually became overcome by hubris and was submerged by the gods. Throughout the centuries, Atlantis inspired ever-changing philosophical, utopian, and esoteric beliefs, with many enthusiasts searching around the globe for physical traces of the lost continent.[7] In the twentieth century, Atlantis underwent yet a new transformation, taking a major role in Tolkien's legendarium as the lost world of Númenor, a nation once

FIGURE 0.4 A view from Glastonbury Tor in 2014. © Wikimedia Commons (public domain).

close to the gods but who fell due to its growing obsession with mortality and eventually engulfed by the sea.

The notion that humans can attain a higher plane of reality in the farthest reaches of the physical world remains an active motivator, if not for exploration, for creation and for careful consideration of what it means to be human. Stanley Kubrick's 1968 masterpiece *2001: A Space Odyssey* shows man pitted against machine on that very last frontier of the human world, space. The story is couched in Odyssean terms and, interestingly, ends with a return to a reality that is entirely beyond the normal world, beyond the limitations of linear distance and time.

CHAPTER ONE

Knowledges

Knowledge of the Sea in Greco-Roman Antiquity: "Oceanography" and the Physics of Water

GEORGIA L. IRBY

INTRODUCTION

The Alexander Romance (compiled six centuries after Alexander's death) recounts the great general's apocryphal descent into the deep in a spherical glass submarine so that he could discover what was on the seabed. He purportedly reached a depth of about 154 meters (500 feet) (Dowden 1989: 708–9; Oleson 2008: 129). However fanciful the tale might be, it does speak to intense curiosity regarding the dominant geographical feature of the Mediterranean world, the sea, which permeated culture, literature, and society: through commerce and trade, military defense, fishing, and as the setting for tales of adventure and wanderlust. Nautical and hydrological metaphors are sprinkled throughout the literature.[1] At least two hydrological treatises entitled *On Ocean* are known, composed respectively by Pytheas of Massilia (fl.320–305 BCE) and Poseidonius of Apamea (fl.110–51 BCE). Both, unfortunately, survive only in a few tantalizing fragments. Claiming to have reached "Ultima Thule," a distant, icy land in the northern Atlantic, Pytheas was an intellectual pariah whose works were redacted by hostile successors who (unfairly) delighted in showing up Pytheas's

---

Translations from the Pre-Socratics are from Graham (2010) (*TEGP*); translations of Strabo are from Roller (2014). All other translations are the author's.

(perceived) mendacity. Pytheas's observations, furthermore, did not align with Aristotelian interpretations of the natural world. In contrast, Poseidonius was much admired. Like so much Greco-Roman scholarship, Poseidonius's hydrological treatise was broad in scope, covering not just hydrology (including tidal behavior) but also the earth's climactic zones, the size and extent of the inhabited world, celestial phenomena, terrestrial geography, ethnography, and history, as filtered through a Stoic lens.

Hydrological knowledge aligned seamlessly with geography, astronomy, and meteorology, which were all informed by philosophical prejudice. Vacillating coastlines were long part of the scholarly dialogue, and geographers, from Homer onward,[2] dutifully recorded the lengths of coastlines and the proximity of settlements to significant waterways. Ancient nomenclature, however, was equivocal. Is the Mediterranean a "sea" or a "lake"? Generally believed to have an outlet into the northern Ocean, the Caspian was thus considered a "sea," although it fulfilled criteria for classification as a "lake": e.g., fresh water in which serpents could live (Polyclitus in Strabo 11.7.4).[3] The Pontus (Euxine/Black Sea) was so large that lakes were embedded within it (Herodotus 4.85–6). Moreover, Greek employs several words that can be understood broadly as an open expanse of water. *Ōkeanos* (open sea: the primeval source of all other bodies of water) is typically reserved for the waters that were thought to frame the world (i.e., the Atlantic). Cognate with *pateō* (walk), *patos* (something that is trodden or beaten, as in a path), and *pons* (bridge), *pontus* (open sea) suggests water as a passageway.[4] *Pelagos* (high sea, open sea) can refer to particular seas.[5] *Thalassa/thalatta* (sea, salt water)—possibly cognate with *hals* (salt), and perhaps adopted from a pre-Greek word—was usually reserved for the Mediterranean Sea in Greek sources.[6]

Although two important primary sources are lost, it is possible to tease out Greco-Roman knowledge, understanding, and interpretation of the oceans and seas from a long scholarly tradition that begins even before Thales, the first rational Greek thinker. Curiosity about the natural world, especially the Mediterranean Sea and other large bodies of water, was deep. And here we shall explore that trajectory, the evolution of Greek and Roman conceptions of the sea, from Homer's circumambient river to unified philosophies of hydrology expressed in Aristotle, Seneca the Younger, and others. Valuable sources include geographical authors (Eratosthenes, Pliny, Strabo), travelers' accounts, *periploi* (coasting guides), and poets (Homer, Aeschylus, Vergil, among others).

HOMER AND HESIOD

We start with Homer and Hesiod for whom Ocean provided the world's physical framework.[7] In the *Theogony* of Hesiod of Askra (*c.* 750–650 BCE), the world comes into shape as substances are sequentially withdrawn from primeval

Chaos: Gaia (earth), the solid foundation; Tartarus, the primordial edge of creation; Eros, the cosmic principle of Love, which brings together male and female, thus facilitating subsequent generations. The physical components of the orderly universe are then separated from Gaia: Ouranos (Sky), Mountains, and Pontus (the open Sea). Finally, the sexual union of Gaia and Ouranos produces the first generation of fully anthropomorphized deities, the Titans, who include Okeanos (Hesiod, *Theogony* 133) and Tethys (*Theogony* 136), deities of salt and fresh water, respectively. These siblings enjoy such abundant fertility that they produce 6,000 offspring —3,000 daughters and 3,000 sons so that each body of water might have its own patron deity (*Theogony* 346–70).[8] Among their children were Nereus ("the old man of the sea") and his mate Doris whose union produced a prodigious fifty nymphs (Hesiod lists fifty-one by name: *Theogony* 233–64). Thus, Ocean is a generative principle.

Ocean is also a bounding principle. Deep flowing (*Theogony* 265), deep swirling (Hesiod, *Works and Days* 171), and glorious (*Theogony* 215), Ocean is the "complete" or "perfect" river (*Theogony* 242) that encircles the human world and separates the mundane from the divine. Beyond Ocean are the Hesperides (*Theogony* 215), the haunts of the ancient Graeae (*Theogony* 274), the Elysian Plains (*Od.* 4.563), and the Isles of the Blest (Hesiod, *Works and Days* 170–3) where heroes go after death, and the fabled island paradise of Atlantis where powerful, wealthy men flourished until they descended into *hubris* for which their island was submerged beneath the sea (Plato, *Timaeus* 24e–25d; *Critias* 108e–121c). On Ocean's foundations one can find the dwellings of Zeus's Cyclopic allies (*Theogony* 816) and Poseidon's palace (Bacchylides 17). Ocean is also the de-anthropomorphized boundary of the physical world as first envisioned on Achilles' shield in Homer who described the cosmos as a river that flows around the bipartite inhabitable world (*oikoumene*), comprised of a city of peace and one of war (*Il.* 18.607) (Figure 1.1). The paradigm is repeated on a roughly contemporaneous neo-Babylonian clay tablet that delineates a circular map of the "New Empire" around which the "Bitter River" flows. The human world is distinguished by significant topographical details: a mountain, canal, swamp, and cities. Beyond the Bitter River, seven radiating triangles represent islands: the island of the rising sun; the island from which the sun is hidden and nothing can be seen; and the island beyond the flight of birds (Rochberg 2012; cf. Raaflaub and Talbert 2009: 147). As in Greek mythology, these islands beyond the Bitter River may represent dwellings of the gods.

THE PRESOCRATICS

Thales of Miletus (*c.* 600–545 BCE) may have been the first Greek thinker to consider the physical world in a rational way, explaining natural phenomena without reference to the gods. Water seems to have been the foundation of

FIGURE 1.1 The shield of Achilles by Angelo Monticelli. © The History Collection / Alamy Stock Photo.

his theory of material monism, wherein a single element was the source of all material. Ancient sources disagreed on whether Thales actually wrote anything—three astronomical titles are variously attributed to him (*On the Solstice, On the Equinox, Nautical Star Guide*)—and we know about his theories only from second- and third-hand reports. According to our sources, Thales proposed that the earth was a columnar disc resting on water like a ship (*TEGP* 18–20), and that water was the source (*archē*) of the material world (*TEGP* 15–17), seemingly because nourishment is derived from what is moist. The omnipresence of water on Thales's theory explains earthquakes (subterranean waves shaking the earth) and the plentiful supply of river water. The process of condensation and desiccation accounts for the composition and dissolution of the world (which begins and ends with water), as well as windstorms and stellar motion. We do not know if Thales had a theory of the Ocean's origin or nature.

Hydrology (the study of water) cannot be separated from geography and cartography, or even geology. Increasing knowledge and understanding of the oceans in the fifteenth to seventeenth centuries was incidental to the economic goals of the European age of exploration (seeking alternative water routes for trade with the Far East). Likewise, in Mediterranean antiquity, knowledge of the physical world was advanced during peaks in colonization and international trade. Until its destruction by the Persians in 494 BCE, Thales's hometown of Miletus was a wealthy harbor *polis* and center of trade on the eastern Aegean, well situated for contact with intellectual and cultural achievements (art, religion, science, literature) of the Near East, including Mesopotamia and Egypt. And it was at Miletus, a vigorous center of commercial and colonizing activity, that the first Greek map of the *oikoumene*, the inhabited world, was drawn by Thales's student Anaximander of Miletus (*c.* 580–545 BCE) (*TEGP* 6–8), probably accompanied by a geographical commentary (*Circuit of the Earth*). This map was soon improved by a fellow Milesian, the well-traveled Hecataeus (*c.* 520–490).[9] These early maps followed the Homeric paradigm of an *oikoumene* surrounded by a circular, circumambient Ocean (Herodotus 4.36) (Figure 1.2).

Like Benjamin Franklin who interviewed sailors to collect data for charting the Gulf Stream, one imagines Anaximander querying sailors and visitors in port regarding distant places, weather patterns, and the interstices of land and water. Eratosthenes (Strabo 2.5.24), Hipparchus (Strabo 2.1.11), and Strabo (Strabo 2.5.8, 2.5.24) had all relied on sailor reports. For Anaximander, Ocean was not merely the physical frame of the world. He seems to have also developed a nascent hydrological theory. Anaximander suggested that matter derived from "the boundless" (*apeiron*), a mixture of all opposite qualities from which sensible objects are generated (*TEGP* 9–20). Although rebuffing water, Thales's *archē*, as the material source of the physical world (*TEGP* 10–11—as perhaps too specific), Anaximander retained his mentor's theory of an earth that was originally entirely moist, slowly exsiccated by "the winds and the turnings of the sun and moon," eventually revealing dry land—that is to say, by the heat of the sun and the winds that were generated by the revolution of celestial bodies around the earth in his geocentric cosmos. Primeval moisture settled in the earth's hollows to create the sea (*thalassa*), which, according to Anaximander, continues to evaporate until "finally some day it will be completely dry" (*TEGP* 34–6). Anaximander also built on his teacher's theory regarding moisture and nourishment. If not a proper theory of evolution, it was at least a progression of animal life: as water and land grew warmer, animals were generated in moisture and protected by bark, shells, or embryonic sacs within fishes (in the case of human beings) until they could make landfall (*TEGP* 37–9).

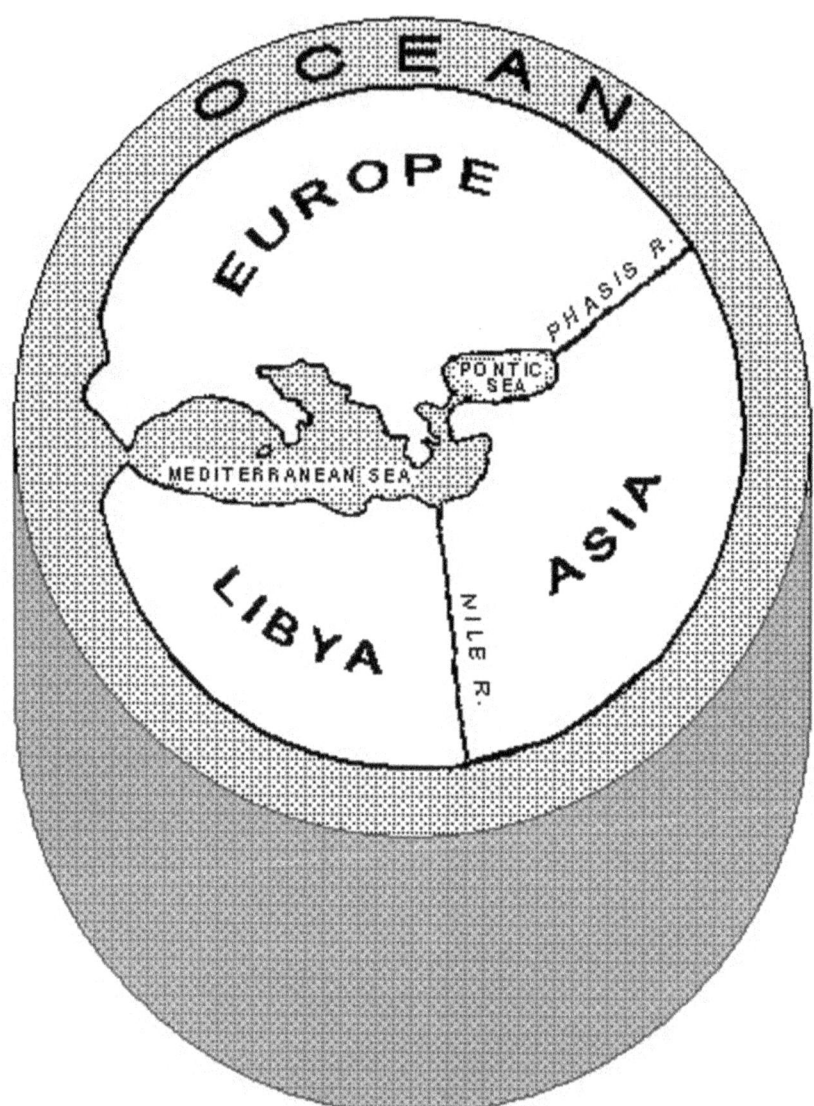

FIGURE 1.2 Theoretical reconstruction of Anaximander's map. © Georgia L. Irby (author).

Further developing the Milesian school of thought was Xenophanes of Colophon, on Turkey's western coast near Ephesus (fl.540[?]–478[?] BCE). Xenophanes traveled widely like Hecataeus, and, unlike most philosophers, he wrote in verse, perhaps to make a living as an itinerant minstrel. Xenophanes asked many of the same questions as the Milesians, employing similar explanations, but using the medium of poetry to interrogate the conventions and assumptions of human knowledge. Rejecting material monism, Xenophanes posited two elements, water and earth, as the generative material for all matter: "all things which come to be and grow are earth and water" (*TEGP* 51). Thus water was an essential component of Xenophanes' cosmogony and physics. Furthermore, as the source of both water (rivers, rain) and weather (clouds, winds), the sea (*thalassa*) was the unifying lynchpin of Xenophanes' natural philosophy (*TEGP* 54–5). As on the Milesian theory, the processes of evaporation and condensation accounted for rain: fresh water was separated from the sea and drawn up as mist into clouds, then felted into raindrops which would finally return to the earth when clouds exhaled their winds.

Xenophanes' hydrology was not just cosmogenic. Xenophanes was perhaps the first Greek thinker to develop a theory of Ocean. Fragments of his text reveal that he queried the nature of the sea, explaining that sea water was salty "because many mixtures flow into it" (*TEGP* 59). Additionally, Xenophanes advanced Thales's theory of a cycle of terrestrial desiccation and moistening on the strength of fossil evidence. He had discovered seashells in mountains, impressions of fish and seaweed in quarries at Syracuse, of coral on rocks at Paros, and of "all sea creatures" on the island of Malta (*TEGP* 59). The process is also geological as earth mixes with sea, thus reflecting the complex interplay between earth and sea that defines malleable coastlines. Finally, Xenophanes saw a link between the sea and celestial bodies: the sun and moon were comprised of "incandescent clouds" (*TEGP* 60–1, 67), and they were formed from evaporation like rainclouds but manifested differently (Mourelatos 2008).

Although he may not have developed a unified theory of hydrology or "oceanography," Heraclitus of Ephesus (*c.* 510–490 BCE), who was "a humanist with scientific interests" (Graham 2010: 136), cut to the heart of the nature of water, which he employed as a metaphor for epistemology and the ephemerality of human reality. Heraclitus compared "existing things to the flow of a river." And he asserted "on those stepping into rivers staying the same other and other (*hetera kai hetera*) waters flow," a maxim famously and cryptically paraphrased as "into the same rivers you could not step twice … for other waters flow on," or more transparently as "all things are in motion like streams" (*TEGP* 62–3, cf. 65–7). This is to say that while the appearance, size, and behavior of the river may remain constant, its waters are continuously replaced by new waters (*hetera kai hetera*) while the river itself remains in continuous flow.[10]

More concretely, on Heraclitus's natural philosophy, the world is governed by opposing binary forces held together in a contentious equilibrium, and this world is comprised of earth and sea (*thalassa*): "the turnings of fire: first sea (*thalassa*), and of sea, half is earth, half fire-burst (*prēstēr*)" (*TEGP* 51). According to Kahn, this fragment may have been "intended to *suggest* some process of world formation or transformation" (Kahn 1979: 139–44). Often translated as "tornado" or "waterspout," a *prēstēr* appears as a lightning storm or "fire from heaven" in conjunction with storms and wind.[11] Kahn concludes that the phrase "half-earth, half-*prēstēr*" refers to the binary forces in play after the production of sea. By means of desiccation, these binary forces convert the sea into earth and vapor, and the resulting vapors in turn nourish the celestial fire. *Prēstēr*, then, seems to be the catalyst for the alteration between earth and sea. Heraclitus did note the diametric relationship between earth and sea: "<Earth>is liquefied as sea and measured into the same proportion it had before it became earth" (DK22B31b). Thus Heraclitus recognized a constant ratio between earth and water. And water (sea) is one of the foundational elements of the material world that is not converted into earth (as in material monism) but rather retains a "strong non-identity" (Graham 2010: 189). In addition to his remarks on Sea as a physical component of the world, Heraclitus also observed the binary tension in the Sea's nature: "Sea (*thalassa*) is the purest and most polluted water: for fish drinkable and healthy, for men undrinkable and harmful" (*TEGP* 79).[12]

The natural philosopher and "religious guru" (Graham 2010: 327) Empedocles of Acragas (fl.460–430 BCE) in southern Sicily was the first to articulate a coherent theory of four elements (roots, *rhizomata*), each of which was connected to a deity: Zeus was fire, Hera presumably was air, Aidoneus (Hades) was earth, and Nēstis ("the mortal spring") was water (*TEGP* 26). Like Xenophanes, Empedocles wrote in verse. His interests were as broad as his theories, and sizable fragments of his poems *On Nature* and *On Purification* are extant. There are, nonetheless, critical gaps. For Empedocles, like his predecessors, Sea (water) was an integral cosmological component, playing a significant role in the development and framework of the earth and its *oikoumene* as the elemental *rhizomata* cycle between total mixture and total separation (*TEGP* 41). But two intriguing fragments suggest that Empedocles, like Xenophanes, was asking questions about the nature of the sea (e.g., why is sea water salty). He offered a clever hypothesis based on an analogy with human sweat: Ocean water grows salty when heated by the sun, as if the earth were sweating: "sea (*thalatta*) is the earth's sweat" (*TEGP* 99–100). Empedocles also posited that the sea was swelling and encroaching onto the land (*TEGP* 101). While suggesting that Empedocles had developed a geological theory on the formation of terrestrial features (including cliffs and crags; *TEGP* 96), surviving fragments fail to preserve any further details of his hydrology. Did he interrogate the causes of the tides, the depth of Our Sea, the nature of its surface, or seabed topography?

Democritus of Abdera (440–380 BCE), founder of the atomic theory (which explained the sensible world and change in the world as combinations of uncuttable atoms and the nothingness of void), was a polymath ascribed with seventy titles on wide-ranging topics including astronomy, geography, and geology. Extant fragments and testimonia suggest a well-developed theory of geology (*TEGP* 78–88), but his hydrology is poorly preserved. As in Thales, earthquakes seem to originate from the uneven distribution of terrestrial waters either because of winds or the incommensurate accrual of water in underground passages (*TEGP* 78–9). Democritus's hypothesis that the sea is receding and would eventually disappear was met with ridicule by Aristotle (*Meteorology* 2.1 353b = *TEGP* 88). It is unclear whether Democritus perceived a cycle of desiccation and hydration, like Anaximander, or if he believed in a teleological senescence of the sea.[13]

PLATO AND ARISTOTLE

As with the pre-Socratic thinkers, knowledge of the sea remained largely theoretical for Plato. Plato's hydrology is cast as a *katabasis* or descent into the underworld. In the *Phaedo* (109b–113d), a dialogue that explores the nature of the soul and recounts Socrates' last day, Plato's Socrates opined on the nature of the sea and its relationship to the earth. Socrates commented only on Our Sea, the waters between the Phasis River (debouching into the Black Sea) at the eastern edge and the Pillars of Herakles in the West. Humankind inhabits only a small portion of the sea which encroaches into littoral hollows. But those hollows are merely impressionistic versions of the true earth:

> It escapes our notice that we dwell in the hollows of the earth; we think that we are living upon it. Just like if someone inhabiting the depths of the sea thinks that he lives on its surface, seeing the sun and other stars through the water, he thinks that he sees the sky; on account of his sluggishness and weakness he would never arrive at the sea's surface, nor would he rise and lift his head from the sea to our world; nor would he see how much more spotless and beautiful it (the earth) happens to be than his (watery world).
>
> (Pl., *Phd.* 109c–d)

The sea in the *Phaedo* is an analogue to the cave of the *Republic* (7.514a–520a). Socrates here repeated the wisdom of the epic poets with reference to the depth and expanse of the watery hollows in Our Sea (but did not speculate on their extent). Just as our atmosphere erodes the objects in it (referring to the weathering of stones), so does brine corrode objects in the sea. Despite a thriving fishing industry (e.g., Hom., *Od.* 19.109; cf., Plato, *Republic* 2.363c) and plentiful vegetation (albeit non flowering and non fruiting), in Socrates' sea nothing "worthy of mention" grows, the mud is measureless, and the swamps, where sea and earth meet, are messy. In his perfect world, even the mountains and stones are smooth and transparent, and the earth's air- and water-filled hollows glitter with a seamless variety of color. Socrates surmised the existence of other areas of human habitation beyond the Mediterranean region, strewn around other hollows:

> some are deeper and broader than the one in which we live, others are deeper than those in our region but with a smaller yawn, some are both shallower than ours and broader.
>
> (Pl., *Phd.* 11c–d)

Underground channels connect these hollows through which flows "a great volume of water" constituted of subterranean rivers of various qualities: hot, cold, fiery, muddy, clear, murky, correlating to volcanic lava flows in Sicily. All these subterranean rivers stream into the deepest and largest chasm, which Socrates identified as Tartarus, the bottomless source of all waters. Perpetual oscillation causes waters to rush from one side of the earth to the other, with no fixed seat. In this way rivers and lakes (including Our Sea) flow and are filled or depleted. Because of this breath-like ebb and flow (resembling tidal activity), bodies of water sometimes return to their sources; at other times they flow toward opposite channels. Socrates specified four significant bodies of water, each with afterlife associations: Ocean, the frame of Homer's world (above); Acheron (river of woe), debouching into the Acherusian Lake, a rallying point for the souls of the dead; the fiery, lava-filled Pyriphlegethon (river of fire); and the Cocytus (the river of wailing) debouching into the Stygian lake. Their currents and courses are geometrically symmetrical: the Acheron flows in the opposite direction of Ocean; the Pyriphlegethon appears between Ocean and Acheron, mixing with no other rivers and spiraling downward until it returns to Tartarus deep within the earth; directly opposite Pyriphlegethon between Ocean and Acheron, the Cocytus spirals in a contrary direction toward Tartarus, also mingling with no other waters. Plato has adjusted the physical world to fit his epistemology. With his dying words Socrates was contemplating the physical boundaries between the worlds of the living and the dead, where newly deceased souls receive their punishments or rewards at the appropriate river. On Plato's theory, despite the apparent disjunction of the underworld rivers, all the waters of the earth originate from and return to Tartarus. On Plato's theory, there is a unified sea that washes over the entire earth, our *oikoumene* and others, and we are in constant contact with those waters, a subtle reminder of our own mortality and Socrates' impending death.

In Plato we have a theory of Ocean and its relationship to other waterways as well as a sense of its variable depth and expanse. Aristotle's hydrology, situated between his discussions of lofty mountain springs and loftier winds, is also cast as a sort of *katabasis*.[14] Aristotle soundly repudiated Plato's oscillating, unified bodies of water as irrational and impossible (*Mete.* 2.3 357a15–23). On Plato's theory, rivers then would flow according to the surging of Tartarus. Would they then flow upward when Tartarus surges? That, of course, is impossible!

Nor do rivers return to their own sources. Aristotle tackled the origins of the sea, its salinity, its distinction from "flowing" waters, and whether seas can be interconnected. *Meteorology* 2.1–3 is a rhetorical tour de force in which the author selectively disproved the "silly" ideas of his predecessors, who seemed to exaggerate the importance of Ocean as the source of nourishment for heavenly bodies (*Mete.* 354b33–55a33). Evoking Hesiod, Aristotle denied the ancient assertion that the sea has "springs" (*pēgai*: running water, sources; cf. Hes., *Theog.* 736–41), which must belong to artificial (that is, non-flowing) bodies of water. Hesiod likely had in mind something akin to Anaximander's *apeiron* or indeterminate sources of moisture. Aristotle's interpretation was anachronistically filtered through Plato's more deterministic view of Tartarus with its physical subterranean passages (West 1966: 361; Wilson 2013: 182). For Aristotle, Ocean/Sea is neither flowing nor artificial, nor is natural spring water ever found on such a large scale (*Mete.* 1.14 352b29–353b30). Flowing waters *flow* from springs. Standing waters either have no source (lakes, swamps) or they are artificial (wells). The point is partly intended to buttress Aristotle's architectonic view of the world where the heavens assume the highest importance and the sea is relegated to "the bottom of the meteorological cosmos" (Wilson 2013: 190).

For Aristotle, the sea is stagnant, unflowing, and it is isolated from rivers and the cycle of weather. Aristotle's predecessors believed "that the remaining heaven had been contrived around earth and for its sake, and that earth was the most honorable and primary source (*archē*) of it." Thus the cosmological role of earth and sea is elevated (Arist., *Mete.* 353b3–5). Some seas are landlocked, such as the Hyrcanian and Caspian Seas, which Aristotle correctly recognized as "separated" from the outer ocean. Should these seas have sources, the inhabitants would have observed them (354a3–5). Nor can the fresh rivers that debouche into the salty seas be their source because of the difference in the quality of the waters (fresh/salty: 354b20). Fresh river water, furthermore, settles on top of salt water, according to the tenets of Aristotelian physics, where the sea is restricted to a cup-like container. Moreover, the Red Sea is linked with the "the Ocean outside the Straits" only by a narrow channel. Thus, these seas have no sources. Aristotle resolved the debate by borrowing from Heraclitus's river. Bodies of water are one and the same: the sea is one in form and volume; but it is also comprised of discrete parts that are in continual change: some parts change more rapidly, others more slowly. While the bulk remains constant, the parts do not.

According to Aristotle, however, the Mediterranean does flow as do the other bodies of water that are bounded by the circumambient Ocean (Arist., *Mete.* 354b24). In accordance with Aristotelian physics, sea water finds its natural place (weighed down by heavier, earthy salt), flowing into the deepest hollows of the earth (355a33–b5, 355b17–19). Aristotle outlined a progression of seas from shallow to deeper: Maeotis, Pontus, Aegean, Sicilian, and the Sardinian and Tyrrhenic seas (*Meteorology* 354a14–21).[15] Intense alluvial activity makes the northern seas shallower and the outer seas deeper.

Refuting Empedocles' analogy of salt water as the sweat of the earth, Aristotle maintained that sweat implies a failure of digestion. There is, however, no need at all for the earth to digest anything, nor is there any indication that the earth is currently "sweating" (357b7–13). Instead, Aristotelian physics demands that elements seek their natural place: only the lightest (fresh-) water would evaporate and return as rain, and the sweetest waters would be evaporated daily (354b29). Heavier, thicker salt water remains in the ocean and sinks below the overlying lighter, fresh water. The sun's warmth attracts the sweeter parts up. The process of evaporation and re-condensation also accounts for the interplay between ocean and weather: autumn rains are brackish; cool north winds drive away the clouds (358a29–358b6). Aristotle's experiments proved that vaporized sea water does not re-condense into salt water but becomes sweet (358b12–17). Empirical evidence also demonstrates the greater density of brine: once a sea-going vessel enters a fresh-water river, it sits lower with the same cargo (sometimes nearly sinking), and eggs sink in fresh water but float in brine (359a6–15). Aristotle also rejected the theories of Xenophanes (*TEGP* 59), Anaxagoras (DK59a90), and Metrodorus (DK70a19) that salinity increases as water is filtered through different types of soil, leeching out minerals. Nor can the evaporation of fresh water result in higher concentrations of salt and a diminished extent of sea since the sea is inert and clearly not receding, as Anaxagoras and Diogenes of Apollonia had argued. Why, then, is the sea salty? Because of the admixture of moist (watery) and dry exhalations, which are earthy, containing residues that result from the natural process of generation on analogy with a bladder (358a16–26; Taub 2003: 102). As proof that earthy stuff in water makes it salty, Aristotle cited a fabled Palestinian lake where nothing sinks, with waters so bitter that no fish can survive and clothes can be cleaned simply by dipping and shaking.[16]

TIDES

According to Poseidonius, Aristotle had also developed a tidal theory: that the high rugged headlands off Spain and Morocco caught the ocean waves and hurled them back to sea. Poseidonius, however, had seen first hand the low sandy beaches along that coast (f220): there was nothing against which the waves could bounce. Aristotle, whose only experience of tides was in the gentle Mediterranean, had likely formulated no hypothesis of oceanic tides. Nor is Poseidonius's conjecture substantiated in the *Meteorology* (Kidd 1972: 790). But Aristotle's authority was unimpugnable, and a popular belief that tides were caused by the winds may also go back to him (Aëtius 3.17.1).

Tidal activity has always been a source of curiosity. Praised by Strabo for his knowledge of flood tides (1.1.7), Homer discerned the "ebb and flow of Ocean" near Scylla and Charybdis (*Od.* 12.1–2, 235–43) and "soft flowing" Ocean (*Il.* 7.422; *Od.* 19.434). Tidal activity varies widely from nearly imperceptible to dramatic. The striking tidal activity of the "Great Ocean" and the Atlantic respectively caught both Alexander of Macedon and Julius Caesar unaware. In 325 BCE, Alexander's fleet on the Indus River suffered damage because his troops were unprepared for the amplitude of water at high tide (Arrian, *Anabasis* 6.19.1). In 55 BCE, Caesar lost several ships that flooded or collided because of the unfamiliar effects of spring tides in the English Channel (*Gallic Wars* 4.29; Kidd 1972: 774–5; Mohler 1944–5).

From the late fourth century BCE, Greek thinkers recognized the connection between phases of the moon and tidal activity.[17] Close observation of tides could be of great strategic advantage: Scipio Africanus deliberately waited for low tide before giving the order for his men to scale the defenses at New Carthage in Spain in 210 BCE (Polybius 10.14; Livy 26.45.8; Lovejoy 1972). The seafaring Venetians of Aremorica (Brittany, near modern Vannes, Roman Belgica) built broad-bottomed boats with high sterns and prows that were well suited to withstand dramatic Atlantic tides (Caesar, *Gallic Wars* 3.12–13; Strabo 4.4.1).

The first Greek thinker to study tidal activity systematically was probably Pytheas of Massilia, who was intrigued by the dramatic tides around the British Isles, among the largest in the world. Pytheas allegedly reported tidal swells of up to 80 cubits (37 meters [118 feet]: Pliny, *Natural History* [*NH*] 2.217).[18] Pytheas may have correlated the half-daily tides to phases of the moon ("fullness and faintness"; Aëtius 3.17.3). He was more likely observing a spring tide (when the sun and moon are together in the earth's equatorial plane, exerting a greater, combined gravitational pull) that coincided with an equinoctial tide, together yielding dramatic tidal amplitude.[19]

A stoic natural philosopher who promoted heliocentricsm, Seleucus of Seleucia on the Tigris river (165–135 BCE) was the first to write a monograph on tidal theory.[20] Seleucus suggested that the moon's orbit and the earth's rotation disturbed the intervening *pneuma* that pervaded the cosmos, which in turn caused sea levels to fluctuate; seasonal tidal variation depended on the lunar zodiac sign and location. This theory was favored by Hipparchus of Nicea (F4), but rejected by Strabo, for whom the ocean in general and tides in particular exhibited uniform behavior (1.1.9; Dicks 1960: 115; Kidd 1972: 760–3; Roller 2006: 115–17). Seleucus also observed uneven diurnal tidal activity on the Red/Babylonian Sea (Indian Ocean): tides are "regular" (neap, with only slight differences of amplitude between high and low tide) when the moon is in equinoctial signs (Aries and Libra, the signs that rise after the equinoxes), but "irregular" (with extreme differences in amplitude) when in solsticial signs (Cancer and Capricorn), proportionate to the moon's distance from the earth's equinoctial (on the equator) and solsticial planes (greatest north/south declination). When the moon is over the equator (equinoxes), the Indian Ocean has two daily cycles of equal highs and lows; when the Moon is at 90 degrees to the equator (solstices), the diurnal highs and lows are unequal. Diurnal inequality in the Atlantic is practically nonexistent (Darwin 1898: 86–7).

This account likely intrigued Poseidonius, who may have visited Gades in order to test Seleucus's claims (Kidd 1972: 776). Poseidonius spent thirty days on the southern Spanish coast, where the tidal swells exceeded those in the protected Mediterranean Basin. Poseidonius's theory of diurnal and monthly tides, marshaled from empirical evidence, is a "remarkable contribution" and substantially correct (f217b; Kidd 1972: 281, 775–6). When the moon is in one zodiac constellation above the eastern horizon (30 degrees), the sea rises visibly until the moon reaches the meridian (90 degrees). Water levels then begin to recede until the moon is 30 degrees above the western horizon, remaining steady until the moon is 30 degrees below the horizon. Water levels again rise until the moon reaches the meridian below the earth (270 degrees). At that point they start to ebb, holding level as the moon travels from 30 degrees below to 30 degrees above the eastern horizon (Figure 1.3). In addition to the diurnal cycle, Poseidonius correlated varying tidal amplitudes to phases of the moon, noting that sea levels are greatest in conjunction with full and new moons,

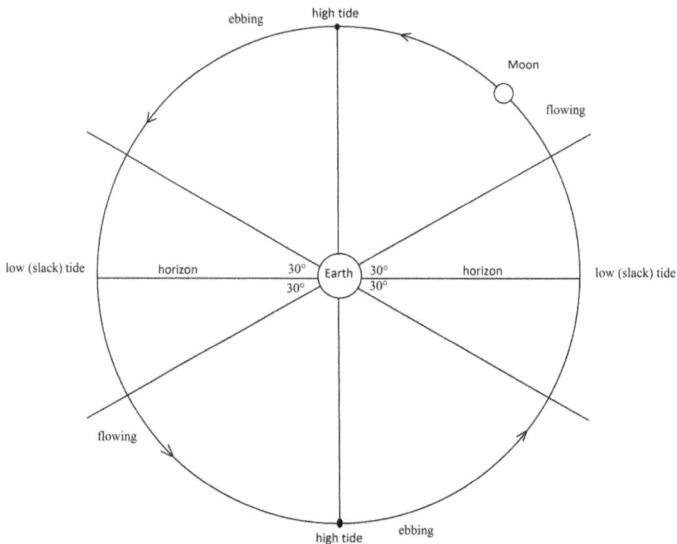

FIGURE 1.3 The diurnal tidal cycle according to Poseidonius. © Georgia L. Irby (author).

smallest in conjunction with quarter moons. On the authority of local evidence, Poseidonius also recorded (erroneously) that the highest annual tides occurred in conjunction with the solstices (these coincide instead with the equinoxes).[21] Poseidonius, however, had observed another high sea at the summer solstice (f227), due to a volcanic eruption on Sicily, and this may have reinforced the high solsticial tides that he was deliberately searching for at Gades (Strabo 3.5.9). The error was corrected by Seneca the Younger (*Natural Questions* 3.28.6) and Pliny (*NH* 2.215), who both likely followed Poseidonius. Seneca and Pliny correctly gave the maximum high tides at the equinoxes.

CURRENTS

Also of great interest was the behavior of the currents in the straits, most famously at Cape Pelorus (Strait of Messina), the treacherously narrow passage between Italy and Sicily (Vergil, *Aeneid* 3.414; Strabo 1.3.10; Mela 2.115; Pliny, *NH* 3.87; Seneca the Younger, *Epistle* 79). Here were the lair of a sailor-snatching sea-monster (Scylla) and the site of a dangerous natural whirlpool (Charybdis). In harrowing detail Homer described the Strait as framed by two sheer cliffs through which no ship could pass (except the Argo, and only with divine aid: *Od.* 12.59–110). One cliff reaches the sky with a pointed peak, perennially crowned by a dark cloud, against which "crashes the heavy swell of dark-eyed Amphitrite" (12.60). Midway up is Scylla's cave. The lower cliff marks the whirlpool, "deadly Charybdis," which promises certain death for the entire crew. Circe advised Odysseus:

> May you not happen upon that place when she sucks down water, for not anyone could rescue you from beneath that evil, not even the Earth-shaker (Poseidon). But sail your swift ship towards Scylla's mound and drive past her, since it is far better to regret six companions in your ship than all.
>
> (12.106–10)

Aristotle attempted to account for refluent currents in the Mediterranean Straits as resulting from the contraction of water within the narrows:

> The sea seems to flow in the narrowest places where through the framing coastline the open sea contracts from a large to a small space, because it (the water) often sways back and forth. In a large quantity of sea, this is unobserved. But in the narrows of the land, a scant passage restrains (the water), there the shores constrict the swaying which seemed small in the open sea but now seem great.
>
> (*Meteorology* 354a5–10)

The swift currents at the Chalkidean Strait (Euripos) that separate Euboea from the Greek mainland, where strong tidal currents reverse direction about four times a day, was particularly troubling. Ancient biographers suggested that its apparently inexplicable behavior (reversing direction several times a day) provoked Aristotle to commit suicide.[22] Eratosthenes recorded that the currents here reversed direction seven times a day (f16). The Hispano-Roman chorographer Pomponius Mela (fl.30–60 CE) doubled Eratosthenes' seven shifts of current, with seven alternations occurring both daily and nightly (2.108). Regarding the underlying reason for this ostensibly unusual behavior, Strabo demurs: "the cause must be investigated elsewhere" (9.2.8).

Eratosthenes seems to be the only ancient thinker to explain the vacillation of currents in narrow straits: as owing to discrete surfaces for each sea (f16). Strabo dismissed the postulate as impossible. In accordance with Archimedes' proposition that "the surface of all fluids that remain immovable will have the surface of a sphere, having the same center as the earth,"[23] the sea cannot be sloped, but it must be spherical. How then can the oscillation of the currents in the straits be explained? Strabo considered the question too scientific for the scope of his work, suggesting that explanations are ad hoc: "it is sufficient to say that there is no single explanation for the currents in straits that corresponds to their form" (1.3.12).

Like the "notoriously treacherous" Charybdis (Pliny, *NH* 3.87), which Apollonius of Rhodes histrionically described as an endless roar and upsurge (4.923) in his harrowing litany of "ship-smashing horrors at the sea's crossroads" (4.921), whirlpools occur naturally where opposing currents meet or where tides affect the fast currents of waters in narrow straits. Charybdis was described as a deep eddy "into which the reflux of the Strait cleverly pulls down boats, which are swept away with the twisting around and a great whirling." The wreckage would land at the Tauromenian shore, giving the place its name: *Kopria* (Refuse) (Strabo 6.3.2; Seneca, *Epistle* 79.1–2; Silius Italicus, *Punica* 14.254–7). Together with a violent storm, the whirlpool was responsible for the destruction of Octavian's fleet in the Strait in 36 BCE (Appian, *Civil War* 5.90).[24] And the anonymous author of *The Periplus of the Erythraean Sea* warned his readers of violent whirlpools in a bay near the Sinthos (Indus) River (40).

Homer and other poets described the Charybdis with three daily cycles of ebbing and spouting, Polybius (34.3.10, without explanation), Eratosthenes (fr. 16; Roller 2014), and Strabo (1.3.11) corrected this to two cycles. Strabo defended Homer, whom Vergil followed, by ascribing the erroneous triple gushing to either a copyist error (1.2.16) or to rhetorical hyperbole that was intended to induce greater fear (1.2.36). Other whirlpools are described: at Genethlium in Argolis where bridled horses were once drowned to propitiate Poseidon (Pausanias 8.7.2), at Cape Caldone on the Persian Gulf (Pliny, *NH* 6.147), and abutting Apollo's sacred grove in Lycia where worshippers sought oracular guidance (Athenaeus 7.333c–f). The locals believed that a fresh-water spring produced the whirlpool. The Aristotelian author of *Problems* 23.5

correctly ascertained that whirlpools are products of the currents. And he explained currents as factors of the winds:

> Now a current occurs when—the earlier wind having stopped—wind blows in the opposite direction over a sea that is flowing under the influence of the earlier wind, and especially when it is a south wind blowing in the opposite direction.

A complex phenomenon, currents are generated by many determinants including variable densities of contiguous bodies of water that differ in salinity or temperature (e.g., the warm Gulf Stream flowing through the colder waters of the Atlantic Ocean). Surface currents, the only ones likely observed by the author, are largely fashioned by the winds together with coastal geography and the Coriolis force (inertial force) resulting from the earth's rotation.[25] The interplay between the winds and coastal geography was described by Homer: for example, "there the Southwest Wind thrusts the great wave towards the leftward headland" (*Od.* 3.295). And the (unknown) author of *The Periplus of the Erythraean Sea* recognized that winds blowing from mountains on Diodorus Island contributed to the strong currents in the Strait there (25).

REEFS

Reefs are another notorious danger for ships at sea, and some had names: such as the "Ass of Antron" below Antron in the Euboean Strait (Strabo 9.5.14); the "Midland" on the way to Lesbos, where colonists were supposed to sacrifice live bulls to Poseidon and virgins to Amphitrite (Plutarch, *Dinner of the Seven Wise Men* 163a–b); and the "Ant" between Sciathus and the Magnesia archipelago where Persian ships went aground in 480 BCE (a stone beacon was then erected to mark the reef: Herodotus 7.183). On his return from Troy, Menelaus lost half of his fleet to a reef (*Od.* 3.291–300), Sergestus ran afoul of a reef thus losing a ship race (Vergil, *Aeneid* 5.202–6), and Ovid lamented his shipwreck on a reef in the Pontus (*ex Ponto* 4.15–24). Fishing boats were destroyed when fishermen carelessly or ignorantly floated over reefs (Alciphron, *Letters of Fishermen* 1.7). Fishermen, nonetheless, took advantage of rich reef habitats to harvest anchovies (Oppian, *On Fishing* 4.468–87) and the reef-purple snail (Pliny, *NH* 9.131).

SEA DEPTH

There were also attempts to measure sea depths. In Herodotus we have the earliest textual evidence of taking soundings (2.5.2), an essential tool in navigation, especially regarding where it is safe to sail or anchor.[26] Archaeological evidence predates 2000 BCE: Egyptian boat models from the tomb of Meketra, chancellor to Nebhepetra Mentuhotep II, feature crewmen holding sounding lines in the bows (McGrail 2001: ix; Vinson 1994: 31). Paul's storm-savaged crew also took soundings by heaving a lead line (Acts 27.28). Several varieties have been recovered, designed to lift samples of bottom sediment. The nature of sediment changes at the mouths of river beds and other geological phenomena, and this knowledge can enable navigation according to seabed topography when visibility is impaired.[27] The author of *The Periplus of the Erythraean Sea* described the sandy bottoms of the anchorages around Muza (24).

Aristotle recorded that the "Deeps of Pontus," 54 kilometers from land (33.5 miles), were unfathomable: "no one has yet been able to find the bottom by soundings" (*Meteorology* 351a9–14; cf. Pliny, *NH* 2.224). As Oleson observes, readings taken so far from land probably formed part of a larger scientific project (Oleson 2008: 130). The emperor Nero was also unable to take soundings in the Alkyonian Lake near Lerna, despite attaching his sounding weight to several lengths of rope (Pausanias 2.37.5). With a lead line attached to a rope (thousands of *orguiae* long), Psammetichus, king of Egypt, aimed to prove that the sources of the Nile (between Elephantine and Syene in the Thebaid) are bottomless (Herodotus 2.28.4). Poseidonius reported the Sardinian Sea as about 1,000 *orguiae* deep (1.8 kilometers [1.16 miles], in reality closer to 3 kilometers [1.86 miles]), "the deepest of those that have been measured" (f221). We do not know how the reading was taken (Kidd 1972: 794–5). In contrast, a shallow sea in the Arabian Gulf is about two *orguiae* deep (3.75 meters [12 feet]), and it "appears grassy with seaweed and other weeds showing through" (Strabo 16.4.7), perhaps the Sargasso described by Avienus (122–9), through which vessels go slowly and sluggishly.

DIVING

As early as the Minoan era, artwork reveals a sensitive, realistic treatment of marine creatures and their habitats (including octopods and other mollusks, a variety of fishes, and dolphins) (Figures 1.4 and 1.5). Much of the ancient knowledge of seabeds and sea life would have been collected by divers (Figure 1.6). According to Oppian (*On Fishing* 1.82–9; cf. Aelian, *On the Nature of Animals* 9.35), men have explored the sea to a depth of 300 *orguiae* (about 550 meters [1,804 feet]), but the sea, where no fewer tribes or herds dwell than on the dry earth, is otherwise infinite and unmeasured, and "many things are hidden." Oppian also implied that fishermen have mapped the seabed through autopsy (1.9–12), despite the fact that ancient divers, whose vision naturally would have been occluded in the depths, lacked goggles (Frost 1968: 182). Nonetheless, the best divers, especially sponge divers, had keen eyesight (Aeschylus, *Suppliants* 408; scholiast ad loc). The author of Aristotelian *Problems* also queried why

FIGURE 1.4 Fresco of dolphins in a seascape in the Megaron of the Queen, Knossos, Crete. © Bildagentur-Online / Getty Images.

divers' eardrums burst in the deep (32.2) and why some divers deliberately punctured their eardrums (32.5).[28]

Watermen dived for mollusks, including scallops and oysters (Aristotle, *History of Animals* 603a; *Il.* 16.745–7), seaweed (Theophrastus, *History of Plants* 4.6.4), murex purple (Pliny, *NH* 9.131), pearls (especially in the mouth of the Persian Gulf: *The Periplus of the Erythraean Sea* 35; cf. Athenaeus 3.93e; Arrian, *Indika* 8.11), and sponges (Pliny, *NH* 9.153; Plutarch, *On the Cleverness of Animals* 981e). They also dived for salvage and military purposes: to deliver supplies or messages (Thucydides 4.26; Appian, *Spanish War* 6.91); to release a fouled anchor (Lucan 3.699–700); to sabotage an enemy fleet (Thucydides 7.25.608; Cassius Dio 75.12.2); or to repair sabotage (Cassius Dio 42.12.2; Arrian, *Anabasis* 2.21.6).[29] Within the Euboean Strait, false beacons would lure ships to collision so that wreckers could salvage the cargo (Dio Chrysostom, *Oration* 7.31–2), and under Septimius Severus a guild of fishermen and divers enjoyed exclusive rights to debris on the Tiber's bed (*CIL* 6.1872). We have the names of two famous Greek divers: "Skyllus" who sabotaged Xerxes' fleet by cutting the moorings (Pausanias 10.19.1–2); and the apocryphal "Skyllias," whose legendary nine-mile (14.5-kilometer) underwater swim may be a doublet for Pheidippides' day-run from Athens to Sparta, seeking help against the Persians at Marathon in 490 BCE (Herodotus 8.7) and whose name suspiciously recalls the historical Skyllus.

FIGURE 1.5 Fresco of Minoan fisherman with tuna and mackerel, Akrotiri, *c.* 1600 BCE. © Wikimedia Commons (public domain).

FIGURE 1.6 Fresco from the Tomb of the Diver, Paestum, *c.* 470 BCE. © Wikimedia Commons (public domain).

SCHOLARLY ACCOUNTS

Knowledge of the sea was also gathered on a systematic, global scale. During the hegemony of Aristotle's famous student, Alexander of Macedon, as well as in the scientific "golden age" immediately following the general's death, theories and mathematical models came to be correlated with a growing body of facts about the world, including in hydrology. Scholars in numerous disciplines accompanied Alexander, who was eager to conquer and explore the entirety of the *oikoumene* east of the Aegean in his endeavor to extend Greek culture as far east as the Punjab. His coterie included biologists, zoologists, physicians, historians, geographers, and surveyors who were instructed to collect data and to produce full records of their observations. Nearchus overruled Onesicritus's order to sail directly to Cape Maceta, admonishing the helmsman for not understanding Alexander's purpose in sending out the fleet:

> not because of any difficulty in getting his whole army safely through by the land route, but because he wanted to investigate the beaches along the line of the coast and the anchorages and islets. (Arrian, *Indika* 32.9–13; Pearson 1960: 83)

Nonetheless, Onesicritus made the claim that his team "examined many things about nature" (F17). From this endeavor there survive fragments of the historian Callisthenes's *periplus* of the Black Sea (and probably beyond), as well as of two accounts of Alexander's expedition to India by his admiral Nearchus (*FrGrHist*

133) and helmsman Onesicritus (*FrGrHist* 134), valuable eye-witness sources for Eratosthenes, Strabo, and Arrian on India (Roller 2010: 178–80, 193–4). Following Juba II's précis of Onesicritus's *Indika*,[30] Pliny (*NH* 6.96) criticized both Nearchus and Onesicritus for omitting toponyms and distances. To what degree Onesicritus engaged with hydrological theory is difficult to ascertain from the brief fragments. Cited by Strabo over thirty times, Nearchus did comment on weather patterns (f18), riverine siltation (f17), the annual flooding of the Nile as compared with rivers in India (f20), and the large sea creatures in the Indian Ocean, including whales up to twenty-three *orguiae* (43 meters [140 feet]) who were easily chased off by loud noises (Roller 2018: 848):

> what was most troubling was the spouting that produced great streams and a large body of mist from the eruptions, so that they could not see the area in front of them.
>
> (f1b=Strabo 15.2.12)

With reconnaissance and a shore party, Nearchus was also able to disprove his crew's misconception that sailors disappeared near a certain island (f1c), an island that Arrian reported as inhabited by a Nereid who turned sailors into fish (*Indika* 31.6–8).[31] Nearchus also listed the shoals along the coast of Sousis (f25), and he remarked on the lack of anchorages between Babylonia and India (f26). Over the years, knowledge accrued and the details came into sharper focus. Arrian, for example, made reference to seasonal winds that prevented sailing (*Indika* 21.1) and the violent action of the open sea against the coast at the Indus' mouth (21.5). He gave particular attention to safe harbors and good anchorages (26.2, 29.1, 39.6).

Although Arrian seems not to have visited India, he did in fact command an expedition in the Euxine where the prevailing counterclockwise current may explain his route (King 2004: 16). His account of the expedition is rich in hydrological detail, including the direction and effect of the winds (Arrian, *Periplus* 3.2, 6.1), harbors that protected ships from the Thracian winds (4.2, 18.3), and waves crashing over the sides of his ships (3.3–4, 6.1).

THE PERIPLUS OF THE ERYTHRAEAN SEA

Aimed primarily at merchants, *The Periplus of the Erythraean Sea* (between eastern Africa and the Indian subcontinent: first century CE) explicates the imports and exports of various settlements.[32] But it is also a valuable source for the hydrology of the Erythraean Sea. The interplay of water and weather was recognized: at Spice Port, for example, growing turbidity of the waters indicates an oncoming storm (12). The author was careful to note seabed topography, including the rocky stretches along the territory of the Kanraitai (20) and the alternation of sheer drops with rocky, shallow bottoms at Baraké (40). And he observed that the appearance of snakes indicated proximity to land (38). Riverine topography was altogether a different matter, and pilots were often employed to guide ships from the open sea into harbors, as at Barygaza (44, 46).

CONCLUSION

Greek and Roman seafarers and natural philosophers were observant and curious. Data gathered from the seas were marshaled into hydrological theories (including lunitidal theories) as well as useful compendia for sailors, merchant mariners, and naval fighting forces. Alexander's bathysphere aside, the technology could only take them so far. Divers did possess some aids: snorkels (Aristotle, *Parts of Animals* 659a8–12); a *lebes* (cauldron) worn over the head, lip down, could extend the supply of oxygen, possibly doubling the length of a dive (Aristotelian *Problems* 32.5);[33] and tether-lines connected divers to crews topside (Oppian, *On Fishing* 5.612–74). The ancients, nonetheless, lacked the means of exploring deep sea floors, measuring salinity or temperature, and thus they were unable to develop an accurate understanding of currents. Further, despite the fact that most marine fauna in Our Sea are harmless and non-poisonous (Pliny knew that sharks could be frightened away by aggressive divers swimming directly at them: *NH* 9.152–3), the perils of the submarine environment were exaggerated: Oppian described *iulides* (rainbow wrasses) swarming and nipping at sponge divers by the thousands (*On Fishing* 2.434–53); and Pliny recounted how *nubes* (*nubila*, perhaps benign manta rays?) would obstruct divers from returning to the surface (*NH* 9.151). Many dangers were real—reefs, storms, treacherous currents within straits—and the sea remained a place of danger and mystery: the abode of gods, and the stage for the heroes of epic and saga.

CHAPTER TWO

Practices

Religious Practices at Sea in Antiquity

MIRELLA ROMERO RECIO

"Yet it is a terrible thing to die among the waves." This is one of the best-known sentences from Hesiod's *Works and Days* (Hes., *Op.* 687; Hesiod 2016). The Greek poet summarized the feeling that tormented those who risked their lives at sea since time immemorial. Those who needed to sail regularly or punctually until the beginning of the archaic period and those who would carry on until late antiquity, even many centuries later, would share the same fear. Dying at sea implied much more than losing one's life; it entailed a body that would disappear, devoured by fish, and, therefore, that would not be receiving the funerary rituals preparing access to the world of the dead. The famous shipwreck krater from Pithekoussai, dating from the eighth century BCE, portrayed this drama with clarity by representing one of the victims that had fallen in the sea with his head in the mouth of a large fish (Basch 1987: fig. 394; Ridgway 1992: 58, 150, fig. 10). The family of the deceased would find no solace in visiting their sepulchers as their souls would roam in totally alien parts. In similar terms, book VII of the *Palatine Anthology* collected a numerous series of epigrams of people that had died at sea, showing their despondency and lamenting an eternity that, with an empty sepulcher, would provide no relief.[1]

This paper is the result of the Research Projects: HAR2015-65451-C2-2-P (MINECO/FEDER) and Andalusian Agency of Knowledge, FEDER/UPO-1260377.

Even though the perception of risk probably changed as trips became more frequent, fear to set forth in an enterprise that remains dangerous to the present day forced those involved to seek solutions to all the threats to which they were exposed. Some of these could be overcome more successfully with nautical and port engineering developments; a better knowledge of geography, the currents, winds; and the observation of the stars and the sun in the different seasons of the year. However, there were many contingencies that could not be foreseen and, at a time when communications across the sea were totally necessary, preventing and solving them was indispensable. The only solution to controlling storms, wrecks, adverse currents, dangerous straits, or even sea monsters that would menacingly be lurking at the borders of the known world, was to resort to religion and magic.

Phoenicians, Greeks, Etruscans, Romans, and the rest of the peoples that sailed the seas during antiquity, all sought the help of deities.[2] In the following pages we will see how the religious experience of the people that traveled the sea was conditioned by different factors that shaped a characteristic way of expressing piety and that determined the choice of some gods over others.

Fear of the sea turned the majority of divinities into accomplices of these individuals that were able to express their devotion by dedicating votive offerings and performing ceremonies and rituals in spaces consecrated to their benefactors. Although it is possible to observe some transformations in time, there exist a number of characteristics that persisted in the religiousness of mariners throughout the centuries. As we will see, the dangers that confronted sailors were perceived in a uniform manner: therefore, the mechanisms applied to appease uncontrollable phenomena were persistent and analogous among diverse communities, even universal in some of their expressions.

In the literature generated around the travels of Greek heroes, it is common to find reference to sacrifices of animals in improvised coastal altars, both upon landing as an expression of gratitude or before weighing anchor, seeking the help of the divinities. The Argonauts, for instance, resorted to Apollo (*Embasios, Aktius, Ekbasian*, of the Dawn, Savior of ships, and the Gleamer) (A.R. 1.353–62, 400–4, 964–7; 2.688–702, 924–8; 4.1714–17), the Twelve Gods (A.R. 2.531–3; Mela, 1.19.37; Plb. 4.39.6) and the Sons of Zeus (the Dioskouroi, Castor, and Pollux) (A.R. 4.649–54). But as mythology reveals, the first exploration trips presented sailors with an insecure world filled with strange manifestations that could alter the religious rhythm of the voyage. The heroes, Jason and Odysseus among others, saw themselves forced to face moving rocks, the Kyanean Rocks; lurking monsters, Kharybdis and Skylla; or hybrid creatures, sirens, who devoured sailors.[3] In fact, this was a mere interpretation of inexplicable singularities, weather circumstances, adverse winds, or treacherous straits, granting them a supernatural hue that needed to be countered in the real world by divine intervention. It was then considered, since very ancient times, that these rituals had to respond to those improvised needs; it implied a readjustment in the manifestations of the sailors' piety that had to attend to the cults of their original community; to those of the places where they were docking, whether they belonged to their own or a different culture; as well as to the sites consecrated to divinities that could be sighted from their ships as they journeyed.

Many of the places that appear in mythology associated with the piety of mariners must have been settings that were sacralized in ancient times and that perpetuated this function over time. In this way, a pertinent example would be the Hieron at the mouth of the Black Sea, a sacred space since the beginning of the first explorations of the Pontus Euxinus in which, presumably, the Argonauts had dedicated their offerings and where there remain material vestiges that allow us to corroborate the existence of a cult to the Twelve Gods. In this same locale, similar veneration was shown to other deities favorable to sailors such as Artemis, Poseidon, and Zeus/Jupiter *Ourios*, that can be dated from between the seventh century BCE and the sixth century CE (Moreno 2008).

Minoans, Mycenaeans, and Phoenicians explored the Mediterranean trying to improve the safety of their journeys by means of the sacralization of a coastal site in which the sailors' material expressions of piety were going to be defined. These locations easily adapted to the requirements of the seafarers so that coastal caves, springs, promontories visible from the ship or capes and straits of difficult navigation became sacred places in which constructions were erected to identify them as sanctuaries linked to seagoing piousness. The "White Rocks," with their luminescent effects and which were the only visible landmarks, especially during nocturnal storms, served as geographical signposts, but also were home to phosphoric divinities, mainly Leucothea and the siren Leucosia (Giangiulio 1996: 260 ss. Cf. Nagy 1973: 147). Some sea routes that connected Greece with Sicily were marked by reference to the "white rocks" that guided sailors in their course and identified as a benevolent divine intervention (Nenci 1973: 387–96).

Consequently, in these sacred places of the coastal geography it was not indispensable to erect a construction for sailors to identify them as a place of worship. The appearance of shells and other maritime motifs was associated since Minoan times with the Goddess of the Sea and with the desire to secure a continuity of the activities related to navigation. P. Faure confirmed a long time ago the presence in several Cretan caves, such as Tsoutsouros and Skotino, of dedicated shells and other offerings such as fish and small clay boats that led to the belief that they were offerings presented by mariners (1964: 165–6, 1969: 192, 199).

Furthermore, studies on Phoenician and Punic expansion across the Mediterranean have also substantiated the existence of caves associated with sailing cults (Grottanelli 1981). In the cave of Es Culleram, northeast of the island of Ibiza and dating between the fifth and second centuries BCE, in an area from which it was possible to monitor maritime traffic with Sardinia, an important votive deposit was located (Aubet 1982; Marín Ceballos, Belén, and Jiménez 2010). In addition to bell-shaped figures of enthroned goddesses, perfume burners, terracottas, pottery, and ivory and metal objects, the site presented some altars, incinerated remains, cisterns next to the entrance, and cone-shaped stones identified as baetyls. Undoubtedly, the offerings were made by sailors who came to this part of the island to receive the favors of the deity in the cave, probably none other than Astarte-Tanit.

The cave of Es Culleram holds parallelisms with other locations in the Mediterranean, for instance Gorham's Cave (Gibraltar), regularly visited since approximately the eighth century BCE by those navigating the hazardous waters of the Strait: offerings appear here from sailors to Melqart and Astarte-Tanit (Belén 2000; Belén and Pérez 2000; Zamora López et al. 2013). Another well-studied example would be the Grotta Regina in Monte Gallo, near Palermo (Sicily); it was visited between the fifth and first centuries BCE by worshippers connected to the cult of the same goddess, as portrayed in inscriptions and graffiti found on ships, and with a probable cult of Isis that has been suggested by several scholars.[4] In relation to the study of this sacred place, it has been pointed out that the cult must have involved a part-time religious team, trained to carry out the essential rituals in these extra-urban locations and aboard the ships as well, a frequent activity to which reference was made above and will also be made below (Christian 2013).

The representation of vessels in sacred sites was part of the everyday religious life of sailors during antiquity and became important elements within a ritual (López-Bertrán, García-Ventura, and Krueger 2008) that is found in Phoenician (such as Kition), Minoan (for example, in Malia), Greek (Delos), or Roman (Ostia) temples (Romero Recio 2000: 18–22).[5] This kind of religious expression saw continuity in time. During the Middle Ages and later in modern and contemporary times, more graffiti of ships have continued to appear in Christian churches, illustrating the devotees' hopes to secure the protection of the deity or of the patron saints, as with Saint Nicholas or Saint Mark (Basch 1978: 40–54; 1987: fig. 533 (grafitto at the church of Saint-Luc in Phocis); Ovtcharov 1995: 327–33 (examples between the fourteenth and eighteenth centuries). Even if it is difficult to classify some of these graffiti as votive offerings,[6] the continuity of their presence in sacred sites is significant along the centuries.

A cave implied a circumscribed physical space, but there were other sacred areas created by sailors that have left no archaeological traces because rituals took place in the open air. Strabo (3.1.4) alludes to a ritual that took place on the Sacred Promontory, between Cape Saint Vincent and Sagres (Portugal) (Figure 2.1), according to which those reaching it would turn the stones

FIGURE 2.1 The sacred promontory between Cape Saint Vincent and Sagres (Portugal) with the lighthouse at present. © Mirella Romero Recio (author).

that were scattered on the ground, in groups of three or four, changing their position. Strabo, following Artemidorus, stated that there was no altar or sanctuary dedicated to any divinity, though I believe, taking into consideration references made by classical authors to different gods in this geographical area, that it may have been consecrated to one of the sailing gods such as Baal Saphon, and to an agrarian one, Baal Hammon, to whom powers are attributed in relation to natural disasters and endeavors that are hard to achieve (Romero Recio 1999). The association between chthonic and agrarian divinities with deities of navigation was also present in other Mediterranean sanctuaries, some as important as the one known as Kothon of Motya, where Baal 'Addir, who had a great sanctuary with a sacred pool since 770–750 BCE, shared space with Astarte (Figure 2.2). Baal 'Addir was identified with Poseidon and Astarte with Demeter, as recent archaeological excavations have revealed (Nigro 2013; Nigro [with the contribution of Spagnoli] 2014; Nigro and Spagnoli 2012; Spagnoli 2013).

The celebration of sacrifices was forbidden in the Sacred Promontory, and so was access during the night, the moment in which it was occupied by the gods.[7] Those wanting to participate in the ritual had to camp at dusk in a nearby spot and come during the day carrying water for the libations, as none could be found in the vicinity (and water was essential, as proven by the findings

FIGURE 2.2 The kothon at Motya (Sicily). The sacred pool of Baal 'Addir/Poseidon. © Mirella Romero Recio (author).

in excavations of sanctuaries such as Baal's 'Addir/Poseidon in Motya). As I proposed elsewhere, it is likely that those stones that believers used to turn were nothing other than stone anchors that the first sailors coming to this site had offered, as had happened at the temples of Ugarit, Byblos, or Kition, where they are placed in different positions and even seem to be trying to cause visitors to trip over (Frost 1969: 425–42; 1970: 14–24; 1991: 355–410), and in colonial Greek sanctuaries (Gianfrotta 1975: 311–19). Anchors were one of the favorite offerings made by sailors in the Mediterranean during Phoenician and Punic times, as well as in the pre-Hellenic, Greek, and Roman eras, with their religious importance thoroughly established (Romero Recio 2000: 29–61). Some scholars have proposed that this interpretation of the ritual to which Strabo refers is highly plausible, and it could have also taken place in other locations of the Atlantic coast such as Punta do Muíño do Vento (in Vigo, Galicia) (Suárez Otero 2017) and also in sacred sites associated to the sea where no archaeological remains have been found. Whether this possibility is accepted or not, it is a fact that in the west coast of the Iberian Peninsula there were places of worship that developed into navigational landmarks for the Phoenicians, as was the case of the Setubal Peninsula and the mouth of the river Sado (Portugal) (Gomes 2012: 99, 121, 124–5).

Undoubtedly, one of the oldest and most important sanctuaries that is associated with Phoenician sea travels in the westernmost part of their area of operations is Heracles-Melqart in Gades, where those arriving from the sea would carry out sacrifices (Strabo 3.5.5). It is, however, possible that the Heracleion, surrounded by other places of worship regularly visited by sailors (Romero Recio 2008: 79), might not only have been a place where mariners would come to thank and/or request salvation at sea, as well as the benefits obtained from their commercial transactions. As indicated by Manuel Álvarez Martí-Aguilar, it is probable that the temple's inscribed pillars, which are mentioned in Philostratus's *Vita Apollonii* (5.5), were imbued of a magical condition that would make them serve as talismans against tsunamis (Álvarez Martí-Aguilar 2017). The *Vita Apollonii* indicates that "their capitals were inscribed with letters which were neither Egyptian nor Indian nor of any kind which he could decipher" and that there "are ties between earth and ocean" (Philostratus [1912] 1989: 5.5), which could be interpreted as a religious response of apotropaic magic against a natural disaster perceived to have a cosmic essence (Álvarez Martí-Aguilar 2017: 978–93).

This attractive hypothesis may not be surprising if one considers that amulets were very present in the sphere of navigation, intending to fend off any kind of calamities that could take place during a voyage. For instance, a piece of coral placed on top of the mast with a seal skin granted protection against the winds, waves, and other mishaps to prevent shipwrecks, in addition to resisting lightning, typhoons, winds, and storms; seal and hyena skins kept away lightning from the ship's mast; red diamonds protected sailors; cinaedia had prophetic abilities as it could let sailors know beforehand whether the sea would be tranquil or stormy;[8] travelers carried along amulets, even offering them to the divinities that represented protective gods, such as Zeus Casio, or anchor-shaped ones, etc. (Romero Recio 2000: 33, 59–61) (Figure 2.3). This device, referred to above as a typical sanctuary offering, had a particular magical connotation onboard. Submarine excavations have uncovered numerous anchor clamps with inscriptions of "Savior" deities, such as Aphrodite *Sozousa*, or that were decorated with four astragali that were associated with good luck during navigation (39, with bibliography) (Figure 2.4). Moreover, the "sacred anchor" was only employed in extreme circumstances of peril, being the last resort when trying to drop anchor and calm the storm.

Further, mariners had the habit of attributing human qualities to their ships, in some sort of belief or superstition which later, in medieval and modern times, went as far as granting a soul to the vessel, a concept that reached the present day in different forms (Ovtcharov 1995: 329; Medas 2010). A ship could have the ability of speech, for instance the Argo of the Argonauts, consecrated by Jason in the sanctuary of Poseidon at the Isthmus, and many other votive vessels of which we have evidence through texts and archaeology (Dio Chrys., *Or.* 37.15);[9] or it could be sight, through the eyes at the prow, which could also ward off ill fortune (A. *Suppl.* 716–18; Péron 1974: 30, 143n6; Carlson 2009: 347–65). It is still nowadays common for sailors to paint these eyes seeking

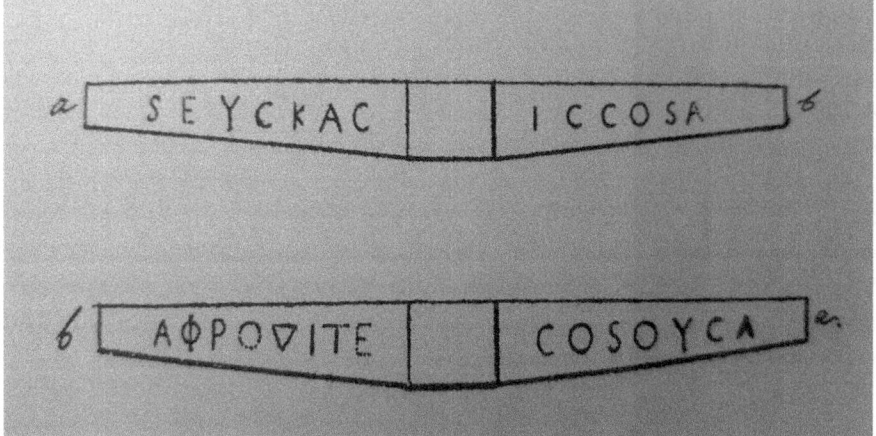

FIGURE 2.3 Anchor discovered at Cape Palos (Murcia, Spain) with inscriptions to Zeus Casio and Aphrodite *Sozousa*. In Laymond and Jiménez de Cisneros y Hervás (1906).

FIGURE 2.4 Lead anchor stock. © Museo Archeologico Regionale Lilibeo Marsala-Baglio Anselmi.

some type of supernatural protection (Filgueiras 1995: 149–66; Medas 2010). The apotropaic nature of the prow eye seems to be universal, as it is found as much in the Mediterranean as on the shores of Asia.

Magic was, therefore, part of seafaring religious practices at the individual and collective levels, using amulets and apotropaic eyes in the former, the latter ritualized through onboard practices (animal hides, precious stones, sacred anchors) and at the sanctuary (talisman-pillar), as a means of confronting grave perils, such as storms or tsunamis, that could affect not only the mariner but those left ashore as well. Relatives that had not taken sail and had invested in ships and cargo similarly suffered the risks taken by their loved ones. This resulted in the common consultation of cathartic astrology, which added to the consultations made by the sailors themselves at oracular sanctuaries (Alvar Nuño 2017).

The Phoenician god Melqart, identified with his Greek counterpart Herakles,[10] was venerated as the protector of sailors in the Strait of Gibraltar, not only in the aforementioned famous sanctuary of Gades, but also at other locations along the coast. Avienus (*Ora* 358–61) indicated that near the Pillars of Herakles/Hercules there were temples and altars dedicated to this divinity where sacrifices were made by those approaching on their ships, promptly leaving afterwards. Other authors correspondingly mention worship sites consecrated to protective divinities such as Astarte, with her veneration corroborated by archaeology and whose adoration was present with that of Melqart's, as stated earlier, in Gorham's Cave or in Motya, and successively assimilated by local communities (Dominguez Monedero 2018; Ferrer 2002; Mederos 2009). Phoenicians and Greeks alike participated in the experiences of the journey that affected the religiousness of sailors and the places where their piety was manifested. As a consequence, the majority of religious practices and coastal sacred sites that are mentioned in the sources and/or that have left archaeological vestiges were shared, assimilated, and integrated to such an extent among these mariners that they became consolidated in the Mediterranean region by Roman times, perpetuating in many instances their existence within Christian devotion. In the same manner that Greco-Roman gods and heroes traveled the seas while protecting their sailors (Bonnet and Bricault 2016), there were also Christian saints that sailed and were venerated by mariners (Orselli 2010). Ellen Churchill Semple observed almost a century ago that sailors built sanctuaries at locations where shipwrecks used to be frequent, and some of these resulted in shrines dedicated to both saints and the Virgin in her different advocations (Semple 1927: 28, 530, 624; 1931: 369–74).[11] (Cape) Maleas,[12] (Mount) Athos, Cape Nimphaeum, (Cape) Tainaron (also Matapan, or Tenaro), (Cape) Caphereus,[13] and (Cape) Pelorus are just a few of them.

Pelorus, who emerges in the sources as Hannibal's helmsman was, according to Servius, buried at the homonymous promontory in Sicily, by the Strait of Messina.[14] His case is by no means exceptional: literature, first, alludes to other sepulchers dedicated to heroes at coastal locations; secondly, to sanctuaries dedicated to pilots in particularly dangerous capes and promontories, where sailors expected to find the protection of those who had made good on their task of bringing their vessels safely to harbor; and, lastly, to festivities. According to Plutarch, Theseus chose Nausithous for his pilot and Phaeax for his lookout man and created in their honor the festival of the Cybernesia, or Pilot's Festival, held in the month of Boedromion (September/October) (Plut., *Thes.* 17.6–7).[15] Another steersman, Phrontis, for Menelaus's ship and who had died returning from Troy on Cape Sounion (Attica), was buried here by the hero and probably received worship in a heroon near the temple of Athena (Hom., *Od.* 3.278–85; Paus. 10.25.2; Abramson 1979: 1–19). Similarly, Elpenor was buried by Odysseus in a tomb near the sea with his oar piercing his tumulus, next to the stela, in commemoration of his occupation in life.[16] It was traditionally said that his tomb was on Mount Circeo, in Lazio (Italy), where he was venerated at least since the fourth century CE, though his myth can be found in this area at least two centuries earlier.[17] Yet another example is that of the companions of Aeneas. First, Misenus, who was laid to rest next to his oar, arms and trumpet, on a dangerous promontory next to Cumae (Italy), which then took his name.[18] Secondly, Cinaethus died upon leaving Troy and was buried on the Cinaethion promontory (D.H. 1.50.2). Thirdly, his pilot, Palinurus, was buried after falling into the sea and venerated on the homonymous cape, near Velia (Campania, Italy).[19]

Even if it were possible to continue listing other renowned pilots, it is now convenient to return to the case that named Cape Perolus (Punta del Faro), due to its paradigmatic nature. At this point of the northeastern end of Sicily, on the Strait of Messina, where the currents caused by the meeting of the Tyrrhenian and Adriatic Seas were so treacherous, that the first Greeks to sail those waters populated them with two terrible monsters: Kharybdis and Skylla (Figure 2.5). Fear of crossing the strait resulted in the need to create sacred sites so that sailors could implore the assistance of the gods through their signs of devotion. However, when this version of the deed of Pelorus took place, as Hannibal's pilot, there already existed signs of worship associated with seafaring in the area; there was even another character with the same name of Pelorus, from Thessaly, son of the god of the sea, Poseidon, who on this promontory had a famous sanctuary erected by Orion (Hes., Frg. 149; Merkelbach and West; Giangiulio 1996: 257). Athenaeus (14.639d–640a), according to writings by Baton of Sinope, refers to the existence of sacrifices in honor of Zeus *Peloros* and of festivities known as the Peloria, introduced after an earthquake devastated Thessaly (Mili 2015: 239–41; Robertson 1984: 7–8). Near this promontory there is also knowledge of a nymph identified by the name of Peloria who appeared on coins (Vian 1952: 140–2). Upon discussing the myths of Orion, Diodorus connected the formation of the Strait of Messina with the earthquake and stated the following:

> In Sicily, for instance, for Zanclus, who was king at that time of the city which was called at that time after him Zanclê, but now Messenê, he built certain works, and among them he formed the harbour by throwing up a mole and made the Actê, as it is called. And since we have mentioned Messenê we

FIGURE 2.5 The strait of Messina from Torre Faro (Sicily). © Wikimedia Commons (public domain).

think it will not be foreign to our purpose to add to what has been set forth thus far what men have written about the Strait. The ancient mythographers, that is, say that Sicily was originally a peninsula, and that afterward it became an island, the cause being somewhat as follows. The isthmus at its narrowest point was subjected to the dash of the waves of the sea on its two sides and so a gap (*rhegma*) was made (*anarrhegnusthai*), and for this reason the spot was named *Rhegion*, and the city which was founded many years later received the same appellation as the place. Some men say, however, that mighty earthquakes took place and the neck of what was the mainland was broken through, and in this way the Strait was formed, since the sea now separated the mainland from the island. But the poet Hesiod states the very opposite, namely, that when the sea extended itself in between, Orion built out the headland which lies at Peloris and also erected there the sanctuary of Poseidon which is held in special honour by the natives; after he had finished these works he removed to Euboea and made his home there; and then, because of his fame, he was numbered among the stars of heaven and thus won for himself important remembrance.

(Diodorus Siculus, *Library*, 4.85.1–5 [translation Oldfather 1939].)

On the Sicilian side of the Strait of Messina, therefore, there was a sanctuary dedicated to Poseidon by Orion, a character to whom the construction of a harbor and of the Pelorus promontory is owed, and who had ascended to the heavens in the form of the famous constellation. In addition, we are aware of the existence of a colossal statue that, according to Olympiodorus of Thebes (Fr. 15; Müller 1961), had been erected by the ancients to stop the eruption of Etna and to prevent crossing by sea to the island.[20] The statue had an ever-burning flame on one of its feet and a water fountain on the other. The most likely possibility is for the statue to represent Zeus *Peloros*, as paintings found in the small pagan sanctuary within Santa Lucia's catacomb in Syracuse would indicate, and it would have served as a lighthouse (Caruso 2017). The divinity, represented with his right foot on the prow of a vessel and with his name, Zeus *Peloros*, written in Greek over his head, was surrounded by other images that signified sea-related worship: Porthmos, the personification of the Strait, holding a rudder in his right hand, Apollo *Archegetes* and, probably, Isis (Caruso 2017: Tav. 5–7).[21] The presence of these deities in another enclave of the Sicilian coast highlights the importance of the sacred sites of the Strait for all of those traversing the sea to or from Sicily. Taking into account the relationship between the formation of the strait with an earthquake and large waves, as mentioned by Diodorus, it is possible to suggest that the statue of Zeus *Peloros*, hindering eruptions from the Etna and invasions across the sea, could have also stayed tsunamis (sea earthquakes resulting in huge waves), akin to the columns at the temple of Heracles-Melqart in Gades.[22] That transcendence would make the cults at Pelorus reach a degree of relevance in the entire island, including Syracuse, where veneration of sea-related deities was commonplace.

It is in this famous colony that we find a practice that must have been common throughout the Mediterranean: the throwing overboard of objects as offerings in sight of a temple consecrated to a protective deity. According to Athenaeus (11.462b), following news provided by Polemon, when sailors set sail from harbor they would contemplate the golden shield decorating the frontal pediment of the temple that Athena had in Ortygia. Once far enough and unable to see the shield, they would fill a number of ceramic cups, previously taken from an altar located next to the sanctuary of Gaea Olympia outside the city, with flowers, honeycombs, frankincense, and other spices and would subsequently throw them into the sea. Athena was one of the favorite deities for mariners because she protected shipwrights and pilots (as with Odysseus, who had her assistance), guided the ships, would take bird form to help sailors, received rudders and rams as offerings, and had temples on promontories where she received veneration with advocations such as *Promachorma, Aithuia, Ekbasía,* or *Pronoia*.[23] Over her temple in Ortygia, situated on the highest place in the city and perfectly visible from the sea, now stands the Cathedral of the Natività di Maria Santissima.

This type of offering mentioned by Athenaeus is not unusual. Both literary and archaeological sources show that these cups and other offerings in honor of protective deities were thrown into the sea, as happens with the adoration of Achilles in the Black Sea.[24] It is possible that the recipient of these receptacles in Syracuse was Dionysos *Morychos*,[25] who probably had an altar in the area of the isthmus near the temple of Gaea, a key location between land and sea, between the farmers growing vines and producing wine and the sailors who drank it to then return the cup to the god by tossing it overboard (Caruso 2012).[26] The worship of Dionysos *Morychos* may have been related to the festival of the Anthesteria (Caruso 2012), held in the month Antesterion (February/March), which included a procession of the god atop a ship. In this celebration, Dionysos appears in all his facets: agricultural divinity bringing wine, deity of hell who dragged the deceased with him, and sea god arriving by ship (Caruso 2012).[27] This way, the farming and sailing aspects occur again side by side, now in the Greek world, as was previously observed for the Phoenicians.

The Sicilian coastline offers numerous testimonies of religious manifestations associated with divinities that sailors correlated with their day-to-day life across the Mediterranean. The Dioscuri (Castor and Pollux), for instance, were revered in many places, such as Syracuse, among others, and Tyndaris,[28] a city consecrated to them and opposite which we find the island of Didyma (present-day Salina). According to Strabo (6.2.11), it owed its name to its double shape, for the twin volcanoes could be identified with the representation of Castor and Pollux, also twins. Undoubtedly, the small landmass was a location sacred to mariners, maintaining such nuance until contemporary times, this is indicated by the many offerings presented by sailors in the Santuario della Madonna del Terzito.[29] The Dioscuri, as they are commonly known, were deities that could directly intervene during navigation by saving the vessels.[30] According to the *Homeric Hymn to the Dioscuri* (33.8–11), to prompt the arrival of these divinities when storms were lashing the ship, seamen had to sacrifice white lambs set at the highest part of the stern. A white animal was sacrificed because these were the bearers of light and, consistent with tradition, in addition to materializing in the form of Saint Elmo's fire[31] (an atmospheric phenomenon that originates due to an electric overload and which heralds the end of the storm) they formed a constellation that served as guide for sailors at nighttime (Lycoph., *Alex.* 510; Aratus, *Phaen.* 147; Chapouthier 1935: 256–7).

Light and stars were indissolubly bound to the mariner's religiousness. Light could be artificial, through the fires that illuminated lighthouses or the altars of temples oriented to the sea, like that of Astarte-Aphrodite in Eryx. Aelian said in *On the Nature of Animals* (10.50) that the goddess, who received plentiful offerings, had an open-air altar in the sanctuary where many animals were sacrificed. The fire of this altar was always burning, day or night. The same author also mentions the celebration of festivities known by all inhabitants of

Sicily as the "Festival of the Embarkation" and the "Festival of the Return" (Aelian, *On Animals* 4.2). We know that Aphrodite frequently appears accompanied by sea epithets, *Pontia* (Of the Sea), *Limenia* (Of the Harbor), *Epilimenia* (On the Harbor), *Pelagia* (Of the Sea), *Acrea* (Of the Peak), *Euploia* (Smooth-Sailing), that made reference to her marine purview, and sailors presented objects, anchors for example, that are reminders of her activity. All facets of the goddess were put to the service of sailing, including her role as protector of sexuality and of the prostitutes found in the harbors, and focused through a lens that allowed for the contemplation of the goddess as one of the most important ones in the nautical scope (Romero Recio 2000: e.g., 15 ss., 38 ss., 123 ss.; Demetriou 2010: 67–89). The temple of Eryx is but one example among many others in the Mediterranean where the goddess received the reverence of sailors. Previously, the cult to another goddess had developed, Astarte, well known to travelers; later, the heir to Aphrodite in the Roman world, Venus, would be adored.[32] This type of worship associated with a spot visible from the sea and firmly established on a coastal promontory would have its profuse continuation elsewhere. Among others, a well-studied case is that of the temple of Astarte in Capo Sant'Elia (Cagliari, Sardinia), which would also probably have served as a lighthouse-temple near which the church of Sant'Elia al Monte was later built (Ibba et al. 2017).

The light that mariners expected could also have a natural source and come from the shining rocks that were mentioned before, from divine manifestations as those involving the Dioscuri in the middle of the storm, or from the sun or the stars. The appearance of deities associated with light expressed a positive presence which was linked to the imminent assistance to be provided to devotees; this was reinforced during navigation and in the darkness of a storm or at night. Phosphoric deities, such as Leucothea or the siren Leucosia, but also other deities, such as Artermis or Hecate, who bore the *Phosphoros* epithet, helped sailors (Romero Recio 2000: 65). The light through which these divinities showed themselves could be related to the nimbus surrounding Helios or Apollo, but also crowning the Catholic Virgin or saints in the offerings made by sailors in Christian churches (Tripputi 1995: 28–9; Caruso and Di Blasi 2017). In these places of adoration there were painters dedicated to producing paintings representing the shipwreck endured by the client and his miraculous salvation favored by the apparition of the Virgin, Christ, and other saints floating in the sky surrounded by light.

In addition, there is also knowledge of the offering of votive tablets in gratitude for survival after a shipwreck, a dreadfully traumatic experience that led to presenting the gods with items as personal as hair or clothing (Romero Recio 2000: 109–12). Cicero reports an anecdote of Diagoras, according to which a friend had asked him how it was possible for him not to believe that the gods were looking after men when the sanctuary of the Great Gods on

Samothrace was full of votive pictures brought by those who had survived a shipwreck, to which Diagoras wittily replied that it was due to the fact that the dead at sea could not paint (Cic., *de nat. deor.* 3.37, 89; cf. D.L. 6.2.59). Isis also received this kind of offering, as Juvenal and Tibullus mention (Juvenal, Satires, 12.26–29; scholia 12.27–28; Tib. 1.3.23–4, 27–8; *Anth. Pal.* 6.231), and even though no material remains have reached us it is possible to conjecture that those paintings must have been similar to the archaic painting of wood panels dated from between the seventh and third centuries BCE, which were found in a cave in Pitsa, near Corinth, and show a sacrificial scene (Larson 2001: 232–3, 261, fig. 5.18; Nilsson [1921] 1967: 248). Isis was a goddess with strong links to the sea. She took epithets such as *Euploia* (Smooth-Sailing), *Pelagia* (Of the Sea), and *Pharia* (Of the lighthouse), she was venerated as the inventor of navigation and sails, she controlled the sea winds and in her honor the *navigium Isidis* "ship of Isis" was held, a celebration that opened the sailing season on March 5.[33] Although we are uncertain as to what was represented in those votive tablets dedicated to the Great Gods on Samothrace and to Isis, one can suppose that, as in the case of the offerings made in Christian churches, the paintings could portray the scene of the shipwreck. A relief belonging in the collection at the Museo Lapidario Maffeiano (Verona, Italy), which was studied by Margherita Guarducci, depicted a scene in which a sailor was thanking the Dioscuri for his survival after a shipwreck (Guarducci 1984: 136–41, Tav. V). Moreover, we know that the shipwrecked who merely scraped out a living in the harbors reminding passers-by of their misfortune, shaved their heads, bandaged their chest as if they were injured so as to generate more compassion, and carried, hanging from their necks, a painting of the shipwreck they survived.[34] This last piece of information leads us to interpret that the tablets dedicated in sanctuaries by those who survived the disaster analogously represented that scene, and it is possible that, as in the case of the relief of the Dioscuri, the helping deity would also be represented in them.

Whether the representation of the deity was surrounded by light on these tablets or not, marine divinities such as the Dioscuri manifested themselves with a grandiose luminous effect and Isis was also associated with light. One of the steps in the Isiac initiation, described by Apuleius in his *Metamorphoses*, represents the moment in which the faithful sees the sun shining in the middle of the night, in reality, the manifestation of Isis.[35]

Another trait shared by the Dioscuri, Isis, and other gods and heroes associated with the sea was their relation with celestial bodies. So far we have made mention of the Dioscuri and Orion as constellations, but Isis was also known for being responsible for cosmic order, giving instructions to the stars, as we see in a Greek inscription from *Supplementum epigraphicum Graecum* (SEG 9 [1944], 192). The observation of the stars and the sun's position during the different seasons of the year held great relevance. For nighttime navigation, the Phoenicians depended on the location of the Little Dipper and Ursa Minor; and the Greeks on the Big Dipper and Ursa Major (Medas 2004), and they both attributed immaterial qualities to the stars that could easily be identified with divine beings; consequently, astronomical knowledge would have to be collected at temples (Stiglitz 2014).

Archaeoastronomical studies have resulted in interesting data relating to the orientation of sanctuaries dedicated to sailors in their alignment with the stars. For instance, it is known that worship at the temple of Kothon at Motya, referred to above in connection to sailing, had an astral nature. The excavations produced baetyls and aligned stelae, as well as an object, fixed to the pavement, that was probably presented as an offering and which has been interpreted as a measuring device similar to an astrolabe. Studies conclude that the temple was oriented toward the constellation of Orion and it is possible that Baal might have been identified with this character that also had an important presence in sea-related cults in the Strait of Messina (Nigro 2010).

There are myriads of elements involved in the religious practices developed by mariners during antiquity and that responded to an inner logic derived from the practice of a professional activity that constantly called for divine intervention. The expressions of the sailors were varied, permissive, and flexible, as contact with a wide variety of cults and the everyday exposure to danger allowed for the integration of all divine forces able to contribute to the success of navigation. In the end, seafarers prayed and showed gratitude in a resolute dynamic that left nothing to chance and tried to bind together everything that could preserve their existence, passing from land to sea, from the heavens to the underworld.

CHAPTER THREE

Networks

Maritime Trade in the Ancient World from the Hellenistic through the Byzantine Periods

ZARAZA FRIEDMAN

INTRODUCTION

The Greeks realized that by controlling the seas, the luxuries of foreign goods obtained by the intercommunication would be theirs. Thucydides (1.15.1) understood that those who paid attention to the navies gained in power with revenue and control over others:

> Such were then the navies of the Hellenes, both those of early and those of later times; nevertheless, those who paid attention to such matters (to naval business) acquired not a little strength by reason both of revenue of money and of control over other people.

This, of course, was also true for the Roman–Byzantine periods. Trade allowed not only the movement of goods but also the dispersion of peoples, extended political contacts, and exchanges of ideas, thus contributing to cultural diffusion. The role of the sea in the spread of ideas in antiquity is mostly evidenced by shipbuilding technology and navigation. The Mediterranean Sea played an important role in cultural development and its diffusion from prehistory until nowadays. The Mediterranean Sea is unique and had a great importance in antiquity because it connected three continents, namely Africa, Asia, and Europe, through sea trade, and also geographically. The Romans called the Mediterranean Sea *Mare Internum* (Internal Sea) and *Mare Nostrum* (Our

Sea). The first attestation of the name *Mare Mediterraneum* (Landlocked Sea) was stated by the Roman grammarian Gaius Julius Solinus (third century CE), whereas Isidore of Seville (sixth century CE) converted this term *Mediterraneum* to the proper name as it has been known since the sixth century CE (Kahlaoui 2018: 24 and n7). This name came into common usage in the twelfth to thirteenth century CE. Aelius Aristides, a Greek sophist and rhetorician, when visiting Rome in 143/4 CE, expressed his vision on the role of the Roman Empire and the importance of the Mediterranean Sea:

> The sea (Mediterranean) is like a belt that extends in the middle of the *oikoumene* (the inhabited world), as well as in the middle of your empire (Roman). Around this sea, the great continents extend far and wide, constantly augmenting your wealth with something of their own.

The Roman Empire founded by Augustus after the Battle of Actium (31–30 BCE) expanded via the Mediterranean, which became the main seaway of communication. Therefore, the Roman Empire was "built on water" (Rickman 1996: 1). The height of the Roman sea trade in the Mediterranean is considered to be between 200 BCE and 200 CE.

WHAT WAS TRADED IN THE MEDITERRANEAN WORLD IN ANTIQUITY?

The most vital merchandise traded in the Mediterranean world in antiquity was grain and wheat. The supply centers for these products from the Hellenistic through the Byzantine periods were the Black Sea, Egypt, and North Africa. Other commodities were olive oil; wine; copper, tin, and lead ingots; as well as glassware, woolen, and silk textiles and a great variety of other products. Fine wines were produced in many places, such as the islands of Lesbos, Samos, and Chios off Asia Minor, Thasos in the northern Aegean, many regions in Italy, as well as Spain and France. Cnidus, on the southwest coast of Asia Minor and the Island of Rhodes sent shiploads of wine to Athens, Alexandria, and other centers where the demand for wine was too great to be fulfilled by the local vineyards. Olive oil, an important merchandise for the Roman population, had its main centers of production in Greece, Spain, and Italy.

The main spice in the Roman diet was *garum*, a type of condiment made of fermented fish (it was processed by fermenting fish in salt for up to three months). Greek sources mention fish salteries being in activity as early as the fifth century BCE. *Garum* itself starts being mentioned in the first century BCE, when Horace praised the *garum* "made from the sweet fish of Spain" (Curtis 1988: 205). Pliny (*NH* 31.94) wrote that the best *garum* was produced from *scomber* (mackerel) by the *socii*[1] (allies of Rome) of New Carthage (31.94). These products also reached units stationed along the *limes*[2] (207). Migdal on the western shore of the Sea of Galilee, Israel (*c.* 5 kilometers north of Tiberias), in the Hellenistic and Roman times was known as *Migdal Nunia* (Aramaic) or *Tharichaea* (Latin)/*Tower of Fish*. This site was also a center for the production of *garum* in the Eastern Mediterranean. Strabo (16.2.45) mentions that "in *Tharicaea* (Migdal Nunia) the sea (Sea of Galilee) provides the best fish for pickling" (Raban 1988: 323; Friedman 2008: 45).

Other products traded in the Roman Empire were metals such as lead, copper, marble, and wood (Figure 3.1).

The location of commercial centers in the Mediterranean evolved with time. In the fifth century BCE Athens was the main commercial center of the Eastern Mediterranean and her port at Piraeus was flooded with ships coming in from as far as Marseilles in the Western Mediterranean and the Black Sea from the east (Casson 1981: 38). In the third century BCE Ptolemaic Egypt became the main center of maritime trade in the Eastern Mediterranean, especially as the grain supplier of the ancient Mediterranean. The Nile was an important trade highway for the transport of grain from the fertile lands of the Fayum to Alexandria and thereafter shipped to Rome and other hub ports in the Mediterranean. The Roman hegemony in the Mediterranean started after First Punic War (241 BCE) when the Carthagian thalassocracy was crushed. Later, however, the Roman leadership in the Mediterranean in turn was to be shattered by the Vandal conquest in the mid-fifth century CE (Scheidel 2011: 29).

The political unification of the Roman Empire brought a major diminution of piracy in the second half of the first century BCE. The safe passage of goods and people all over the Mediterranean was guaranteed by well-organized military

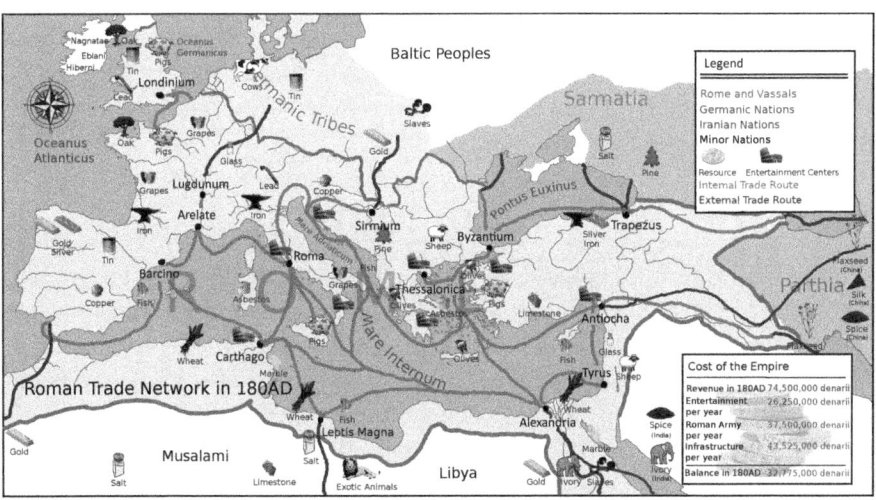

FIGURE 3.1 Map of trading goods in the second century BCE. © Wikimedia Commons (public domain).

fleets. Aelius Aristides (mentioned above) wrote that Rome became prosperous and abundant with varied merchandise due to the intensive sea trade coming from all over the Mediterranean:

> Of all that is grown or manufactured by each and every people, there is nothing that would not be here in abundance [Rome]. So many freight ships arrive here from everywhere, carrying every merchandise, throughout all seasons until the very end of the autumn [...]. Arrivals and departures of ships never cease, so much so that one may wonder how sufficient room can be found for the freight ships not merely in the harbors but in the entire area. (Rickman 1996: 3)

Before Rome had established its port at Ostia and later at Portus, Puteoli was Rome's port in the late Republican period and in the early empire. The famous arched mole in the port of Puteoli was probably built on Augustus's orders. It not only was a wonder of hydraulic engineering, with flushing channels to prevent silting of the inner basin, but also a tourist attraction (Rickman 1996: 9). The wax tablets discovered at Murecine, near Pompeii, confirm that under Emperor Gaius Caligula in the first century CE, the grain merchantmen coming from Alexandria were shipped to Puteoli (9). This grain was the most important merchandise to be shipped to Rome to feed the growing population.

The grain trade reached far and wide in the Mediterranean. Some Oxyrhynchus papyri provide important information on grain trade and how it reached ports on the Nile. Apparently, heavy river transport of grain occurred during the harvest season. These papyri mention that at some ports of the Oxyrhynchus Nome during a period of nine days, from Choiak 9 to 17, about 10,000 *artabas* of grain were loaded on boats and shipped to Alexandria (Adams 2018: 187 and table 6.2). When the cargo of grain arrived in Alexandria it was transferred from the authority of the *naukeros* (shipowner/captain) for the testing for impurities (188 and n67). The samples of wheat were sent to the *cheirismos*[3] in Neapolis (a part of the port of Alexandria).

WOOD TRADE

Another important trading good in antiquity was the wood or timber needed for shipbuilding, monumental construction, expensive furniture, heating for the bath-houses, cooking, and a variety of other industries. Metal production required huge quantities of wood to heat furnaces. In the Eastern Mediterranean wood mostly came from the area of modern-day Lebanon (ancient Byblos), Syria, and Turkey. The Assyrian relief of Sargon II (722–705 BCE) from his Palace at Khorsabad (now at the Louvre Museum) is the earliest pictorial evidence of seaborne trade in timber. The wooden logs are loaded and transported in the typical Phoenician Hippos Ships (Figure 3.2).

FIGURE 3.2 Timber transport by sea; Sargon's II palace at Khorsabad. © Wikimedia Commons (public domain).

The heavy cutting of timber in the Apennines during the two Punic Wars brought the Romans to look for new woodlands to supplement their wood industry. The dramatic increase in population at Rome during the Republic intensified the demand for wood. Therefore, the construction of *porticus inter lignarios* outside Porta Trigemina in 192 BCE was to bring wood logs up the Tiber to Rome (Meiggs 1980: 186). Cargoes of woods logs probably came from the coast of Lazio, as they did in the fourth century CE (Harris 2018: 218). The well-established commerce and organized trade of wood in the Roman Empire is illustrated by a mosaic floor in the office of wood shippers at Piazzale delle Corporazioni, Ostia (third century CE). Two sailing ships facing one another are placed on either side of a large rounded structure set on a raised rectangular podium. Flames are coming out from the top of the structure, probably indicating a lighthouse. The two-line inscription set into a *tabula ansata* indicates the function of the office—*Naviculariorum Lignariorum* (Friedman 2011: 94, fig. 3.7.3).

Great quantities of wood were needed for various industries. Considering that tiles and burnt bricks were the standard materials for roofing and construction, the production of these fired tiles and bricks for public and private constructions required enormous quantities of timber for the furnaces (Meiggs

1980: 187). Wood was also very much needed in the shipbuilding business to build merchant ships and war galleys. Dionysius of Halicarnassus (c. 60–7 BCE), when describing Italy's agricultural wealth, mentions that Italy was still rich in wood supplies:

> Her (Italy) woodlands on precipitous slopes, glens, and on unfarmed hills are most impressive; they provide a plentiful supply of ship timber and of timber for other purposes. (Dionysius of Halicarnassus, *Roman Antiquities*, 20.5)

Dionysius also mentions that timber can be transported without any obstacles:

> The abundance of rivers in all parts of the peninsula makes the transport and exchange of the products of the land easy [...] mountainous district called Sila (southern Italy), which is full of timber suitable for the building of houses and ships and every other kind of building. (20.5) Of this timber, that which grows nearest the sea and rivers is felled at the root and taken down in full length to the nearest harbor, sufficient in quantity to serve all Italy for shipbuilding and the construction of the houses. That which grows inland is cut up in sections for the making of oars, poles and all kinds of domestic implements and equipment, and is carried out on men's shoulders.
> (Dionysius of Halicarnassus, *Roman Antiquities*, 20.6)

Timber from the Alps was brought to Rome from the Adriatic ports of Aquileia and Salona in Dalmatia (Meiggs 1980: 192). Wood was also imported to Rome from the forests around the Black Sea, especially boxwood from Mount Cytorus in Mysia (192). By the fourth century the wood supply was quite reduced and therefore, in 364 CE, an order was sent by the emperors Valens and Valentinianus to allow shippers from North Africa to bring logs needed for the bathhouse furnaces (193).

SEA TRADE IN METALS

The Greeks had mined gold, silver, and lead from the rich deposits of the Lipsada mines near Stageira in southern Macedonia. Silver was mostly exploited from Laurion in Attica, as early as the sixth century BCE. Silver ore was found close to the surface, thus the earliest means of mining was in trenches and shallow caves (White 1984: 114). Other kinds of metals, mostly lead, gold, silver, and copper, were among valuable merchandise imported by the Romans. These metals were required for the minting of coinage throughout the Roman Empire, the production of military equipment, as well as expensive jewelry. The most useful information on Roman mining comes from a chronologically limited span covering the late first century BCE and the first century CE. Pliny (*NH* 32II and 34), as procurator of Hispania Tarraconensis, had first-hand experience of the large-scale gold mining operations in northwest Spain

(Edmondson 1989: 85). Early Christian writers also provide some hints on mining operations in the third to fourth centuries CE, when they discuss the condemnation of Christians to hard labor in gold and silver mines in Numidia, copper mines in Cyprus, Palestine, and Cilicia (86). Certain regulations for gold mining appear in the *Codex Theodosianus* between 365 and 392, and 424 CE (86). The northwest of the Iberian Peninsula, especially the sites of Gallaecia and Asturia were among the richest gold fields known to the Romans, and their exploitation started soon after the final conquest of the area by Augustus. These gold mines were very important sources of precious metal for the Roman Empire during the first and second centuries CE, and they were the property of the Roman state. The mining districts were under the control of *procuratores metallorum* (metals officers). The procurators managed the mines, according to the imperial policy adapted to the local conditions, or were authorized to lease single mines to individuals or associations (Healy 1978: 130; Edmondson 1989: 88). The procurators were also responsible for the collection of the revenues due for the imperial treasury. They were usually *equites* (citizens who originally formed the cavalry of the Roman army and later had a great political importance) or freedmen (Healy 1978: 131). The *tabularii* (scribes) recorded the quantity of metal mined. Slaves and locals were in charge of the technical tasks of mining (131). According to recent studies in ancient mining it is suggested that one region (the Duerna) produced 3,000 kilograms of gold per annum for 130 years; thus in total it is estimated that the northwestern region of Roman Spain provided approximately 7 percent of the state revenue under the Flavians (Edmondson 1989: 88). The Romans also extracted gold from the mines in the Iberian Peninsula, at Las Medulas, *c.* 60 kilometers west of the military colony of Asturica Augusta, in modern Astorga, Spain (White 1984: 116). In Britain, the mining business was well organized after the Roman invasion in 43 CE. The areas rich in lead were Mendip, Wales, and the Midlands. Mining in Britain and its exploitation was restricted by legislation (124). Pliny (*NH* 39.49) mentions that black lead (used for pipes or in sheets) was extracted with great labor in Spain, and in all the Gallic provinces; but in Britannia it was found close to the surface in such abundance that a law was passed prohibiting anyone from working more than a certain amount. In Britain the Dolaucothi gold mines were worked intensively starting soon after the conquest of Claudius and continued until the Antonine period, but numismatic evidence suggests that some exploitation took place at least as late as the reign of Gratian (375–83 CE) (Edmondson 1989: 92).

Some pictorial evidence from mosaics and reliefs offer a better understanding of metal trade in the Roman period. One such pictorial representation is nicely rendered in a mosaic found near Sousse, Tunisia (third century CE), now displayed at the Bardo Museum (Figure 3.3). A ship anchored near the shore is suggested by the stevedores walking in shallow water, and the static position of

FIGURE 3.3 Weighing lead or gold ingots by the shore. © DEA PICTURE LIBRARY / Getty Images.

the ship with the mast lowered on deck; no mooring nor anchor line is visible; this ship just brought a cargo of lead, or iron, or gold ingots that is unloaded by stevedores, who bring the bars to the shore where they are weighed. Many lead ingots were found within several shipwrecks around the North African coast, Spain, Croatia, and Italy, as well as in the Eastern Mediterranean. A cargo of five lead ingots was found in 1994 around the submerged northern breakwater in Area K at Caesarea Maritima, Israel. These ingots revealed that they were made during the reign of Emperor Domitian (81–96 CE), as attested by the long inscription on the top of the bars "IMP.DOMIT. CAESARIS.AVG.GER" (Imperator Domitianus Augustus Germanicus) (Figure 3.4). Different marks on the ingots attest their manufacture and weight (each ingot weighs 200 Roman *libra* = *c*.70 kg). The inscription "MET. DARD" (*metallum Dardanicum*) attests that their place of origin is from the rich lead and silver mines from the Roman province of Dardania, in the region of the Kosovo (Raban 1999: 70). These ingots offer conclusive evidence to indicate that in the last decade of the first century CE, a rather large area of the northwestern breakwater of the Herodian harbor was submerged and this created traps for the ships entering the harbor.

TRANSPORT OF AMPHORAE AND THEIR PACKING

Amphorae bring evidence of seaway transactions of goods consumed on a large scale in antiquity, especially wine and oil, as well as different food stuffs, such as salted dried fish, olives, dates, *garum*, etc. In order to manage shipping contents, amphorae were utilized for easily and systematically recording loads. Herodotus reports that before the Persian conquest in 500 BCE, an extensive trade in wine came to Egypt from Greece and eastern Phoenicia. The fact that the Egyptians reused empty imported wine jars, indicate a system that was well organized by the king's order:

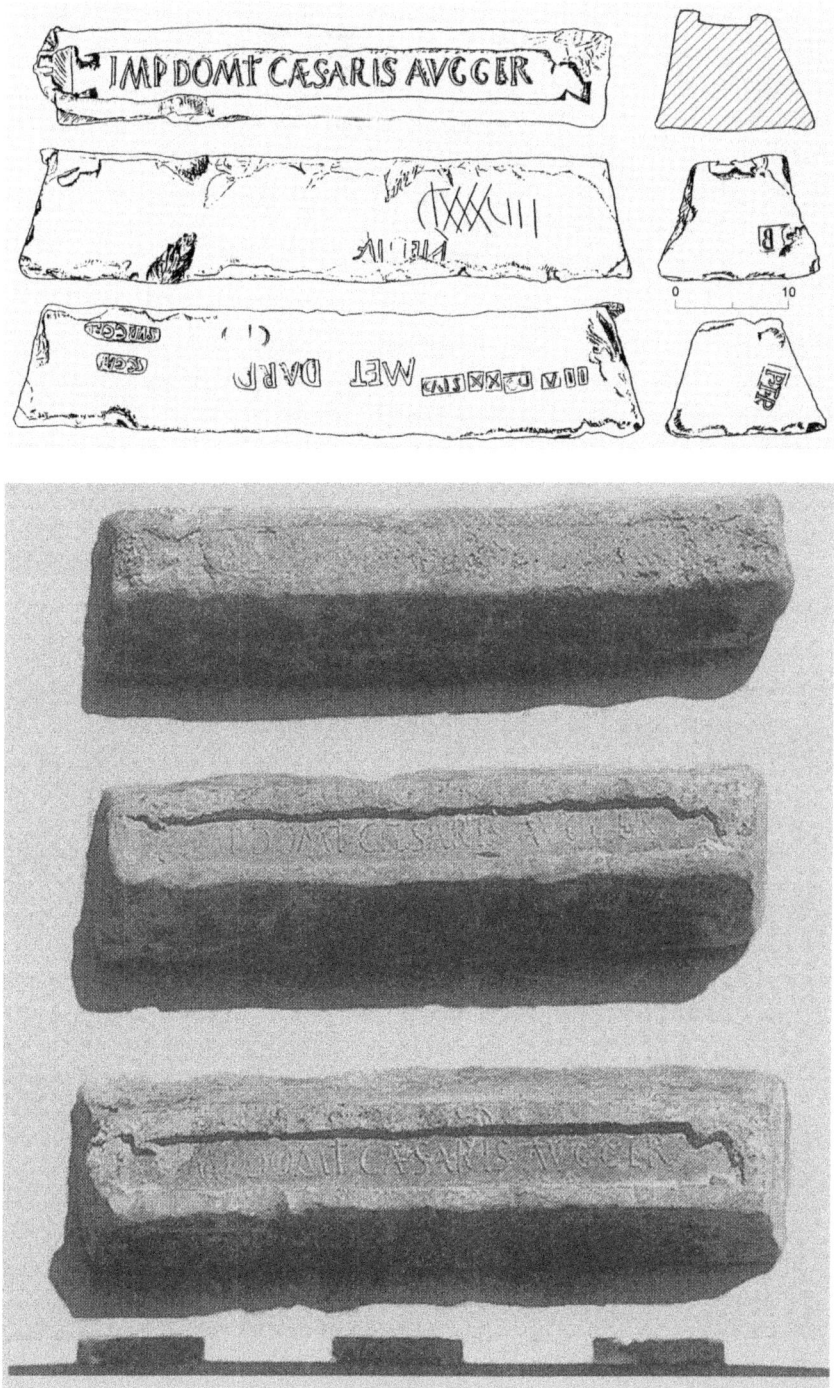

FIGURE 3.4 Lead ingots from Caesarea Maritima, Israel. © Zaraza Friedman (author).

Earthenware jars full of wine are brought into Egypt twice a year from all Greece and Phoenicia beneath; yet one might safely say that there is not a single empty wine jar anywhere in the country [...]. Each governor of a district must gather all the earthen pots from his township and take them to Memphis, and the people of Memphis must fill them with water and carry them to those waterless lands of Syria; so the earthen pottery that is brought to Egypt and unloaded or emptied there is carried to Syria to join the stock that has already been taken there.

(Herodotus 3.6)

The transportation and packing of amphorae cargo in sea trading is evidenced by several mosaics. Some of these representations show amphorae sealed with clay lids or stoppers. Three mosaics from different sites in the Mediterranean dating from the third to sixth centuries CE show how amphorae cargoes were packed on board of merchantmen:

1. *Fortuna Redux* mosaic (third to fourth century CE) from Thebessa, modern Algeria; North African jars are packed in vertical position in two horizontal rows on the deck of a merchantman (*navis oneraria*) with their necks and rims projecting above the gunwale. These jars with egg-shape shoulders, long necks, and outer inverted rims are sealed with clay stoppers, deduced from the white covers (Ferdi 1998: 172, bottom). They may be associated with the Dressel type 1B or 2B, which were liquid containers for wine, olive oil as well as *garum*. The ship bears some adornments that characterize Hellenistic warships: the *proembolion* (upper ram) is adorned with the bronze head of a wolf or fox, and three open branches *aphlaston* (upward curving) sternpost (Friedman 2005/6: 126). These elements became the characteristic adornments of Roman merchantmen. The prow of the ship is pointed to the left, thus the entire port side is revealed lengthwise. Nine large rowing oars project through square oarsports beneath the outrigger oarsbox. One large rudder oar is mounted on either quarter. The shaft of the port rudder projects through a square oarsport at the end of the outrigger oarsbox. The same arrangement was found on the starboard side; thus the ship was equipped with eighteen rowing oars and two rudders. Oars in merchantmen were auxiliary equipment and were used for rowing when entering/leaving harbors and also when the wind conditions were not favorable in the open sea. The ship is rigged with the main mast still stepped amidships. The sail is furled but the standing rig (forestays, backstays, and shrouds) is still in place, thus securing the mast in its vertical position. This ship is also rigged with an *artemon* (fore) mast and sail. The mast is inclined forward above the stempost and the sail is furled beneath the yard. The load capacity of such a vessel could range from 20 to 200 tons.
2. Haditha/Lod, Israel (first half of the sixth century CE). The sailing ship is in the process of leaving the shore, carrying onboard torpedo-like jars known as the Gaza type; the jars are sealed with conical lids. They are packed in

two superimposed rows (as can be seen in the National Maritime Museum, Haifa, Israel). This cargo of amphorae was probably loaded in the hold of the ship as well. The ship is leaving the anchorage, probably in the Nile Delta (as indicated by the Nilotic flora) as deduced from the effort of the helmsman to work the steering oars to stabilize the ship on its sailing course. The figure on the foredeck, holding the lower end of the forestay passed over his shoulder, is in charge of setting the sailing rig properly when the vessel reaches open waters. The standing figure on the shore facing the ship and waving his right hand to the crew on board also indicates that the ship is leaving the anchorage. The rounded spoon-shape hull is built with long, thin planks, as indicated by the strips of light and dark brown tesserae. Beneath the bow is depicted a symbolic and distorted cutwater, which may have resulted from the mosaicists' lack of nautical knowledge and also not understanding the function of this element. This element is the forward elongation of the keel and was meant to give better hydrostatics and hydrodynamics to the hull. The ship may be associated with a specific type known as *linter* or *kerkouros* type.[4]

3. The mosaic floor of the Church of Saints Lot and Procopius (557 CE) at Mount Nebo, Jordan, depicts a maritime scene. A rower facing the stern rows the boat with two oars mounted on either side of the gunwale. He works the oars in two oars/sit/pull technique with his back turned to the bow and the sailing direction. In the hold of a rowboat, fore and aft from the rower, bag-shaped jars are packed, sealed with conical lids (Piccirillo 1993: 160, fig. 209). The boat brings a cargo of wine or oil to a city enclosed by city walls and with gates opening to the river or seaside. The boat may represent a *scapha*[5] or *stlatta*[6] type.

Archaeological evidence of cargoes carried on board of ancient merchantmen (*navis oneraria*) and amphorae packing within the hold are provided by shipwrecks and tumbles of amphorae still preserving the outline of the ship on the bottom of the sea revealed during underwater surveys and excavations. The efficiency of cargo packing depends on maximizing the net volume to weight ratio, especially of liquid cargo. The egg-shaped amphorae provide a strong structure, thus supporting and dividing the weight of their contents and resistance for transportation, as well as from the stress of their repeated handling and tight packing within the hold of ships and storerooms. The handles and the base of the jars are ergonomically designed to provide a better grip by letting handlers curl their fingers around these handles. The earliest Greek or Roman amphorae sealed with cork lids or stoppers date back to the third century BCE and were found on the sea bottom (Twede 2002: 184). The shape of the amphorae enabled them to be packed in layers in storerooms on the deck or within the hold of ships. In general the toes (pointed end) of the jars in the first layer were secured in sand, pebbles, or dunnage. Once the first layer was secured and braced in place then the subsequent layer could be packed by fitting the toes into the space between the necks of the layer below (186).

One of the results of the Roman expansion in Greece, Asia Minor, and North Africa was the ability to export wine worldwide from the Italian regions of Latium and Campania. For comparative evidence, only two examples of shipwrecks with their packed cargo are discussed in this chapter due to limited space.

1. The *Kyrenia* wreck was discovered by a sponge diver in 1965 off the northern shore of Cyprus. The excavations of the site found 1 kilometer offshore and at a depth of 30 meters were carried out by the University of Pennsylvania under the direction of Michael Katzev from 1967 to 1969. The hull, preserved to about 75 percent, provides information on the construction of the ship and the repairs it bore through its sailing activity until it was wrecked. Negative impressions and small pieces of lead attest the lead sheathing of the hull at least up to the water line and also as part of repairs that had been made. The lead plates were attached to the outer hull with copper nails. The carbon 14 analyses indicate that the ship was built around 385 BCE with Aleppo pines, while Turkey oak was used for tenons, pegs, and the false keel. The ship was built in the traditional Mediterranean method of shell-first with planks jointed together by mortise and tenons. The original length of the ship was 14 meters; its width was 4.2 meters with an estimated load capacity of 25 tons. The cargo comprised more than 400 jars of distinct types. Among them, 343 jars originated from the island of Rhodes. Fore and aft above the keelson were found 29 millstones originating from the island of Kos, as they were also used as ballast (Muckelroy 1980: 43, middle). The small crew of the ship comprised four men, as evidenced by their personal belongings. The dating of the coins on board indicates that the ship was wrecked around 305 BCE, after eighty years of sailing in the northeastern Mediterranean.

2. *Madrague de Giens* (sank around 70–65 BCE), one of the largest ancient shipwrecks ever found, was discovered off the southern coast of Marseilles in 1967 by divers from the French Navy. Excavations were carried out between 1972 and 1982 by the Centre National de la Recherche Scientifique (CNRS) and the University of Provence, France (Muckelroy 1980: 55, bottom). The cargo of 6,000–6,500 jars of Dressel Type 1B, were manufactured in Italy and bore stamps mostly of *Publius Veveius Papus*, whose pottery shop was near Terracina in Latium, south of Rome (Tchernia et al. 1978: 14). Local stones from Latium used as ballast were found among the lower layer of the jars. The amphorae were stacked in four staggered rows, reaching a height of 3 meters. They showed remains of stopper sealing. Three lead ingots were found among the cargo on board. The ingots probably date to the second or first century BCE and were produced in Carthage (69, 71). Each ingot weighs 30/34 kilograms, and bears the inscriptions: "L.CAVLI.L.HISPALLI.MEN (Luci CARVLI Luci Fili HISPALLI MENENIA tribu), C.VTIVS.C.F. (Caius VTIVS Cai Filius), and C.VTI.C.F.MENEM (Cai VTIVS Cai Fili MENENIS tribu)" (71). The family of Manenia probably originates from the southern area of Campania and came to the region of Carthage were they mined lead (70–1; Pl., XXIV).

The presence of kitchenware, tableware, and other objects indicates that the cabin was placed near the stern of the ship. The double-planked hull was built in the traditional Mediterranean shell-first technique. Sheeting with lead plates on the outer planking reached at least the height of the waterline. The reconstructed size of the vessel indicates that its original length was about 40 meters, abeam was 9 meters, and the depth of the hold was 4.5 meters; the total cargo weight was 400 tons and the ship's displacement was 520 tons. *Madrague de Giens* was a very large Roman merchantman that may be associated with a type known from ancient literature as the *myriophoroi* type, capable of carrying about 10,000 amphorae (Delgado 2001: 252).

HARBOR ACTIVITIES

Our understanding of sea trading is directly linked to harbor activities in the ports of destination, such as the modalities of ships entering harbors, loading/unloading facilities of cargoes, or their recording for taxation and validity (Friedman 2005/6: 126–7, 131–2). The visual perception of such activities is well preserved in several mosaics and reliefs dating from the second to sixth centuries CE.

When ships entered or left the harbor they were guided by tugboats quite similar to the modern ones. The Rimini harbor mosaic (second to third century CE), made with black and white *tesserae* (mosaic stones) depicts a complex harbor scene. Two large sailing merchantmen with their sails in the process of furling are guided by a tugboat to a two-storied structure, probably the customs for checking in, near the harbor entrance (Municipal Museum, Rimini, Italy). On the flat roof of the first floor of the two-storied building a man is setting or controlling the flames set in a rounded short structure. The flat roof of this building may also have been used as a lighthouse.

Three oarsmen are depicted on the port side as rowing the tugboat, while the helmsman works a long steering oar. We may assume that the boat was rowed by six men, three seated on either side. The left-hand merchantman (behind the tugboat) tows astern a small rowboat without oars with a rope pulled taut from its prow to the root of the ship's sternpost. Several thwarts are shown from above, in bird's-eye view. On the quarter deck of the ship is placed a large capstan without its working bars. The sail of the left-hand ship is still fully open and the crew is engaged in furling it. The sail of the right-hand ship is furled beneath the yard. The crew still works the running rig. The *artemon* sail and yard are not visible on either ship; probably the crew removed them and stored them on the deck. Each sailing ship is rigged with a bowsprit projecting forward and almost perpendicular to the stempost. It was a device to secure the *artemon* rigging and also to tighten the running rigging during sailing in open waters. Either merchantman is inhabited by three crew members working the running rig to furl the sail. A long structure with pitched roof extending almost the entire length of the deck depicted on each ship indicates the storeroom. The quarter deck of the right-hand vessel is raised. A tall and rather fancy structure with pitched roof is placed on this deck. The arched entrance to the cabin is shown on the port wall, while three small, square windows are depicted on the lower side of the cabin. This structure may have been used by the helmsman/captain and also as an additional storeroom or as a kitchen. The quarter cabin in the left-hand vessel has a flat roof where a kneeling sailor works the brails and the starboard brace.

A more detailed harbor complex is depicted on the Kelenderis mosaic, Turkey (sixth century CE). A large sailing vessel is anchored within the inner harbor with its prow pointed to the arching colonnade quay (Friedman 2011: 43, fig. 3.4.7). Although no mooring or anchor lines are visible, the static position of the vessel indicates that it is anchored. On the mid-deck is depicted a large rectangular structure with a flat roof, which may indicate the storeroom for the cargo on board. The sail is still fully open and billowing before the mast, thus one may deduce that the wind blows from astern or port quarter. Large sailing ships could not enter into the harbor with a fully open sail because it was a burden on the ship's maneuvering to reach the quay for mooring. This anachronistic depiction is symbolic because the mosaicist wanted to show a fully rigged sailing vessel entering the harbor. The harbor scene is depicted though as being seen from the stern of the ship entering the harbor. The ship tows astern two ship's boats, one is a rowboat minus its oars (left-hand) and the second is a small sailing boat rigged with a fully open quadrangle sail (right-hand). The towline of each boat is secured to either quarter of the large vessel. These boats were used to carry cargo and/or passengers from/to the ship and the quays.

RECORDING AND LOADING/UNLOADING CARGOES

Cargoes that had to be shipped away by sea were first recorded for customs and tax payment. Such a rare scene appears in a black-and-white mosaic in the Shippers Office 51, at Piazzale delle Corporazioni, Ostia. A *tabularius* seated on the quarter deck of a merchantman holds a large wooden wax tablet on his lap, whereas the other end of the board is supported by legs laid on the deck. He holds a *stylus* in his right hand, while he uses his left hand to count the cargo of bag-shape jars on the deck (Figure 3.5). Similar loads of jars would have been stored in the hold of the ship. When finished with the recording, the tablets were stored at the custom-house for inventories and checking at the harbor entrance, a practice quite similar to the modern era. When the ship arrived at its destination the cargo was unloaded from the ship by stevedores to be carried to the warehouse, as at the same time it was recorded again by a *tabularius* as indicated by a relief found at Portus, and now in the Torlonia Museum, Rome

FIGURE 3.5 Tabularius recording of a cargo of bag-shape jars; Piazzale delle Corporazioni, Ostia, Italy. © Parco Archeologico di Ostia Antica.

(third century CE). Each stevedore was given a tally-piece for every amphora carried on his shoulder down the gangplank and then to the storeroom. They were paid according to the number of tallies they collected (Casson 1994a: 103, fig. 76).

When very large merchantmen arrived in Rome they could not sail on the Tiber due to the shallow depth of the river. They had to anchor in the open sea opposite the mouth of the Tiber. Small service boats, *schaphae*, *lenunculi*, or *caudicaria*, were used to unload the cargo from the merchant ship and then to ship the cargo on the Tiber to Ostia or Rome. The unloading and transferring of the cargo of amphorae was made by stevedores in a similar way as it appears on the floor of the Shippers Office 25 at Ostia (Friedman 2011: 110, fig. 3.7.23). When a merchantman was moored to the quay or anchored near a warehouse, a crane was used to load/unload the cargo from/into ships reaching or leaving port. A unique scene showing the use of a crane from the quay appears in the mosaic floor of the Shippers Office from Narbonne (France) at Ostia. The ship faces a two-story tower structure. On the flat roof of the first floor there is a crane facing the ship; it is in the process of loading/unloading a large bundle in/from the ship (113, fig. 3.7.27). The *artemon* mast (foremast) or the main mast in a merchantman could also be used as a crane when the ship anchored alongside the quay as it appears in the Torlonia relief (Casson 1994a: 112–13, fig. 84). These uses of a crane for loading/unloading cargo from ships onto the quay are consistent with Vitruvius's description of the operation.[7]

CAPSTAN

When conditions were not favorable to sail upstream on the Tiber or when different operations were carried out within the harbor basin, service vessels were towed by a towline. This line coiled around the mast was controlled by passing it through the capstan set on the poop of the service vessels—*scaphae, linter,* or *caudicaria*. The left-hand ship depicted in Station 25 at Piazzale delle Corporationi, Ostia, shows the capstan mounted on the quarter deck and the bars are inserted into the shaft of the capstan, which may suggest that the vessel will be towed when completely loaded (Friedman 2011: 111, fig. 3.7.25). Vessels were towed by towlines from the Tiber's banks by men or oxen. The left-hand merchantman in the Rimini mosaic has its capstan missing its bars, indicating that it is not in use at the moment (Municipal Museum, Rimini, Italy).

MERCHANT SHIPS

Roman merchantmen had a round hull and were known as *navis oneraria*. These ships were beamier with a length to width ratio of 5.5:1 or 6.5:1 (Casson 1971: 158). They were rigged with one main mast and a square sail. An *artemon* rig (foremast and sail) and four to six row oars were found as auxiliary rigs, especially used when leaving or entering a harbor, due to the fact that the full open main sail was a burden in maneuvering the ship. A pair of large steering oars or rudders was mounted on either quarter for steering the ship on its route or in any harbor activities. When anchored, these rudders were lifted out of the water and secured to the side of the upper quarters or they were completely removed and stored on the deck.

The most common type of merchant ships was the *keles* (Gr.)/*celox* (Lt.), built particularly for speed, having few rowers, and carrying a modest amount of cargo; *akatoi* (Gr.)/*actuaria* (Lt.) was a merchant ship, or sometimes it referred to a small boat (Casson 1971: 160). It was propelled by oars but its main rig consisted of a single mast and square sail. A papyrus concerning a maritime loan (*Sammelb.* 9571.2; second century CE) mentions that the *akatos* type plied between Ascalon and Alexandria (Casson 1971: 159, and n11). The *lembos* (Gr.)/*lembes* (Lt.) was usually associated with the ship's boat (towed astern), fishing boats, river craft, or as auxiliary in war fleets. It could be propelled by fifty rowers seated on one bank or sometimes from two superimposed banks. The *lembos* was used for carrying cargo both across open waters and on rivers (162, and n36). The *kerkouros* (Gr.)/*cercurus* (Lt.) is attested as a naval auxiliary (see endnote 3 at the end of this volume). Some Greek papyri from Egypt attest that this type of vessel was the standard large grain carrier on the Nile. The *phaselos* (Gr.)/*phaselus* (Lt.) plied the Mediterranean and transported as many as six hundred passengers rather than cargo. Josephus when he traveled to Rome in 64 CE wrote that the ship carried on board six hundred passengers and was wrecked in the Adriatic Sea:

> I reached Rome after being in great jeopardy at sea. For our ship foundered in the midst of the sea of Adria, and our company of some six hundred souls had to swim all that night. About daybreak, through God's good providence, we sighted a ship of Cyrene, and I and certain others, about eighty in all, outstripped the others and were taken on board.
> (Josephus, *Life*, 15.3)

Sallust mentions that a cohort of soldiers was carried in a large *phaselus* (Casson 1971: 167 and n55). The *phaselus* was propelled by a large square sail, along with *artemon* rig, and used row oars only when the wind conditions were not favorable, or entering/leaving a port. They were in use in the Mediterranean in the first centuries BCE to CE (Torr 1964: 120).

The size of ancient merchantmen had no universal units. The size of grain-carriers was known by different measures of grain: the *artab* at Egypt; *medimnus* at Athens; or *modius* at Rome. The Roman merchant ships' cargo capacity varied from 70 to 600 tons of load. The port regulation from Thasos attests that in the third century BCE ships under 3,000 talents (80 tons of load) were of negligible size, whereas ships with a load of 5,000 talents (130 tons) were the average size of merchantmen (Casson 1971: 183). Most ships had a cargo capacity of 100 to 150 tons; 150 tons being the capacity of a ship transporting 3,000 amphorae (183–4). A ship with a cargo of 450 tons was 35–40 meters long and 10–12 meters wide. The Romans were capable of building ships with a capacity of 300 to 400 tons, and it is most likely that ships with a capacity of over 1,000 tons were also built.

During the Roman Empire it was quite common to see the huge galleys of the Roman Navy comprising of *liburna* and *triremes* patrolling the Mediterranean Sea to prevent any pirate attacks and escorting other large merchant ships. The Mediterranean Sea trade routes remained quite safe up until the collapse of the Western Roman Empire in the fifth century.

CONCLUSION

The purpose of this chapter was to shed light on different aspects of maritime trade and what we can learn from historical, archaeological, and iconographic sources throughout the centuries. Well-preserved pictorial evidence from mosaics and reliefs and the archaeological remains from Hellenistic to Byzantine shipwrecks and their cargoes, provide us with information and a better understanding of ancient sea trade in the Mediterranean, as well as preserved techniques of ship construction. These vessels also allow us to connect them with types known from ancient literature. Current research on shipwrecks and their cargoes, especially amphorae, indicates that the heyday of Mediterranean Sea trade corresponds with the Roman thalassocracy from 200 BCE to 200 CE. This period was marked by the stability of the Roman Empire and free seaways trade, without the fear and threat of piracy. Traders, merchants, and entrepreneurs were the heart of the economic system, which provided for the needs of the population and their rulers in all provinces throughout the Roman Empire. Combined pictorial evidence from all arts, especially from mosaics and reliefs, and from the archaeological remains of shipwrecks and their cargoes, contribute to the developing field of "nautical experimental archaeology." The reconstructed *Kyrenia II* and the *Kyrenia Liberty* merchantman (Figure 3.6) and the packing experiment of amphorae and millstones cargo bring us a better understanding of the transportation methods of cargoes and sailing conditions in antiquity. Mosaics and reliefs with depictions of nautical and maritime scenes may be considered as open windows of the ancient maritime societies in the Mediterranean.

FIGURE 3.6 *Kyrenia Liberty* sea trial, Cyprus. © Zaraza Friedman (author).

NAUTICAL GLOSSARY

aphlaston: sternpost, ornament atop the sternpost.

artemon: foresail, bow-sail.

bowsprit: a large spar projecting over the stem, used for securing the foremast. The bowsprit itself is held in place by shrouds secured at each side of the bow.

brace: a line attached to the end of the yard whose use is either to square or traverse the yard horizontally.

brails: lines for controlling the area of the sail exposed to the wind; ropes used to furl a sail rapidly.

capstan: a winch with upright spindle (in ancient ships) set either on the forecastle deck or quarter deck and used for heavy-lifting work, particularly when working anchors and cables.

cutwater: the forward curve of the stem of a ship; the forward extension of the keel to provide a better hydrostatics and hydrodynamics to ship.

false keel: the false keel was constructed in several pieces, which were scarfed together, and attached to the underside of the keel by copper or iron staples.

forestay: part of the standing rigging; a line running from the mast forwards.

gangplank: a plank temporarily extended from ship to shore for embarking and disembarking.

gunwale: the uppermost course of planking on a ship's side, which covers the heads of the timbers between the main and fore drifts.

hull: body of a ship.

keelson: an internal longitudinal timber or line of timbers, mounted atop the frames along the centerline of the keel; it provides additional longitudinal strength to the bottom of the hull, similar to an internal keel.

lembos: a general class of small boats, propelled by oars or sails or both; it is also referred as a rowboat that ferried people out to ships anchored in deep waters.

lenunculus: a heavier boat manned by several oarsmen.

mast: spar used to support a sail by means of associated rigging.

mortise-and-tenon join: a union of planks or timbers by which a projecting piece (tenon) was fitted into one or more cavities (mortises) of corresponding size.

oarbox:	the projection on each side of a polyreme, which is required by the oar system *passim*.
oarport:	an opening in a vessel's side through which the looms of oars or sweeps pass.
plank:	a long, flat piece of timber, thicker than a board.
port:	the left-hand side while facing forward.
proembolion:	upper ram.
quarter:	either side of the ship near the stern.
quarter rudder:	one or a pair of rudders placed on either side near the stern. They were permanently mounted and turned about a fixed axis.
ram:	a heavy beak or spur projecting from the bow of a warship for penetrating the hull of the enemy ship.
rigging:	the lines fitted to the mast, yard, or sail.
rudder:	a steering device that is placed aft (quarters) and is pivoted about a (usually vertical) axis to generate a yawing moment from the hydrodynamic forces that act on the rudder blade when it is angled to the flow of water over it. Until the middle of the medieval period, the fashion was to mount rudders on one or both stern quarters; these were known as *quarter rudders*.
running rigging:	the lines that control the movement of the sail and spars.
shrouds:	standing rigging, to support the mast laterally.
square sail:	sail that is set athwart ship.
standing rigging:	rigging that supports a mast.
starboard:	the right-hand side while facing forward.
stempost:	a vertical or upward curving timber scarfed to the keel, into which the two sides of the bow were joined.
stern:	the after end of a vessel.
sternpost:	a vertical or upward curving timber or assembly of timbers stepped into, or scarfed to the after end of the keel or heel.
waterline:	line on the hull that the water reaches when the vessel is floating normally.
yard:	a large wooden or metal spar, crossing the mast horizontally or diagonally, from which a sail is set. Usually, the yard is made of two pieces scarfed together in the middle, thus providing the desired length to fit the large square sail.

CHAPTER FOUR

Conflicts

Conflict at Sea in the Ancient World

JORIT WINTJES

INTRODUCTION—OR, ADRIFT IN A SEA OF DEFINITIONS

The sea mattered to antiquity in much the same way as it does to the globalized world of the twenty-first century. As soon as trade developed beyond local boundaries, humans were invariably drawn to the sea as a means of connecting local and regional networks, thereby gaining access to commodities unobtainable in their own communities. Sea routes made long-range contacts a viable proposition and allowed for the transportation of commodities in quantities that would have been difficult to carry over land—or which, given the location of their source, could not be accessed by travel over land at all. In the history of early human civilizations, venturing out to sea therefore constituted one of the greatest revolutions in mobility and connectivity, and rapidly growing communities would soon establish contact—either directly or via intermediaries—with far-away places. The establishment of trade contacts with Arabia by communities in the Ancient Near East, which were in place as early as the first half of the third millennium BCE, is an early testimony to this development (Magee 2014: 89–93; Potter 2009: 31).

Despite the enormous opportunities sea routes offered, everything was not plain sailing: maritime trade looks impressive when seen through the eyes of a twenty-first-century observer looking at a map charting artifactual evidence for such contacts; but for those actually involved in establishing and keeping up these contacts it meant having to brave treacherous seas in small ships. The greatest danger an ancient seafarer would have encountered on his way, however, was invariably fellow man. It is probably safe to assume that as soon as someone realized that sailing out to sea could, by implementation of hard work, result in material gain, someone else realized that the implementation of *force* could result in a transferral of that material gain to himself in an easier way than the hard work required for its original procurement. In other words, the first mariners were soon—very soon, one is tempted to think—followed by the first pirates, thereby extending human conflict to the sea.[1]

A history of conflict at sea could therefore begin with the very first case of an unnamed pirate forcefully—and presumably rather unpleasantly—separating an unnamed fisherman or merchant from his worldly possessions. This would, however, be based on an extremely broad definition of "conflict," a definition that—at least for the purposes of the present chapter—is quite impracticable given that one is unlikely to find evidence for such an encounter. Modern understanding of conflict at sea often focuses on the distinction between state actors and non-state actors, according to which the history of conflict at sea between the former is generally called naval history, whereas the activities of the latter are often seen as being part of the history of crime.[2]

While applying this distinction to antiquity is tempting—and would allow us to focus on the actions of organized communities, from which tangible evidence is more likely to be produced—it is not as clear-cut as one would want it to be. In fact, right down to the latter half of the nineteenth century there are huge gray areas where activities by state and non-state actors overlap, as for example the employment of privateers up to the 1856 Declaration of Paris shows.[3] Moreover, conflict at sea regularly saw state and non-state actors on opposing sides, and while such conflicts often only involved token forces or even individual ships fighting each other, sometimes significant amounts of resources could be mobilized to fight non-state actors. Pompey's famous operations against Cilician pirates in 67 BCE are often seen as a typical example—though the Cilician communities living off the sea could probably also be classified as state-actors[4]—but such constellations are not alien to modern times either: during its heyday in the late 1840s and early 1850s the Royal Navy's West African Squadron, which was employed on an antislavery mission, included nearly a sixth of the Royal Navy's peacetime strength.[5]

The present chapter aims at presenting a brief chronological overview of key aspects of conflict at sea in antiquity from the emergence of organized communities producing written sources in the third millennium BCE to the end of antiquity in the late sixth or early seventh century CE; essentially, the overview given below runs from the Egyptian pharaoh Pepi I and his near-contemporary Akkadian kings Maništušu and Naram-Sîn to the Roman emperor Justinian and his contemporary and ally, the Axumite king Kaleb. Traditionally, studies of seafaring in antiquity mostly concentrate on developments in the Mediterranean; given, however, that the Bronze Age saw the rise of civilizations in the Mediterranean that were clearly the result of developments originating further East, it seems advisable to at least include the Ancient Near East into the present overview and hence to include Maništušu and the early history of Akkadian seafaring.

As for the overall structure of the present chapter, after two general sections on the evidence available and the operational capabilities of ancient naval forces, I will mainly follow two lines of development, that of naval technology—which includes both ships and the specialist infrastructure required for keeping them and their crews operational—and that of the operational capabilities developed around that technology. Throughout history, naval technology and operational capabilities have tended to influence each other: while technology drives the development of new tactics, operational procedures instigate the development of technology specifically designed to meet operational needs; this interdependence between technology and tactics is illustrated for example by the development of purpose-built landing craft in the Roman Army, which will be discussed below.

The present chapter argues that there is a fairly distinct line of development discernible in the naval history of antiquity, with simple operations gradually being supplemented by more complex ones, culminating in the Roman imperial period when operations reached a hitherto unseen level of complexity. Naval warfare took on staggering proportions already well before the Roman imperial period. Perhaps the largest battle at sea, as far as the number of participants is concerned, took place in 256 BCE off the Sicilian coast, more than two hundred years before the beginning of the Roman imperial period (Lazenby 1996: 87). By the end of the first century BCE, however, Roman naval forces had also mastered what in terms of complexity are perhaps the most difficult of naval operations at all—amphibious assaults. Throughout the following centuries, the Romans regularly undertook amphibious operations on a scale and of a complexity unseen before and only matched again in the twentieth century. Rather than a mere synthesis of what happened at sea between Pepi and Maništušu on the one hand and Justinian and Kaleb on the other, the present overview is mainly about the development of naval capabilities and the technology required to sustain these.

KNOWLEDGE AND ITS LIMITATIONS – SOURCES FOR THE NAVAL HISTORY OF ANTIQUITY

By and large, the sources for ancient naval history are the same as those for the history of antiquity in general. Apart from the all-important written evidence, be it literary or documentary in character, archaeology has contributed greatly to the understanding of the material aspect of maritime history in general and naval history in particular. The remains of coastal installations, shipwrecks, and trade goods continuously add to the evidence available and allow insights into how both individual communities and whole trade networks were connected by the sea and how the material aspects of such connections—ships and harbors—looked in reality, a question for which iconographic evidence can be of key importance as well. As a result, at least for some periods, it is possible to get a fair understanding of ship types, harbor structures, and many of those commodities that were moved on the sea.

While there is material of at least significant quantity, it comes with a serious qualification that considerably limits the insights into the *naval* history of antiquity one can gain from it. Most of the surviving evidence, be it iconography, material culture, or written sources, usually provides little if anything at all in the way of clues for operational matters. Depictions of ships or pieces of naval infrastructure can yield valuable information on technological aspects of warfare at sea, information that then can be further supported by archaeological material. This, however, only provides insights into the individual elements used for implementing, so to speak, ancient naval warfare—*how* these elements actually operated together is unlikely to be understood from iconographic and material evidence alone, even if it may be possible to gain information about an individual element's function. For information about operational issues one would then instinctively turn to written sources—only to be badly disappointed. Ancient historiographers, our main source for what actually happened at sea in antiquity, were seldom interested in operational details, and while there are some examples of authors directly involved in the running of major operations writing about these—Julius Caesar's account of his invasions in Britain in 55 and 54 BCE would be a case in point—they are few and far between. As a general rule, ancient literary sources usually confine themselves to giving accounts of events and rarely, if ever, cover operational details. Other written sources on ancient naval warfare, such as handbooks on naval tactics, will have existed—yet, apart from a very small corpus of extremely late Roman texts, none survive.

One might argue that operational questions are only matters of detail, as in the end it is only the outcome of naval operations that eventually might have an influence on the course of the history of an ancient community. Yet in fact the—for certain periods nearly total—lack of evidence on how ancient naval operations actually worked is quite a serious issue: understanding naval operations is the key to understanding naval capabilities, and it is the evaluation of these capabilities that must have played a major role in political and military decision-making processes of communities involved in conflict at sea. Because we are not able to understand ancient naval operations properly, we are therefore also missing an important element to understand general political history as well.

In recent decades, full-scale reconstructions of ancient warships have become an additional source of information on the naval history of antiquity. In principle, reconstructions should provide some insights into the technical capabilities of, for example, a specific ship, which then allows conclusions to be drawn about its operational use. However, while reconstructions can indeed provide important information, these insights are mostly confined to tactical capabilities—which should not come as a surprise, as there is usually only one reconstruction of a particular ship type available.

Without doubt the most important example of such a reconstruction is the *Olympias*, an attempt at reconstructing a Greek *trireme*, a warship in use from the late sixth century onward. Originally built as a "floating hypothesis," as Boris Rankov famously put it (Rankov 2007), in order to find out how the oarage of this particular type of warship worked, the *Olympias* not only made it possible to finally end a controversy over trireme design that had been going on for more than a century, rigorous testing also produced much evidence on its tactical capabilities. These in turn shed some light on operational issues as well, though key aspects of operating trireme fleets still lie in the dark, as they are beyond what can be found out by using only one reconstruction.

To give but a few examples, many of the logistical problems of operating a squadron of triremes can at present only be extrapolated from information gained from *Olympias*, while information on all issues related to the movement of larger numbers of ships in formation is nearly impossible to come by. In particular problems such as station keeping, minimum distances between ships or formation change would, if studied experimentally, require the employment of at least three *Olympias*-type reconstructions, something that is unlikely to materialize in the near future. Perhaps the most important question, however, that working with a single reconstruction cannot answer, is how ancient naval commanders exerted control over formations that could number hundreds of ships and stretch over large areas; the available literary evidence strongly suggests that they did—indeed, the large-scale operations attested for various periods are extremely difficult if not impossible to make sense of if ancient naval commanders were *not* able to exert command—while providing very few clues on how that might have happened.

Reconstructions, which in recent years have become rather popular, thus have considerable limitations when it comes to information about operations—reconstructing ancient operational procedures based only on individual ship reconstructions is a daunting proposal at best and likely to be impossible. In addition, there is another important qualification that also has an impact on the information a reconstruction can yield about the capabilities of an ancient warship—both the operational environment and the operators themselves are "modern," so to speak. In the case of the operational environment this is quite obvious—for example, experiments with reconstructed Roman ships on the Rhine and the Danube have to face the fact that the rivers nowadays are different from ancient times in many respects that could have a direct impact on the functional, tactical, and operational capabilities of Roman ships.[6] Likewise, the crews operating modern reconstructions invariably have very different backgrounds compared to ancient crews—as David Schaps pointedly put it: "The most salient fact about the world of the ancient Greeks and Romans is that it no longer exists [...]. We can never speak to an ancient Greek or Roman, never visit them in their homes, never walk through their streets as they knew them. They are situated in the past" (Schaps 2010: 176)—which will similarly have a significant impact on the capabilities of a reconstructed ship.

As for the limitations posed by the availability of only one reconstruction at a time, digital approaches may in the future offer some further insight into ancient naval operations. Computerized simulations of warship squadrons might yield information on issues such as station keeping or minimum distances, while being able to put an observer—at least virtually—on the deck of an ancient warship inside a larger squadron could help to get a clearer picture of the command and control challenges ancient naval commanders faced.

The above remarks on the sources for the naval history of antiquity do not sound exactly optimistic, and this is due to the simple fact that the available sources nearly always fail to provide sufficient information for properly understanding ancient naval operations. This does not prevent modern observers from sometimes gaining a fairly clear picture of the complexity of ancient naval operations and the operational challenges that ancient naval commanders faced, but one should not forget that there is very little if any information on how these challenges were overcome.

ULTRA POSSE NEMO OBLIGATUR—OPERATIONAL CAPABILITIES OF ANCIENT NAVAL FORCES

Given the limitations of the available evidence it comes as no surprise that discussing ancient naval history from an operational perspective is fraught with difficulties. However, perhaps the single most important obstacle to a proper understanding of ancient naval operations is not so much the dearth of evidence but rather a set of modern preconceptions about what naval warfare fundamentally is about, or should be about; preconceptions that are quite at odds with the realities of ancient naval—and indeed general seafaring—capabilities. In other words, modern observers have in the past all too often used early modern or modern concepts of warfare at sea as an analytical instrument with which to understand ancient naval warfare—an approach that is methodologically questionable, to say the least.

In understanding naval warfare and measuring the success of naval operations, modern observers are invariably drawn to the complementary strategic concepts of sea control and sea denial.[7] Indeed, in the present-day world it is hardly conceivable to think of any priority higher up on a navy's agenda than guarding shipping lines in times of war and peace, and attacking and possibly denying shipping lines to the enemy in times of war. Throughout the past three centuries the control of seaborne lines of communication has not only become a central mission for all large and many medium-sized navies, it has also driven technological development to an extent that weapon systems originally meant to serve in other roles—such as the submarine—became mainly geared toward controlling the sea. To put it slightly pointedly, sea control is all important for naval forces in the twenty-first century, and it has been ever since the eighteenth century at the latest.

The importance of sea control on a strategic level is matched by the development of operational capabilities geared toward defending or contesting sea control throughout the past three centuries. The employment of individual raiders specifically designed for operating against enemy merchant shipping, the implementation of convoy and patrol tactics to counter the use of raiders, and the use of naval forces to blockade enemy coasts are key examples of the influence that the thinking about sea control has on developing operational capabilities. It is a testimony to the importance of sea control-oriented missions that the history of amphibious operations, if compared to convoy or blockade operations, is a fairly young one, with operations achieving any degree of integration of landing and support forces only appearing for the first time in the latter half of the nineteenth century.[8] Even then, amphibious operations still lacked mission-specific technology, the development of which only began in earnest during the First World War.[9]

The importance of seaborne lines of communication and the missions of sea control and sea denial associated with it pose significant challenges for modern observers trying to understand ancient naval warfare—*because there was no such thing as sea control in antiquity*. At first this may appear to be a bold statement given the importance of the sea for many ancient seafaring communities. Indeed, the key role access to and the use of the sea played for communities such as Athens can hardly be overrated, and neither can the attempts at dominating the sea resulting from the importance of seaborne commerce and communications. The influence exerted over large areas in the Aegean sea by Athens in the fifth and fourth centuries was a direct result of the importance of the sea for a city whose wealth was based to a great extent on maritime commerce—in other words, if there ever was an Athenian empire, it was a naval one. It comes as little surprise, then, that the ancient Greeks not only distinguished between land and sea powers in practice, but also saw fundamental conceptual differences between communities exerting dominance primarily over inland territories and those who controlled coastal and island communities, coining the term "thalassocracy" for the latter.[10]

Even so, however, there is a crucial difference between the naval empires of antiquity and those of the early modern and modern period. Ancient naval powers exerted control over the sea by controlling—either directly or indirectly—its *access points*. In addition, they were able to project power by transporting soldiers across the sea and by striking at enemy fleets. By destroying the latter they could even deny an enemy the use of the sea to some extent—provided he was unwilling or unable to come up with a new fleet. Such was the case, for example, at the end of the First Punic War, when Carthage, having lost its last fleet in the Battle of the Aegates in 241 BCE and being unable to finance a new one, had to ask for peace after a struggle of twenty-three years (Lazenby 1996: 156–8). What ancient naval powers could not do, however, was deny the sea to an enemy who had access to it.

Early modern and modern naval powers, however, could do so by patrolling the seas, hunting down enemy merchantmen and warships, and, ultimately, by maintaining a blockade of the enemy coast. Indeed, looking back from the twenty-first century, naval operations directed at contesting sea control by either blockading a numerically inferior enemy or by using raiders to attack a superior enemy's merchant shipping have been at the core of naval warfare at least since the eighteenth century. Safeguarding or contesting seaborne lines of communication are today perhaps the single most important way of using sea power. The primary technological requirement for such operations in a warship is the capability of staying at sea for prolonged periods of time. Only by having ships "on station" is it possible to blockade an enemy coast, while the employment of raiders requires an even greater capability of staying at sea, as for a raider operating against a numerically superior enemy naval infrastructure is likely to be unavailable for replenishment or damage repair.

Staying at sea, then, is a necessary requirement both for exerting and contesting sea control—*and ancient warships were incapable of doing so*. Both patrolling and blockading operations of the type so often seen in the naval history of the eighteenth to twenty-first century would have been impossible to undertake with ancient warships, as they were basically tied to land-based infrastructure. This should not come as a surprise given the design characteristics of ancient warships, which were designed around their main element of propulsion in combat—large numbers of rowers. In order to balance weight, speed, and maneuverability they tended to be fairly long, shallow-draught ships of light construction; as a result they had neither storage capacities worthy of any mention nor seakeeping qualities, something attested by the large numbers of ancient warships lost not to enemy action but to the weather.[11] This is not to say that ancient warships were only capable of making brief, day-long voyages; in fact, there are many examples for operations requiring ships to cover distances of several days, some of which will be given below. However, there is a fundamental difference between, for example, an amphibious operation requiring a force of warships to run across a larger body of water once and the upkeep of a blockade, which would make it necessary for ships to stay at sea for weeks and months on end, something for which there is zero evidence.

Another technological requirement only slightly less important than staying at sea was the capability of detecting and identifying a potential enemy over long distances. Until the advent of beyond-visual-range technologies around the middle of the twentieth century, this meant relying solely on human sight. While both ancient and modern warships thus employed basically the same type of "sensor"—lookouts—their capabilities differed considerably: ancient lookouts had only their eyesight to rely on, while early modern and modern lookouts could, if required, resort to glasses, thereby significantly increasing the detection range. Both in patrolling and in blockading operations, being able to identify a threat as early as possible was of crucial importance, and even if they had been able to stay at sea for longer periods of time—which they were not—ancient warships would have been markedly less effective in such operations; their effectiveness suffered even further from the fact that they were generally of lower construction than modern warships and hence offered a lower vantage point for lookouts.

Of course, the lack of key technology—seakeeping and long-range detection capability—for the specific set of operations outlined above does not mean that ancient naval operations generally lacked complexity and were as a consequence simple and easy to undertake. In fact, quite the opposite is true, as already the sheer size of some ancient naval operations shows, be it measured in the numbers of ships or men involved—the former could be well in excess of 1,000, the latter reaching staggering six-digit figures. While incapable of blockading a coast, ancient naval forces could be used for blockading harbors in what were essentially naval sieges, thereby lending a second dimension to siege warfare. Ancient naval forces could also cover considerable distances during operations, thus offering military and political decision makers an instrument capable of long-range power projection. And—perhaps most importantly—in the field of amphibious operations, ancient naval forces by the time of the Roman imperial period had reached a remarkable degree of cooperation, with warships offering direct support to landing forces in ways seen again only from the beginning of the twentieth century onward. It is particularly in the field of amphibious operations that over the course of nearly three millennia a clear development is visible from operations that were nautically challenging yet operationally fairly simple to those which due to their scale and complexity presented challenges even the late nineteenth century would have found nearly impossible to overcome.

BEFORE THE WARSHIP—NAVAL WARFARE, c. 2300–c. 600 BCE

While the beginnings of the history of conflict at sea are lost to human memory, *recorded* ancient naval history begins in the latter half of the third century BCE. In the Old Kingdom Egyptian pharaoh Pepi I (2295–2250 BCE) used ships to project power to the Levantine coast; one of his generals, a man named Uni, memorialized in an inscription how he moved the pharaoh's forces by sea into the enemy hinterland, possibly landing near Mount Carmel (Pritchard 1969: 228). While the inscription does not give the impression of something totally out of the ordinary it is unclear whether such an expedition was commonplace or exceptional; certainly there were trading contacts between Egypt and the Levantine coast as early as the twenty-seventh century BCE. The Egyptian pharaoh's ability to project power by sending armies across the sea rested partly on an infrastructure making such campaigns possible if not at short notice then at least with no excessive preparation; during the Old Kingdom the harbor at Ayn Sukhna saw the construction of massive storage facilities effectively turning it into what may well have been the world's first naval base (Tallet 2012: 148–51).

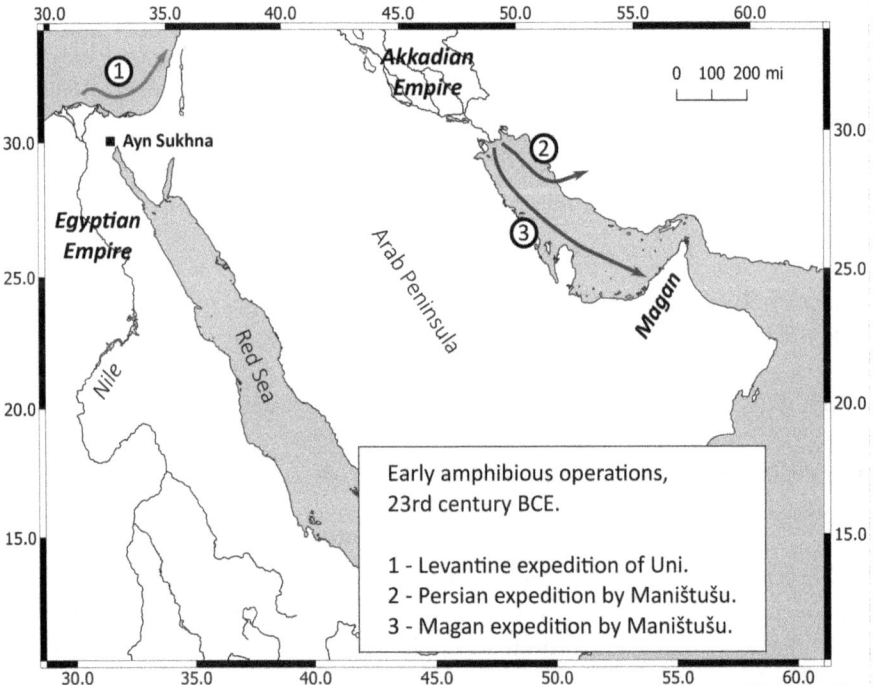

FIGURE 4.1 Early amphibious operations, twenty-third century BCE. © Jorit Wintjes (author).

Further East in ancient Mesopotamia, rulers of the Akkadian Empire had, beginning with its founder Sargon the Great (*c.* 2334–2284 BCE), grown quite fond of black diorite, which was the material of choice for the statues and stelae of the Akkadian kings. However, as the material was alien to ancient Mesopotamia, it had to imported from sources outside the Akkadian Empire. Already during the reign of Sargon there is some evidence for seaborne trade along the Persian coast, though its exact extent is unknown (Potts 1993: 384–94). Sargon's successor Maništušu (*c.* 2270–2255 BCE) then apparently decided to go directly to the source of the precious stone—and to do so by force.[12] After a successful campaign against communities on or near the northern coast of the Persian Gulf he led a force across the sea, defeated a coalition of various enemies, had quantities of diorite quarried, and eventually returned home, where he had his campaign recorded in an inscription on a statue made from the diorite captured abroad. Both the size of the forces involved and their intended target are not obvious from the inscription. The former may not have been all that great—the cities defeated by the Akkadian king could well have mustered only a few hundred men of fairly low capabilities between them, allowing Maništušu, who was able to field experienced warriors, to prevail even with inferior numbers of his own. For the intended target of the campaign, however, there is additional evidence from the reign of Naram-Sîn (*c.* 2254–2218 BCE), one of Maništušu's successors, who, according to an inscription on one of his statues found at Susa, campaigned against Magan, a region usually located in modern-day Oman, to gain diorite (Potts 1989: 131–7); it is thus quite likely that Maništušu had directed his campaign against ancient Magan as well.

While the forces of both Maništušu and Naram-Sîn may have been as small as a few hundred men, covering a distance of well over 1,000 miles was a considerable achievement, even if the Akkadian ships hugged the coastline during their voyage. The capability of projecting power by sea over such a distance speaks for a considerable nautical experience among Akkadian seafarers, something that should not come as a surprise given the existence of seaborne trade in the Persian Gulf. From an operational perspective the campaigns of the Akkadian kings are best described as transport operations; they were clearly aimed at transporting contingents of the Akkadian army to a point from which they could proceed on land, defeating the enemy, who did not venture out to sea, in a land battle; in that they were very similar to Egyptian operations off the Levantine coast.

The following millennium probably saw many operations of this type—carrying land forces to a point where they could defeat enemy land forces—launched by both larger and smaller polities with access to the sea. At the same time, actual fighting at sea in the form of boarding actions will have gained importance as well. While for much of the late third and early second millennium there is practically no evidence for boarding, it was the only combat tactic available for ship-to-ship action—and an extremely simple one at that: one had to get hold of the enemy ship and then to beat down the enemy crew while avoiding meeting an untimely end at the hands of the latter. The middle of the second millennium then saw the rise of communities in the Aegean whose power and wealth was clearly based on their ability to use the sea both for commerce and for projecting power; as a consequence, the concept of thalassocracy has been variously applied both to the Minoan civilization based on Crete and the Southern Aegean and to its successor, the Mycenaean civilization.[13]

While there is iconographic as well as artifactual evidence for Minoan and Mycenaean ships, of which the Thera fresco depicting several Minoan ships is probably the most famous single piece (Wachsmann 1998: 86–99), nothing is known about the operations of Minoan or Mycenaean naval forces; this should not come as a surprise given the general lack of narrative sources from the Minoan and Mycenaen periods. The surviving textual evidence from the Mycenaean civilization is entirely documentary in character and mostly consists of material connected with the centralized palace economies of the time. It is quite noteworthy though that while weapons and other military equipment feature quite prominently in the surviving evidence, ships and equipment necessary for naval operations do not. One could therefore wonder whether military operations across the sea really played such a prominent role in the Minoan and Mycenaean world; however, unless narrative material appears, the exact nature of Minoan and Mycenaean power is likely to remain in the dark.

Whatever the true capabilities of the Minoan and Mycenaean civilizations, by the last third of the second millennium BCE developments were underway that would eventually result in maritime conflicts of significant scale; conflicts that, for the first time since the campaigns of Pharaoh Pepi I and the Akkadian kings, left tangible traces in the available evidence—and quite monumental ones at that. In the reliefs and inscriptions adorning the walls of the Egyptian temple at Medinet Habu, Pharaoh Ramesses III (c. 1186–1155 BCE) recounts his great victory against foreign invaders who, coming from the sea, attacked the Nile delta.[14] According to the inscriptions, the attackers in their thousands embarked in a great number of ships. The Egyptians, on the other hand, had forces aboard Egyptian ships as well as troops on land, and their plan was to lure their enemy into the shallow waters of the Delta, where they could then be attacked both from land and from the ships hidden in the Delta's maze of reed and papyrus. From reading the inscriptions one gets the impression that the Egyptians did not want to engage the enemy outside the Delta, possibly because they thought the enemy to be superior in ship-to-ship action. Therefore, they tried to lure the enemy forces into a trap, and succeeded rather brilliantly—at least according to the inscriptions, which, it has to be admitted, represent the official Egyptian

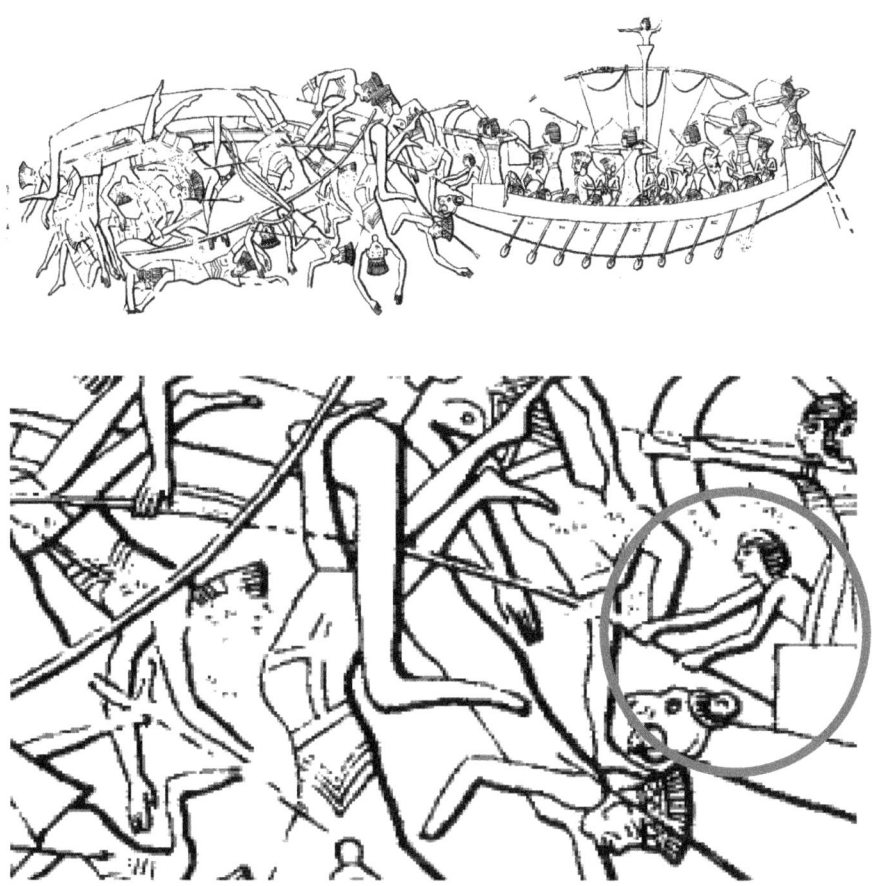

FIGURE 4.2 The battle in the Delta. *(a)* Egyptian ship turning over a ship full of enemy warriors (detail from Medinet Habu reliefs); *(b)* Egyptian sailor using a rope or a grappling hook to overturn an enemy vessel. © Jorit Wintjes (author).

version, which was unlikely to dwell longer on anything that may have gone wrong on the Egyptian side.

The Battle of the Delta, as it is often called, was of key importance in eventually repelling the foreign invaders—foreigners that elsewhere in the Eastern Mediterranean overran communities and civilizations by the score. While their exact composition is unclear, they are usually grouped together under the term "sea people," suggesting that in their raids and campaigns the sea played a crucial role, even if there are no traces of anything that could be interpreted as a new "thalassocracy" in the Eastern Mediterranean. In fact, from evidence elsewhere it is clear that these raids could come in very different scales;

thus, the last king of the Syrian coastal city of Ugarit, Ammurapi, described in a letter the grave danger enemy ships posed to his realm—enemy ships that were seven in number, thus carrying at most a few hundred warriors (Wachsmann 2000: 104). While this was a far smaller force than the one that suffered a catastrophic defeat at the hands of Ramesses III, it was apparently still sufficient to make an end both of Ammurapi and Ugarit.

Operationally, large-scale raids like those launched by the sea peoples displayed a considerable level of complexity. Moving any large body of troops required not only the collection of sufficient transport but also the establishment of certain routines covering the embarkation and disembarkation of soldiers and their equipment. In addition to that, considerable nautical expertise was necessary, ranging from the ability to sail in formation to that of choosing a landing place suitable for putting large numbers of soldiers on land. All these capabilities, as was noted above, were already available to the Egyptians and Akkadians in the third millennium BCE as well as to the Bronze Age civilizations of the Mediterranean in the second millennium BCE.

In one respect, however, the early Iron Age brought about an important change—evidence for large-scale naval activities largely vanishes after the twelfth century BCE. Only from the eighth century onward is there again tangible evidence for the use of ships to project power or wage war against an enemy beyond the reach of one's land forces. During the last decades of the eighth century the Assyrian king Sargon II (722–705 BCE) operated against Cyprus in support of one of his allies,[15] while a generation later his son Sennacherib (705–681 BCE) waged a successful campaign in Phoenicia, making use of ships that are depicted on the walls of his palace in Nineveh.[16] The Phoenicians had by that time begun to explore the Mediterranean, establishing trading posts and founding colonies on the way, the most famous of which, Carthage, would eventually rise to become the Western Mediterranean's foremost naval power. By the latter half of the seventh century BCE, Greek communities both in mainland Greece and in Ionia appear as naval powers. According to Greek historical tradition the first battle at sea took place around 660 BCE (Thucydides 1.13.4), while the rise of the Persian Empire in the following century caused a rise in the scope of conflict both on land and at sea in the Eastern Mediterranean; famous examples include the flight of the Phocaeans who according to Herodotus evacuated their city and moved their whole community in their ships to one of their colonies in Italy (Herodotus 1.164–168).

While conflict at sea could thus already be of considerable scale—even if it was often better described as conflict *from* the sea—one element that is usually seen as of primary importance for naval activities was only slowly emerging during the early centuries of the Iron Age: the warship. Shipbuilding itself had seen a considerable development between the ships of the early pharaohs, those of the Akkadian kings and the vessels of Mediterranean seafarers in the early first millennium.[17] While little iconographic evidence survives for early Akkadian ships, Egyptian ships appear to have been of lashed construction and without a keel, requiring hogging trusses for structural integrity. By the late Bronze Age ships appeared with a keel, and from the tenth century onward iconographic evidence begins to appear for ships with a pronounced forefoot. Apart from sails, ships were initially propelled by rowers sitting in single file, though by the eighth century ships had been developed in which rowers were located on two levels[18]; by the sixth century the *penteconter*, a fifty-oared vessel with rowers on two levels, had become a standard warship type in the Eastern Mediterranean.

However, despite these key developments, when it came to conflict, the sole purpose of a ship was still the movement of warriors, either to attack an enemy on land or to board an enemy ship. As a result, characteristics such as speed and loading capacity needed to be balanced out, as the ships themselves were neither carriers of weapon systems nor weapon systems themselves—in other words, attacking a ship meant going after the crew rather than trying to damage or destroy the ship.

By the sixth century BCE this was beginning to change due to two key technologies. One—oared propulsion—was not a new one and had only indirect relevance to the development of warships. Oared propulsion gave ships not only a certain capability of movement independently of wind but also allowed, depending on the construction of the hull, for fairly high speeds, if only for brief periods. Compared to sailing ships, which throughout much of antiquity relied on square sails without the capability to tack, oared vessels had a distinct edge in maneuverability, which made them attractive for anyone intending not only on swift travel but also on preying on other seafarers. The other technology was new and crucial for turning ships into warships: the ram.[19] For the first time in maritime history, the ram gave ships a weapons system with which it was possible to seriously damage or even destroy an enemy ship. While boarding still remained an option—and continued to be in use throughout antiquity—the invention of the ram allowed an attacking ship to go for the enemy ship without having to fight the latter's crew in direct combat. The invention of the ram therefore opened up the way for the development of ships with the primary or even sole purpose of fighting other ships at sea—with the ram, the warship was born, and with it began a new important phase in the history of conflict at sea.

THE DAWN OF THE WARSHIP—NAVAL WARFARE, c. 600–c. 300 BCE

Around the middle of the sixth century, probably in 546, the Greek city of Phocaea was captured by the founder of the Persian Empire, Cyrus the Great (Herodotus 1.164.1–2; Strabo 6.1.1). As mentioned above, the Phocaeans evacuated their population, since much of their possessions were moveable—and presumably lightweight—aboard a fleet of penteconters. Moving first to Alalia in Southern Corsica the Phocaeans soon faced an alliance of Etruscans and Carthaginians trying to curb Greek influence in the Western Mediterranean in general—and to put an end to the Phocaeans in particular who apparently had embarked on a rather piratical lifestyle. Around 540 BCE a large Etrusco-Carthaginian fleet of 120 ships attacked the Phocaeans, and it is in the context of this battle that the ram is first mentioned. While the Etruscans and Phoenicians enjoyed a two-to-one superiority in numbers, the Phocaeans initially succeeded in driving them off, if only at a heavy price: two-thirds of their ships were lost, the remaining twenty ships were heavily damaged, "their rams twisted awry," as Herodotus notes (1.166.2). As a result the Phocaeans loaded their belongings onto their ships again and retreated to Southern Italy, eventually founding the city of Elea.

The use of the ram by the Phocaeans suggests that both the technology itself and the tactics necessary for making use of it were already available around the middle of the sixth century; they may have been invented a few decades earlier perhaps at the beginning of the century. While the ships of the Phocaeans were still ordinary pentecontes, only around a generation after the Battle of Alalia the Samian tyrant Polycrates introduced triremes to the Samian fleet. The trireme, a shallow-draught, long and slender oared ship in which oarsmen sat on three levels was the first true warship and stands at the beginning of a new phase in the history of conflict at sea in antiquity.[20]

On a tactical level, the trireme was the first ship capable of incapacitating or even sinking enemy ships without requiring a boarding action. While initially triremes still carried contingents of warriors, by the middle of the fifth century these had been reduced to small numbers of a dozen at most, the trireme's main weapon being the ram. Whereas in earlier centuries the ability of the warriors or their sheer numbers would decide over the outcome of a naval engagement—the boarding battle going one way or the other—key factors in trireme battles were the quality of the ships themselves, finding an expression particularly in their maneuverability, and the ability—or lack thereof—of the crews to exploit these qualities; as a consequence, both complex formations like the *kyklos*, a defensive circle where the rams pointed outward, and complex tactics to break formations were developed. In other words, whereas boarding battles were decided by the fighting qualities of the warriors, trireme battles were decided by the nautical qualities of the crews.[21]

On an operational level, larger campaigns invariably now involved considerable logistical support. As the warships were by themselves incapable of carrying enough provisions for longer periods of time, other ships had to be tasked with transporting water, food, and other necessities. Even then, however, given the huge amount of manpower required even for a modest-sized trireme fleet, longer-range operations had to be planned ahead to allow for places on the coast where ships could be put ashore and crewmen could stay for the night.

On a strategic level, the construction of a trireme fleet meant a vast outlay of money and resources. The construction of ships required timbers, rope, pitch, paint, leather, cloth, and bronze, and money had to be spent to gain these resources; as a consequence, aspiring naval powers started to project power into areas where these resources could be found; the Athenian activities in Northern Greece from the mid-fifth century onward are a good example of a foreign policy at least partly geared toward securing resources for keeping up a trireme fleet. Also, in order to protect warships from both the weather and the shipworm they had to be hauled out of the water during their longer periods of inaction. The need to protect this substantial investment in money and resources led, already in the sixth century BCE, to the construction of shipsheds, where warships were safe from adverse weather and where maintenance work could take place.[22] By the fourth century at the latest, whole harbors were exclusively devoted to supporting fleets of warships, with separate harbor installations made available for commercial shipping; building such an infrastructure only raised the already enormous cost of a trireme fleet, and as a result only wealthy communities could afford to maintain large numbers of warships. For those who were able to afford significant naval forces, however, they proved to be extremely useful tools for the projection of power.

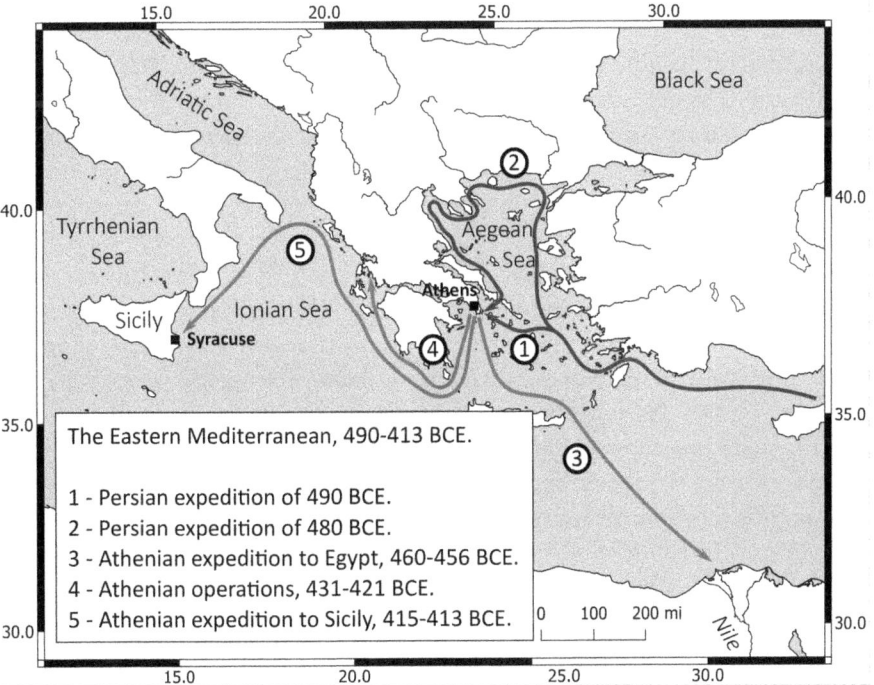

FIGURE 4.3 The eastern Mediterranean, 490 to 413 BCE. © Jorit Wintjes (author).

As a result, most large-scale conflicts of the period had a significant naval part to them: thus, the Persian War of 490 was essentially a large-scale naval expedition, even if it culminated—at least from the Athenian point of view—in a battle won due to the fighting qualities of Greek hoplites; ten years later, Xerxes' campaign had a significant naval component as well, and it was the failure of his fleet to defeat the Greeks in the Battle of Salamis that prompted him to return to Persia (Herodotus 8.97.1). The wars of the Delian League during the following decades would have been impossible without the Athenian capability to project power in the Aegean and the Eastern Mediterranean, and the Peloponnesian War saw arguably more decisive actions at sea than on land. The Aegean continued to be a major theater of operations after the Peloponnesian War, with Athens soon trying to regain its position as Greece's foremost naval power. Likewise, the wars between the Sicilian Greeks and Carthage also included significant naval operations, culminating in a large-scale invasion by the Syracusan tyrant Agathocles in 310 BCE, who sent 14,000 elite troops across the sea in an—ultimately futile—attempt to attack the city of Carthage itself (Diodorus 20.3.1–18.3).

As far as actually using the new warships is concerned, there was much continuity with previous centuries. Large numbers of ships were used to either project power directly by moving armies across the sea, as the Persians did in 490 BCE during their campaign in the Southern Aegean, which eventually culminated in the Battle of Marathon, or to support armies moving on or near the coast, as the Persians did a decade later when a huge fleet accompanied Xerxes both to be able to outflank an enemy blocking his way and to prevent the Persian Army from being outflanked—an operation that Uni, Pharaoh Pepi's general, would have understood perfectly. During the following decades the Athenians not only launched several large-scale expeditions—around 460 BCE against Egypt and in 415 BCE against Syracuse—but also made extensive use of their warships for harassing the coasts of an enemy incapable of meeting their fleet on equal terms. During the early years of the Peloponnesian War, Athenian warships attacked the coasts of the Peloponnese while Spartan-led Peloponnesian land forces launched futile invasions of Attica intending but never managing to fight the Athenians on land. During the second half of the war, when a Persian–Spartan alliance gave the Peloponnesians access to money, resources, and consequentially warships, the character of the naval war shifted slightly, as Athens' enemies tried to force the Athenian fleet to battle; they eventually succeeded, and the loss of its fleet in 404 BCE in the Battle of Aigospotamoi resulted in Athens' collapse and the end of the war (Xenophon, *Hellenica* 2.1.21–28).

Throughout the fourth century the pattern of operations continued to be broadly similar to those of the fifth century. Fleets of warships were used to project power by moving soldiers from one point to another, and even if not actually employed in that way a trireme fleet could constitute a powerful threat—unless an enemy met it with a fleet of his own. As a consequence, searching and attacking enemy fleets with the aim of destroying them and thereby removing the threat they posed was the second main type of operation common in the fifth and fourth centuries BCE. While this could result in sea battles, in quite a number of cases Greek commanders actually managed to attack the enemy fleet while sheltering on a coast; thus the nearly total destruction of the Persian fleet in the Battle of the Eurymedon in the early 460s was achieved by the Athenian general Cimon while the Persian ships, which had been beaten earlier in a naval engagement, had been hauled onto the shore (Diodorus 11.61).

At the turn of the fifth to the fourth century new warships were developed that together with the trireme were to form the standard warship types throughout the following centuries (Bugh 2006: 275–6). The tetreres had two levels of rowers with two men to each oar, with the number of rowers roughly comparable to that of the trireme; compared to the older ship type, the tetreres was more heavily built and could accommodate a larger number of soldiers. In Syracuse, the penteres was developed, which had three levels of rowers, with two men to each oar on the upper two levels and one man to each oar on the lowest level.[23] This resulted not only in a crew significantly larger than that of a trireme but it also caused the ship to be beamier and offering even more space for soldiers than on the tetreres. This increase in space available on board allowed for greater operational flexibility, as not only boarding action again gained considerably in attractiveness due to the larger number of soldiers available, it also made the transport of larger numbers of troops in warships possible.

GAINING COMPLEXITY—NAVAL WARFARE IN THE HELLENISTIC PERIOD, *c.* 300–30 BCE

In addition to the advances in ship design just mentioned, by the beginning of the Hellenistic period early in the third century BCE technological progress—which would eventually have a significant impact on warfare on land—made itself felt at sea as well (Sabin and De Souza 2007: 441–3). Artillery, and specifically torsion artillery, first conceived for sieges, soon saw use both during battles on land and mounted aboard ships (Marsden 1969: 169–73). Already in 306 during the Wars of Alexander's Successors, Demetrios I Poliorketes employed artillery during a battle off Salamis against the fleet of Ptolemy I. Using both stone and bolt throwers, Demetrios's ships were able to hit their opponents at a distance of several hundred meters and thus capable of inflicting damage before the ships could attack each other directly (Diodorus 20.51.2.). This long-distance strike capability—torsion artillery could easily outrange archers—brought a new dimension to naval warfare, which up to that point had invariably been a close-range affair. While battles during the Hellenistic period would still be decided by close-range fighting, this would now often only follow an exchange of missiles during which the ships themselves could already take damage and the crew casualties. Much more important in terms of operations, however, was the possibility to hit targets on land, which would eventually develop into true naval fire support, the very first type of "joint" operations, where warships not merely offered logistical support by carrying soldiers but actually engaged the enemy in direct coordination with friendly land forces. Looking back from operations such as Caesar's invasion of Britain in 55 BCE, where the fire support provided by his warships proved to be one key factor for success in battle, the introduction of torsion artillery to warships, therefore, was a crucial development in ancient naval history as it opened up a whole new spectrum of operations.

During the last decades of the fourth century, warfare at sea initially showed little difference to that from earlier decades. Both the support lent to the Macedonian Army during its crossing of the Hellespont in 334 BCE and the cruise of Nearchos carrying back home a sizeable contingent of Alexander's army in 326–324 BCE were operations of a type very similar to those undertaken by the Persians 150 years earlier[24]; indeed, Nearchos's cruise, while impressive in terms of distance, differed little operationally from the power projection operations by Pharaoh Pepi I or those undertaken by the Akkadian kings. The use of warships to gather intelligence during the preparation of Alexander's Arabian campaign—which was eventually cancelled after his death in 323—likewise was a common type of operation.

Throughout the third century, conflict at sea also followed familiar patterns, with fleets either transporting soldiers or trying to destroy enemy fleets to prevent an opponent from using warships to his operational or strategic advantage. On a tactical level, as already noted, missile exchange, ramming, and boarding were commonplace; in the Western Mediterranean the Romans during the First Punic War for a time resorted to an extreme version of boarding tactics by equipping their ships with boarding bridges that would, if applied properly, form a permanent connection between their Carthaginian opponents and the Roman ships and allow Roman commanders to flood enemy decks with soldiers. The *corvus*—a large and heavy contraption, which apparently had catastrophic consequences for the already bad seakeeping qualities of Roman warships—eventually gained a reputation out of all proportion and is even in the twenty-first century probably the most iconic piece of Roman naval technology.[25] The Romans themselves, having had it in use for around a decade, got rid of it as soon as they could build ships that were a match for those of the Carthaginians with regard to speed and maneuverability. Elsewhere in the Mediterranean, during the latter half of the third century the Rhodians experimented with the use of fire as an offensive weapon by equipping their ships with "fire pots," vessels filled with pitch or tar, which were projected from the bow of a warship in a manner similar to late nineteenth-century spar torpedoes, to be dropped onto an enemy's deck (Casson 1971: 122–3). Apparently they proved to be quite successful for some time, though whether the Rhodians developed any special tactics for their new weapon system is unclear. The case of the Rhodians serves well to illustrate a general problem—while the Hellenistic period brought about the publication of dedicated military manuals dealing with all aspects of war on land, some of which actually survive, next to nothing survives on naval warfare. This is somewhat ironic, given the huge importance of the sea in general and naval warfare in particular for many Hellenistic states.

It is worth noting, however, that, while Hellenistic navies did develop new tactics tailored to the new technology available, older tactics were far from outdated. During the Second Punic War, a force of Roman and Massaliote warships fought a Carthaginian fleet off the coast of Spain, probably near the mouth of the Ebro. By sheer chance the only surviving fragment of a Greek history of Hannibal's war against Rome describes what happened during the battle and notes that the Massaliote commander countered Carthaginian tactics with a maneuver which had already been successfully used against the Persians by Heracleides of Mylasa in the Battle of Artemision in 480 BCE.[26] While the text leaves many questions unanswered—for example, how did the Massaliote commander gain knowledge of these tactics? Were they transmitted in a tactical handbook?—it is nevertheless a crucial piece of evidence showing that, for all the new developments the Hellenistic period brought about, there was also much continuity, right down to tactics more than two centuries old still proving to be eminently useful in the 210s.

Looking beyond the tactical level one finds that operations of prior centuries were now if not dwarfed then certainly often surpassed in scale by the massive struggles involving hundreds of ships during the conflicts between Hellenistic powers in the Mediterranean. Whereas Athens had been Greece's foremost naval power during the fifth century with a trireme fleet of 200 ships, two centuries later the Ptolemaic kings were able to muster more than a thousand warships (Adams 2007: 42). As a consequence, fleet actions could involve hundreds of ships and thousands of men. Thus, in 256 BCE a Roman invasion fleet of 330 ships clashed with a Carthaginian fleet of 350 warships off the coast of Sicily; the so-called Battle of Ecnomus could well have been, at least going by the number of participants, the largest naval engagement in human history—nearly 300,000 men were involved in this huge battle.[27] More than two centuries later, the last civil war of the Roman Republic culminated in another huge battle between two opposing fleets, this time off the Epirotian coast, the Battle of Actium in 31 BCE. On both sides nearly 400 warships fought, while apart from the crews nearly 40,000 soldiers were embarked aboard the ships.[28]

On a strategic level there was much continuity from preceding centuries. Many of the conflicts of the fourth to first centuries involved naval activities,

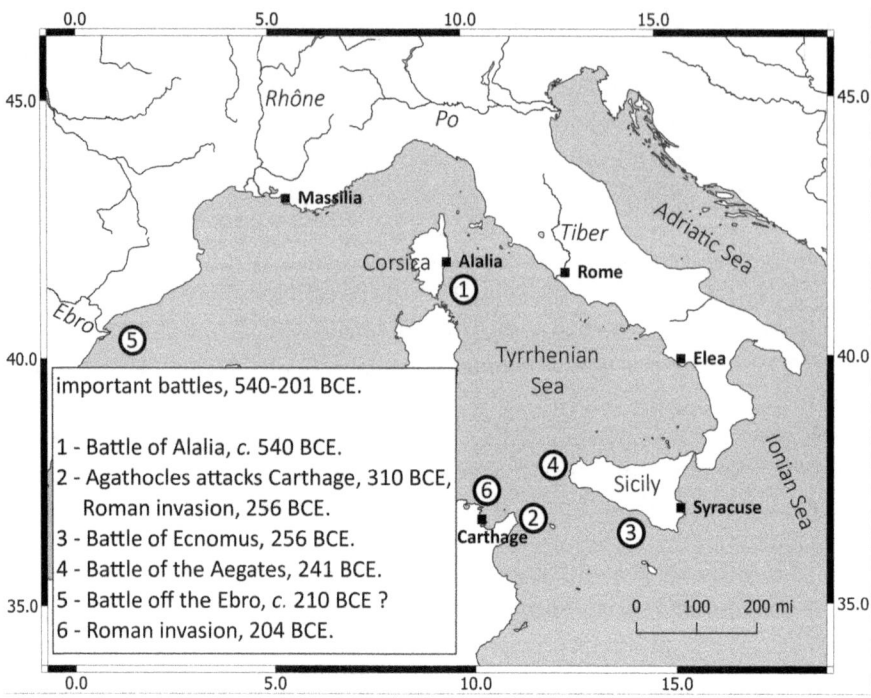

FIGURE 4.4 Important battles, 540 to 201 BCE. © Jorit Wintjes (author).

which in some cases were of equal or even greater importance than warfare on land. Thus, Ptolemaic attempts at establishing a hegemony over the southern Aegean in the early third century—which were ultimately unsuccessful—rested exclusively on the Ptolemaic Navy's capability to project power into the Aegean.[29] In the Western Mediterranean, the first Punic War (264–241 BCE) between Rome and Carthage was essentially a naval war, even if it also saw significant fighting on land in Sicily and Northern Africa; it was, however, eventually decided at sea in the Battle of the Aegates in 241 BCE (Lazenby 1996: 152–6). The Second Punic War (218–201 BCE), while nowadays mostly known for the exploits of the Carthaginian general Hannibal and his Roman adversary Scipio Africanus, also saw key events taking place at sea, with the Romans eventually moving a large army across the sea to North Africa in 204 BCE.[30] In the Eastern Mediterranean, Roman success in the war against the Seleucid king Antiochus III was partly due to Rome wresting control of the Aegean from Antiochus in two key battles in 190 BCE, where Rome's Rhodian allies made good use of their firepots.[31] During the civil wars at the end of the republic in the second half of the first century naval forces were used by the belligerents in a struggle that encompassed the whole Mediterranean[32]; eventually, the civil wars ended in the already-mentioned Battle of Actium.

The increase in size and scope of naval forces had three important consequences for states involved in conflict at sea. First of all, naval warfare had grown ruinously expensive. Ships, crews, and the infrastructure necessary to support their operations required vast amounts of money; as a result, only extremely well-off states could field large fleets—and even they had to resort to measures smacking of desperation, like collecting money from the aristocracy, if they suffered losses in large numbers (Polybius 1.59.6–7). As a second consequence—and a direct result of their value—warships were seen as important strategic assets, and peace treaties could include specific provisions about the numbers of warships left to a side that had lost a war. Perhaps the most important consequence, however, was the potential impact on society large-scale naval warfare could have. With crews of several hundred men per ship, combat losses could easily amount to thousands of men. In addition, due to the limited seaworthiness of ancient warships, storms posed a constant danger—in 255 BCE a Roman fleet of 270 ships and more than 100,000 men perished in a storm off Camarina. According to Polybius the Romans lost a staggering total of 700 quinqueremes during the First Punic War, which would have been crewed by more than 200,000 rowers; Polybius records Carthaginian losses at around 500 quinqueremes with up to 150,000 rowers. Losses on such a scale would not only have a significant demographic impact on the societies suffering them but also their visible effects on everyday life—a noticeable lack of young men—had psychological consequences as well: it kept the memory of what the enemy had done to one's own community alive, putting considerable obstacles on the road to a possible reconciliation; perhaps the most famous example is the "implacable hatred" with which Cato the Elder declared at the end of every speech that Carthage had to be destroyed (Florus 1.15.4).

While both fleet actions and large-scale troop transport operations over longer distances followed earlier patterns, the Hellenistic period also saw the development of a new type of naval operation: the naval siege.[33] Among the most famous examples was the siege of Tyre by Alexander the Great in 332 BCE, an island city only accessible by ship (Arrian, *Anabasis* 2.16.1–24.6). Ships were not only used to transport troops but also to attack the city walls by bringing siege engines close to them. In doing so, ships were for the first time in the history of conflict at sea in antiquity employed as directly supporting attacking land forces. While full-scale amphibious assault operations involving naval fire support were still a thing of the future, naval sieges were a first step toward such operations.

PUSHING THE BOUNDARIES—NAVAL WARFARE, 30 BCE–600 CE

The Battle of Actium in 30 BCE marks the beginning of what is perhaps the most underrated period of ancient naval history. Indeed, interpreters have gone so far as to claim that "proper" naval history essentially came to an end—with the Mediterranean turned into a peaceful lake and the days of huge polyreme fleets trying to outsmart each other by employing complex maneuvers gone for good, naval forces were relegated to secondary duties, carrying persons and commodities around and performing dull day-to-day duties on the frontiers.[34] To put it slightly pointedly, naval forces during the centuries between the Battle of Actium and the early seventh century CE, or so it is implied, had reverted to a simple life of carrying out simple operations.

While there is a certain attractiveness to the line of reasoning outlined above, closer inspection of the period in question reveals that the notion of naval history largely coming to a halt with the onset of the principate is simply, and utterly, wrong. Quite on the contrary, during the first five centuries CE naval warfare reached a level of complexity that was both unknown before and only approached again during the latter half of the Middle Ages. Far from being relegated to second-line duties, Roman naval forces not only quite literally pushed the boundaries by operating in waters as far away as the Baltic and the southern part of the Red Sea—and doing so often on a scale comparable with modern large-scale operations—they also fulfilled a key role for any emperor; this role is highlighted by the fact that demilitarized Italy was not only the home to the Praetorian guard in Rome but also to two large and highly capable naval units stationed in Misenum and Ravenna, which were primarily tasked with guarding Italy and the emperor against any possible threat from outside Italy—a threat that could quickly materialize during times of civil war.[35] While during the first centuries CE the Roman Empire lacked an enemy with a comparable level of naval organization, making major naval battles unlikely, interior conflict could result in such large-scale naval engagements, as in the war between Constantine and Licinius in 324, when a Constantinian fleet of eighty warships defeated a Licinian fleet of two hundred warships.[36]

On an organizational level, Roman naval power now rested on three pillars: the first one consisted of the standing naval forces called *classes*, which were stationed in Italy and some of the frontier provinces. While the Italian *classes* were large units containing dozens of ships and thousands of men and their commanding officers consequentially high-ranking officials, the *classes* in the provinces in contrast were, as far as can be told from the limited evidence surviving for them, mostly small units with limited capabilities led by fairly junior commanders.[37] While the Italian *classes* were large and presumably well equipped, even they were incapable of running some of the large-scale operations typical for the early and high empire simply on their own resources. Rather, for flinging several legions across a large body of water, large numbers of ships were required, which were provided during the preparatory phase of a campaign.

The second pillar of Roman naval power therefore consisted of ships specifically built for the purpose of a particular campaign. While this aspect

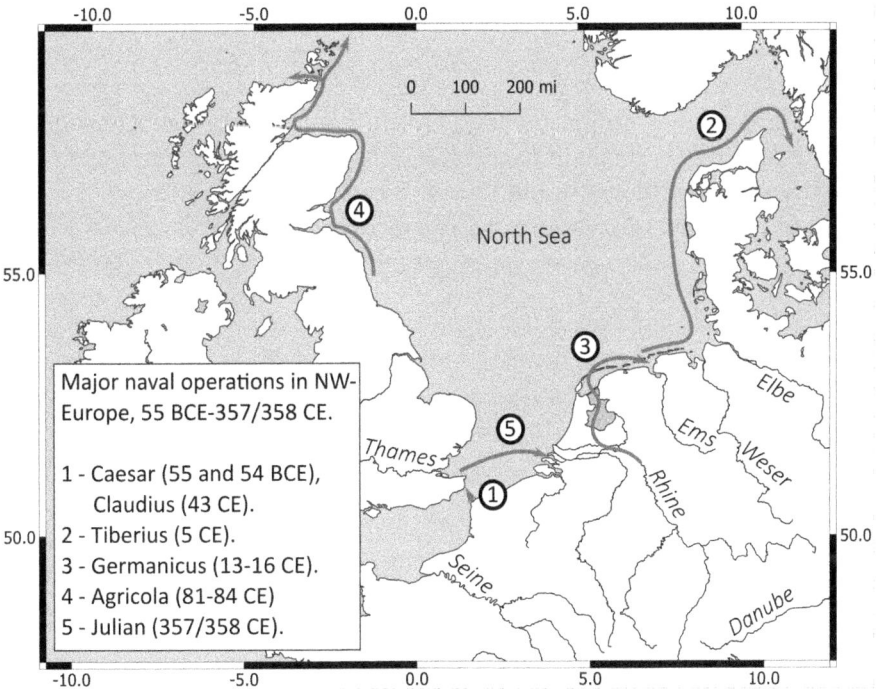

FIGURE 4.5 Major naval operations in northwestern Europe, 55 BCE to 357/8 CE. © Jorit Wintjes (author).

of Roman sea power was of key importance for large-scale operations, which could involve more than 1,000 ships,[38] it does not get as much attention as the standing naval forces do and is as a consequence rather poorly understood. In particular, crucial questions such as the recruitment of crews—which for hundreds of transports could number thousands of men—or the eventual fate of those ships surviving the operations they had been constructed for have never been properly addressed.[39] Although it is clear from the meager evidence surviving that for larger campaigns ships could be both purpose built and collected from available merchant shipping, where the crews originated from lies largely in the dark. Also, the precise legal status of crews recruited— for short-term service—is unknown, as is the system of payments and rewards applied to them. The crews of the ships transporting Roman soldiers across the seas in and around the Roman Empire thus serve well to illustrate how little we actually know about Roman naval operations.

Much the same can be said about the third pillar of Roman sea power, which has attracted even less attention than the ships and crews mentioned above. While the Roman emperor had largely monopolized military force in the standing army that was sworn only to him, and while private citizens were not allowed to raise and keep armed forces, this does not mean that outside the Roman Army organized military forces did not exist within the Roman Empire. Quite on the contrary, in the highly urbanized Greek-speaking part of the empire, cities maintained local armed forces tasked mostly for fighting banditry. In coastal communities, some of these were in fact naval units with broadly similar missions—while Pompey's famous anti-piracy operation had removed the threat from large-scale, organized piracy, on a much smaller level piracy continued to be a problem just as banditry was on land (De Souza 1999: 195–210). The existence of local naval forces, which might best be described as some sort of militia-type coast guard, went some way to counter the threat posed by piracy, but it also had two other important consequences. In coastal communities, it helped to underscore the "regionalized," so to speak, character of the Roman Empire on its lowest level: for anyone confined to the coastal waters of his own community—local fishermen, ferrymen, etc.—the authority of keeping the waters safe would have a Greek "face."

The three-tier structure outlined above allowed for the execution of large-scale operations both after a longer period of preparation and at comparatively short notice. It is these large-scale operations that are quite typical for Roman naval history during the first five centuries CE, occurring with considerable frequency. While "traditional" fleet operations did not feature as prominently as they did during the Roman Republic—there was no major enemy with a significant naval capability in the Mediterranean or its neighboring waters—they did occur. Thus in 267, Herulian pirates, who had entered the empire by crossing the Danube and capturing a significant amount of shipping on the Black Sea coast, tried to move through the Dardanelles into the Aegean, where they were successfully fought by the Roman general Venerianus, who led a force hastily gathered together from local sources.[40] Around half a century later the emperor Constantinus removed the last obstacle to sole rule in the empire by defeating his opponent Licinius in the civil war of 324. Crucial to his eventual success on land in the Battle of Callipolis was a prior success at sea, which Constantinus achieved by defeating his enemy in the Battle of the Hellespont; both sides had prepared for several months in advance by building new ships as well as collecting ships from local sources (Kienast 1966: 133–54). The Battle of the Dardanelles serves as a reminder that, while large-scale fleet action may have been rare, the threat of it was not, particularly when it came to civil war—which is why Augustus had stationed extremely powerful naval units in Italy.

Outside fleet action, the Romans used ships to move even larger bodies of troops around on a regular basis. There is ample evidence showing that the establishment of the province of Britain in particular saw troops being moved to and from the continent on a regular basis, while the same will have been the case for units stationed in Northern Africa. Transport operations could cover large distances—much of the logistical support for the Parthian campaigns of

CONFLICTS

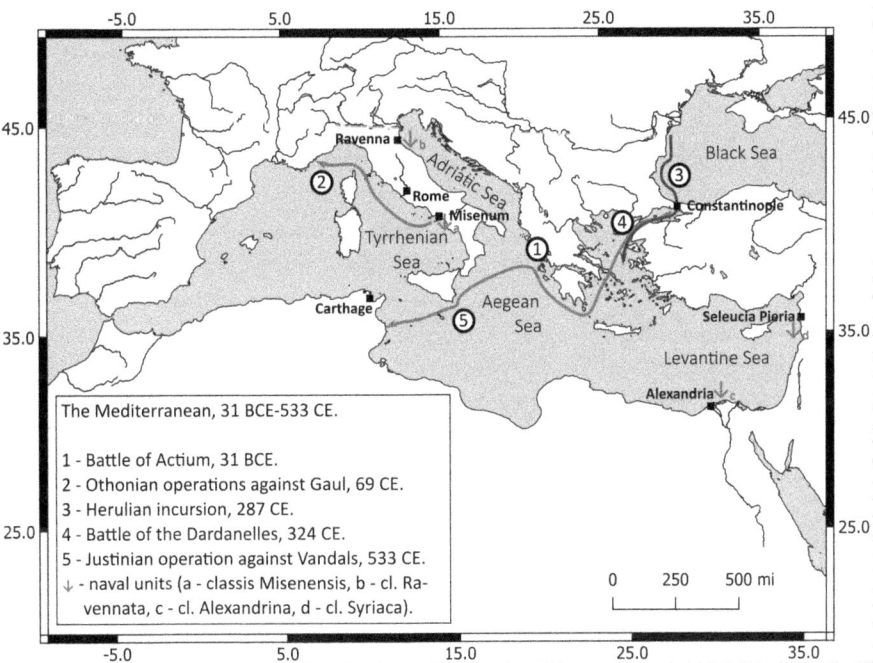

FIGURE 4.6 The Mediterranean, 31 BCE to 533 CE. © Jorit Wintjes (author).

several Roman emperors in the second, third and fourth centuries went through the key port of Seleucia Pieria on the Syrian coast, and this will have included the transport of troops (Kienast 1966: 133–54). In the early sixth century CE emperor Justinian recovered Roman North Africa, which had fallen to a Vandalic invasion, by launching a long-distance operation in 533 CE, in which a force of around 15,000 men was successfully transported from Asia Minor via Greece and Southern Italy to the coast of modern-day Tunisia (Procopius, *Gothic Wars* 3.12–13).

While transport operations in principle harked back to the days of Pharaoh Pepi's general Uni and the Akkadian kings, it was with amphibious operations that the Romans surpassed all their predecessors in terms of both scope and complexity. The first recorded example of an amphibious assault against a defended beach is Caesar's first invasion of Britain in 55 BCE, where his soldiers encountered an enemy keen on preventing them from gaining a foothold on the beach. In the confused fighting that followed the first Roman landing, direct fire support provided by Roman warships proved crucial for eventual Roman success (Caesar, *Bellum Gallicum* 4.24.2–26.5). While the invasion of 55 BCE is the very first recorded example for naval fire support, already in the following year Caesar had prepared a large fleet for another invasion attempt, which included both purpose-built landing craft designed to facilitate the easy landing of mules and horses and warships accompanying the invasion fleet to provide fire support (5.2.2). Around half a century later, in 16 CE, the Roman general Germanicus, who had already made intensive use of naval forces during operations in Northern Germany, sailed to the mouth of the Elbe with a huge invasion fleet of more than 1,000 ships, again including large numbers of purpose-built craft designed as fire-support vessels with platforms sporting artillery pieces (Tacitus, *Annals* 2.6.1.). Both the Caesarean landing craft and the Tiberian fire support vessels are testimony to the Roman willingness and ability to mass-produce mission-specific equipment for amphibious operations—something only achieved again in the twentieth century.

While the available evidence for operations is extremely patchy after the first century CE, it is obvious that the Romans had overcome crucial challenges such as retaining command and control over a large force landing on a hostile beach or target identification and fire control for shipborne artillery in a combat situation—or at least felt confident about having done so. Outside the Mediterranean, the Axumite king Kaleb around 525 CE led a successful campaign across the Red Sea and conquered the Southern Arabian kingdom of Himyar (Anonymous, *Marthyrium Arethae* 43). While Kaleb's invasion force apparently did not have an artillery capability, the operation nevertheless occupies an important place in the history of amphibious operations, as the Himyarite king tried to prevent the Axumite landing by using beach obstacles similar to those encountered by Allied troops on the beaches of Normandy in 1944—the very first time such obstacles are recorded in literary sources.

During the first five centuries CE, the Romans were pushing the boundaries not only operationally but also quite literally in the sense that waters outside the Mediterranean became operational theatres, seeing large-scale operations

FIGURE 4.7 Graffito from the Roman fort at Vechten, possibly depicting a Roman warship. © Jorit Wintjes (author).

at times. Thus the waters around Britain frequently saw large bodies of troops transported or major campaigns supported by naval units, which in the years following 77 CE pushed as far as the Shetlands.[41] Off the coasts of Germany, Roman naval forces not only supported the large-scale amphibious operations noted above but early in the first century also sailed around the Jutland Peninsula and penetrated into the Baltic during long-range reconnaissance missions.[42]

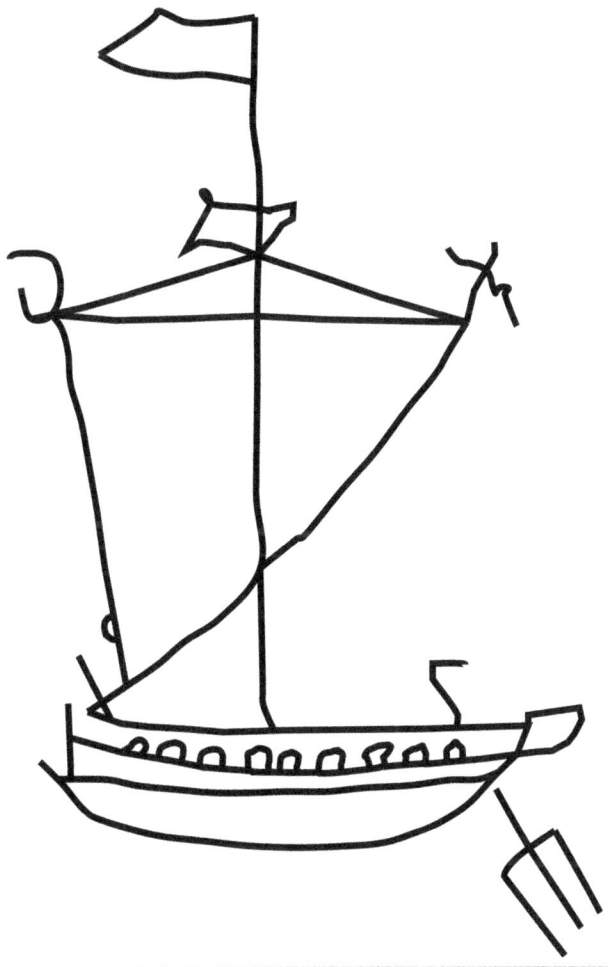

FIGURE 4.8 Graffito from the Roman harbor of Berenike (Egypt), possibly depicting a trading vessel on the Indian route, *c.* 25 to 50 CE. © Jorit Wintjes (author).

In the Red Sea, large numbers of troops were already moved under Augustus during the—ultimately not very successful—attempt by the Roman general Aelius Gallus to conquer the Arabian peninsula (Strabo 16.4.22–4). Later, during the early second century, Rome appears to have projected power well into the Southern Red Sea by establishing a military base on the Farasan Islands; while nearly all the details about this post lie in the dark it is quite obvious that maintaining even only a small presence in the Southern Red Sea, a good 1,000 miles away from the southernmost harbor of Roman Egypt, must have involved considerable naval activities (Speidel 2007). By the early sixth century, the Roman naval presence in the Red Sea may have been wound down, but, as noted above, Rome's ally Axum quite handily filled the gap by undertaking large-scale operations of its own.

CONCLUSION

Looking back from Justinian's North African expedition and the Himyar campaign of Axumite king Kaleb to Pharaoh Pepi and the Akkadian kings, it becomes clear that the three millennia separating the four rulers saw both great continuity and significant progress. Technologically, progress was both driven by developments in naval technology—the development of keeled ships with a strong forefoot was a prerequisite for the invention of the ram, which in turn had significant consequences for the development of true warships—and by technological advance originating outside the maritime world—the invention of torsion artillery not only allowed ancient warships to effectively engage an enemy from a considerable distance, it also made naval fire support possible, first during naval sieges and then during amphibious operations. The implementation of new technology drove tactical and operational progress, which in turn could lead to further technological progress as shown for example by the development of Roman landing craft, which led to further sophistication of naval operations. By the time of the Roman principate, standing naval forces were in existence with an organization and an infrastructure to match the complexity of their operations. At the same time, however, there was also much continuity—power projection by means of transporting soldiers to fight on a foreign shore was something empires of the third millennium BCE were already capable of.

CHAPTER FIVE

Islands and Shores

GABRIELA CURSARU

Islands are a cultural rather than a physical reality of ancient Greece. The Greeks were not all islanders and our following remarks come not only in the wake of a geographical and historical empirical observation, but notably in reaction against interpretations animated by an excessive geographical determinism. Moreover, space is one of the fundamental concepts of human thought, yet it is always socially and culturally determined. Therefore, instead of inquiring "what *is* an island for the ancient Greeks?," a more nuanced view has to obviate the potential danger of imposing coherency of such heuristic concepts on the Greeks. We can only hope to try to retrace "how did the Greeks perceive νῆσος 'island' and how did they *represent* islands and thus insularity?"[1]

Representations sometimes have more reality than reality itself. Almost by definition, space and landscape representations are semantically charged to the extent that they acquire or spark clusters of symbolic associations, which, sometimes, become so dominant that we are dealing with imaginary instead of real spaces. The Greek insular landscape, throughout the literary tradition, is a particularly strong codified image imbued with symbolism (Vilatte 1991: 21). It is more enlightening to understand the shape, the structure, the function of a mythical/imaginary island, for example the islands that dot the journey of Odysseus through a mythical world, than that of a real island. This is why we will discuss the concept of insularity within the context of mythical rather than historical geography. Even a simple reading of Herodotus, Strabo, or Pausanias lets us see to what extent the geographical/historical/periegetical genres imbricate both mythical and geographical knowledge onto distinct topographies and landmarks and unlock mini–mythological narratives at every step of their specific accounts, at each and every insular key point along the way. Despite their "imaginary" and "conventional" character (as literary tropes), the mythical islands, as cultural constructs, are more apt to define both the ways the Greeks envisaged the insular landscape and represented it through the most accurate forms of expression of the Greek spatial thought: myths, poetry, and imagery.

THE FORMATION PROCESS OF ISLANDS

At the beginning, every island was only a piece of land floating indefinitely on an unspeakable immensity of water. Half-continental, half-marine, without roots and without relays with the mainland, encircled by the sea and carried randomly by its flow, residing both everywhere and nowhere, the "primitive" islands (or the islands to become) thus inherit the swirling qualities of the germinal stage of the world, still undifferentiated.

The original name of these floating islands, Πλανησία/Πλανασία (from πλανάω "to (make) err") directly qualifies their "wandering" nature. The idea of the floating islands appears early in Greek thought,[2] with the *Odyssey* and the island of Aeolus (*Od.* 10.3: πλωτῇ ἐνὶ νήσῳ), the winds' master who would only live on an island "moving" along with the waves and whose nature mirrors that of its "Aeolian" inhabitants. Floating is not magical, but permanently given to Aeolia because it is part of its condition, it refers to the unstructured state of space in the early stages of its formation. Only an exceptional intervention can put an end to this kind of movement, either a divine act or a heroic and "civilizing" event. Patmos, a small island in the Aegean Sea, would have remained hidden in the depths of the sea until Orestes established the cult of Artemis there, a founding and "civilizing" gesture. When Zeus and the Olympian gods were dividing the earth among them, the island of Rhodes was not visible in the extent of the sea, but hidden in its salty depths. It was only after Helios claimed it and after Lachesis "spoke, correctly and earnestly, the great oath of the gods" and consented with Zeus, that the island "grew from the waters of the sea" and was allotted to Helios (Pind., *Ol.* 7.54–71).[3] In both those cases of "invisible" islands, it is only due to a divine/heroic intervention that they are rendered immobile and that they fix themselves in a definite place.

Callimachus's *Hymn to Delos* (30–5) offers the complete image of the "manufacturing" process of the islands as an act of foundation belonging to the cosmological "program" of the Olympian reign concerning the ordering of the elements and spatial structures of the world (Barchiesi 1994; Depew 1998; Nishimura-Jensen 2000). "At the very first" it was Poseidon who "smote the mountains with the three–forked sword which the Telchines fashioned for him, and wrought the islands in the sea, and from their lowest foundations lifted them all as with a lever and rolled them into the sea. And then in the depths he rooted from their foundations that they might forget the mainland." The complete cycle of island formation is thus described as follows:

1. a preexisting elemental material (the mainland) is divided into entities of the same nature;
2. without roots, those entities are thrown into the water and doomed to wander on the sea waves; in a raw state, these blocks of stone are deprived of all form, and therefore of everything related to stability, limit, and order; thus, they represent a form of hybrid space where land and sea are not yet plainly separated;
3. a divine artisan connects the newly created entities to the land (the land base bordering the seabed).

This three-step process illustrates the progressive structuring process of the islands' cosmos. The original/"primitive" material (the mountains) is reduced to pieces that are detached from their support, dislocated and set in motion, then attached back to another base, similar in nature to the first (the underwater seat of the earth). The agent who ensures the transition from one fixed structure to the other is the sea stream, par excellence figure of change, of passage, but also of instability and disorder. The divine work that puts an end to this confused coming and going is defined by a double opposition: to the "fast and resounding" waves, Poseidon opposes the centripetal and silent force of the sea depths and the incessant floating of the island is opposed to its rooting. Thus, the divine craftsman creates space and a new order.

The image is grandiose: we see the land base located in the marine abyss offering ties to an entity of the same mineral nature, tossed by the surface waters. The island is thus immobilized forever, rooted in and bound to the material to which it belongs by its nature. The stability and balance it gains are nothing but the signs of a process of world ordering, carried out according to the cosmological principles of axiality. The centripetal force comes from below, from the bottom of the sea and from the earthly foundation that supports the whole universe and guarantees its order.

The role assigned to the founding intervention of Poseidon within the narrative economy of Callimachus's *Hymn* is not surprising considering his functions related to stability and order, respectively to the foundations. If the traditional image of Poseidon is that of a violent god who shakes the earth and the sea and who splits and shatters the rocks with his trident, Poseidon is also honored as one who supports the earth and its foundations. His divine interventions are often related to a foundation and cosmic regulation process: according to an episode of Apollodorus's *Gigantomachy* (1.6.2), Poseidon broke off a rock from the island of Cos and hurled it on Polybotes, one of the hubristic early beings opposed to the Olympians, in order to punish and to crush him, but he founded thereby the island of Nisyros (about sixty stadia distant from Cos), where a temple dedicated to Poseidon was founded; according to Strabo (10.5.16) and by a contamination process highly specific to the foundation narratives, a fragment of Cos dislocated and turned into a missile, became an island, Nisyros, with the Giant lying beneath it, while "some say that he lies beneath Cos" (Figure 5.1). It is thus not haphazardly that Poseidon has total control of both the terrestrial and the maritime space. Founder of the islands that he rooted in the earth amidst the waves, he is also ruler of the seas surrounding the islands. Moreover, by this founding act of divine origin and essence, the new Olympian cosmic *ordo* acquires stability and equilibrium, the architectural firmness of the whole universe is guaranteed.

FIGURE 5.1 Poseidon holding a trident, with the island Nisyros on his shoulder, battling a Giant (probably Polybotes). © Wikimedia Commons (public domain).

(IS)LAND VS SEA, ISLAND VS MAINLAND

As a result of their formation process, the islands are characterized by their distinctiveness: islands are constantly depicted as sea-circled pieces of land, distant and distinct from the mainland, surrounded by water on all their sides and situated somewhere *in the middle* of the vast and indefinite space of the sea. It is precisely the presence of the sea that encloses the island within its own limits and its own insular interiority, which separates it from its surroundings while defining its own territory and forging its own identity, a territorial identity by virtue of which any island is insular, so to speak. A sea-wrapped world closed to its surroundings and folded onto itself. Distinctiveness, uniqueness, isolation, and self-containing enclosure on itself are inscribed in the nature of any island (Braudel 1972: 150; Constantakopoulou 2007: 3; Febvre 1932: 207; McKechnie: 2002: 127) (Figure 5.2).

Emerged from and rooted in the bottom of the sea, the island ends up defining itself by opposition to the sea: νῆσος "island," and especially its shoreline,

FIGURE 5.2 The map of the Cyclades. Compiled by the Danish cartographer Johann Lauremberg (1590–1658). © Wikimedia Commons (public domain).

ἤπειρος, define the island as a terra firma opposed to the sea (Ceccarelli 2009). Ηπειρος has a large semantic field, from "shoreline," "land," "mainland," to "continent," hence even "island"; without being assimilated to it, νῆσος ends up being identified by or with its own ἤπειρος, and both are defined by delimitation from the sea. One does not go without the other. In order to explain the way in which islands emerge, Pliny (NH 2.88) stresses the "earthly" affinities between land and island, both defined by opposition to the sea and as extensions of the earth: "Land is sometimes formed in a different manner, rising suddenly out of the sea, as if nature was compensating the earth for its losses, restoring in one place what she had swallowed up in another." The Earth (islands and continents combined), encircled by Okeanos, which eternally rolls its perfectly circular waters around it, is then insular.[4] Apparently, and by a sort of reversal of the conceptual *ratio* between ἤπειρος and νῆσος, it is the figure of the island that serves as an intellectual tool to imagine and to think, by analogy, of the Earth as an enlarged image of the island, as a totally circular continental entity surrounded by Okeanos (Vilatte 1991: 165).

One must never underestimate the significance of the concepts of edge, border, or boundary in the ancient Greek spatial and conceptual horizon, let alone when it comes to islands, micro-universes overbounded. While the outermost edges of the Earth were commonly believed to be surrounded by the mythical river Okeanos, any island was also surrounded by the sea on all sides.[5] Calypso's island is a "sea–girt island" (*Od.* 1.50, 198 and 12.283), as are Ithaca (*Od.* 1.386 = 1.395 = 1.401 = 2.293), Cyprus (Hes., *Th.* 193), Crete, "a fine and rocky land, sea-girt" situated "in the middle of the wine–dark sea" (*Od.* 19.173–4) or Libya (Hdt. 4.42.2); Paros stands "amid the encircling waters" (*HHDem.* 492); the mythical island of Erythea is "surrounded by water" (Hes., *Th.* 290 and 984); Lemnos, as well as Rhodes are "sea–wrapped" (Pind., *Ol.* 7.61; Soph., *Phil.* 1464); round Sicily flow the barren and unharvested plains of the sea (Eur., *Phoen.* 209), etc.

The insular isolation, also including the autarkic policy of "self–reliance," led to the creation of the idea of the island as a coherent enclosed ecosystem, which is highly prized by the utopian narratives applied to insular locations. The encirclement by the sea is often duplicated and even multiplied by other types of encirclement, under the form of rocky, sandy, or vegetal circular boundaries supposed to protect the islands' inland space. All these successive "belts" confine the islands into a perfectly closed space and reinforce their distinctiveness and thus their insularity.

THE ISLANDS' INLAND

As Greek sailors generally feared the "boundless sea" as a dangerous wasteland, they tended to travel within close proximity of the coast (Thuc. 1.7) and thus viewed the coastline marking its edge as a familiar and orienting space. Seen from afar or from a certain distance, the islands look, almost without exception, like impregnable citadels because of the rugged coastlines that form a first rock belt surrounding and enclosing the insular inland space, while doubling the sea belt. At first sight, the coastline landscape of the Phaeacians' island is rather inhospitable: there are "no harbors, ships' holders, not even roadsteads," but it is surrounded by "jutting spits, stony rocks, and reefs" (Hom., *Od.* 5.404–5 and 416), the shore is "rugged" (425), there are "sharp rocks running up smooth" and "dashing waves / bellow about them" (411). Aeolus' island is surrounded by an unbreakable bronze wall doubling "the smooth rock running sheer up" (*Od.* 10.3–4). These rocky features highlight the "continental" nature of the islands, their earthly texture, and therefore their "opposition" to the sea.

The insular rocky coasts are often doubled by the presence of a mountainous landscape, wooded or bare, that dominates the center of the islands. Ithaca's landscape is dominated by the wooded Neriton (*Il.* 2.632 = *Od.* 9.22); Creta's by its snowy mountains (*Od.* 19.338); Troia's by the "shadowy mountains of Ida" (*HHAp.* 34); Maleia's by its sheer mountain (*Od.* 3.287 = *Od.* 4.514), etc.[6] The dramatic landscapes of these islands, their rugged interior with high mountains and notoriously inhospitable coastlines enhance their insulation. However, by their double encirclement, marine and coastal, and thanks to the central high point of the iconic mountains dominating their landscape, the islands are all symbolically centered.

Stony reefs and rocky mountains are not so much marks of the wildness of a place, but rather serve to signify its otherness, the particular nature and status of that qualitatively different place. The high precipitous opposite rocks of Calpe and Abyla form the narrow entrance from the Atlantic to the Mediterranean, the renowned "Pillars of Heracles": originally, they were one mountain, which was torn asunder by Heracles,[7] together yet opposed to each other they stand like a veritable *axis mundi*, marking the eastern extremity of the Greek *oikoumene*: sailing past the Pillars of Heracles is either forbidden, since it is an inappropriate intrusion upon divine territory,[8] or is accessible only "under divine guidance" (Hdt. 4.152.2): according to Herodotus's description of the passage of Colaeus of Samos through the Pillars of Heracles, a constant and consistent wind "did not abate" until Colaeus and his crew had passed through.[9] While the two sheer cliffs, the winds, and the "invisible" divine presence serve to mark the sacred nature of the narrow strait and its particular status as the edge of the known world, its periphereal position and the strongness of the current that runs through it disclose the "primitive" nature of the place and its links with the mythical space–time of the origins.

The shoreline is the most important element of the periphery of any island and thus is unmissable from the Greeks' conceptual horizon and from their cognitive insular landscape. Dividing line between land and sea, the shoreline serves as the orienting border of the sea. Early *periploi* and sailing or colonizing expeditions construct their narrative accounts in the form of a point-to-point itinerary along the shoreline,[10] rarely venturing far inland from coastal areas. Seen from the point of view of the island's inland, the shore is a place both peripheral and preliminary, whose function is to reinforce the qualitative differences between the outside and the inside. This is why the shoreline easily becomes a narrative frontier, the diverse literary accounts of sailing expeditions describing it thoroughly through the sailors' actions. Each time Odysseus or the Argonauts reach a new land, generally an island, the description follows the retrospective gaze of the main hero/narrator in a kinetic way, as in a tracking shot: while at first, the space is dilated and panoramic, generally from the coastline to the island's promontory (ἀκτή), the frames eventually become more and more condensed around the heroes: we see the landing operations in functional or non-functional harbors, either natural[11] or built. The non-functional harbors are specific to the fictional geographical network: one cannot anchor his ship there, but only crash or be driven there.[12] Such harbors, as well as the rugged shore, the rocky coasts and the ἀκτή, signal a liminal place and work within an ambivalent spatial logic[13]: they are actually true breaking points and narrative borders that both separate and act as links to a qualitatively different space. As any major topographical border, the shoreline (together with its specific elements) serves both to draw the frontier between land and sea, and to mark the passage from one to another (as well as from outside to inside, from one spatial/temporal/narrative level to another, sometimes from one realm/world to another), but also to mark or categorize the nature/quality of the insular space it borders.

Finally, dense thickets, forests, or groves form another kind of belt, a vegetal one this time, but dense and compact.[14] They are a constant of the mythical islands' landscape where they cover the summit level,[15] surround the central area of the islands, separate the periphery from the center, and, at the same time, ensure the spatial link between these extreme points. Calypso's island is abundantly forested, a luxuriant wood grows around the cave in which she lives (*Od.* 1.51, 5.63–4); Circe's palace is surrounded, too, by "dense thickets and a forest" (*Od.* 10.150, 197 and 251), which will be crossed several times, in both directions, both by humans (Odysseus and members of his crew) and gods (Hermes, but also an anonymous god, τις θεός, 10.157).

This play of concentric "belts" draws a geometry dedicated to perfection, especially in the case of mythical islands, perfect settings for mythical events. Far from sketching out a fragmented space devoted to multiplication and made of scattered elements, the model of this rigorously arranged spatial partition proves to be a real "pictogram of order" (Figure 5.3). The spatial motifs appearing in the description of the insular landscapes and the characters who inhabit it mutually shed light on each other and, together, provide a significant endorsement of the narrative's intended plot.

FIGURE 5.3 Mosaic of Haidra (Tunisia) representing cities and islands of the Mediterranean (*c*. the end of the third or the beginning of the fourth century). © Fathi Bejaoui. Institut National du Patrimoine de Tunisie.

ISLANDS AND THE BEYOND

In addition to distinctiveness as a dominant feature of the spatial–cognitive model of the island in ancient Greek thought, another dominant feature stands out: the island's remote, isolated, and sometimes undefined position, somewhere in the middle of the sea or indefinitely "far away" over the sea, at the very edges of the "real" world, beyond the Ocean or at the ends of the "civilized world."[16] From this position, the insular landscape could therefore be used to negotiate the real and the imaginary (Fowler 2017) and becomes a perfect tool for building and mapping the Beyond.

The more remote/isolated the island is, the higher is its degree of "imaginary"; the higher is its "fictional" status within the web of Greek imaginary geography, the more its remote/isolated/undefined position is emphasized. Distance is a precondition of islands as imaginary topography and insularity and islands are archetypal remote areas (McKechnie 2002: 128). Remoteness also serves to reinforce the impervious character of the "out of this world" islands whose untouchability or inviolability stress their unique status: for instance, the one-off status of Delos as Apollo's birthplace is reinforced by Hera's oath to let her rival give birth "only in a place that will never reach the rays of the sun" (Hyg., *Fab.* 140).

Remote and isolated islands are perfect locations for exiles, whether banished or voluntarily self-exiled[17]: desert islands where banished heroes are left behind to become the spoil for birds of prey, to die without burial, like the singer banished by Aegisthus (*Od.* 3.270–1), or Philoctetes, left behind on Lemnos, the insular witness of his agony (Hom., *Il.* 2.721–3).[18] These desolated insular landscapes, remote and wild places of solitude and seclusion, mirror the protagonists' loneliness and despair (Soph., *Phil.* 686–706 and 1452–67); likewise, as the islands where they are doomed to insularity, the banished become "islands," enclosed on themselves in their own interiority. As spaces encircled by the sea and often prone to a geometric structure formed by successive concentric "belts," the islands can easily be transformed in veritable prisons[19]: Menelaus and his crew are "bound" (*Od.* 4.380 = 469) and kept from their journey for twenty days on the island of Pharos (*Od.* 4.351–7, 373–81, 466–80) and they can't leave until Menelaus ambushes Proteus, binds him, stops the cycle of his metamorphoses, and coerces him to tell them how to put an end to their captivity. Besides circling for so long around the edges of the earth in his attempt to return home, Odysseus is held back from his *nostos* (return) on the islands of Calypso (for seven years, cf. Hom., *Od.* 5.13–15, 7.259–263) and Circe (for one year, *Od.* 10.467–471), while Penelope is kept prisoner by the suitors in Ithaca.

Perfectly isolated, sealed, and impervious, islands are also perfect settings for utopian narratives. In fact, distance and separation from the "real" world are preconditions for imaginary or paradisiacal islands, utopias, and even dystopias (see Sulimani's chapter in this volume). What are the main elements of these narratives? (a) first, the "natural" ones: exceptional soil fertility, delicious crops flourishing several times yearly, temperance of climate and mildness of the air, luxurious vegetation and wildlife, ocean breezes and sweet scents, radiant light, nourishing springs and rivers[20]; (b) timeless felicity, unfading serenity, eternal good never mixed in with evil, endless songs, dances, and music; (c) supernatural and bizarre phenomena, spatial and temporal paradoxes enhancing the islands' isolation and their own insularity, their remoteness from normality (of both the mainland and the "real" world) and from any sense of normality (Lätsch 2005: 222–8), but also their potential as seats for alternative ways of life.

Nothing is natural in these distant, eccentric islands, situated outside the physical categories of space and time, outside the boundaries of humanity and mortality. While all these islands appear as veritable other-worldly Wonderlands/Fairylands located at the very ends of the earth, where we witness the (con)fusion of fundamental landmarks and levels of the world, they are in fact closed off and timeless spaces where the perimeters of space–time are stretched or where time is brought to a standstill. They are all aspatial and atemporal figures of the Otherworld/Neverworld. The far-away island of Ogygia (*Od.* 5.55), Calypso's divine residence, takes on traits from lands at the western limits of the world, beyond Ocean, but is located "where the sea's navel is" (*Od.* 1.50). The island takes on many aspects of the hereafter as well,[21] since it is there that Calypso promises Odysseus immortality and agelessness (5.135–6). It thus offers, in poetic form, an alternative to a human life locked in the cycle of birth and death. The marks of the isolation and remoteness of this island closed in and centered on itself are of definite importance. Ogygia is completely disconnected from the "real" world, nothing and nobody can upset its eternal equilibrium: there is no movement to and from, and Calypso can't convey Odysseus anywhere on the broad back of the sea for "she has not oared ships or comrades at her side" (5.140–2); "no one mixes with her, neither gods nor mortal men" (*Od.* 7.246–247). The fabulous apple-bearing shore of the Hesperides, which apparently did not break with the golden age, because "holy Earth, with her gifts of blessedness, nourishes the felicity of the gods" (Eur., *Hipp.* 750–1), is situated at the edges of the world (Soph., *Trach.* 1100), sometimes at sunset, in a beautiful island, sometimes in the Far North, in the land of the Hyperboreans, sometimes in the Great South or in Libya.[22] The passage farther up the Ocean's stream is forbidden by Poseidon, who fixed the sacred boundary of the skies, the pillar held up by Atlas, the Hesperides' father, as well as Calypso's. The soul must cross a narrow bridge to reach the land of the Blessed, however, the island is located "outside the boundaries of mortality, namely, in the Underworld and in the afterlife" (Beaulieu 2016: 30).[23]

ISLANDS AS STORIED LANDSCAPES

Sea journeys, islands, and male ritual initiation

Whenever it's about an island, there is a narrative built right in. Insularity is so invaluable in Greek thought and imagery, it is so closely associated with the ideas of exceptional, atypical, and fabulous that most of the Greek heroes are islanders and the islands have the particular role of setting and frame in mythological narratives of heroic journeys as well as a symbolic role for radical changes in destiny. By far the commonest destination or transit point in mythical sea expeditions is a remote and inaccessible (or accessible only to privileged heroes and under the guidance of the gods or their divine agents) island.[24] In fact, in these narratives, the islands prevail over the sea: while the sea has a role as setting, scenic backdrop, and secondary narrative frame of the action, it is the island that constitutes the main stage and primary setting.

The tempests that the mythical heroes have to confront during the crossing of the sea[25] are much more than a backdrop and the liminal places they have to surpass are more than accidental obstacles in their way toward their destination. If one sails out of the sea to Melos, one approaches Cape Malea at the southeast coast of the Peloponnesus. That the sea around this promontory is notoriously treacherous and difficult to navigate, with its high cliffs and powerful storms, is clear from the *nostoi* of several Greek heroes, mentioned in the *Odyssey*: several sea journeys are short circuited or deviated in this liminal place, such as those of Odysseus (Hom., *Od.* 9.80–1, 19.186–7), Menelaus (3.284–90) or Agamemnon (4.514–8). Cape Malea is one of the canonical narrative and spatiotemporal points from which a state of total confusion and the complete disruption of order are triggered, which bypasses the linear path of mythical heroes' sea journey and interrupts the narrative thread. Another conventional place symbolic of danger at sea is Gyrae, as it is known, for example, from the story of Ajax (*Od.* 4.500–11). Many scholars have tried, in vain however, to geographically locate it, while Gyrae, like Malea, rather than referring to a real, geographical location, is an *in-between* point, both spatial and temporal, where a level break occurs, where the unreal bursts into reality. It is *then and there* that the heroes are put to the trial of the sea, that they experience the ritual of coming of age, as their rites of manhood are compressed into the ritual of their sea journey. Thus, the sea crossing and the arrival on the shores of a remote island located beyond the limits of the known "world" are part of the heroes' ordeal and reveal their role as liminal and transitional passage from one register of spatiality and/or temporality to another, from one level of the heroes' personality to another, from one status of their "social persona" to another (Sourvinou-Inwood 1995: 115–17), whether it is to obtain κλέος "glory", royal prerogatives, or immortality, access therefore to a new or renewed identity and condition.

Islands, divino-human sexual unions, and female ritual initiation

The illicit unions between gods and humans, particularly between the former and παρθένοι ("maidens"), are particularly consummated in isolated islands and in their lush meadows/gardens, veritable *loci amoeni* (Motte 1973: 198–232) and *loci communi* of the symbolic topography of the narratives of divine–human unions. These extraordinary unions lead not only to the sexual initiation of the maiden but also to the radical change of her status, since they typically produce exceptional offspring who eventually take their rightful place in the history of an ancient race or city related to that island.

Prior to their abduction and sexual intercourse, the young maidens are generally playing or plucking flowers on the seashore or on the riverbanks. The scenes take place in a ritualistic environment animated by ritual dancing, choruses, and feminine games. The gesture showing the παρθένος cutting flowers is prior to her abduction and transport to a remote and insular uncut meadow and to her maidenly body being "ruined." Persephone was "playing with the deep-bosomed daughters of Oceanus and gathering flowers over a soft meadow," in the plain of Nysa, when Hades sprang out upon her and bare her away (*HHDem.* 5–21); in Euripides' *Helen* (1310), Hades drags Persephone out of a cyclic ritual chorus of παρθένοι. Kreousa was abducted by Apollo and carried off to a sacred cave while she was plucking flowers (Eur., *Ion* 885–901). Chloris/Flora is seized by Zephyrus and carried over the sea to the Island of the Blessed (Ov., *Fast.* 5.193–222). Aegina, the youngest daughter of the river-god Asopus, was seized by Zeus, in the guise of an eagle, and taken off from Phlios to a "virgin" and unviolated, not yet inhabited island that was named Aiegina after her; lying with Zeus on this island, she gave birth to Aiakos who became its king.[26] The young and wild Kyrene was abducted by Apollo and carried off from Pelion in Thessaly to the shores of Africa, to be queen of Libya (Greek colony founded around 620 BCE), where Aphrodite joined them in marriage (Pind., *Pyth.* 9.5–13); thus Kyrene became by Apollo the mother of Aristaeus, and the place welcoming this divine–human union became a flourishing landscape, which took the maiden's name as if her virginal body was equated with the land of the newly settled colony witnessing the "marriage" between the god and the παρθένος, now a tamed, fully acculturated γυνή (woman). Europa is seized by Zeus metamorphosed in a Cretan bull (or by a bull sent by Zeus to fetch the maiden)[27] and carried off from Phoenicia to Crete, across the sea. On one iconographical representation of this scene, we even see the arrival of Europa on Crete, represented by an island planted with trees, with a running hare.[28] The liminal space between the air and the surface of the sea represents a transitional space which is delimited, on one side, by the Phoenician shore, now out of sight, which the heroine is leaving; on the other side, there is far-off Crete. Between these two points, Europa finds herself suspended in air in a space far from any point of land, an image that signifies both the separation phase of the παρθένος (from her social setting, family, her old life) and her passage (toward the home of her future husband, toward another social status, a new, or renewed, life, and another world), without possibility of return. Her abduction, followed by marriage, is to be identified with her symbolic death; the aerial-aquatic space is perfectly suited to denote the particular ritual passage that she undergoes. As the chosen object of Zeus's desire, Europa has a fate that is entirely exceptional, that is, union with the god in his divine refuge in a mythical Crete, the gift of immortality, a change of status, a new, radically different life, and posthumous honors.

This is the lot reserved to a whole plethora of heroines excelling in beauty, who have aroused the desire of the gods and are abducted and subsequently transported to the insular destination intended by the divine abductor, usually one of the divine refuges that dot the mythical geography of the edges of the earth. All these privileged, but peripheral insular spaces, help to define otherwise undefined divine *elsewheres*, the eternal dwellings for those favored mortals whom the gods choose, snatch from the earth, release from their existence and their status as mortals, and promote to a deathless life or to heroic honors after death. In this way, all these islands elaborate spatial models of the hereafter.

Abducted by gods and having sexual intercourse with them, the maidens benefit from divine protection, and with them, their offspring and the insular space welcoming the divine union. By deflowering a maiden's body in a certain sacred place, the divine being appropriates and consecrates the very virginal island itself (Karakantza 2004: 44). By producing legitimate heirs of divine origin thanks to a violent but extraordinary divine intervention, the new γυνή and her offspring are the roots of a new place—now sacred and consecrated to the gods—and the stems of a new social body of the new *polis*. The new *polis* uses this narrative nucleus of the myths of marriage by abduction as a myth of its divine origins and to legitimize its civic and religious identity. With its powerful ideological and political background, the very same myth of origins of the newly founded city establishes its legitimacy through the idea of autochthony. Moreover, as all new *poleis* are generally insular, that says a lot about the strength of the island's representations in ancient Greek thought, the first to define the city in the Ionian and Aegean world insofar as the island is seen as the territorial expression of the centered circularity, guarantee of defense and protection, freedom, sovereignty, and unity.

THE SHORES

The seashore constitutes the intermediate space separating and, at the same time, joining water and earth, sea and land, contiguous realms yet opposed in many respects. A variety of divine actions occurs along the shoreline (mythical encounters between gods and mortals, epiphanies, miraculous rescues, metamorphoses, omens, and prophecies), passageway for the gods, nexus, and at the same time frontier between the respective worlds of the gods and of mortals, and between the world of living beings and the hereafter. A study of these actions will allow us to emphasize the religious connotations of this *in between* space located *betwixt and between* land and sea.

The seashore is one of the main narrative frameworks of the Homeric poems and of epic poetry. In the *Odyssey*, as well as in other famous tales of maritime adventures, the seashore serves mainly as border and nexus between land and sea, inside and outside, gods and mortals, as well as serving as passageway from one level of reality to another and from one world to another. In the *Iliad* it serves mainly as border and communication channel between the human camps (between the Achaeans' and the Trojans' or between different sides of the same camp) or between gods and humans, especially in critical circumstances, including life or death situations or in liminal contexts where things are not yet decided. The messengers sent by Agamemnon to Achilles' shelter went against their will "beside the beach of the barren sea" (Hom., *Il.* 1.327), while the embassy led by Odysseus to the same Achilles "walked along the strand of the sea deep–thundering" (9.182): their mission is more than difficult, considering the narrative context, the high stakes, and the inflexibility of both sides (cf. 9.179–84). Sometimes the shore forms part of the narrative setting during a climactic scene of battle and often it sets the scene for veritable situation reversals and passages from life to death. In *Iliad* 15, the battle at the ships takes place on the shore and the dark earth reddens with the blood of both Achaeans and Trojans (715). In Bacchylides 13, the Trojans drove the Greeks back to the shore after Achilles' withdrawal and fought them by the ships while the dark earth of the shore reddened with the blood of the Greeks slain by Hector (149–54): on the shore, seen as a place of despondency, the Trojans turn from victors into victims. Odysseus and other sailors gladly step upon the land, escape misfortune at sea, fleeing death's agents (windstorms, dashing waves, reefs and sharp rocks, hostile gods), and finally reach their homeland or other welcome lands. Or gladly sail, getting out of danger and escaping monstrous beings that inhabit hostile islands, the shore representing a place of relief as well as a place of a happy-ending outcome from a situation reversal.

Ἐπὶ θῖνα πολυφλοίσβοιο θαλάσσης, "shore of the loud–roaring sea" is often a place of solitude and sadness. The loud noise of the sea mirrors the emotional inner agitation of several downhearted people walking along the shore, silently or lamenting. Their gestures show that they are in critical situations where things that cause their torment are far from being settled or resolved: in *Iliad* 23.59, Achilles is groaning heavily on the "shore of the loud-roaring sea" over the loss of Patroclus and later, mourning for his friend in swelling tears, he roams "along the shore of the sea" (24.12), lying sometimes along his side, sometimes on his back, and then again prone on his face. It is on the shore of the sea-washed Lemnos, harborless, untrodden by men, and desolate island (Soph., *Phil.* 1–2, 220), that Philoctetes was abandoned, it is on the shore that he resides in complete solitude (145; 227–8: "so wretched and so lonely, a castaway, so friendless and so miserable"; 1018: "friendless, abandoned, citiless, a corpse in the eyes of the living"), "crying out a far-sounding howl as he stumbles, perhaps, from tortuous pain, or as he scans the haven unvisited by any ship" (215–17; see also 1456–61). After Proteus told him about the lot of the other Achaeans who left Troy, Menelaus "sat weeping on the sand," no longer wishing to live (Hom., *Od.* 4.538–42). After Hermes' visit, Calypso finds

Odysseus "sitting on the shore" (*Od.* 5.151, 156–8, see also 5.81–4) mourning for his return, as he was spending his time since his forced arrival in Ogygia and while the goddess was holding him there back from his *nostos*; his situation is about to change radically, and it is also on the border of the island (5.238) that Calypso leads the way and shows Odysseus the tall trees with which he will make the raft that will take him to Ithaca. In *Odyssey* 13.220, Odysseus is pacing by the "shore of the loud-roaring sea," mournfully longing for his homeland, without even realizing that he has arrived in Ithaca and that its shoreline itself was the very place of this extraordinary situation reversal in the economy of his long *nostos*.

A place of solitude and introspection, the shore can sometimes be a place of meditation and prayer, of inner conversation with protective divine figures. The banks of Ilissos, counterpart of the seashore, are seen as the perfect setting for philosophical reflection, far from the troubles of life: Socrates feels the sanctity of the place and is not afraid to meet the Nymphs (Pl., *Phaidr.* 238c–d) on the riverbank, situated on the outskirts of the city, since such a liminal place can be frequented and even inhabited by such intermediate figures divine in essence but close to humans, with the power of mediators between gods and mortals. Besides, Socrates notes the presence of a sanctuary dedicated to the Nymphs and Achelous (230b) and an altar of the Muses was also situated along the river (Paus. 1.19.5), the two groups of divinities and their cult being probably associated in several places. There are therefore rituals enacted actually in the very heart of this space (seashore as well as riverbanks), during a public event of ritual significance. Purifications and sacrifices to the gods take place on the shore, despite its marginal position beside the heart of the *polis*, but according to its liminal and thus particular status: in *Iliad* 1.313–6, Agamemnon "told his people to wash off their defilement. / And they washed it away and threw the washings into the salt sea. / Then they accomplished perfect hecatombs to Apollo, / of bulls and goats along the beach of the barren salt sea."[29] The sacrifice was effective: "The savor of the burning swept in circles up to the bright sky" (317), as if sea, water, and sky would be united during this special moment of ritual encounter with the divine through the sacred ritual operated in a liminal space–time of transition and communication.[30]

The seashores, as well as the riverbanks, are often inhabited by nature deities, especially by semi-divine beings either situated on the margins of the divine world or close to the human world and thus playing an important mediation role between the two realms. There is thus a perfect complicity between (a) the ambivalent nature of these deities representing inherent and natural sacredness, (b) the *in between* nature of the space they inhabit, the shores, which also constitute their field of action, and (c) their main characteristic, namely mediation, since they act between the worlds of men, heroes, and gods in various ways. There are caves on the shore of Circe's island, caves inhabited by Nymphs (*Od.* 10.404, 424) whose presence is justified by their *in between* functions related to the *in between* situations of the embarking/debarking scenes on/from the ground: they welcome and introduce the heroes to the land at which they have arrived, making from the indefinite shorespace of an unknown land a place definable and inviting, facilitate their access to, soften their arrival/departure and offer them natural hospitality, mediate between land and sea, wild nature and its adaptability, between mortals and protective gods, etc. (Malkin 2001). Philoctetes found shelter, all along his captivity on Lemnos, in a cave of the Nymphs situated upon the shore (272): before his departure, he hails the land of the island, the cave-asylum that "shared his watches," the Nymphs and their watery meadow, and the chorus adds his prayers to the Nymphs of the sea "to grant them a safe return" (Soph., *Phil.* 1454–71). The "pleasant dusky cave" of the Nymphs on the seashore of the *Odyssey*'s Ithaca is a veritable "physical" meeting point for men and gods: "It has two doors, / one leading down for men toward the North Wind, / but the other, towards the South Wind, is holy, and men / never enter by it, since it's a path of the immortals" (13.102–12). Through its two entrances, the cave gives direct, although differentiated access to both the divine and the human, as well befits any place inhabited by *in between* deities and situated in a liminal space which is both border and nexus.

If not inhabited by divine beings, seashores are frequented by them and sometimes constitute their field of action. If, in the second *Homeric Hymn to Dionysus* (2–3), the Tyrrhenian pirates witness Dionysos's epiphany "upon the unharvested seashore / high on a prominent headland," the Argonauts, upon disembarking on the shore of the island of Thyniade (*Arg.* 2.669–93) witnessed Apollo's appearance. The spatial interval between sea and land is an important *locus* of divine epiphanies, which are striking on more than one level. The physical attributes of this space, furthermore, are conducive to the epiphanies' scenery: the transparence of the air, the translucence of the water, and the effects of iridescence match the sparkle, brilliance, but also the mist of which the gods are so fond during their manifestation in human form to the world.

Given the unbridgeable gulf that separates the divine from the human, the contacts and the encounters between gods and mortals are anything but extraordinary, yet they are possible in certain places and at a certain time. As liminal and *in between* space, the shore can be the setting of actual and direct encounters between gods and mortals or of the noetic contact between human thoughts and divine inspiration. The scenes of the encounters frequently play out in the dark, at noon, or at the rising of the sun, giving the encounter a mysterious quality. They are intimately connected with instances of liminal time as well as crucial moments in the destiny of mortals. It is on the seashore that Thetis, after hearing her son weeping and after emerging "like a mist from the grey water," came and sat beside Achilles, stroked him with her hand, speaking to him (Hom., *Il.* 1.357–61). The mist could stand here for the invisible presence of the goddess (to anyone except her son), but it fits perfectly with the liminal and *in between* nature of the place. After his *nostos* was deviated at Cape Malea, Menelaus was held back from his journey by the gods, in the harbor of Pharos, for twenty days. One day, Eidothea, the daughter of Proteus—the old man of the sea and Poseidon's underling—approached Menelaus and offered him a solution to escape, devising a whole ambush to capture the divine old man. This encounter between Menelaus and Proteus, mediated by Eidothea, takes place at noon (*Od.* 4.400), "beside the edge of sea's surf" (4.449), *when* and *where* Proteus came out of the sea and laid down to sleep beneath the hollow caves on the shore (450–3). At that moment, Menelaus and his comrades, throwing their arms around the old man, witnessed his six-stage metamorphosis (lion/serpent/leopard/boar/water/tree), followed by their conversation during which Proteus gave advice to Menelaus, urging him to offer hecatombs to Zeus and the local gods, revealed to him what happened with other Achaean leaders after their departure from Troy, and uttered his prophecies regarding the fate of Menelaus himself.

By virtue of its liminality, the critical importance of the shore is confirmed by other divine actions that occur there: the seashores, as well as other spaces situated in the proximity of the (sea)water—seen as an element of untamed nature—are canonical places for abductions and rapes, sexual unions between gods and young maidens,[31] exposure of their illegitimate infants of divine descent (as well as of the banished mothers), in fact a liminal experience preliminary either to their salvation and legitimization either to their death: the young mothers abandoned to the sea are tossed between life and death; as for the children, they must prematurely experience the ritual of coming of age, because it is the rite of their exposure that fulfills its functions: well before adolescence, they receive either physical death (in addition to civic death), or life and a new status in accordance with their divine birth status.[32] The exposure and ordeal by the sea undergone by the victims form the epic kernel of these legends, that is their ritual initiation and coming of age, even the passage from a world to another and the transition from one condition to another, which are qualitatively different. The setting of all these multiple passages is precisely the seashore, that of the victims' native city (which expelled them) and that of the new (is)land toward which the sea carries them. The shoreline where the victims arrive or not gives an account of and seals, by its liminal nature, the liminal nature of the ordeal imposed to the heroic protagonists. The shores where the survivors are deposited (by the sea itself), then fished and brought to land (by different rescuers)—all of that with the gods' consent—are by definition *in between* liminal spaces between the sea and the land, places that ensure the passage from their old life and potential death to a renewed life.

Most of the survivors change their name or obtain it only after their arrival in a safe place, where the new name refers to the change of identity and the radical transformation undergone by the heroes who have been put to the ordeal of the sea. Places that have witnessed their rescue and which legitimize the exposed children, are sometimes named after them. The exposed children, henceforth legitimized, thus revalorized, are adopted, as a rule and not by accident, precisely by the kings of the host lands of which they become the heirs; or they themselves become the founders of the cities in the new lands they approach and give them their name. Therefore, it is not surprising that most legends concerning the exposure of newborns on the sea are etiological: the sea has legitimized them, the gods have given them their consent, they are ready to become founders or illustrious kings. Other newborns, fruits of divine births, are taken care of by the gods themselves: some lose their status as mortals and become heroes or demi-gods worshipped by specific cults; others become gods in their own right, notably marine; others, finally, become their servants and practice in particular the art of divination.

All these examples show that it is not enough, then, to consider the *in between* space located *betwixt and between* land and sea simply in aesthetic terms. As a place of wonder and a veritable spot of sacredness, it is endowed with a very specific sort of sacrality: the (sea)shore is ambivalent at every level, yet clearly invested, by the presence and actions of the gods who manifest themselves there, as religious.

CHAPTER SIX

Travelers

Sea Routes and Seafarers in Antiquity

RAIMUND SCHULZ

INTRODUCTION

After the destruction of Troy—according to Homer—Menelaus, Nestor, and Diomede discussed on the island of Lesbos which route they should take home: "whether we should go north of rocky Chios, hard by the island Psyra, keeping it on our left, or south of Chios, past windy Mimas. We kept asking god to show us a sign – and he did so, telling us to cut right across the open sea to Euboia" (*Od.* 3.169–76). The astonishing thing about these lines is not the fact that the heroes intend to go home across the sea but that as a matter of course they could choose from several routes: a shorter one to Chios and then along its northern coast and to Euboea via the island of Psyra (Psara); the longer one along the southern coast ("below") Chios, passing the Mimas foothills, and via the Cyclades. On the other hand, the divine order told them to take the direct route, from Lesbos to the West. As the narrative progresses we find out that Menelaus decided on a fourth, southern, route via Crete (4.514) to return to Sparta while Odysseus preferred to sail along the coast of Thrace (9.38–40). In this way, a whole network of routes within a territorial–maritime spatial continuum is revealed, allowing the heroes to return to their homes or to seek new adventures.

The phenomenon of the council on Lesbos is based on what was understood in all the regions where seafarers roamed: in the eighth century BCE the Mediterranean had been made accessible via much frequented sea routes. Greek captains sailed into the Black Sea and explored the coastlines of Sicily and Italy. One generation later a Greek ship sailed through the Straits of Gibraltar and to Spain's Atlantic coast, where centuries earlier Phoenician seafarers had established their first outposts. The speed of this maritime networking was continuously increased, until about four hundred years after Homer the Arabian and Indian waters were also connected to the Mediterranean routes. The history of antiquity is thus also a history of ever-growing seafaring and condensed maritime connectivity. The sea provided a network of overlapping routes for the transportation of goods, knowledge, and technologies. These routes not only took merchants and colonists to their destinations but they were also used by pirates, mercenaries, and generals. Because seafaring allowed for mobility across great distances, it connected far-flung civilizations and fostered their development. Sophocles (*Antigone* 332–8) placed seafaring at the top of man's cultural achievements; only this way can man become well rounded with no limitations (except death).

All this is not a matter of course, and Sophocles shivers when recognizing man's successes, particularly on the sea. Even for the most skillful seafarer the sea remained a place of horror, hostile to man and unpredictable. "There is nothing worse"—one of Homer's Phaeacians confesses—"than the sea to break a man, however strong he may be" (*Od.* 8.138–9). And even 700 years after Homer, St. Paul in the safe world of the Roman Empire got caught by a storm during his passage from Asia Minor to Italy that almost cost his and the crew's lives. There must have been some particular factors that allowed humans to dare going to sea again and again. The following chapter is meant to explain the reasons why and the purposes for which the seafarers of antiquity made ever further maritime spaces accessible. I will present the historical stages of connecting the Mediterranean to the oceans to the West, the South and the Far East. In the first centuries CE, even a crossing of the Atlantic from Spain was considered. The question of why this last great goal of antiquity was never realized is intended to contribute to a final, epoch-spanning historical assessment of the successes and limitations of seafaring in antiquity.

THE GENERAL CONDITIONS FOR SEAFARING IN ANTIQUITY AND THE BASIS OF OUR KNOWLEDGE

Homer's heroes find their way along the coasts and through the islands, and what is favorable for seafaring in the Aegean is also true for other places on the Mediterranean: its northern coasts are much segmented, vast peninsulas divide the water into smaller basins and the surrounding coasts into ecological subspaces. Sailors were able to cover long distances without losing sight of the land, while mountains immediately in the hinterland—as indicated by the debate on Lesbos—provide orientation. Huge islands such as Cyprus, Sicily, and Sardinia as well as the Balearic Islands serve as important stations for both East–West and North–South connections.

In addition to these favorable geographical conditions there were nautical advantages: the greater Mediterranean is a comparably predictable maritime area. In summer the sky is mostly clear, fog is rare and mostly restricted to the winter, which allowed the seafarers to orient themselves by the sun and stars. Tides and dangerous currents appear only in a few regions (Strab. 17.3.20); there are heavy storms, but they are short and the waves are by far not as gigantic as in the Atlantic. Even if each maritime subarea had its own particular hydrological and ecological conditions, particularly in the Eastern Mediterranean, in summer one could count on stable water and air currents (Arnaud 2005: 16–68). The great currents moved counterclockwise from the West to the East and to the North, which corresponds to the wind coming mostly from the West or Northwest (Horden and Purcell 2000: 137). Thus, westward trips along the northern routes took longer than trips to the East which were rather oriented toward the southern coast. The system of winds and currents supported the development of real *carreras* that, on the inside line, allowed for faster and easier transportation of bigger loads than the land routes.

However, these route networks were subject to regional and seasonal changes that the seafarers had to take into account. Since the seventh century BCE ships were capable of tacking up to 65 degrees upwind, and in case of a lull and against unfavorable currents they could revert to oars for a certain span of time (Fabre 2004: 117). Near the coast one could exploit the landward sea breeze, which started shortly after sunrise, as well as the nightly land breeze to pick up the pace and tack up to the predominant wind on the sea (Arnaud 2005: 22–3). In any case, the idea that seafaring in antiquity happened exclusively or predominantly along the coast and never in winter has long been exposed as a myth by researchers (Arnaud 2005; Beresford 2012). Actually, since the Middle Bronze Age there existed oceangoing vessels. They found their way without a magnetic compass, without log or sextant and exact marine maps, just orienting with the stars and the "signs of nature", namely, by the smell, color, temperature of the water, with the winds and the atmosphere, the movements and appearance of birds, fish and plant remains, as well as by sending out birds (to find out how far away the coast was). Trips across the open sea did not only save time and money (harbor dues) but also provided opportunities to ride out storms on the high sea, whereas on the coast it could well be that shallows and reefs, unpredictable currents, maelstroms, and downward draughts (particularly on a leeward coast) as well as pirates put a sudden end to a trip.

The hydrological, nautical, and geographical conditions on the Mediterranean were important preconditions for shipping, but as they allowed for trips both along the coasts and across the open sea, they left sufficient leeway for creative variations. However, there must have been people who were ready to exploit the resulting advantages while at the same time making a reasonable risk assessment. The epics and the (few) firsthand accounts have a tendency to present journeys to far-away places as heroic enterprises by individuals. In reality, however, seafaring over longer distances is not only a risky but also an expensive and technically demanding business, requiring long-term planning and capable supporters. In particular it requires being backed up by a community that maintains and passes on the knowledge of routes and destinations, rewards those making the step onto the sea with social recognition, and is not discouraged by failures. Such communities of seafarers developed mostly in urban centers. Coastal cities were the starting points and destinations of seafaring in antiquity, and important routes for sea trade were mostly established where the coasts provided urban contact points. Both phenomena supported each other and were largely responsible for the dynamic connectivity covering the Eurasian seas in the course of antiquity.

Cooperation with territorially oriented powers was also important. They hired the captains from the coastal communities to purchase metals and luxury goods as well as to explore objects for possible expansion. In return, they funded such enterprises and hoped to benefit from collecting duties from an ever-intensifying traffic on the sea. This combination of nautical expertise in the coastal cities and the interests of bigger land powers was an essential driving force for opening the seas and for maritime networking. It was also an important precondition for the constant expansion of seafaring peoples and for the improvement of the technological aspects of seafaring—indeed in many cases it reached a level that could compete with the early modern age.

The (usually) monarchic patrons of trips to far-away destinations are also significant for our understanding of extensive seafaring in another respect. Captains and coastal municipalities usually communicated their knowledge orally and at best passed it on in intricate ways in the form of epics. However, public sponsors expected the heads of their expeditions to deliver detailed reports about routes and ecologic conditions, as well as about the political and social situation of the explored coastal zones and their hinterlands, because only in this way was it possible to organize conquests and assess risks and chances of success. In this context there developed a literary genre of describing coastal regions (the "periplus," "sailing journey"), which on the one hand followed the principle of listing the names of places and peoples as it was common in the Near East (*Gen.* 10; Hes., Frg. 98) and on the other hand to the linear records of coastal places the seafarers sometimes used themselves. All this was included in the intentional context of the states' comprehensive need for information and planning.

In the Western Mediterranean, where until the rise of the Romans there was no imperial territorial power of this kind, port cities such as Carthage or Massilia adapted this principle when sending out their captains on expeditions to far-away destinations. Much of this was kept in archives and assessed. However, unfortunately, no firsthand expedition report from there has survived. All we have are excerpts and rewritings by authors who were able to reach back to original documents, but in most cases exploited them for completely different purposes, thus integrating them into new contexts. At least they preserved crucial facts as well as structuring principles, such as the calculation of distances and traveling times (Arnaud 2005: 63, on Herodotus). That is why already in antiquity these texts were essential sources for systematically grasping the horizon of experiences and knowledge available. Together with oral information from the seafarers, they served as the foundation for Greek geography, ethnography, and natural sciences when attempting to classify and explain a growing world. And given that archaeological finds are often insufficient and difficult to interpret, even these days we would know much less about the success (and failure) of seafaring in antiquity if we could not reach back to these texts.

THE EASTERN POWERS AND THE PHOENICIAN CONNECTION

Since the third millennium BCE, rulers in the Near East needed many resources they did not (sufficiently) find within their immediate sphere of influence: at first, tin and copper for making bronze, gold and silver from Southern Spain and Nubia, then iron from Cyprus, Northern Italy, and from the northern coasts of Asia Minor to build up their armies, for furnishing their palaces, and for making artwork and temple equipment. Then there were exotic plants such as incense and myrrh from South Arabia and Somalia. The Pharaonic Empire organized journeys to the legendary country of incense (Eritrea and Ethiopia). But the supply of metals from the Western Mediterranean required such a high degree of nautical-maritime expertise that it was left to the coastal cities of the Levant, which were prepared for such a task. The most famous example is the "mercantile oligarchy" of Tyre (Aubet 2001: 31–125). Like those of nearby Byblos and Sidon, their inhabitants called themselves Canaanites (*kinahhu*), while the Greeks called them Phoenicians after one of their most famous products, the red color of the purple snail. Apart from bulky sailing ships for the transport of goods over longer distances, their master craftsmen also constructed leaner vessels, endowed with a marked keel and driven, in addition to the sail, by two rows of oars with twenty-five men on each side (Figure 6.1). These ships were less dependent on winds and currents and they could defend themselves against pirates while still having a considerable tonnage.

These ships were the standard model for long-distance trips, even to waters such as the Red Sea, which, due to its dangerous reefs, waterless coasts, and terrible heat, was a unique problem for sailors and did not allow for island hopping. Furthermore, at Bab el Mandeb the monsoon system of the Indian Ocean was waiting for the captains. The Phoenicians were the only ones who were thought to be capable of mastering these difficulties. For example, King Hiram of Tyre

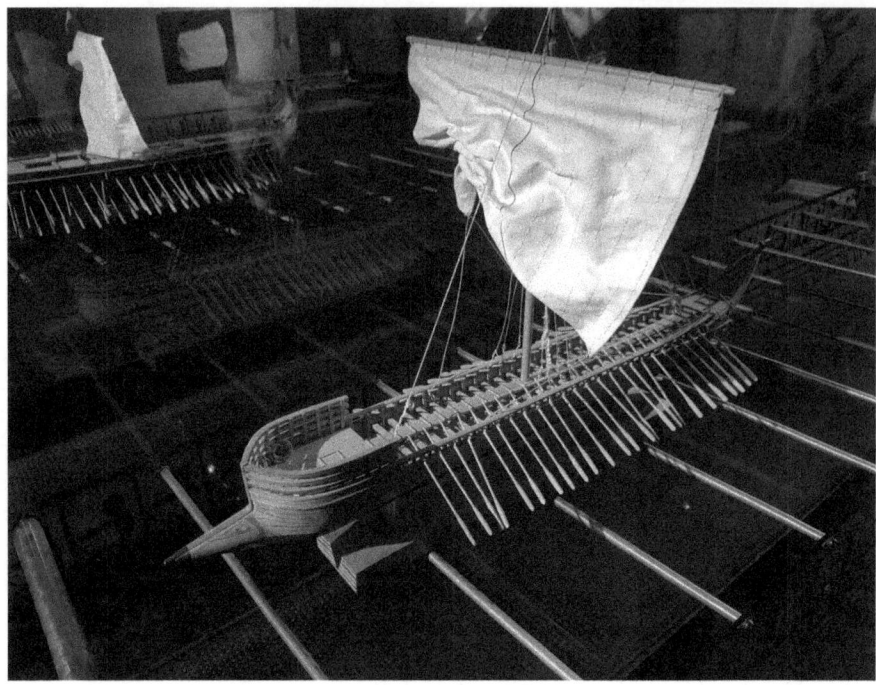

FIGURE 6.1 Model of a penteconter ("fifty-oared"), the standard galley of colonization and sea battles in the archaic period. © Wikimedia Commons (public domain).

(971–939) is said to have provided King Solomon with ships and sailors who went from Ezeon Geber (Aqaba on the Red Sea) to the country of Ophir and returned with great amounts of gold, sandalwood, and precious stones.

The Greek historian Herodotus reports that Pharaoh Necho II sent Phoenician sailors on an even more spectacular expedition. They were supposed to follow the coast of Africa (Lybia) even farther, to the West, until they would reach the Pillars of Heracles (Gibraltar) and could sail into the Mediterranean. According to Herodotus (4.42), this sailing around Africa was a success, although he expresses some doubts. However, we have no reason to doubt that such a journey could be made, even if we must assume that there were preliminary stages and that the enterprise happened in several attempts which tradition condensed into one event. Necho did not pursue any scientific interests; the sources do not offer any indications of this. Rather—like in the case of other long-distance trips (Beaulieu 2016: 8)—the sources indicate that there were material goals. The Old Testament tells of a "Tarsis fleet" that returned "full of gold, silver, ivory, monkeys and peacocks" after having been away for three years (I Kings, Old Testament book of Kings 10.22; Old Testament book of Chronicles 9.21). Tarsis probably refers to Tartessos in Andalusia in far-away

Spain, an urban culture that was famous for mining silver. The other products may be supposed to have come from West Africa and to have been traded at Tartessos (Cunliffe 2002: 44). As early as the tenth or ninth century the Phoenicians had reached Spain via the northern route of the Mediterranean, and they had established several outposts on the Atlantic coast, such as Huelva and Cadiz, from where they had access to the silver and copper mines in the hinterland.

Obviously Necho was looking for an alternative route in the South. The fact that this did not result in establishing lasting sea connections was not only due to the length of the journey but also to the fact that it could not compete with the Phoenicians's Mediterranean connections. Right from the beginning their enterprises were embedded in a stable network of routes starting out from the Levant. At first it led to copper-rich Cyprus. There, Kition was founded in the ninth century. From there the route led to Rhodes in the Aegean where, among others, the silver deposits of Athens (Laureion) and Thasos were a promising destination. Alternatively, ships made a stopover at Kommos on the south coast of Crete, to then return to Egypt and the Levant. However, the fifty-oared ships also allowed for sailing to Sicily and Sardinia via Malta or to Spain via the Balearic Islands.

Driven by summer west winds, the way back along Africa's north coast was not too difficult, and it was made easier by the founding of colonies (Figure 6.2). Among these, Carthage in particular soon evolved into a rich harbor metropolis and a hub of overseas and overland trade. From there the ships

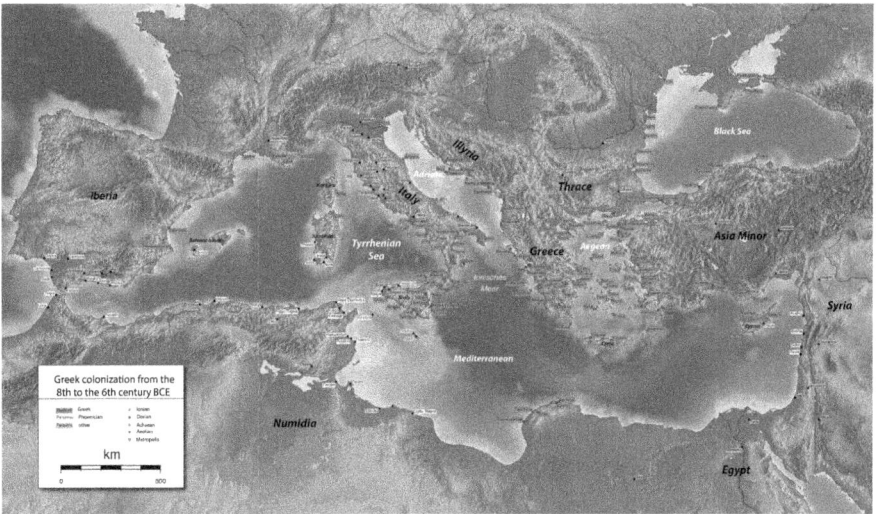

FIGURE 6.2 Phoenician and Greek colonization in the Archaic period (c. 800–550 BCE). © Wikimedia Commons (public domain).

coming from Cadiz could go to Sardinia and Sicily or further to the East. Furthermore, trade routes from Central and West Africa led to the Algerian coast. Africa offered slaves, ivory, and gold, and that was why Carthage extended its influence on the West African coast by establishing colonies as far as Mogador and by explorations further down to the South. The most famous of these explorations is that of the *strategos* Hanno. After founding new colonies, this expedition was supposed to find access to the gold deposits that were assumed to be on the Senegal (Schulz 2017). After a voyage of three days upriver on the Senegal, Hanno moved along the African coast, probably as far as the Gulf of Benin. Obviously he tried to find out if sailing around Africa was also possible from the West. Once in the Gulf of Benin he found out that, contrary to his expectations, the coastline went down further to the South, and that terminated the enterprise.

FROM UNRULY OUTSIDER TO AMBITIOUS PLAYER: THE GREEKS ON THE SEA

Even if the plan to sail around Africa at regular intervals was a failure, nevertheless the enterprises of the Phoenicians seem astonishingly purposeful. Their focus on peaceful gain and on the distribution and processing of valuable metals came along with a skill in shipbuilding that hardly knew any competitor. This specialization allowed the Phoenician cities to prevail against much stronger land powers, and this also explains why, even according to their enemies and enviers, the activities of the Phoenicians were comparably peaceful.

Carthage changed this policy starting in the sixth century. Independently from the claims of competing empires, the city could change the Phoenician trade posts into a colonial rule, thus turning entire maritime spaces into imperial spheres of influence. In the East, the Phoenicians lacked such aspirations, even when it came to the non-imperial periphery. In the Aegean they encountered a population whose elites practiced an archaic variant of purchasing goods by way of exchanging gifts. This was (as yet) far from the profit-oriented mentality of the Phoenicians who measured goods not only by their statutory value but most of all by the profit resulting from purchase, production, and further distribution. Homer shows little sympathy for this attitude; the genre of epic honored the acquisition of goods only in the context of proving one's worth by way of adventures or raiding. Myths and epics are full of young heroes going through adventures on foreign shores to find their places in the community of adult elites. The role model for an aristocratic youth was Odysseus, who confessed that gain (*chremata*) was more important for him than going home (*Od.* 17.248–50). Everyone is full of understanding (and envy?) when he talks incognito to his swineherd, Eumaios:

> Farming was never to my taste, nor tending of house and household which brings up fine children. No, my love was always oared ships and battles and smooth-polished spears and arrows – fearful things which make others shudder. What I loved was what, I suppose, god had put in my mind. (...) Before the sons of the Achaians ever set foot at Troy I had had nine commands of men and speedy ships against the people of foreign lands, and much booty came my way.

Raiding and piracy were connected to another activity that is also based on using trans-regional sea routes. Odysseus tells Eumaios that when looting Egypt he had been taken by surprise and had only been able to save his life by asking the lord of the land for mercy. Seven years later he returned as a rich man. Obviously the pharaoh had hired Odysseus as a mercenary. According to Herodotus (2.163; cf. 2.152–4), at the beginning of the sixth century up to 30,000 Ionian and Carian mercenaries, who had come, like Odysseus, as pirates, were fighting in Egypt. Greek fighters were also much in demand in the neo-Babylonian and the Assyrian Empires. Most of them reached their deployment zones via a sea voyage. One famous assembly area was at Cape Tainaron at the southern tip of the Peloponnese, from where soldiers went to Egypt via Crete and further along the coast to the empires of the Middle East. "Thalatta, Thalatta" (Xen., *An.* 4.7), the Ten Thousand mercenaries shouted at the sight of the Black Sea. After their murderous march from the Euphrates across the Armenian highlands only the sea offered a way back to their homes and to new jobs.

Mercenaries, warriors, and pirates did not only need ships but also protected places for the turnover of goods, where they could sell their booty and spend their pay. We may suppose that many of them gradually learned about the secret of the success of Phoenician sea trade and got an idea of the gain promised by the purchase of valuable minerals. Homer also knew this: disguised as a Taphian guest of Odysseus, Athena says: "I have come here now with my ship and my companions [...]. I am bound for Temese in search of copper, and I carry a cargo of gleaming iron" (*Od.* 1.180–2). Temese may be supposed to have been copper-rich Cyprus. Probably his cargo of iron came from Sardinia or North Italy. There the Phoenicians were already active in the ninth century. A hundred years later they were followed by seafarers from Euboea. It may be that in Central Italy Euboeans and Phoenicians went up the Tiber as far as to a settlement called Rome. Also Carthage was a trading place that was jointly visited by Phoenicians, Euboeans, and Cypriots. At Pithekoussai, founded on Ischia in the Gulf of Naples, Corinthians were living together with Rhodians and Phoenicians who had joined the first, Euboean, settlers. A melting pot of people for whom staying at home meant nothing and success in foreign countries everything. Perhaps it was in this multilingual society that the Greeks adopted the Phoenician alphabet. It had been developed in the late second millennium BCE to provide the merchants with an easier way of setting down and transferring their knowledge instead of cuneiform writing, which was performed by professional scribes.

Thus, in several ways the Phoenicians were important pioneers for the Greeks when it came to long-distance seafaring. The early Greek settlements were founded during a period when the *polis* in Greece itself was only in its infancy. Whereas the influx from Tyre and other Phoenician cities (with the exception of Carthage) was limited and had to be completed by native settlers, from the seventh century onward waves of immigration from the harbors of Greece went not only to the West but also to the shores of the Black Sea and even to North Africa, to live there in *poleis* whose size, often in the course of only a few generations, exceeded that of their home cities. Their motivations were varied: perhaps flight across the sea was the result of an attack by a superior enemy, or inner troubles demanded the emigration of part of the citizenry, or—rather seldom—agricultural hardships made the people leave for foreign shores. However, the establishment of *apoikiae* or colonies—another difference from the Phoenician enterprises—was only one option out of several. After the founding of a colony in Africa had failed, the Spartan Dorieus sought greener pastures as a leader of mercenaries in the South Italian and Sicilian colonies. Like Odysseus, anybody putting out to sea with a crew had to be capable of playing several roles and of taking the opportunities provided by foreign countries. This is the reason the Greeks were so successful, and also because they were not committed to a single goal.

THE EXTENSION OF SEA TRAFFIC AS FAR AS THE ATLANTIC OCEAN

This flexibility was one of the driving forces of the maritime dynamics that went beyond the Mediterranean. One of the most fascinating examples is the enterprise of the men of Phocaea on the Aegean coast of Asia Minor. Herodotus (1.163) says that the Phocaeans "were the first Hellenes to go on long-distance sailing trips," not on "round merchant vessels but on fifty-oars-ships." In the seventh century they arrived at Tartessos, where the Phocaeans became mercenaries of the local king and were so richly rewarded in silver that their home city could afford to build one of the biggest fortifications of the time (Hdt. 1.163).

Something similar happened on the French coast of the Mediterranean. The native king near the Rhône estuary also needed foreign fighting power and permitted the young Phocaeans to found a settlement. The Phocaeans accepted; their decision marked the birth of one of the most famous harbor cities in the West: Massilia. Only two generations later, more colonists from Phocaea had joined them, and the Massilians turned to long-distance trade. Via the Rhône,

Saône, and the lower Loire valley they looked for overland connections to the Atlantic tin deposits. At the same time, captains from Massilia got through the Straits of Gibraltar and to the Oestrymnic Islands (probably Brittany). A certain Midakritos (Plin. Hist. 7.197) is said to have been the first one to take "white lead from *insula Cassiteris*." Some believe him to have been from Massilia and identify the Cassiterides with Cornwall or the British Isles (Schulz 2016: 128–30).

Despite these spectacular individual enterprises, which also took the people of Massilia to West African waters (Sen., *Quaest. Nat.* 4.2.22), they did not succeed in establishing a regular trade route across the sea that would have made them familiar with the waters of the North Sea. All we know is that in the fourth century BCE Pytheas of Massilia started a journey to seek for tin and amber treasures, which took him as far as the Shetlands, perhaps even further to Iceland or Norway (Thule?) (Cunliffe 2002) (Figure 6.3). However, precisely the fact that this expedition was considered so spectacular and that many rejected it as being implausible shows that over the centuries the knowledge of these routes had been forgotten; Pytheas probably traveled as a passenger of Celtic and coastal shipping (Cunliffe 2002: 54–6; Roseman 1994: 148–50). The latter was so well established and competition from Carthage was so strong that establishing one's own sea trade route seemed to require too much effort, even more as the river systems and the eastern "amber routes" provided alternative land routes.

Thus, Tartessos remained the ultimate destination of Greek seafarers. Shortly before or after the Phocaeans, captains from Rhodes and Samos—obviously via other routes—are said to have come to the place and to have taken rich treasures home (Schulz 2016: 130–1). The competition for establishing long-distance routes contributed not only to the further dynamization of sea traffic but also to an increase in the productivity and prosperity of the urbanized coastal zones. Whereas in the seventh century mostly Oriental luxury goods and valuable metals were brought across the sea, now staple commodities and "mass goods" such as grain and pottery were also being shipped. Consumption was evermore driven by taste, fashion as well as the desire to purchase (allegedly or actually) qualitatively better and/or more exotic products (Foxhall 2005: 235). After the Phoenician and Euboean sea trade had focused on the elites as the buyers and customers of products from the Near East and had provided them with new means for distinction, about two hundred years later seafaring was the vehicle for a consumption revolution that not only supported cultural exchange but also stimulated the social differentiation of the consumer societies.

Even if long-distance journeys were still a matter for urban elites (Hdt. 1.163; 4.152), with the diversification of goods and services as well as with the growing number of potential customers now the circle of seafaring people grew considerably. Some shipped their grain surpluses from the colonies of Magna

FIGURE 6.3 Statue of Pytheas outside the Palais de la Bourse, Marseille. © Wikimedia Commons (public domain).

Graecia to the *poleis* of the Aegean and shipped wine and pottery from the workshops of Corinth and Athens to Etrurian cities. Others traded timber from Macedonia and Thracian slaves to the Eastern Mediterranean. Some focused on certain regions, such as Demaratus of Corinth who, after *one* successful trip to Southern Italy, "did not want to go to any harbor anymore" (Dion. Hal. 3.46.3), whereas smaller merchants sailed around coasts and ports, always looking for cheap goods and solvent customers. Most of them went as *emporoi*; as "passengers" or "people going to sea on other people's ships." Among them there were people with different interests having as the only trait in common that their professions required mobility and that they depended on long-distance contacts: singers such as Arion of Lesbos who commuted between Greece and the colonies (Hdt. 1.23–4) or Ibycus from Rhegion in Lower Italy who was employed at the court of the tyrant of Samos. From Samos, scholars such as Pythagoras went in the opposite direction, whereas the physician Democedes of Croton had offered his skills in the Aegean before he made a career at the Persian court in Susa.

All this, however—the extension of the seafaring parts of the population, the dynamic development of sea trade via the pan-Mediterranean routes, and most of all the extension of the geographic and ethnographic horizon that was driven by colonization, long-distance explorations, and trade—not only provided opportunities but also demanded orientation. One of the most urgent questions was to explain the confusing variety of natural phenomena encountered during long-distance trips. The scholars who were looking for answers were usually called natural philosophers. One center of the debate was the trade and port city of Miletus. Many of its inhabitants went on long sea voyages and dealt with geometry, astronomy, and the art of navigation. Thales, who is considered the founder of Ionian natural philosophy, communicated geometric, astronomical, and meteorological knowledge, which was necessary for seafaring. He wrote an astronomy handbook for sailors, in which he calculated—based on geometric evidence—how far away a ship was from the coast, and discovered the significance of the constellation of Ursa Minor for navigation. His younger compatriot Anaximandros claimed that man had originally developed inside fish. He called the origin of that which exists *apeiron*, literally the "unlimited," by which he meant something quantitatively infinite and qualitatively indeterminate, similar to Okeanos, which was not only the origin of life and of that which exists but also the epitome of chaos and disorder (see Irby in this volume).

Another challenge was the gigantic amount of empirical data on far-away coasts that could no longer be communicated by way of epic codes but demanded a comprehensive classification flexible enough to process new insights and add them reasonably to what was already known. Each expedition resulted in a readjustment of existing spatial orders that drove the planning of new trips on the one hand and the geographic recording of the world as a whole on the other. Anaximandros was one of the first to try to depict the extended idea of the world and its oceans by way of a circular map (*ges periodos*). This world was construed around a fixed mental orientation line along the waterways and reached from Gibraltar via the Mediterranean as far as the Black Sea. However, this was not just meant to provide orientation for sailors but most of all it was about harmonically (circularly) organizing lands and oceans. In contrast, by the end of the fifth century Greek and Carthaginian seafarers had to deliver travel accounts to their public sponsors. These reports provided information about travel distances, coastlines, and hinterland; some of them were later evolved into popular descriptions of countries by their authors. They again were exploited by scholars such as Hecataeus of Miletus who added his own explorations and made this into a voluminous overall presentation of the world, thus creating a much more detailed written counterpart to the natural philosophers' speculative and harmony-oriented efforts to interpret the world. Then at about the same time, in the late sixth century, the thesis of a spherical earth was developed in the western colonies and, in the following decades, it was confirmed by empirical observations (Schulz 2016: 145–7). Greek scholars were provided with the basic inventory for a geographic and ethnographic understanding of the world to which new explorations could be added. In this context, seafaring did not only provide food for thought and offer stimulating, if sometimes irritating, discoveries, but also provided crucial preconditions for the various theses on the shape of the world, which were rapidly spread and critically discussed. The maritime connectivity allowed for further forays beyond the limits of the familiar, and it was also essential for the development of a comprehensive discursive space within which these thrusts could be processed and new explanations for the whole of the world could be expedited. It is no coincidence that all the geographic works of antiquity were developed from a maritime point of view (Strab. 2.5.17) and were very much based on information about distances provided by seafaring.

THE FORAY INTO THE INDIAN OCEAN AND THE SIGNIFICANCE OF MONARCHIC WORLD POLICY

Of course the maritime dynamics of the late Archaic period also had a technological aspect. With the growth of the seafaring segments of the population and the specialization of the professions, the ships they used also became more specialized. Whereas Homer made no difference between merchant ships and other ships (Whitewright 2016: 12), vase paintings show, apart from high-boarded merchant vessels and fifty-oared ships, a number of mixed types coming from regional traditions but also constructed according to the requirements of their destinations (Casson 1994b: 60–8). For instance, in the second half of the sixth century technicians from Samos developed a type of ship for the transport of mercenaries to Egypt and grain from there to the Aegean (Wallinga 1993: 93–9). At the same time war ships with an additional third row of oars were developed in Phoenicia and Egypt. This made the ship faster and made ramming with the trireme more effective (see Wintjes in this volume) (Figure 6.4).

The development of a ship exclusively meant for combat (it could only be readjusted for the transport of horses), whereas at the same time merchant vessels were launched, was both a reaction to and the trigger for a fundamental change that had been happening in the Mediterranean since the last third of the sixth century. Seafaring came under the influence of imperial interests and geostrategic considerations. Expansive powers such as Carthage started to push competitors out of their maritime spheres of interest, either by way of treaties or by force. An even more marked turning point was the rise of the Persian Empire in the East. In the 520s, Cambyses had a fleet of about three hundred triremes built for his attack on Egypt. In this way, for the first time an empire in the Near East succeeded in building up naval forces on this scale, in addition to the enormous efforts on land warfare. These forces were successful, but their existence increased the foreign-political pressure and led to internal tensions. The financial burden was a crucial factor in the development of the revolt that followed Cambyses' death.

When finally Darius the Achaemenid pushed through, he needed expansive success to legitimize his rule, but also new financial sources to maintain his

FIGURE 6.4 The so-called Lenormant Relief, *c.* 410 BCE, from the Athenian Acropolis, showing the rowers of an Athenian trireme ("with three banks of oars"). © Wikimedia Commons (public domain).

naval forces. For this purpose he conquered Thrace in the Northwest with its gold and silver mines and rich forests. Controlling the sea trade route through the Bosporus promised duties. In the Far East the Indus valley, rich in wood, was a promising objective, even more so as gold was supposed to be found there (Hecat., Frgs. 3 and 4). Thus, in the 520s Darius organized an expedition to prepare the conquest of the Indus valley. As the head of this expedition he chose the Carian Skylax who probably had earned his reputation as a captain for the Persians on the Shatt al-Arab. The expedition went to Bactria and then, with a fleet built there, down the Indus via the Kabul River. From there it sailed to the Gulf of Hormuz. Then Skylax probably did not sail into the Persian Gulf but rather around the Arabian Peninsula and into the Red Sea until he arrived in Suez (Hdt. 4.44). If these assumptions are true, Skylax was the first seafarer from the Mediterranean who sailed around the Arabian Peninsula.

In the West, on the other hand, Darius's and his successor Xerxes's attempts to extend the Persian sphere of influence as far as the Greek peninsula were a failure. Instead, after having fended off the Persian expansion, Athens succeeded in controlling the sea routes of the Aegean Sea and, with three hundred warships, for some time extended its influence far into the Eastern Mediterranean. This rise to maritime power, was halted by the resistance of the Corinthians and Spartans. The Greek world started a period of about a hundred years of almost permanent struggles for power, which were again and again triggered by the intention to control the important sea routes and burdened the resources of the participating *poleis* beyond all measure. The powers on the fringes benefited from this situation: Syracuse, which in the 410s had destroyed a huge expansionist Athenian fleet and then itself became a great maritime power, and the Macedonian kingdom, which, under Phillip II, exploited its favorable geo-strategic location to gain control over the silver mines of Thrace and access to the Bosporus. In 338 the king defeated the *poleis* of the southern peninsula, which were exhausted by the constant fighting.

Then Phillip's son Alexander turned his gaze to the East and tried, after the conquest of the Persian heartlands, to finish what Darius had once started in India. Like Skylax, the Macedonian went down the Indus via the Kabul valley and had a fleet under the Cretan Nearchus sail to the West. However, the latter then sailed into the Persian Gulf. Immediately after having arrived in Babylon, Alexander made preparations for sailing around the Arabian Peninsula from the Persian Gulf via the Red Sea. These attempts did not result in establishing any regular sea traffic based on one's *own* merchant vessels. From then on, the building of ports on the Persian Gulf (Aginis—Alexandria; later, Spasinou Charax) served for controlling, securing, and tax-taking from the *existing* sea trade, which was run by Indians and Arabs who kept their knowledge secret and competitors away from the routes and trade posts of the Indian Ocean. Thus, Mediterranean seafarers were not able to get any clear idea of how far the Indian subcontinent expanded to the South. Anybody who dared sailing from the Red Sea or the southern coast of Arabia to the western coast of India ran the risk of missing India and of being driven into the vastness of Okeanos (Schulz 2016: 302f).

As is often the case in the history of maritime discoveries, it was the interplay of several factors within an evolving overall constellation that brought change. Around the end of the fourth century, the Ptolemies in Egypt and the Seleucids in the Asian region of the former Persian Empire established two territorial states there that competed for the supply of products from the Far East. In Northern India, after Alexander's death, the Maurya Empire rose, which had good relations with the Seleucids and the Ptolemies. The rise of three economically prosperous empires drove the exchange of goods between India and the Near Eastern Mediterranean to unprecedented heights. After the intensification of trade on the Mediterranean in the Archaic period (see above), this was the second consumer revolution, once again supporting the extension of seafaring: whereas the Mauryas learned how to appreciate wine, slaves, glass, and red corals, in the Hellenistic metropolises there was a growing demand for medical plants from the Far East, cosmetics, and aromatics such as *amomum*, *nard*, *costus*, *cinnamon*, and *cassia*, which came to the West from China and Southeast Asia. The European idea of the magical fragrance of the East, which remained alive in the modern age, dates back to that time.

Simultaneously, the presence of envoys from the Seleucids and Ptolemies at the residence of the Mauryas extended the knowledge of the extent of the subcontinent. When in the first half of the second century the Greeks from Bactria explored the western coast to the South, Western seafarers lost their fear of sailing past India when going to the high sea. Now such considerations were combined with concrete political and material motivations. Because of their costly wars for predominance over the Eastern Mediterranean, both Hellenistic empires had long lost the financial headstart they had inherited from Alexander and the treasures of the Persians. The Roman expansion restricted their leeway for action in the Mediterranean, and thus the kings were looking more intensively than ever for financial resources in places where they expected the least resistance. Whereas the Seleucids turned toward the Persian Gulf, the Ptolemies took an interest in the coasts of the Red Sea. A number of colonies—among them Myos Hormos and Berenice—were initially meant as starting points and shipping ports for elephant hunting as well as for supplying the army with Nubian gold; however, they could also serve as intermediate stations for maritime explorations (Strab. 16.4.5; Plin. *Nat.* 6.167–8).

Gaining insight into the secrets of the Monsoon system, however, required the help of Indian pilots. They came at least as far as the Island of Sokotra at the mouth of the Red Sea and could be guided to Alexandria by Ptolemy's patrols. Just as the Persian king once used the help of a Carian captain, now the king reached back to the know-how of a Greek sailor by the name of Eudoxus, whose home city of Cyzicus had trade relations with India (Schulz 2016: 301–4). Thus, once again, the search for new sea routes was intensified due to the interplay between the goals of a monarchic ruler and the maritime expertise of Mediterranean coastal cities that allowed their citizens to become rich in the service of powerful kings. After the Indian Ocean had been crossed two times, Ptolemy IV could receive valuable goods from India and could expect direct trips to India that would reduce seafaring time by three-quarters of a year and would happen at regular intervals. Duties and fees made sure that there were important intakes for the Ptolemies, and they were a good enough reason for becoming even more committed to the fiscal control of the sea routes and their military security, the latter particularly against Arab pirates. Only now and backed this way, Greek sailors dared going through Bab el-Mandeb and even further to the South along the African coast, and in the generations to come they went even further, as far as the Zanzibar Strait.

THE ROMAN EMPIRE AND THE WAY TO THE SEA OF CHINA

The information that Mediterranean sailors could reach the southern Ocean from its western flank and sail there fell on sympathetic ears in the Western Mediterranean. In parallel to the Ptolemies discovering the Monsoon system, the Roman Republic had extended its rule as far as the Eastern Mediterranean. The victories in the East flooded the city on the Tiber with gigantic amounts of booty and money, and together with the influence of the Hellenistic world culture among elite circles this resulted in a growing demand for Eastern luxury goods.

At first, the civil wars for some time prevented the greed for Eastern exotics from developing into new dynamics of long-distance maritime exploration. Only Augustus's *pax romana* brought a change. Augustus created a politically integrated sphere of rule spanning across the entire Mediterranean and its neighbors, and after having swallowed Egypt he was provided with gigantic financial means that, by way of expenses on the army, building measures, and gifts, stimulated the economy and created new potential demands. The Roman Empire became the most economically advanced empire of antiquity, with a concentration of resources and trade energies in a global space that would only be experienced again at the time of Europe's transatlantic great powers in the seventeenth and eighteenth centuries. The constant influx and provision of liquid assets, a general increase of production, technological inventions in the fields of shipbuilding and harbor construction, a high degree of elementary education and literacy, legal and political stability, as well as a favorable foreign-political overall situation had the effect that long-distance overseas trade reached a volume and a level of organization like never before.

In the East, Alexandria finally rose to be the most important center of sea trade, whereas in the West all roads were leading to Rome and the city developed into a super metropolis of up to a million inhabitants who needed constant supplies from the outside. During all seasons, grain freighters of up to 1,200 tons were moving from Alexandria to the West via the southern tip of Cyprus and Lycia (St. Paul took this route on a grain freighter: Apg. 27.37) or from the African coast around Leptis Magna straight across the sea to Sicily and from there to the port of Ostia.

However, both the upswing of the economy and the shift of the military strength to the borders had the result that maritime activities were extended beyond the Mediterranean. In parallel to Rome's expansion into the interior spaces of Europe, naval forces opened up the North and Baltic Seas. In the East, the incorporation of Egypt as Augustus's Crown land was the geopolitical precondition for the Mediterranean trade energies spreading into the Indian Ocean. The crucial driving forces in this respect were no longer the financial power of elites and their luxurious way of life; spurred by the political and professional security provided by the principate, now the army as well as wide parts of the urban middle class started enjoying the consumption of pepper and eastern cosmetics; some researchers once again speak of a real "consumer revolution"—it would be the third in the Mediterranean region in antiquity.

The fact that in the first century evermore inhabitants of the empire participated in the flourishing trade with the East was due to the growing demands of Western customers and the decline of inner-Arabian caravan routes; there was no need for imperial politics to intervene in this field. It was oriented by the political and fiscal measures of its predecessors. After Aelius Gallus's campaign had proven that the extension of immediate rule to the incense regions of Southern Arabia was unrealistic (like later in Germany), a network of treaties of amity with Arab, Indian, and Ceylonese princes was supposed to protect the Egypt from hostile competitors. At the same time, Augustus and his successors tried to secure the sea and caravan routes connecting the Nile to the Red Sea by way of forts and military patrols and to increase the revenues from duties and fees. The recently discovered prefecture on the Farasan Islands at the mouth of the Red Sea served both purposes.

Thus, on the whole, the emperors continued the policy of the Ptolemies, without officially supporting expeditions across the sea. Instead it was merchants from the eastern parts of the empire who, provided with bigger and more stable ships and goods from the West, as well as the *denarii* of their super-rich clients and investors, set off to benefit from the enormous profits promised by the acquisition of products from the Far East, despite the expensive duties. The main target area of Western seafarers were the port cities of West India. And again, it was not only merchants and craftsmen but also technicians and mercenaries of Greek-Mediterranean origin who, like once at the courts of the kings in the Near East, now were seeking greener pastures at the residences of the rajas.

However, the Bay of Bengal was still dominated by native seafarers and merchants. Nevertheless, the Roman imperial period opened up new horizons in the vastness of the eastern Okeanos. This was, as it is almost always the case, a result of power changes at the macro-level, which happened at the other end of the Eurasian continent. There, at about the same time that the Ptolemies found out about the Monsoon system, a ruler of the early Han dynasty, looking for war horses and allies against the northern nomads, had sent out expeditions to explore the region beyond the Tarim Basin and as far as Bactria and North India. As a consequence, on the evermore condensing "highways", the so-called Silk Road, Chinese goods were traded. Alongside raw silk were also spicewoods and ores for Western products: glass, pottery, wine, as well as reexported silk robes. At about the same time as the Imperium Romanum, the Empire of the later Han dynasty also experienced an economic upswing. Between these two territorial powers, the Kushanas in Northern India established one of the most flourishing empires of antiquity, which served as an additional buyer of Western and Eastern products as well as, simultaneously, a hub for Eurasian long-distance trade as a whole.

In the course of the condensation of territorial connections, the Indian Ocean also developed into a crucial connecting space for world trade in antiquity (Figure 6.5). Around 100 CE an envoy of the Chinese Protector-General of the

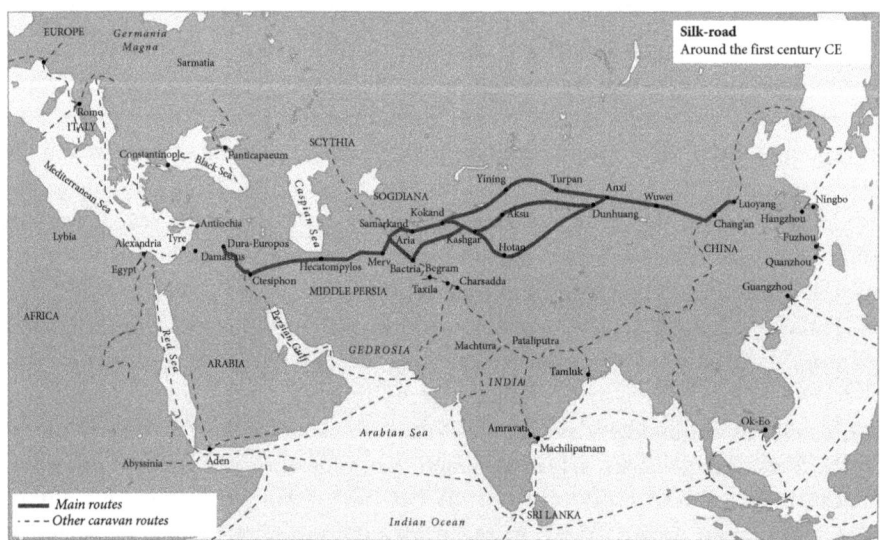

FIGURE 6.5 The connections between the Mediterranean and the Far East (China) in the first century CE over land and sea. © Wikimedia Commons (public domain).

Western Lands appeared on the Euphrates and asked, in the port city of Spasinou Charax, how he could get to the Roman Empire (Ta-tsin). Fourteen years later he would have met Emperor Trajan who stood on the pier and wistfully watched the ships going in the opposite direction, to India. The Chinese envoy was told that the sea route to the West took three months in the case of favorable winds and two years if the winds were unfavorable. This is mostly considered a purposeful deception. As a matter of fact, however, it is quite well in line with the opportunities and risks of the monsoon system that had to be taken into account when sailing around the Arabian Peninsula and the journey into the Red Sea. According to a more recent interpretation of a Chinese document, it may be that in the generations to come Han sailors reached Azania (SeZan?) (Chami 2017: 528). At about the same time a Greek captain from Alexandria probably sailed through the Malacca Strait via Ceylon and into the China Sea to Kattigara, a harbor in the Gulf of Tonquin or in the Hangzhou Bay on the southern arm of the Yangtze Kiang. One generation later again, a group of Western merchants who had come across the sea was granted an audience at the imperial residence of Luoyang (Schulz 2016: 387–90). In this way connections were established that would never be severed, not even in the Middle Ages. With the exception of Japan, the Mediterranean region had knowledge of the world, which hardly came second to that of the time before the African expeditions of the Portuguese and the Atlantic enterprises of the Spaniards.

THE LAST DREAM OF ANCIENT SEAFARING AND ITS HERITAGE—CROSSING THE ATLANTIC OCEAN

But ancient seafaring was not even satisfied with this expansion. It had become second nature to its actors that they were trying to at least theoretically grasp maritime spaces they had not yet explored and to conceptually connect them to what they knew. One favorite dream of ancient geographers and of more than just a few conquerors was the question of whether in the South the Okeanos was a single connected sea and if one could sail from there around the southern *oikoumene*. There were several attempts to explore the sea route around the African continent also from the West; however, all of them were a failure because of the unforeseen southern extension of the coastline below the Bight of Benin. Thus, when, owing to Alexander's conquests, the Mediterranean world became aware of how far Asia stretches to the East and discovered new islands also in the West, in the Atlantic Ocean, another project moved into the focus of the debates, namely an alternative route from Western Europe (Spain) to India or to the Far East via the western Okeanos. Its realization depended on how the West–East extension of the *oikoumene* was measured in relation to the total size of the globe. The smaller the size of the globe and the bigger Eurasia was estimated to be, the smaller the maritime distance between India and Spain in the Atlantic. From this, and referring to Aristotle, many scholars since Hellenism drew the conclusion that a direct voyage could be dared. If on the other hand, like Plato once did, one assumed a gigantic globe, then (for reasons of symmetry) one had to expect further islands in the Okeanos or even a huge continent surrounding the Atlantic Ocean in the West.

Such considerations hardly ever reached the mental horizon of the ordinary coastal captain, but they were part of the knowledge stock of the political and social elites and highly educated expedition leaders as they had been crossing the seas since the fourth millennium BCE. They refuted the old idea that it was not possible to go southward beyond a certain ("burned") zone of the earth. People who were regularly sailing on the Red Sea and the Indian Ocean had no reason to be afraid of going west across the Atlantic. For Hellenistic sailors or those of the Roman Empire navigation by the stars or the sun was no problem; apart from the observation of natural phenomena this still provided the crucial basis of orientation at the time of Columbus and was not replaced but rather completed by the compass.

Yet, still, obviously these more or less favorable preconditions did not result in the realization of the great dream of going to the West across the Atlantic Ocean, at least not opening up *lasting* alternative routes across the Oceans or the discovery of new continents, even if their existence was predicted. The crucial reason was not a lack of technological or nautical skills but the fact that seafaring in antiquity, like at any other time, was a very pragmatic business for which costs and risks had to be balanced. In the Mediterranean and the Indian Ocean the urbanization of coasts and hinterland was a crucial precondition and side-effect of maritime networking. The Atlantic, on the other hand, lacked a comparable, city-based network of sea trade, which integratively connected several sub-seas that were far apart from each other and to which Western actors could connect, whereas in the early modern age the Portuguese and Spanish kings, supported by Italian sailors, had already opened up the Eastern Atlantic as a sphere of interest to such a degree that one spoke of a second Mediterranean.

In antiquity, such a fruitful competition was non-existent in the Western Mediterranean. With the destruction of Carthage, the only power had fallen that could be trusted to have sufficient expertise and ambition for trans-oceanic enterprises. The center of Rome's power was the Mediterranean, not the Atlantic. Thus (other than the Persians and Alexander), it did not seek to establish oceanic connections between the individual parts of the empire and, in the Western provinces, could be satisfied with suppressing the development of competing political dynamics, which in the early modern age were crucial for the Europeans starting out across the Oceans. Other than in the case of the expeditions of the Persians and Macedonians, in the ancient West there lacked any powerful imperial impetus that would have made explorations into the vastness of the Okeanos profitable demonstrations of power. Advances to Britain, to the coasts of the Baltic Sea, and to Morocco were completely sufficient for acquiring the riches of the Oceans and of Central Africa (gold, tin, amber) and for meeting the claim to being an *imperium sine fine*, an "empire without an end," so called by Jupiter in Vergil's *Aeneid*. At the same time, the empire was regularly supplied not only with luxury products from the East but also with gold and silver (from Spain, later from Dacia) to such a degree that neither state authorities nor private persons were ready to take the higher risk of an as-yet-unexplored alternative route. After the incorporation of Egypt and its riches into the empire at last, what was lacking was not money and know-how but definitely any economic or material pressure, not to speak of any kind of religious fervor, which might have driven the Romans and the Mediterranean world they ruled for such an enterprise.

Thus seen, the crucial question is not why ancient seafarers did not (try to) reach the Indian Ocean via the Atlantic—why should they have done so?—but why at all the seafarers of the modern age dared this step? Actually, this is the phenomenon that needs explanation, which is not to say that antiquity is unimportant in this regard. Even if exploration in antiquity did not result in opening up transatlantic (or sub-African) routes, still it provided experiences, opened up horizons, and cleared mental paths on which the later Europeans could then tread. Again and again those planning the oceanic voyages of the early modern age point out how much they were spurred by ancient geographers as well as by the example of the seafarers of antiquity, and not without reason they thought to identify the New World with an old one: Columbus believed Hispaniola/Haiti to be gold-rich Tarsis (Tartessos), and after the discovery of the New World, Spanish authors were sure that Odysseus had already been there (Mund-Dopchie 1998), who—like his companions on Lesbos—really just wanted to go home, but made use of any opportunity for gain and for exploring the unknown.

CHAPTER SEVEN

Representations

The Sea

VALÉRIE TOILLON

INTRODUCTION

In antiquity, the maritime space was essentially linked to the Mediterranean Sea. This vast area was for ancient people mostly related to the experience of seafaring and fishing as well as to the imaginary geography of the maritime space. For this reason, the sea is first depicted as a visual indication, whose meaning oscillates between references to the "real" and the imaginary sea. Yet, the natural space does not occupy an important place in ancient art. In fact, nature is always considered in relation to the human experience of it. Representing the sea refers first to human activity (fishing, war, trade), or to mythological narratives (such as Odysseus's journey, Heracles' labors, or Perseus's exploits). Therefore, naturalistic depictions of the sea for itself, as a landscape, are exceptions. The sea is rather depicted metonymically through its inhabitants, namely, marine fauna, sea creatures, and sea deities.

Depictions of the sea appear on various supports and techniques throughout antiquity: vase-painting, bronze vessels, carving, sculpture, relief, wall painting, mosaics, jewels, etc. Those objects have very specific functions and purposes (funerary offerings, tomb decorations, votive offerings, domestic or public building decoration, etc.), which give information about the significance of the subject depicted on it (i.e., marine themes). Likewise, the meaning of sea-related themes on ancient works of art is strongly attached to the mental idea of the sea itself conceived as a natural and an imaginary boundary, a physical reality and a symbol of the beyond. Therefore, in visual arts, the sea appears both connected to eschatological beliefs and as a strong political symbol promoting the naval power of people, city-states, kingdoms, and empires over the Mediterranean area.

Note that the following subdivision into periods is entirely artificial; its main function is to provide a timeline for the sake of clarity. In addition, due to the limited space allowed for this vast subject, some topics will not be developed as much as they should, but further readings are suggested in the Notes at the end of the volume.

FROM THE "DARK AGES" TO THE "GREEK RENAISSANCE" (*c.* 1200–700 BCE)

The end of the late Bronze Age (*c.* 1200–1100 BCE) was a troubled period for the entire Mediterranean area, especially in the East.[1] Our primary knowledge about that time is recorded by archaeological data that shows what is called "destruction horizons," namely, traces of major destructions of the principal cities in the Levant, Anatolia, and in the Greek mainland (Mycenae, Tyrins, Pylos). The question of the collapse of Bronze Age civilizations is still under debate and no solution, for now, is agreed upon unanimously. According to scholars, the collapse can be explained by invasions, natural catastrophes, climate changes, large population displacements, internal conflicts, and systems collapse. Indeed, the end of Bronze Age civilizations cannot be understood by a single hypothesis. It was a very complex situation, certainly caused by several correlated factors resulting in the progressive impoverishment, then the disappearance of the late Bronze Age kingdoms and societies (Cline 2014: 102–76; Dickinson 2010; Jung 2010; Treuil et al. 2008: 373–83).

For the late Bronze Age period, artifacts are not numerous and mostly decorated with abstracts or stylized patterns. Therefore, depictions that are definitely related to the sea are very few. Octopus stirrup jars (*c.* 1130–1030 BCE) are a good example, very popular in the Dodecanese (a group of islands in the southeast of the Aegean Sea). These jars show elaborate and stylized octopuses placed on the belly of the vase, surrounded by fishes and abstract motifs. As Mountjoy stresses, those vases are a good illustration of the connections between the islands and the South Aegean during the late Bronze Age (Mountjoy 1993: 101–2). These vases also show that sea-related motifs, popular in Minoan and Mycenaean art, still persist in this transitional period as a strong cultural marker. Indeed, marine patterns are at the heart of Minoan and Mycenaean culture. For example, pots of the "Marine style" (*c.* 1500–1450 BCE) decorated with marine creatures (octopods, starfishes, or argonauts) are connected to the palatial administration and perhaps have religious significance (Mountjoy 1984, 1985), just like seals with sea-related patterns (octopuses, squid, cuttlefishes, flying-fishes, dolphins) or the decoration (floor, walls) of palaces inspired by marine patterns, as in Pylos or Tyrins, could have

FIGURE 7.1 Terracotta stirrup jar with octopus, 1200–1100 BCE. New York Metropolitan Museum of Art 53.11.6. © 2000–2018 The Metropolitan Museum of Art (public domain).

been an expression of religious and/or administrative power (Crowley 2013; Marinatos 1993: 229–32; Younger 2010).

The period following the collapse of Bronze Age civilizations is conventionally called the "Dark Ages" (c. 1100–700 BCE) even if that term is further and further away from the actual archaeological reality. Even though the end of the Bronze Age was marked by the brutal modification of the entire economic and political system, this does not mean that the transition to the Iron Age was sudden. Gradually, the features of a whole new civilization were emerging, which can be seen, for example, by new pottery styles and new funerary practices such as individual burial in cist tombs and the growing popularity of cremation (Coldstream 1979; Desborough 1972; Schnapp-Gourbeillon 2002; Snodgrass 2000).

For the period between the eleventh and eighth century BCE, one of the main sources of figurative representations—among ivories, bronze vessels, reliefs, bronze, and terracotta figurines—is vase-painting. Indeed, pottery is by far the most common type of artifact because of its wide range of purposes: preparing, serving, and consuming food and drinks, ritual functions, storage, funerary functions (as an offering or to receive the remains of the deceased), and so on. Of course, pottery is also a very good support for decoration, which, depending on the purpose of the pot, can express religious beliefs, everyday life narratives, or narratives linked to the imaginary or mythical world (Desborough 1972: 289–93).

Visual representations of the sea are attested with certainty starting in the Middle Geometric (c. 850–760 BCE), a time when the human figure is progressively reintroduced in visual arts, on pots widely used as funerary offerings or grave markers. In fact, the sea is pictured metonymically, in connection with human activity and more particularly battle scenes. A Middle Geometric *skyphos*—drinking vessel—(which was a burial offering) from Eleusis shows a battle scene: one on earth, the other on the sea. The sea is indicated by a boat with a high curved stern, the prow is lower and also curved, a bird is perched on it, perhaps indicating the proximity of the shore.[2]

In many respects, the eighth century BCE appears as a turning point (Morris 2009). Trade and colonization start again, especially explorations of the West (see Schulz in this volume). The Greeks establish colonies in Southern Italy and Sicily. They dispute the trade road for tin toward Great Britain with the Phoenicians who had settled in West Sicily, Sardinia, South Spain, and the coast of North Africa (Boardman 1995: 195–257; Coldstream 1979: 221–45) (see Friedman in this volume). In addition, one must not forget that as early as the ninth century BCE, Eastern craftsmen from North Syria and Assyria came into Greece to work and teach their art. Their presence had an impact both on the techniques developed and on the figurative repertoire; in particular, the narrative Eastern art combined with the diffusion of the Homeric poems stimulate the development of the totally unique Greek narrative art (Boardman 1995: 69–103; Coldstream 1979: 358–66).

Sea representations are mostly from the late Geometric period (c. 760–700 BCE), on monumental vessels connected to funeral practices (grave markers, funerary offerings). The sea is pictured by means of representations of boats, birds, and marine fauna, mainly fishes as, for example, a crater from Pithekoussai on which is shown a shipwreck that may have been inspired by a real incident during an expedition on the Mediterranean Sea (Figure 7.2).[3] A boat is depicted upside down while six male figures are floating in the water, symbolized by the numerous fishes of different size. One of the men is being eaten by an enormous fish. One has lost his head, another his arm, while two others seem to be still alive. Here, the swastikas in the field, under the ship, are used to induce dynamism to the scene: they symbolize the rolling effect of the waves (Ahlberg Cornell 1992: 28; Brunnsaker 1962: 199). This representation shows, in a dreadful way, the many dangers of the sea, which is, in some respects, very close to the Homeric epics. Namely a place to travel that can be deadly; as the nurse says to Telemachus "you have no need to suffer ills on the barren sea and go wandering" (Od. 2. 369–70). Death at sea is, in ancient thought, one of the most terrible ways to die since the deceased will not receive a proper burial and will be eaten by fishes as the Ischia crater cruelly evokes (Vermeule 1979: 181–8).

On the other hand, a spouted crater from the British Museum shows a long ship with two ranks of rowers (forty in all), a man, and a woman.[4] The man grasps the woman's wrist—*cheir epi karpô*—(the typical gesture for indicating a wedding in classical times) while preparing to embark. The picture represents an abduction, maybe inspired by a "real-life" event and has been read as an early depiction of the myth of Ariadne and Theseus; the abduction of Helen by Paris or Menelaos; as Jason and Medea; or Hektor and Andromache (Ahlberg-Cornell 1992: 26–7; Coldstream 1979: 354–5; Langdon 2010: 19–32; Snodgrass 2011: 33–5). In this picture, the sea is only indicated by the boat, which acts as a sign of power and recalls, according to Langdon, the experience of Greek colonization across the sea in the eighth century BCE (Langdon 2010: 28–9).

In the Geometric period, the sea is mostly depicted as a place to travel, both in a symbolic and practical sense, as illustrated by numerous representations of

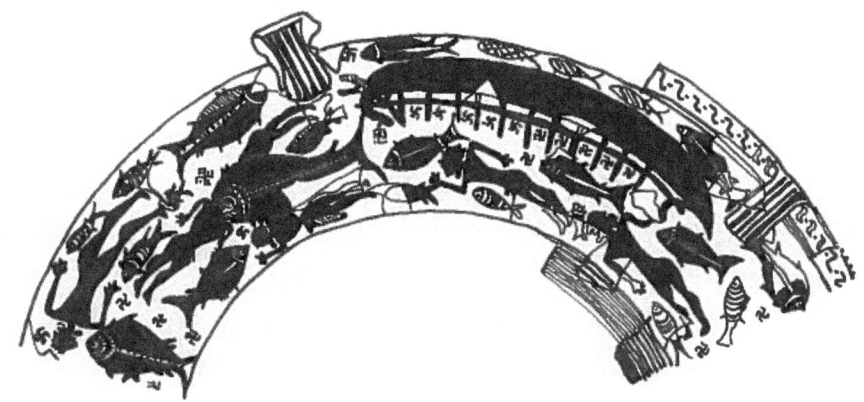

FIGURE 7.2 Shipwreck crater (760–700 BCE). Ischia sp. 1/1. Based on Boardman (1998: fig. 161). © Valérie Toillon (author).

ships on funerary vessels. In other words, the journey on the sea could refer both to the transportation of the dead in the beyond and to seafaring and fishing, a theme known at least since the late Bronze Age (Beaulieu 2016; Marinatos 1993: 230–1; Vermeule 1979: 179–96). For example, on a late Geometric crater attributed to the Dipylon Master now in Paris, a boat is depicted under the right handle and the sea is indicated by four fishes swimming toward the left.[5] Here, the boat is probably referring to the transportation to the beyond and not just to seafaring. This significance is further stressed by a *prothesis* scene (exposure of the body) painted on the main side of the pot which highlights its funerary purpose as a grave marker.

In this picture, a fragment of a large crater from Argos is exceptional since the sea is indicated by zigzag waves, fishes, and water birds.[6] The scene depicts a row of dancers and a man with a horse above a line of zigzags, two fishes, and a water bird. This scene could refer to a local festival by the sea involving a feat of horse-taming and a dance (Coldstream 1979: 141; Langdon 1989: 198).

ARCHAIC AND CLASSICAL GREECE (*c*. 700–323 BCE)

In the present day, most scholars agree to place the beginning of the Archaic period around 750–700 BCE, which has often been named the "orientalizing period" in connection with the multiplication of themes, techniques, and styles derived from Near Eastern models (Boardman 1998: 83–117; Markoe 1996). This period was a time of experimentation and innovation that set the stage for the centuries that followed. Indeed, the Archaic period (*c*. 750–480/479 BCE) saw the birth of the *polis* (city-state), law codes, civic cults, philosophy, mathematics, monumental architecture and sculpture, heroic and mythological narrative representations, which were already in process during the eighth century BCE (Étienne 2017; Raaflaub and Wees 2009; Snodgrass 1980).

During the seventh century BCE, representations of the sea remained fairly consistent with the preceding period. Generally, the maritime space is depicted by means of boats or fishes as for example a proto-attic votive plaque from Sunium (*c*. 700–675 BCE) attributed to the Analatos Painter, which shows a warship[7]; or an ivory plaque from the shrine of Artemis Orthia (Sparta), dated from the seventh century BCE, on which the sea is indicated by a warship, three fishes, and a frieze of spirals.[8] Likewise, on an Etruscan black-figure crater signed by Aristonothos, showing a naval battle (maybe between pirates and a merchant ship), the sea is indicated by zigzags under the ships.[9] This imagery, mostly military, could be related to the intense activity of trade and colonization that continued during the seventh century BCE, and thus encountering piracy and shipwrecks (see the contributions by Friedman and Wintjes in this volume).

At the turn of the seventh century BCE, the foundations of the black-figure technique are developed by skillful craftsmen in Corinthian workshops. The technique consists in incising the inner details upon the silhouette, with sometimes the addition of red and/or white, before firing the pottery (Coldstream 1979: 172–3; Boardman 1998: 85–8). This technique, which developed fully during the last third of the seventh century BCE, offered a new range of possibilities to visualize the sea. Rather than depicting the maritime space by the void and/or sea animals as the craftsmen of the Geometric period did, Corinthian and Athenian vase-painters of the sixth century BCE chose to paint the sea using large black colorblocks, wavy on top (sometimes incised), placed at the bottom of the decorative field, on which ships are sailing accompanied by leaping dolphins. A Corinthian *aryballos* (oil flask) from Boeotia is a good example: the scene is displayed all around the pot and shows one of the earliest depictions of the story of Odysseus and the Sirens (*Od.* 12.154–200; Touchefeu-Meynier 1968: 145–90).[10] Here, the sea is indicated by a black colorblock with an incised wavy line that separates the maritime area from Odysseus's ship. In *c.* 570 BCE, the vase-painter Kleitias used the same technique to depict the sea on his masterpiece, the so-called "François Vase."[11] A black colorblock incised with wavy lines shows the sea in a depiction of young Athenian hostages released by Theseus. The sea is pictured in the same way within a *dinos* rim (mixing bowl) now in Boston.[12] Here the vase-painter has played with the idea of the "wine-dark sea" (*oinops pontos*): when the bowl is full, the ships seem to sail within the vessel on the wine blended with water (see below). On a black-figure *hydria* (water jug) depicting Heracles in his fight with Nereus, the sea is rendered with diluted black, which allows one to see the brush strokes.[13] A dolphin is diving into the water, its head appears only as a shadow while its tail is clearly visible. Thus, the painter has depicted the sea both as transparent and blurry, always in motion and deep. Much earlier the same technique was used on a fragment of a *dinos* (or crater) from the sanctuary of the Dioskouroi (the divine twins Castor and Polydeukes) in Naukratis (Egypt): the sea is depicted by transparent waves with added white under which one can see the shadow of a dolphin.[14] Such depictions stress that the sea is a boundless area, conceived both as a solid body on which ships can sail and as an area in which one can disappear. Indeed, as Beaulieu stressed, the sea is a zone of contact, a passageway to the unseen, both vertically and horizontally (Beaulieu 2016).

From this idea of the sea as a passageway to the unseen, one moves to the idea of the sea as a gateway to the Underworld. Therefore, travel on the sea or a dive in the sea is conceived as a metaphor for death (Beaulieu 2016: 119–57). As, for example, young men riding dolphins on attic red-figure *lekythoi* (oil flask), who symbolize the travel of the soul to the Underworld; or young men swept away by sphinxes over the sea.[15] One of the most beautiful depictions of this idea is painted on the covering slab of the so-called "Tomb of the Diver" in Paestum (Southern Italy), dated *c.* 480–470 BCE (see Irby in this volume, figure 1.6).[16] The sea is pictured as a light blue area, wavy on top. A naked youth dives into the water from a white pillar. The very spare composition of this painting does not diminish its deep meaning. The dive symbolizes the soul of the dead going into the Underworld, while conveying an eschatological message of regeneration and eternal happiness symbolized by the banquet scenes on the walls of the tomb (Holloway 2006).

The *symposion* (communal wine-drinking), which originates in the late eighth century BCE, develops more widely from the late seventh to the fifth century BCE. It is perceived as an aristocratic practice and a social institution related, in certain respects, to the coming of age of young men (*epheboi*). Therefore, the many depictions of symposiasts and wine drinking in sixth and fifth century BCE vase-painting are linked to this aristocratic practice (Calame 1996; Levine 1985; Murray 2009). In this imagery, the sea is often paired with wine drinking. Indeed, being drunk is conceived by the ancient Greeks as a wonderful sailing on the "wine-dark sea" (Corner 2010; Davies 1978; Lissarrague 1987: 104–18; Topper 2012). This idea is well depicted on a bilingual cup (painted in both black- and red-figure technique) now in London (*c*. 510–490 BCE) (Figure 7.3).[17] In the center of the cup, a young man is lifting a pointed amphora certainly full of wine, as an allusion to wine drinking. This scene is surrounded by a large and wavy black colorblock that depicts the sea on which four ships are sailing.

FIGURE 7.3 Kylix (cup) black- and red-figure, 510–500 BCE. London, British Museum E2. © The Trustees of the British Museum.

Between each boat, dolphins are plunging. As on the Boston *dinos*, the vase-painter played with the analogy between the sea and the wine; then, when the cup is full, the ships are literally sailing on the "wine-dark sea."

The development of the black-figure technique does not mean that the craftsmen gave up the "old" way of depicting the sea. On the contrary, the black-figure technique adds new features to the figurative repertoire of maritime themes. Of course, the adoption of the new technique is not the sole explanation for the increasing diversity in the depiction of maritime themes. On the one hand, the Greek colonization of the eighth and seventh centuries BCE both toward the East and the West brought new themes, styles, and techniques to the Greek repertoire. On the other hand, the birth of the *polis*, the development of civic cults, and major Panhellenic festivals and sanctuaries added other symbolic and religious meanings to maritime themes. Thus, representations and visualizations of the sea refer both to the mythological world, religious beliefs, and practices, as well as to social and political realities such as colonization or war.

One of the important innovations of the Greek vase-painters from the late seventh century BCE is the introduction of hybrid creatures, maybe inspired by Near Eastern models, in the figurative repertoire to visualize—among others— sea creatures (Ahlberg-Cornell 1984: 13–25, 1992: 106–8). This creativity is well expressed in the depiction of sea monsters (*ketoi*), which drew on multiple elements such as dog muzzles, lion heads, pointy noses, fish or snake bodies, and sometimes lion feet. Those sea monsters were part of the marine fauna and served sea deities such as Amphitrite and the Nereids. They also appeared in myth, for instance the rescue of Hesione by Heracles or Andromeda released by Perseus.[18] The variety of sea monsters was extensive and did not changed much between the seventh century BCE and late antiquity. One finds sea monsters on sixth century BCE vase-paintings as, for example, a *hydria* from Caere depicting a naked hero (maybe Heracles) combating a sea monster surrounded by a diverse marine fauna (octopus, a seal, dolphins),[19] as well as on red-figure Apulian vase-painting in which sea monsters are ridden by Nereids; and on coins, gems, appliqués, sarcophagi, mosaics until late antiquity (Boardman 1987).[20]

At the beginning of the sixth century BCE, Sophilos, on a black-figure *dinos* depicting Thetis and Peleus's wedding, chose to paint the Titan Okeanos as a hybrid, half-man half-fish, holding a fish and a snake.[21] Okeanos is the father of all waters, the personification of the primeval water encircling the world (Hesiod, *Theog.* 337–70). In this picture, the hybridity of Okeanos highlights his main characteristics as a water god, always in motion. His presence at the wedding ensures the cosmic order of the event. The same characteristics apply to Nereus, the Old man of the Sea, and Triton in depictions of the wrestling match with Heracles. To find the road to the Garden of the Hesperides, Heracles wrestles with Nereus who has the power of mutation and divination. This sea deity is always depicted as a hybrid, half-man half-fish, with flames, lions, or

FIGURE 7.4 Terracotta vase in the form of a ketos, c. 650–600 BCE. New York, Metropolitan Museum of Art 2009. 529. © 2000–2018 The Metropolitan Museum of Art (public domain).

snakes, which break out as manifestations of his power of metamorphosis. For example, a bronze shield-band from Olympia shows the Old Man of the Sea (*Halios Geron*) with flames and a snake coming out of his head.[22] A black-figure *lekythos* in Paris shows Nereus as a fish-tailed creature with a lion forepart coming out of his tail.[23] Later, in the second half of the sixth century (c. 560 BCE), Nereus is depicted as fully human and replaced by the sea creature Triton, son of Poseidon and Amphitrite, maybe for political reasons (Boardman 1989, 2003: 223; Glynn 1981).[24]

In the early fifth century, Triton is pictured as the conductor of Theseus on a red-figure cup by Euphronios and Onesimos.[25] On his voyage to Crete, Theseus dives to the bottom of the sea to recover the ring of Minos as a proof of his divine origin (Bacchylides, *Ode* 17). Here, Triton is pictured not as a monster but as a benevolent sea creature of small size who bears Theseus by the feet. The underwater space is indicated by three dolphins—one leaping up, the two others down—and Amphitrite, the queen of the sea, seated on a throne. Athena acts here as an intermediary, which stresses the ideological meaning of this kind of picture, namely the claim of Athenian supremacy over the Aegean

Sea, especially after the Persian Wars and the creation of the Delian League in 477 BCE (Barron 1980; Calame 1996; Castriota 1992: 58–63; Shapiro 1994: 117–23).

This idea is well illustrated in documents dated from c. 480–460 BCE. At Olympia, in the temple of Zeus, on the god's throne, the personification of Salamis was painted holding a stern ornament (*aphlaston*),[26] as well as the statue of Apollo dedicated by the Greeks at Delphi (Herodotus 8.121; Pausanias 10.14.5), and Athena or Nike (Victory) in contemporary attic vase-painting.[27] This attribute refers to the victory of Athens over the Persians at Salamis in 480 BCE (Völcker-Janssen 1987). Likewise, the economical and political power of the *polis* is expressed on coins (Kraay 1966: 13–15). Therefore, in Greek colonies of Sicilia and Southern Italy, the sea, as a source of power and wealth, was a current theme in sixth- to fourth-century BCE coinage. This one is often symbolized by dolphins as, for example, on coins from Tarentum, Zancle, or Syracuse which show the nymph Arethusa (the personification of the colony's main source of freshwater), surrounded by four dolphins in reference to the island of Ortygia, the place where the founders of the colony settled (Lacroix 1965: 103–8). The sea is also suggested by mollusks, shellfish (as the mussel on the coinage of Cumae, or the crab for Akragas), objects, and divinities related to the sea such as Poseidon wielding his trident (Posidonia) (Fischer-Bossert 2012; Lacroix 1965: 89–100; Rutter 2012; Tsangari 2015).

The development of the red-figure technique from c. 530 BCE brought more artistic freedom to attic vase-painters.[28] The figures were now pictured in line drawings reserved on the background of the pot filled in with black (Boardman 1997: 11–15). This technique allows for increasing and varying the figurative possibilities for picturing the sea, insisting especially on its transparency and depth. On a *pelike* (wine jug) attributed to the painter Myson, Heracles is pictured wrecking the house of Nereus—a story only known through images—with the help of a trident.[29] The sea is depicted with diluted black at the bottom of the decorative field. By transparency, one can see Heracles' feet, while pots (a cup, an oinochoe, a bail amphora) are floating on the water. Just like the hydria in Paris (see above), the painter used diluted black to render the physical qualities of water: a body on which objects can float and in which one can plunge, as well as its transparency. On a calyx-krater from the Polygnotean Group (c. 440–420 BCE) that illustrates the story of Aphrodite and Phaon, the sea is depicted by means of small curved white lines around the boat of Phaon to give the illusion of both depth and infinity.[30] Phaon was a ferryman who took Aphrodite disguised as an old woman across the Aegean for free. As a reward she gave him youthful beauty (Gantz 1993: 103–4).

The red-figure technique continues in Athens until the first decades of the fourth century BCE. It is mostly represented by the so-called Kerch style (after the city in Crimea where a lot of late-classical vases were found), for the finest examples.³¹ Because most late classical vase-painting is of poor quality (Boardman 2000: 190–4) one must turn toward Southern Italy (Lucania, Apulia), where, from the fifth century BCE, Greek vase-painters set up workshops to produce vases for the local community (Metapontum, Tarentum). Those vases were made especially as funerary offerings. During the fourth century BCE, Lucanian then Apulian people started to produce their own vases. In the beginning, images were drawn from attic models, then, little by little, local craftsmen started to express their own identity with new images and models (Carpenter, Lynch, and Robinson 2014).

Just as most of the works of art produced in Southern Italy from the seventh century BCE, the sea in Apulian vase-painting occupies a place of choice, especially in the decoration of large shallow dishes (*patera*), for example, the one attributed to the Phrixos painter, now in Berlin.³² In the center, Phrixos is riding the golden ram above the sea pictured by a squid and a dolphin. All around a frieze of marine fauna (jellyfish, squid, fishes) is pictured in red on the black background, rimmed by a thin band of spiral waves. Likewise, within a basin attributed to the Phrixos Group (*c*. 340–330 BCE), are pictured seven sea animals (dolphin, anglerfish, grouper, skipjack, torpedo fish, cuttlefish, common cerith) that seem to symbolize the sea.³³ In addition, sea animals may evoke the Ocean that separates the world of the living from the Underworld and, when paired with the picture of Phrixos riding the golden ram (Berlin basin), the eschatological meaning is reinforced (see above). Thus, the picture evokes the travel of the soul to the Underworld, especially knowing that those vessels were made only for tomb offerings (Aellen, Cambitoglou, and Chamay 1986: 181–4).

Naturalistic representations of marine animals are common in Apulian vase-painting, especially on fish plates, a special vessel used to serve fish and seafood as a funerary offering (A.D. Trendall lists over 1,000 dishes of this type!).³⁴ It is quite possible that the decoration has a symbolic meaning, perhaps related to eschatological beliefs.

From the seventh to the fifth century BCE onward, in parallel to other artistic techniques, painting on walls and on wood panels was developing and reached its peak during the classical period (middle fifth to middle fourth century BCE). Polygnotos of Thasos, Parrhasios, Zeuxis, or Apelles are, among others, the most celebrated painters of classical antiquity. Unfortunately, those works of art are almost entirely lost. Some paintings are known to us through descriptions (*ekphraseis*) from ancient Greek and Latin authors such as Pliny the Elder and Pausanias. In the past thirty years, archeological findings of funerary paintings dated from the fourth century BCE, especially in Macedonia, have helped us understand what ancient Greek painting looked like. Those paintings are usually centered on the human and animal figure. Therefore, there is little to say about how painters used to represent the sea. An author from the Aristotelian school mentions only that the sea was painted in blue (*kuanos*) in contrast to rivers painted in light yellow (*okhros*) (Ps-Aristotle, *Problems* 23.6). According to descriptions by ancient authors, painters represent the sea in the same way as other artists and craftsmen (boats, marine animals, gods, sea monsters, etc.). We know, for example, that the painter Androkydes of Cyzicus painted a Skylla—a sea monster half-woman half-fish with dog foreparts coming out of her waist (see *Od.* 12.80–100)—surrounded by such naturalistic fishes that they looked alive (Plutarch, *Symposium* IV.665d, 668c; Athenaeus VIII. 411a). Likewise, one of the most famous paintings of Apelles was his Aphrodite Anadyomene (rising from the sea), praised by numerous authors.[35] Sadly, ancient authors were not interested in the rendering of the sea but rather in the beauty of the goddess pressing the sea water out of her hair.

Aphrodite emerging from the sea is a common theme from classical times to late antiquity and refers to her birth.[36] Generally, the goddess is depicted coming out of a shell (a symbol for the sea), accompanied by erotes and/or sea creatures (Tritons, *ketoi*, etc.). For example, a late Hellenistic marble statuette from Greece shows Aphrodite rising from the sea in a very dynamic posture, her left leg still immersed in the water.[37] The sea is depicted by a deep bowl with irregular edges, maybe to evoke the waves. On the lower area of the sculpture remains a fragment of a lost part, perhaps a dolphin. The sculpture may have served as a votive offering in a rock-cut shrine or a fountain (Picón and Hemingway 2016: 282–3, cat. 227).

HELLENISTIC AND ROMAN TIMES
(*c.* 323 BCE–*c.* 300 CE)

The Hellenistic period (323–30 BCE) is one of the most complex periods in all of art history. This is mainly due to the vast geographical area it covers, divided into several kingdoms ruled by different dynasties. This period of about three hundred years marks the complicated transition toward the Roman world in the first century BCE, when Greek and Roman art blended to become the Greco-Roman art of the first century BCE (Picón and Hemingway 2016: 1–7; Pollitt 1986: 150–64).

There is no need to explain at length the impact of Alexander the Great's conquests on the East. On the one hand, the conquests allowed for the opening of the Greek world toward the Far East (Bactria, North India) reviving another orientalizing time both in artistic style and way of life. On the other hand, the large amount of gold and silver taken from the Persian royal treasury by Alexander the Great changed the economic picture of the ancient world, creating a massive demand for luxury goods (Boardman 1994: 75–153; Picón and Hemingway 2016: 16–20, 88–9; Stewart 2014: 206–26). For these reasons, Hellenistic art is mostly characterized by eclecticism due to the fragmentation of the audience (several kingdoms, and so different tastes and purpose), a fast diffusion of taste, styles, and ideas through the different kingdoms, an adaption to the needs of the Hellenistic rulers (worship of the monarch; obsession with victory; need to dominate other communities), the practice of benefaction, the valorization of classical Athens as the default style in litterature and visual arts, the creation of private associations and clubs, predominance of the individual against the collectivity, the idea that art is made to capture and improve appearances, and styles that adapt to specific functions (classicism for gods and heroes, "baroque" for battle and tragic scenes) (Pollitt 1986: 111–26; Stewart 2014: 17–20).

Visualizations of the sea do not differ greatly from classical times: boats, fishes, sea monsters, and sea deities are the usual repertoire. However, new themes came out, related to political needs as for example the depiction of Berenike II (r.246–222/1 BCE) on the mosaic of Thmuis, crowned by a warship's prow and holding a naval flagstaff (*stylis*), her cloak fastened with a naval anchor.[38] The picture seems to stress the naval power of Alexandria during Berenike's reign with Ptolemy III Euergetes and refers to the queen as a naval goddess of Fortune, assimilated to the Tyche of Antioch (Stewart 2014: 174, fig. 101). Similarly, the astonishing *Victory of Samothrace* (*c.* 190 BCE) commemorates a naval victory (maybe of the Rhodians against Antiochos III), and was originally set up in the Sanctuary of the Great Gods in Samothrace.[39] The base of the sculpture was in the shape of a ship prow, the goddess depicted as she is, just appearing on the ship with her clothes flapping in the wind. The whole group was set up theatrically in a two-level pool or fountain, which symbolized the sea and the shore, on a terrace above the theater of Samothrace dominating the sanctuary and the valley below and facing the Aegean Sea (Hamiaux, Martinez, and Laugier 2014; Pollitt 1986: 113–14).

What is changing, in depictions of marine themes, are the style and techniques. The high demand for luxury goods prompts the depiction of maritime themes on jewels and luxurious objects such as a pair of gold armbands representing a triton and a tritoness, each one holding a baby eros with one arm.[40] The spiral aims to encircle the wearer's upper arm. A swirl of fins resembling acanthus leaves marks the transition between the human upper body and the fishtail. The visual solution of acanthus leaves to mark the transition between human and fish parts is typical of Hellenistic art; one finds it, for example, on the Tritons of the Pergamon Great Altar (used as *acroteria*, on the roof),[41] as well as on Roman mosaics and reliefs depicting marine processions such as the frieze of the altar of Domitius Ahenobarbus representing the wedding of Poseidon and Amphitrite (see Figure 7.5).[42] The divine couple is shown on a chariot pulled by two tritons, one blowing into a conch shell, and accompanied by a procession of baby erotes and Nereids riding seahorses and sea bulls. The marine thiasos (Tritons and

Nereids riding sea animals) has, from the fifth century BCE and especially in Roman times, a religious meaning, related to the travel to the Underworld (Barringer 1995: 141–51). The theme is very popular on roman sarcophagi from imperial times (second to third century CE) and illustrates eschatological beliefs in connection with the joys of the afterlife.

One of the most striking particularities of Hellenistic times is the development of the art of the mosaic. First made with pebbles, the technique was rapidly mastered with the invention in the third century BCE of the *opus tessellatum* (mosaics made with cubes of stone, glass, or terracotta) then the *opus vermiculatum* (wormy) made of very tiny *tesserae* (1 milimeter on the side), arranged in curvy lines to create contours and modeling. Thus, mosaics compete with painting in terms of texturing, shadowing, and colors (Dunbabin 1999; Pollitt 1986: 210–29; Stewart 2014: 197–205). The art of the mosaic shows an unprecedented development, especially in the Roman world. One can find mosaics everywhere across the Roman Empire, from Great Britain to North Africa, France, Italy, Bulgaria, as far as the Far East, which was adapted to local styles and tastes, through late antiquity and onward (Ling 2015; Smith 1983).

For Hellenistic mosaics, the most important examples are from Delos, a free port under Athenian control, dated from *c.* 166–100 BCE. Most Delian mosaics have marine themes, certainly because the sea was at the heart of the city's economic activity. The mosaic of the House of the Dolphins shows, for example, a whole decorative program of marine themes.[43] In a square crenelated border is a series of concentric circular bands with waves, meanders, and sea monsters. In each corner, a tiny, winged figure is riding a pair of dolphins and carrying emblems of the gods—thyrsus, trident, caduceus (Dunbabin 1999: 33; Pollitt 1986: 215–16; Stewart 2014: 204–5).

FIGURE 7.5 Altar of Domitius Ahenobarbus. The wedding of Poseidon and Amphitrite, end of second century BCE. Munich, Glyptothek inv. 239. ©PRISMA ARCHIVO / Alamy Stock Photo.

Mosaics were mostly used to decorate private houses and palaces or public buildings, as for example *thermae,* as floor pavement (and sometimes as wall or vault decoration). For the latter, marine themes are particularly popular, for example, the mosaic decorating the Baths of Neptune at Ostia showing a triumph of Neptune entirely realized in black and white *tesserae* (a feature typical of second-century CE Roman mosaics).[44] Here the marine environment is only suggested by the multiple sea creatures evolving on the white background of the mosaic. Typical for North African mosaics, the pavement of the private baths of the "House of Cato" in Utica (Tunisia) shows a polychrome Triumph of Neptune and Amphitrite (see Figure 7.6).[45] The divine couple is rising from the sea on a chariot pulled by four seahorses. The sea is suggested by horizontal parallel lines that show the lower part of the seahorses by transparency. The same theme is represented on another mosaic from Tunisia (la Chebba). Neptune is depicted alone on his chariot pulled by four seahorses and conducted by a triton and a tritoness.[46] The scene is inscribed in a circle surrounded by allegorical representations of the four seasons, giving a cosmic meaning to the whole composition. Here, the sea is pictured in a more naturalistic way, with shades of blue, gray, white, and brown with an illusion of transparency that reveals the lower body of the seahorses.

There is, unfortunately, no space here for a lengthy discussion of the great diversity and originality of the arts of the Roman period.[47] Generally, representations of the sea used the same features as classical and Hellenistic art, namely fishes, boats, sea monsters, Nereids, Tritons, seahorses, etc., on various techniques and supports such as sculptures, carvings, mosaics, luxury items, reliefs, sarcophagi, and wall paintings. The latter, however, are worth a longer discussion, mainly because Roman wall painting provides the only examples of landscape, where nature takes over the human figure (Lorenz 2015; Pollitt 1986: 185–209). One of the best examples are the paintings that depict Odysseus's wanderings on the wall of a Roman house found on the Esquiline Hill in 1848, now in the Vatican Museum (see Figure 7.7).[48] The paintings were set on the wall divided into eight landscapes, positioned against the background of a double colonnade painted in trompe l'oeil. In those paintings, we are dealing with true landscapes in which the sea, especially for the episodes of the Laestrygonians, takes a major place.[49] The sea is painted in blue, with subtle hue variations near the ships and the rocky shore, to create an illusion of movement, depth, and immensity. A clear skyline is indicated, separating the sea from the sky (painted in a grayish blue) in a very naturalistic way. At the forefront, the Laestrygonians hurling rocks toward Odysseus's ships add to the illusion of depth. Likewise, the paintings that decorated the *triclinium* (dining room) of the House of the Priest Amandus, show mythological scenes set in a vast landscape, especially Perseus and Andromeda, in which the sea takes a major part of the pictorial

FIGURE 7.6 Detail from a mosaic with the God Oceanus and the triumph of Neptune and Amphitrite, from Utica, Tunisia, second to third century CE. Tunis, Musée National Du Bardo. © DEA/G. DAGLI ORTI / Getty Images.

space.[50] Here the sea is rendered by green and blue hues that blend with the sky resulting in a foggy atmosphere. This kind of painting marks the taste for landscape itself, as a window opened toward an idyllic outside, possibly charged with symbolic meaning (Clarke 1996).

FIGURE 7.7 Odysseus's ships destroyed by the giant Laestrygonians. Scene from the Odyssey. Wall painting from a private house on the Esquiline Hill, Rome, first century BCE. Rome, Vatican Museum. © Culture Club / Getty Images.

Of course, these examples are exceptional with respect to the vast majority of maritime depictions since the Archaic period, which favor metonymy and stylization rather than naturalistic depictions. Therefore, most of the Roman representations of the sea draw on themes that were well known for centuries, while adding new meanings, especially in funerary iconography. For example, sarcophagi from the second to the seventh century CE show depictions of Odysseus and the Sirens whose significance could be related to philosophical and religious ideas about the afterlife (neo-Platonism, neo-Pythagorism, or Christianity).[51] Odysseus symbolizes the soul of the deceased, confronted to deceitful pleasures such as unlimited knowledge impersonated by the Sirens. The victory against the Sirens could also symbolize, in a Christian context, triumph over death (Touchefeu-Meynier 1968: 188–9).

One must now turn briefly to the early Christian art of the second to mid-fourth century CE, which reworks classical subjects while infusing them with symbolic religious meaning. Among popular subjects of early Christian art is the depiction of Jonah swallowed then spat out by the sea monster, and finally resting under a grapevine. The sequence was painted, for example, in the Catacombs of Callixtus (third century CE).⁵² The subject is related to death, resurrection, and eternal bliss (Ferguson 2012). It is interesting to note, with John Boardman, that in those representations the "Great Fish" is depicted just like a classical *ketos* (see above) (Boardman 1987).

CONCLUSIONS: LATE ANTIQUITY (*c.* 300–500 CE)

Late antiquity is often characterized by change, a constant tension between continuity and rupture, conservatism, and transformation, which leads in the course of the sixth and seventh centuries CE to a new form of visual expression specific to the early Middle Ages (Bravi 2015; Reece 1983). Theses specificities

FIGURE 7.8 Thalassa. Personification of the sea. Mosaic from the Church of the Apostle, Madaba (Jordan), *c.* 568 CE. © Art Directors & TRIP / Alamy Stock Photo.

are naturally expressed in representations of the sea, which balanced between classical patterns, new forms of expression, and new meanings. Thus, for example, on the silver plate of Mildenhall, a very classical marine procession, and then a Bacchic procession surround the mask of Oceanus.[53] Yet the meaning, which in classical times would have been related to eschatological beliefs, is here related to celebrating eternal and invigorating rejoicing (Bravi 2015: 137–40).

To conclude, this overview of visual representations of the sea through antiquity has shown the incredible diversity of styles and techniques but also of meanings. The sea is a place which has caught the imagination of ancient people from the Bronze Age onward, giving it powerful significations related to eschatological beliefs, political realities, philosophical or moral values. The sea was at the heart of ancient life as a way to communicate as well as a boundary, a source of food but also a source of fear, inhabited by marvelous and dangerous creatures. This idea is well conveyed on a floor mosaic in the Church of the Apostles in Madaba (Jordan), which shows in its center a personification of the sea (Thalassa) as a half-naked woman emerging from the water, surrounded by fishes and sea monsters (see Figure 7.8).

CHAPTER EIGHT

Imaginary Worlds

Maritime Fictional Spheres Located at Cardinal Points

IRIS SULIMANI

INTRODUCTION

The sea occupied a central place in the imaginary world of the ancients. Odysseus made his journey from Troy to Ithaca by sailing in the Aegean and the Mediterranean Sea and passing through the lands of mythical peoples such as the Lotus Eaters and the Cyclopes. The Argonauts, in their quest for the Golden Fleece, navigated the Aegean and the Black Sea and, on their return voyage, wandered in the Mediterranean Sea, encountering hazardous figures such as Scylla, Charybdis, the Sirens, and Circe. Aeneas and his companions sailed from Troy to Italy in the Aegean and the Mediterranean Sea, landing, among other places, in the harbor of the Cyclopes and at Cumae, where Aeneas met the Sibyl, who instructed him on how to reach the Underworld. The dates when the versions of these tales were written range from the Archaic period through the Hellenistic age to the Roman era. Homer, for instance, told the adventures of Odysseus probably in the eight century BCE, mentioning also Jason and the Argo, as well as Aeneas, while Apollonius Rhodius composed his version of the Argonautica in the third century BCE, and Virgil wrote his *Aeneid* in the Augustan period (i.e., at the end of the first century BCE). Interestingly, these authors created imaginary worlds but, at the same time, drew on real geographical information.

This chapter concentrates on the descriptions of imaginary worlds found in a variety of ancient literary works, with an emphasis on their maritime characteristics. It shows that these fictional spheres were located in different parts of the universe, whether in the Mediterranean basin or at each of the four corners of the earth. It also demonstrates that the accounts of the imaginary worlds varied in accordance with the time of their writing, as they were influenced by the realities of the authors' own day. Hence, these accounts may also shed light on the history, thoughts, and mentality of the period in which they were written.

THE MEDITERRANEAN BASIN: LAKE TRITONIS AND THE RIVER TRITON

The imaginary world on the Mediterranean coast of Libya, as described by various authors from the fifth century to the first century BCE, evolved from a place where sailors became trapped into a utopian site. At all stages, fantasy is mingled with reality. To begin with Herodotus, in his discussion of the peoples living along the Mediterranean coast of Libya, he mentions the Machlyes, whose land stretches to a great river named Triton that empties into the great Tritonian lake, in which an island called Phla lies. He then relates the story of Jason who, sailing around the Peloponnese with the Argo and intending to reach Delphi, was caught by a north wind near Cape Malea and carried away to Libya. The ship ran aground on the sandbanks of Lake Tritonis and, when Jason was at a loss to find a way out, Triton appeared to him and promised to show him a safe outlet from the lake if he gave him the tripod that he was carrying to Delphi. After Jason had handed the tripod over to Triton, the latter prophesized that if any descendant of the Argo's sailors were to take away the tripod, he would found a hundred Greek cities on the shores of Lake Tritonis. Triton then instructed Jason and his crew how to get out of the sandbanks of the lake, setting the tripod in his own temple. But the Libyan inhabitants of the region, upon hearing this story, hid the tripod (Hdt. 4.178.1–79.3).[1]

Written about two hundred years later, Apollonius Rhodius's description of the Argonauts's arrival in Lake Tritonis is somewhat different. Blown off course, the Argonauts landed on the coast of Libya and were caught in the Gulf of Sirtis. Three nymphs came to their rescue, informing them that in order to survive they should carry the ship across the deserts of Libya. After an arduous journey, the Argonauts reached Lake Tritonis and the Garden of the Hesperides, where the singing of the nymphs was charming. Responding to the request of the Argonauts for drinking water, these nymphs first caused grass to spring from the earth, above which rose up tall sprouts and then flourishing trees. Then, the Hesperides guided the Argonauts to a rock near Lake Tritonis, from which a torrent of water broke out. As in Herodotus's version, the Argonauts looked despairingly for an outlet from the lake, but it was Orpheus who suggested offering Apollo's tripod to the gods of the land as conciliation. Consequently,

Triton appeared to them and, giving them a clod of earth as a gift,[2] showed them the way out (*Argon.* 4.1228–600).[3]

In the first century BCE, Diodorus Siculus incorporated a version of the *Argonautica* in his universal history. Diodorus stands out among the authors mentioned in this chapter. Not only does he depict many imaginary voyages and not a few fantastic maritime sites, but he also presents accounts that differ considerably from those of other writers. It is therefore worth discussing Diodorus and his work first. Most of the information on the historian is derived from his own writings. He was born in Agyrium in Sicily (1.4.4) and, although it is well known that he lived in the first century BCE, the dates of his birth and death cannot be determined with any precision. He visited Egypt, evidently in 60–55 BCE (1.44.1–4, 1.83.8–9, 17.49.1–2), where he was engaged in doing research for his historical work (3.38.1). Settling in Rome (before 45 BCE)[4] and using a variety of sources and records available to him there, Diodorus probably completed his composition (1.4.2–4). His work, titled *Bibliotheke*, "Library," consists of forty books, of which only 1–5 and 11–20 are preserved in their entirety. The first six books are devoted to the myths; three of them are concerned with the mythologies of the non-Greeks, while the other three deal mainly with those of the Greeks. The remainder of the books embrace the affairs of both the Greeks and the non-Greeks starting with the Trojan War to the beginning of Caesar's wars in Gaul, 60/59 BCE (1.4.6–7).[5]

When referring to the Argonauts being carried away to Libya in his version of the *Argonautica*, Diodorus does not mention either Lake Tritonis or the river Triton. He points out that they were driven to the Sirtis, from where they escaped with the help of Triton, king of Libya. As a token of gratitude, the Argonauts granted Triton a bronze tripod (Diod. Sic. 4.56.6). Yet Lake Tritonis and the river Triton are described at quite some length by Diodorus in two other mythical tales.[6] The first is the story of the Libyan Amazons, who lived on an island called Hespera that lies in Lake Tritonis. Receiving its name from the river Triton that empties into it, this lake is situated near the Ocean that surrounds the earth, in the vicinity of the Atlas Mountain that touches the Ocean, as well as near Ethiopia. Unlike his predecessors, Diodorus obviously places the lake farther west, emphasizing that the Amazons lived on the edges of the *oikoumene*, the inhabited world. He also dwells on the characteristics of the island that lies in the lake. It was of great size, contained an abundance of fruit trees of every variety and a multitude of goats and sheep, thus providing the inhabitants with all the food they needed. The peculiar traits of the inhabitants, the Amazons, are also set forth. Being a race ruled by women, the latter both served in the army and administered all the affairs of the state, whereas the men spent their days about the house like married women, bringing up the children and carrying out the orders given them by their wives. It was their custom that when a girl was born, her

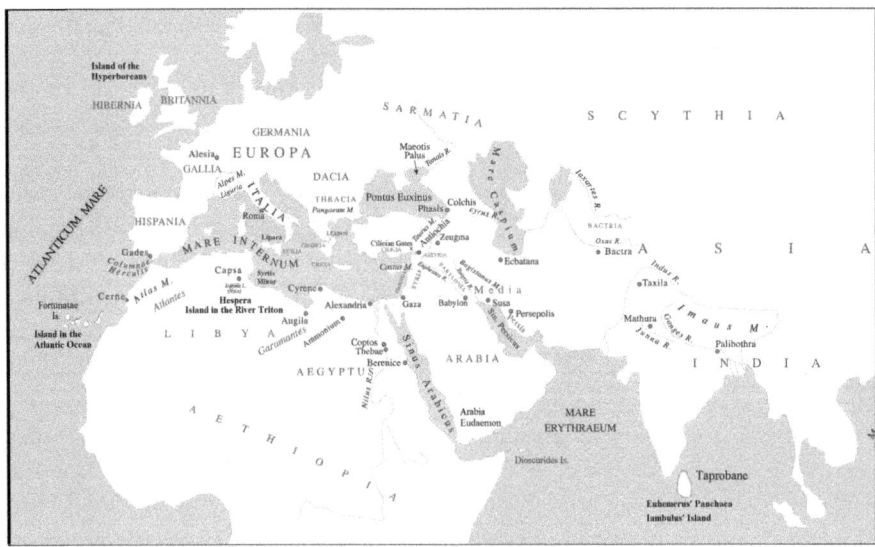

FIGURE 8.1 Imaginary islands. © Iris Sulimani (author).

breasts were seared to prevent them from developing at the time of maturity, for the breasts, as they stood out from the body, were a disruption in warfare (3.53.1–5).[7] Diodorus concludes the story with the destruction of both the people and the lake. Wishing to benefit all mankind, Heracles thought it would be inappropriate for any people to be under the rule of women. Thus, he entirely destroyed the race of the Amazons. The lake disappeared from sight in the course of an earthquake (3.55.3).[8]

The river Triton is mentioned by Diodorus in the story of Dionysus. Fearing Rhea's envy, Ammon brought Dionysus, the son born to him by Amaltheia, to Nysa, a city situated on an island surrounded by the river Triton in the western part of Libya near the Ocean. Like the island of the Amazons, the soil of this island is fertile and produces fruit-bearing trees of every kind. It is well watered by many streams from springs of sweet water and wild vines grow there in abundance. The air is wholesome, and thus the inhabitants are the longest lived in those parts of the world. In addition, Diodorus describes a marvelous cave, in front of which grow wonderful trees, some fruit bearing and others evergreen. Birds of all kinds nest in these trees. The color of the birds is pleasing and their song most charming. Inside the cave there are all types of plants, especially aromatic plants such as cassia.[9] It is in this cave that Ammon entrusted the nymph Nysa with the care of Dionysus, while Athena was given the task of protecting him from Rhea. Diodorus adds that shortly before this Athena had been born of the earth and, having been found near the river Triton, she was called Tritonis (Diod. Sic. 3.67.5, 68.4–70.1). Diodorus is not the first to associate Athena with the river Triton. Apollodorus, for instance, describes the birth of the goddess from Zeus's head at the river Triton (*Bibl.* 1.3.6; cf. Aesch., *Eum.* 292–3), whereas Euripides mentions Lake Tritonis (*Ion*, 872).[10]

The fictional world on the Mediterranean coast of Libya, depicted by Herodotus and Apollonius as a dangerous place, evolved into a utopian site in Diodorus. Both Herodotus and Apollonius emphasize that people were trapped in Lake Tritonis, being unable to get out until the god came to their rescue. Although Diodorus does not mention the lake in his story of the Argonauts, the trap motif appears in his account when he refers to the incapability of the Argonauts to get out of the Syrtis, the location of the lake according to Apollonius. All authors mingle imagination with reality, yet even more Diodorus, who integrates the site of Lake Tritonis and the river Triton into his tales of the Amazons and Dionysus respectively, painting them in idyllic colors. Whereas Herodotus and Apollonius incorporate real geographical places into the Argonauts's route to Lake Tritonis (the Peloponnese, Delphi, Libya, Cape Malea, and the Gulf of Sirtis), Diodorus precisely locates the imaginary sites in real geographical space. Interestingly, Strabo, in his description of Libya, mentions Lake Tritonis in which there is a small island (17.3.20 C 836; cf. Paus. 9.33.7). Diodorus's location, however, is different, for he situates both the lake and the river farther west. As the discussion of other imaginary sites below shows, this is not a coincidence, nor is the fact that the place becomes utopian in the first century BCE.

THE WEST: THE ISLANDS OF THE BLESSED

Although ancient authors use various names for the Islands of the Blessed, and although they do not agree on the number of the islands, there is consensus among them concerning the location and the nature of this imaginary site. Naming it the Elysian plain in the *Odyssey*, Homer writes that Menelaus's fate was not to die but to be carried to the Elysian plain that lies at the western edge of the world. The climate in this place is temperate, for there is no snow there, nor rain nor storms, but always a refreshing western wind, and life there is easy for human beings (*Od.* 4.560–8). A similar pastoral portrayal characterizes Hesiod's description of his Islands of the Blessed (μακάρων νῆσοι), where some of the Trojan heroes were taken instead of facing death. The inhabitants of these islands—located at the ends of the earth, along the shore of the Ocean—are free of sorrows and enjoy the fertility of the soil that produces the sweetest fruit three times a year (*Op.* 167–73). Indicating only a single island (μακάρων νᾶσος), Pindar also situates it by the Ocean and regards it as a place where the good (such as Peleus, Cadmus, and Achilles) are sent in the afterlife.[11] He highlights its golden flowers, splendid trees, and the Ocean breezes that blow around it (*Ol.* 2.68–74).

The Islands of the Blessed appear not only in poetry but also in other literary genres. Plato emphasizes that these islands were a place to which the righteous, including the philosophers of his ideal state, are transferred upon their death, in contrast to Tartarus, to which the wicked depart (e.g., *Grg.* 523a–24a, 526c; *Resp.* 7, 540a–c; cf. 7, 519c). Advancing in time, one finds the islands in historical and geographical treatises with additional features. Diodorus defines in detail the location of an unnamed island in the Atlantic Ocean, indicating that it lies out at sea off the coast of Libya, situated in the Ocean a number of days' voyage from Libya to the west. Although Diodorus does not name this island, the similarities between his description and those of the authors mentioned here (notably its location and natural resources) imply that he probably meant the Island(s) of the Blessed. The land of the great island is fertile and contains both mountains and a vast beautiful plain, filled with parks and gardens. The climate of the island is mild and it is traversed by navigable rivers and many streams of sweet water and therefore is covered with dense thickets and fruit trees of every variety. Additionally, the sea that washes the shores of the island supplies a multitude of every kind of fish. There are also wild animals excellent for hunting and valuable private villas in which the inhabitants pass their time during the summer season. Hence, the island contributes to the health of the inhabitants, providing them with everything that allows pleasure and luxury. Consequently, Diodorus concludes, the island seems like a residence of the gods, not of men (Diod. Sic. 5.19.1–5).

Diodorus obviously took a step forward in the portrayal of the island as a paradise but, concomitantly, he places it in the real world. Not only does he offer actual geographical data—whereas his predecessors regard it as a faraway place to which those who were close to the gods arrive in the afterlife—but he also presents historical information and alludes to contemporary historical figures. Continuing his account of the island, Diodorus relates the story of the Phoenicians, who made voyages for commercial purposes during which they founded many settlements in Libya and the western regions of Europe. Following their successes, they decided to travel beyond the Pillars of Heracles into the Ocean, establishing the city of Gadeira. They built there a temple of Heracles that was held in extraordinary honor down to Diodorus's own day, when it was visited by distinguished Romans (the allusion is probably to Julius Caesar). While exploring the coast outside the Pillars, the Phoenicians were carried off by strong winds into the Ocean. After many days, they were brought to the island under discussion and, learning of its nature and prosperity, they revealed it to all (Diod. Sic. 5.20.1–3).[12]

Diodorus is not the only author who incorporates the imaginary site into a journey made by real people. A little earlier, Posidonius, recording Eudoxus of Cyzicus's third attempt to circumnavigate Africa, states that Eudoxus set out from his homeland, visiting Dicaearchia and Massalia whence he followed the coast as far as Gadeira and sailed into the open sea. But Eudoxus was forced to abandon his plans and, on his return journey, saw a desolate island, well watered and well wooded. He noted its location, but failed to persuade the king of Maurusia to support a voyage there. Strabo, who preserves Posidonius's narrative, criticizes him for believing in Eudoxus's tale, comparing him to Pytheas, Euhemerus, and Antiphanes, who were accused of having included falsehoods in their works (Str. 2.3.4 C 98–102). Pliny the Elder cites Statius Sebosus, another first century BCE writer, who, in his description of various islands in the Atlantic Ocean, integrates the *fortunatae insulae* and specifies their location: they lie at a distance of 250 miles from the islands of Pluvialia and Capraria, opposite the left side of Mauritania, in the direction of the sun at the eighth hour (i.e., west of northwest). He adds that the circumference of one of the islands is 300 miles and its trees grow to a height of 140 feet (Pliny, *HN*, 6.202).

The fragmentary *Historiae* of Sallust provide another contemporary reference to the *fortunatae insulae*. Discussing Sertorius, the Roman general who fought against Sulla and his followers during the civil wars, the historian mentions two neighboring islands at a distance of 10,000 stades from Gades. The earth of these islands, celebrated in Homer's poetry, spontaneously produces nourishment for human beings. Sallust adds that Sertorius planned to flee to the remote parts of the Ocean, and yet, because of the fragmentary condition of the text, one can only guess that Sertorius had the *fortunatae insulae* in mind (*Hist*. 1.90–2 [100–2]).[13] Plutarch's *Life of Sertorius*, probably based on Sallust's *Historiae*,[14] may reinforce this supposition. According to the biographer, Sertorius was told by sailors about two neighboring islands located in the Atlantic Ocean at a distance of 10,000 stades from Libya and called the Islands of the Blessed. Their climate is moderate, as a result of which the air is healthy, while the rich soil is both excellent for cultivating and produces an abundance of wholesome natural fruit. Plutarch concludes the idyllic description by remarking that a belief was spread according to which these islands were Homer's Elysian plain. He then stresses Sertorius's desire to live there free of unceasing wars (*Sert*. 7.2–8.3, 9.1).

Writing from the same perspective, that of the Roman civil wars, Horace suggests the *beatae insulae* as a place where the Romans could find refuge. His description of these islands resembles that of Plutarch, noting their location in the Ocean, their mild climate, and their fertile land that spontaneously produces grain and a variety of fruit trees. Additionally, goats and sheep produce milk for human consumption of their own accord (*Epod*. 16, 41–66).[15] Horace is the third author (perhaps the fourth, if indeed Statius Sebosus was his contemporary) living through the vicissitudes of the first century BCE to elaborate on the Island(s) of the Blessed. Unlike Sallust and Horace, Diodorus was Greek, but he dwelled in Rome during this turbulent period, engaged in writing his universal history, and was evidently affected by the events of the civil wars.[16] There are, however, differences between his treatment of the Island(s) of the Blessed and that of his contemporary Romans. While Diodorus makes the remote utopian island reachable by locating it at a defined geographical site, Sallust and Horace recommend the *fortunatae/beatae insulae* as a sanctuary. Diodorus wrote from the viewpoint of a Hellenistic writer, inspired by Alexander the Great's campaign and its subsequent geographical, political, and social developments, as well as by the politics of his own day. As his *Bibliotheke* shows, he was quite interested in the "utopian genre" that was widespread in his day, and therefore used it to convey the idea of a better world that is within reach.[17] Sallust and Horace, on the other hand, were Romans and thus, out of a narrow concern for their fellow compatriots,[18] suggested the Islands of the Blessed as a place to which they could escape.[19] The poet, however, differs from the historians in that he does not emphasize the location of the islands in the real world, but only notes that they lie in the Ocean.

However confused the details given by the historians may be, and whether their island(s) in the Atlantic Ocean can be identified with the Canaries or the Madeiras,[20] the fact remains that they locate them on the actual map. This tendency to mingle the imaginary world with the real world may also be noticed in Strabo. At the beginning of his *Geography*, he mentions Homer among those who treated the science of geography in earliest times and, quoting him concerning the West, he notes that it was there that the poet locates the Elysian plain. Following this, Strabo also refers to the Islands of the Blessed, explaining that they lie west of the western part of Maurusia, and that their name demonstrates that, because they were close to blessed countries, they themselves became blessed (Str. 1.1.4–5 C 2–3). This treatment of the imaginary islands probably led Lucian to discuss them in his satirical novel written in the second century CE. Describing a voyage made by himself and his companions beyond the Pillars of Heracles, Lucian recounts various incidents that diverted their ship from its course. For instance, they were caught up by a whirlwind and taken to the moon; returning to earth, they were swallowed by a huge whale, and, having escaped, they sailed in a sea of milk, entered blue salt water, and reached the pastoral Island of the Blessed (*Ver. Hist.* esp. 2.4–6, 11–16).

As the above discussion clearly shows, there are certain characteristics common to all descriptions of the Island(s) of the Blessed. First, the poets and Plato present the Island(s) as a place beyond death, to which only the chosen men arrive in the afterlife. Second, all authors highlight the extreme happiness of the islands by naming them Islands of the Blessed and/or by portraying them as places where people live happily. This is particularly evident in the accounts of the Roman writers who, living through the vicissitudes of the civil wars, possibly used their depiction of the islands to convey their longing for happiness. As will be seen below, the theme of happiness is central to descriptions of the imaginary worlds of other cardinal directions.

THE EAST AND THE SOUTH: PANCHAEA AND IAMBULUS'S ISLAND OF THE SUN

It is told that Euhemerus (*c*. 300 BCE), best known for his theory on the nature of the gods, took a trip southwards to the Ocean. Having set sail from Eudaemon Arabia, he made a voyage in the Ocean for many days and put in at the islands in the open sea, one of which was called Panchaea. Similarly, Zeus made his way to Panchaea, after he had visited Babylon, while passing through Syria and arriving in Cilicia on his way back. According to Diodorus Siculus, who bases his account on Euhemerus' work,[21] Panchaea lies in the Ocean, opposite the extremities of Eudaemon Arabia that borders on the Ocean toward the eastern part of the Ocean, and from its easternmost promontory one can catch sight of India (Diod. Sic. 5.41.4, 42.3; 6.1.4, 10). Diodorus clearly places this imaginary island on the southeastern extremity of the universe.[22]

Embarking upon a detailed description of the island (Diod. Sic. 5.41.4–46.7), Diodorus dwells on the features of the land, the composition of the population (in terms of ethnicities), the social structure, and the political regime. The whole land is fruitful, being especially rich in vines of every variety, and possesses rich mines of gold, silver, copper, tin, and iron. A plain, where the temple of Zeus stands, is full of springs and thickly covered with trees of every kind, both fruit-bearing trees and trees that please the eye, such as cypresses and plane trees. Near the sacred precinct, a spring of sweet water of considerable size bursts forth from the earth, creating a navigable river named the "Water of the Sun." The

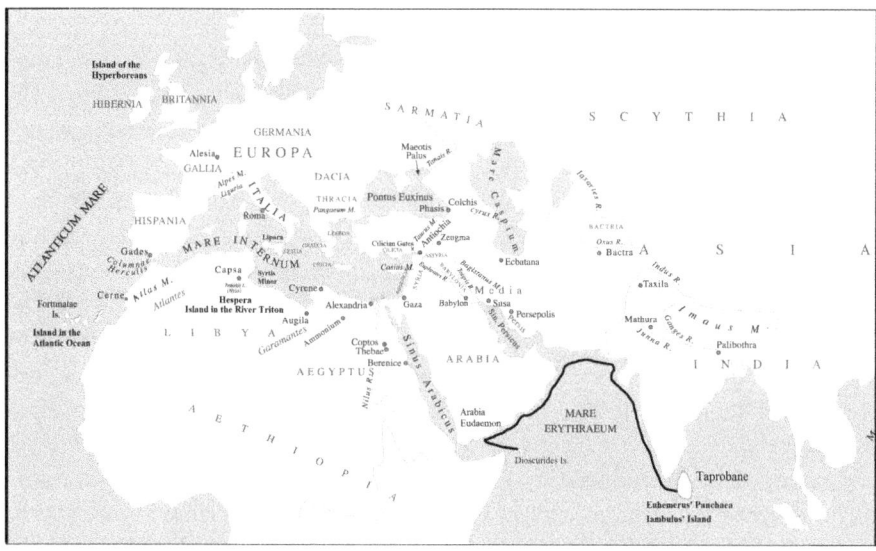

FIGURE 8.2 The voyage of Euhemerus. © Iris Sulimani (author).

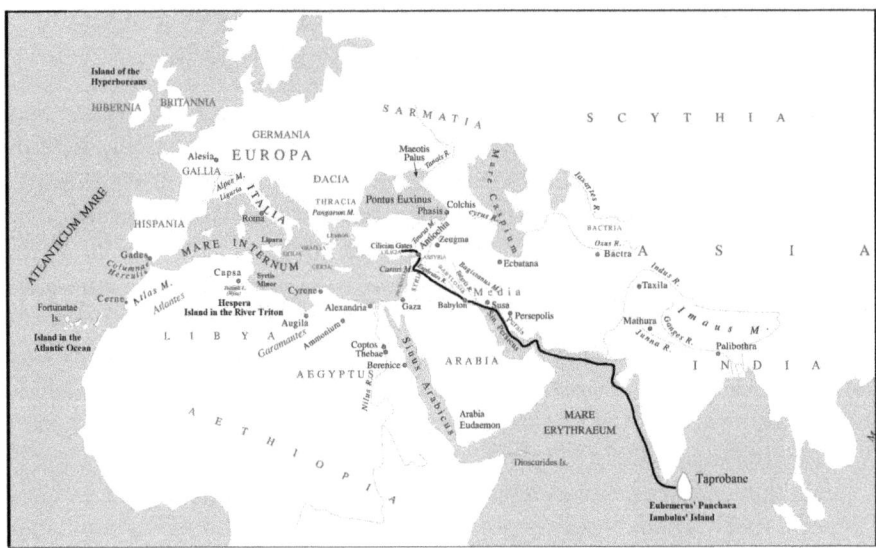

FIGURE 8.3 The journey of Zeus. © Iris Sulimani (author).

water of this river irrigates many parts of the plain, causing continuous forests of lofty trees to grow, where a multitude of birds of every kind, delighting the ear with their song, make their nests and men pass their time in the summer. The plain is also rich in gardens and meadows with varied plants and flowers. The natives are provided with abundant subsistence from the palm trees and many varieties of nut-bearing trees, enjoying the grape vines that are found there in great number and are of every variety. In addition, the water of the river is extremely clear and sweet, thus contributing to the health of the inhabitants. Beyond the plain there is a high mountain, beyond which and throughout the rest of the island there is a multitude of various wild animals (such as elephants, lions, and leopards).

In the description of Panchaea, as in the case of the island that lies in Lake Tritonis and the Island(s) of the Blessed discussed above, one may find the notion of great quantity and diversity of trees, fruit, animals, and water resources as something extraordinary and desirable. This notion appears also in the account of Iambulus's island dealt with below. It thus seems characteristic of Diodorus's versions of utopian places, although Horace also speaks of a variety of fruit trees in his depiction of the Islands of the Blessed. In describing the landscapes of these islands as pastoral, the authors present each island as a *locus amoenus*, a pleasant place. Introduced by Ernst Robert Curtius, the literary convention of *locus amoenus* includes certain basic components that make a place idyllic, especially trees, fruit, meadows of grass, flowers, and water. Emphasizing the diversity and the abundance of each component by Diodorus enhances the idealization of the islands and further strengthens their presentation as *loci amoeni*.²³

The population of Panchaea consists of natives, called Panchaeans, and foreigners, namely, Oceanites, Indians, Scythians, and Cretans. The body of citizens is divided into three parts: the priests, the farmers, and the soldiers. The priests, to whom the artisans are assigned, are the leaders. They hold the final authority in all the affairs of the state, including rendering decisions in legal disputes and performing the rituals of the gods. Moreover, the priests excel in luxury and in their elegant way of life. Their robes, for instance, are made of sheer and soft linen, and they also wear garments of the softest wool. Their headdress is interwoven with gold, their sandals are of varied colors, and they wear gold ornaments as do the women, except earrings. The farmers are engaged in tilling the soil and bring the fruits to the common store. The fruits are apportioned by the priests, who also rank the best farmers from one to ten; to encourage the rest, the outstanding farmer receives a reward. The soldiers, supplemented by the herdsmen, protect the land using forts and posts located at fixed intervals, since part of the country is infested with robbers. The soldiers receive pay for their work, while the herdsmen, like the farmers, give all the animals to the treasury of the state. In general, all the products and the revenues are apportioned justly by the priests, for the inhabitants do not own private property, except a home and a garden.

There are some notable cities on the island. One of them, called Panara, is exceedingly prosperous. Its citizens are the only inhabitants of Panchaea who live under their own laws. They are not ruled by a king, but each year they elect three chief magistrates, who render judgment in all matters except capital crimes. These, and other exceptionally important affairs, the magistrates refer of their own accord to the priests.

Similar to Panchaea, Iambulus's Island of the Sun is located on the southeastern limit of the world and may be also identified with Taprobane (present-day Sri Lanka).²⁴ The story of Iambulus, a Greek merchant,²⁵ is again preserved by Diodorus, who recounts at length Iambulus's journey to an island that has been discovered in the Ocean to the south and the marvels told concerning it (Diod. Sic. 2.55.1–60.3). After embarking on a trip inland to the spice-bearing region of Arabia, Iambulus and his companions were captured by robbers. Later Iambulus and one of his companions were kidnapped and taken to the coast of Ethiopia, since the Ethiopians were in need of two foreigners for the purification of the land. As was their custom, they built a boat of suitable size and strength to withstand the storms at sea. Having loaded it with food sufficient to maintain two men for six months, they ordered Iambulus and his companion to navigate toward the south until they came to a certain fortunate island, inhabited by men of honorable character, where they would live a happy life. The Ethiopians believed that if the foreigners arrived at the island safely,

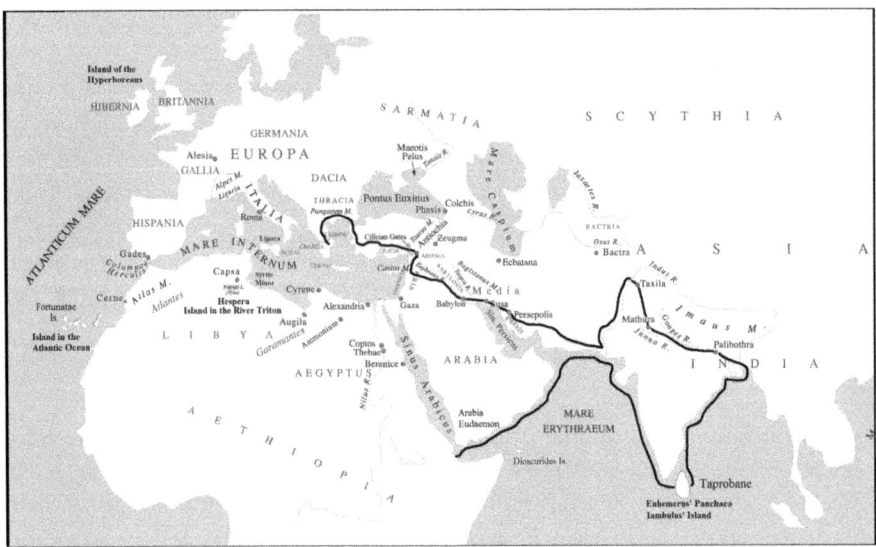

FIGURE 8.4 The journey of Iambulus. © Iris Sulimani (author).

their own people would enjoy peace and prosperity for six hundred years. However, if they were terrified of the vast sea and turned back, they would be severely punished as the destroyers of the entire nation. The Ethiopians, therefore, held a festive assembly by the sea and, offering costly sacrifices, they crowned with flowers both Iambulus and his companion and sent them out.

Having sailed for about four months, during which they faced storms, Iambulus and his companion reached the aforesaid island. It is round in shape and its circumference is about 5,000 stades. The sea around the island has strong currents and high and low tides and its taste is sweet. Although situated at the equator, the climate of the island is temperate and the inhabitants suffer from neither heat nor cold. The day and night are always equal in length and, since at midday the sun is in the zenith, no shadow is cast by any object. There are many warm and cold springs of water in the island; the warm springs are used for bathing and the relief of fatigue, whereas the cold, excelling in sweetness, also contribute to good health. Moreover, because of the fertility of the land and the mild climate, the fruits ripen throughout the year and food stuffs are spontaneously produced in abundance. A certain kind of reed, for instance, grows there in profusion, from the fruit of which the natives make surprisingly sweet loaves of bread. Another type of reed is used for making clothing; mixing it with crushed seashells, the inhabitants prepare extraordinary purple-colored clothing. Fish and birds of every variety in great quantities are found on the island, and there is also an abundance of fruit trees growing wild, including olive trees and vines, from which they make olive oil and wine. Additionally, birds of great size exist there, as well as peculiar animals small in size but distinct in the nature of their bodies, having four eyes and many mouths and feet.

The people of the island, according to Diodorus, differ greatly in their physical and mental characteristics from those in his part of the inhabited world. Stating that they are remarkably beautiful and well proportioned in the outline of the body, Diodorus details their peculiarities. The bones of their body, for example, have the ability to bend to a certain extent and then straighten again, like the sinewy parts, and, when they seize an object in their hands, it is impossible to take it from the grasp of their fingers. Their tongue is double, and thus they can express various sounds, imitating not only every articulate language used by man but also the varied chattering of birds. Furthermore, they can converse simultaneously with two persons; using one division of the tongue to address each interlocutor, they can both answer questions and discourse on current affairs. Their letters are also unique. They use only seven characters but, since each one of them can be formed in four different ways, the letters are in practice twenty-eight in number. They do not write their lines horizontally but vertically, from the top to the bottom.

The inhabitants are long lived, living even to the age of 150 years, and suffer no illness most of the time. According to their law, a man who has become crippled or suffers from any physical disability is forced to take his own life. Another law states that the natives should live only for a specified number of years, and that at the completion of this period they should remove themselves from life by lying down upon a plant, the peculiar nature of which is that anyone who lies on it gently falls asleep and dies. They are accustomed to bury their dead in the sand along the beach at the time when the tide is at the ebb, consequently at flood tide the place has fresh sand heaped upon it.[26]

Diodorus emphasizes that, although the land spontaneously produces food in abundance, the dwellers of the island show restraint and lead a life of simplicity, taking for their food only what suffices for their needs. Their diet is prearranged, since their food varies and is not taken by all at the same time. It has been ordered that on certain fixed days they should eat at one time fish and at another time fowl, but sometimes the flesh of land animals and sometimes the simplest side dishes, such as olives.

As for the social and political regime, the islanders live in groups based on kinship and political organizations. In each group, consisting of no more than 400 kinsmen, the oldest man usually exercises the leadership as if he was a kind of king. When this ruler completes his 150 years of age and ends his life according to the law, the next oldest succeeds to the leadership. Diodorus further mentions some social characteristics, attesting to the existence of a certain communal life. First, the inhabitants, except for those who have reached old age, take turns in tending to the needs of one another, some occupying themselves in fishing, others in various crafts, and the rest in other useful tasks, as well as public duties. Second, the inhabitants do not marry; they possess their children in common, sustaining them as if they belonged to all, and loving them equally. Moreover, the women who nurse the infants often change them around so that not even the mothers may know their own offspring. Consequently, there is no rivalry among them, and thus they never experience civil disorders, always placing the highest value upon internal harmony. They are also a kind people, treating the strangers who come to their island fairly and sharing with them the necessities of life that their homeland affords. Referring to religion, Diodorus says that the natives worship as gods the sun and all the heavenly bodies. They hold festivals and feasts, in which they pronounce laudations and sing hymns in honor of the gods, especially the sun, after whom both the island and its people are named.

Following his detailed account of the island, Diodorus continues his story of the adventures of Iambulus and his companion. Having lived on the island for seven years, they were compelled to leave on the grounds that they were harmful and ill mannered. Having resumed their voyage, Iambulus's friend lost his life when they were shipwrecked on a sandy and marshy shore of India. Iambulus was brought by the natives to Palibothra, a city that was many days' journey from the sea, and with the help of Palibothra's philhellene king, he passed over into Persia and later arrived in Greece.

Panchaea and the Island of the Sun are two imaginary, utopian, worlds described by Diodorus as being at the southeastern end of the universe. However, his description has a real dimension. First, he places the imaginary islands in real geographical space. Second, each of the islands is incorporated into journeys that are based on actual geographical data. The account of Euhemerus's voyage reflects the actual features of the Red Sea[27]; it is also clearly situated within Hellenistic history and relates to the geographical developments following Alexander's campaign. Euhemerus, Diodorus states, was a friend of King Cassander and, since he was required by him to carry out certain royal duties, as well as great journeys to foreign lands, he took a trip southward to the Ocean (Diod. Sic. 6.1.4). Leaders throughout the Hellenistic period sent men to explore foreign lands, both out of curiosity and for commercial purposes.[28] The journey of Iambulus, likewise, is interesting from both the geographical and historical point of view. Evidently, the geographical details, even the geomorphological data of the Indian coastline,[29] included in the description of this journey are accurate. As for its historical reflections, the imaginary inhabitants of the Island of the Sun are described by Diodorus as benevolent men, who treat strangers kindly (2.55.4, 56.1). The reference to Julius Caesar and his *clementia*[30] is clear, for Diodorus conveys this motif, expressed in almost the same wording, recurrently in various parts of his work.[31]

The third feature indicating a real dimension mingled in Diodorus's imaginary description is the striking resemblance of the portrayal of both Panchaea and the Island of the Sun to his depiction of real islands, namely, Lipara (Diod. Sic. 5.7.1–10.3) and Lesbos (5.81.1–82.4). Lipara, for instance, possesses healing springs, an abundance of fruit-bearing trees, and rich mines, while its inhabitants consist of natives and various other peoples who coexist. Moreover, the land of Lipara and the possessions of its inhabitants are made common property. The Liparaians are divided into two groups, one of which cultivates the land, while the other fights the Tyrrhenian pirates. Lesbos has a fertile land, good crops, wholesome air, and a mild climate, and its population consists of various peoples.[32]

In the writings of other authors, Panchaea is only briefly mentioned, and yet in some of them one may clearly see a different approach. Whereas the Roman poets—Virgil (*G.* 2.139), Tibullus (3.2.23), and Ovid (*Met.* 10.308)—refer to Panchaea as a land rich in aromatic plants such as frankincense, both Strabo and Plutarch stress their criticism of Euhemerus. Quoting Apollodorus's censure of poets and historians who invented marvelous tales, Strabo counts Euhemerus among such historians, because of his "Land of Panchaea" (Str. 7.3.6 C 299; cf. 2.4.2 C 104), and Plutarch argues that Euhemerus produced an incredible mythology and made a voyage to Panchaea, which does not exist anywhere on earth (*De Is. et Os.* 23 = *Mor.* 360a–b). As for the Island of the Sun, Diodorus's is the only detailed story about it. However, Iambulus is also mentioned by Lucian, who refers to him as the author of a false story, as noted, adding that he wrote strange things about the countries in the great sea. Diodorus, then, is the only writer who not only does not regard the stories of Euhemerus and Iambulus as false, but also makes an effort to locate their islands on the real map of the world. Again, one may question the reason for this treatment of the imaginary islands in the first century BCE, and yet it will be best to deal with this issue at the end of this chapter.

Like the Islands of the Blessed in the western part of the world, extreme happiness characterizes Iambulus's Island of the Sun. In addition, both Panchaea and Iambulus's Island of the Sun are extremely rich in resources and extremely fertile. Extreme characteristics, it seems, are typical of the utopian sites and are found also on the imaginary island that lies in the North.

THE NORTH: THE ISLAND OF THE HYPERBOREANS

The Hyperboreans are mentioned by various authors, but in most cases only briefly.[33] Two of the longer descriptions are found in Pindar and Diodorus. Since each of these authors has his own unique approach, it is worth focusing on them in the present chapter. In his tenth Pythian (27–49), composed in 498 BCE in honor of the Thessalian Hippocleas's victory in the boys' double-course foot race at Delphi, Pindar recounts Perseus's visit to the land of the Hyperboreans.

While ordinary mortals cannot find the exceptional road to the Hyperboreans either by ship or on foot, Perseus (also called "the son of Danae" by Pindar, emphasizing his mixed nature as the offspring of Zeus and a mortal woman) visited their homes and participated in their banquet. He went there with the help of Athena and, after slaying the Gorgon, he brought her stony head to these islanders. The Hyperboreans, according to Pindar, live a happy life and the Muse is always present among them. Adorning their hair with golden laurel branches and praising especially Apollo, they celebrate their joyous festivals, during which the girls dance everywhere, and the lyres and flutes are loudly played. Furthermore, the Hyperboreans, referred to by Pindar as a sacred race and blessed men, do not suffer any illness or any anguish of old age. Living without troubles or battles, they are free of the fear of Nemesis.

Citing Hecataeus of Abdera, Diodorus states that the Island of the Hyperboreans, situated in the north and lying in the Ocean beyond the land of the Celts, is no smaller than Sicily. The moon is seen from this island as though it was merely a short distance from Earth and one can observe the prominences upon it like those of Earth. The island is rich in crops and, since its climate is remarkably mild, its soil produces two harvests each year. The name of the Hyperboreans is derived from the location of their homeland beyond the north wind (Boreas), and they have a language peculiar to them. Moreover, they revere Apollo above all other gods, since Leto, his mother, was born on their island. In a manner, the inhabitants act like priests of Apollo, since they praise this god daily in song and honor him exceptionally. There is a magnificent precinct of Apollo on the island, as well as a spherical temple, adorned with many votive offerings. There is also a city sacred to this god, and most of its inhabitants play the cithara. They continually play this instrument in the temple and sing hymns, glorifying the god's deeds. The rulers of this city and the supervisors of the precinct are called Boreadae, since they are descendants of Boreas, and these offices are always kept in their family. Apollo visits the island every nineteen years, the interval in which the return of the stars to their original place in the heavens is completed. Upon his appearance, the god plays the cithara and dances unceasingly through the night from the vernal equinox until the rising of the Pleiades, celebrating his own accomplishments.

Diodorus adds that the Hyperboreans have been most friendly toward the Greeks from ancient times, and especially toward Athens and Delos. It is said that certain Greeks visited the Hyperboreans and left costly votive offerings inscribed with Greek letters, whereas the Hyperborean Abaris came to Greece in ancient times and renewed the good relations of his people with the Delians (Diod. Sic. 2.47.1–6).

The accounts of Pindar and Diodorus resemble each other with respect to the religious practices of the Hyperboreans. Both highlight the central position of Apollo, the joyful nature of his cult, and especially the musical festivities in his honor. While Pindar concentrates on the traits of the people—whom he depicts as sacred and happy—Diodorus dwells on the utopian characteristics of the island, which are similar to those of his other imaginary islands mentioned above. There is, however, an essential difference between the two authors. Pindar describes the voyage of Zeus's son to the Hyperboreans with Athena's guidance, stressing the inability of ordinary human beings to find the route thither. Conversely, Diodorus not only locates the island of the Hyperboreans on the actual map of the world, comparing it to Sicily, but also describes diplomatic relations between the Hyperboreans and the Greeks, including exchanges of delegations. To put it bluntly, whereas Pindar detaches the island from the real world, Diodorus regards it as part of the actual world. The explanation for this distinction lies in their individual purposes.

Pindar aims at praising Hippocleas's excellence and his Thessalian aristocratic lineage, using, as elsewhere in his work,[34] the sea and sea voyages of heroes as metaphors. The sea, according to the poet, signifies the boundary between humans and the gods, as well as between life and death, whereas a man's journey to happiness is parallel to a sea voyage. Thus, Perseus, being the son of a god, can cross the Ocean and reach the perfect land of the Hyperboreans, but Hippocleas, the son of Phricias, is restricted by his mortal ancestry. Yet Hippocleas also enjoys the advantages of his father's descent, demonstrating the same virtue and achieving success.[35] Unlike Pindar, Diodorus makes an effort to locate the island of the Hyperboreans on the actual map of the world, turning it into a place reachable by human beings. It is difficult to discover Diodorus's motives for his unique treatment of this island, and yet three factors may help to understand his approach. The first is the fact that he incorporates six utopian islands into the real map of the world, the second is his awareness of the influence of Alexander's campaign and its resulting developments, and the third is the influence of the events of his day on his writing. The explanations for all Diodorus's imaginary islands mentioned above are, therefore, bound together. In addition, however, there is an exclusive justification for the island of the Hyperboreans.

Placing the imaginary islands at well-defined sites on the real map of the universe, Diodorus highlights their position at the edges of the known world and depicts voyages of historical figures thither. Hespera, the Island in the river Triton, and the Island in the Atlantic Ocean mark the western extremity of the universe, Panchaea and Iambulus's island are placed on the southeastern boundary of the world, and the Island of the Hyperboreans, identified by some scholars with Britain,[36] lies on the northern edge of earth. It is plausible that Diodorus, recognizing not only the expanding geographical knowledge of his age but also the longing of his contemporaries for a better world after years of wars and their destructive consequences, is implying that, although far away, these idyllic islands are within reach.[37] Furthermore, Diodorus, whose admiration for

Alexander and Caesar is manifest throughout his work,[38] may have been inspired by their accomplishments. Hence, for instance, he may have intended to offer an ancient and well-established precedent for the conquests of both leaders. The case of the Island of the Hyperboreans is interesting in this respect, for it is quite possible that Caesar's invasion of Britain motivated Diodorus to include it in his work. Additionally, Diodorus seems to utilize his utopian description of the imaginary islands to convey contemporary notions. He recounts the coexistence of natives and foreigners in a certain place and states that, although the inhabitants of this place have cultures different from that of the Greeks, they are situated within the same world. This recalls the notion of the unity of mankind, and the change in the treatment of the "other" in the Hellenistic era. By the time of Diodorus, when Caesar's accomplishments had become no less influential than those of Alexander, there were two conflicting approaches toward the "other": acceptance of and tolerance toward the "other," on the one hand, and distinction between peoples according to racial and cultural factors, on the other.[39] Diodorus expresses both these approaches in his work (Sulimani 2011: 315–30, 342–3).[40] Finally, Diodorus, himself an islander, may have had a personal motive, that is, to glorify islands as the best place for human beings to live. Significantly, he compares both the island of the Hyperboreans and Britain with Sicily, his home island (Diod. Sic. 2.47.1, 5.21.3).

Both Pindar and Diodorus use images of the sea and sea crossings as a means of expressing their ideas, but, whereas the poet employs these images to articulate men's limitations as compared to those of the gods, the historian utilizes them to show how men, like gods and heroes, can reach faraway utopian places. This fundamental difference is revealed elsewhere in their work. Making metaphorical use of the Pillars of Heracles, Pindar writes that, by winning the chariot race (476 BCE), Theron of Acragas reached the farthest point by his excellence, as though he touched the Pillars of Heracles. Any attempt to go beyond these pillars, he adds, would be foolish (*Ol.* 3.43–5). In another ode, Pindar even warns outstanding men not to pursue excellence any farther than the Pillars of Heracles (*Isthm.* 4.12–13; cf. *Nem.* 3.20–3, 4.69).[41] In contrast, sailing beyond the Pillars of Heracles, according to Diodorus, is not only possible but seems to be a routine matter among human beings. Recounting the story of the setting up of the pillars by Heracles, who then crossed the pillars into Iberia (Diod. Sic. 4.18.2), he states, as already noted above, that the Phoenicians used to explore the coast outside the pillars and that during one of their voyages they discovered the idyllic Island in the Atlantic Ocean (5.20.1–3). Moreover, this description appears in Diodorus's fifth book, devoted to islands, where he discusses the islands beyond the Pillars of Heracles as part of the *oikoumene*. Living in different periods, Pindar and Diodorus had a rather different agenda.

The Northern imaginary island, similar to the utopian places mentioned above, is depicted as extremely happy by the authors. While Pindar explicitly states that the Hyperboreans live a happy life, this is implied by Diodorus's description of Apollo's cult, characterized by continuous singing and dancing. Moreover, while Diodorus paints the island of the Hyperboreans as extremely fertile, like his other utopian islands, Pindar portrays it as close to the gods.

CONCLUSION

The sea played an important role in the real life of the ancients; it is thus conceivable that it constituted a significant element in their imagination as well. The scope of this chapter allowed me to concentrate on a single aspect of this imagination, and yet the discussion of the fantastic islands and the voyages to them opens a window for understanding the making of the imaginary world. These islands are usually described as idyllic: they are well watered, fertile, healthy, and provide men with food of every kind, a description that reminds the reader of Hesiod's "Golden Age." At the same time, these accounts also include real elements, increasingly in the Hellenistic era, and especially in the first century BCE, when the changes in the actual world affected the presentation of the imaginary world. Hence, the authors living through the Roman civil wars created a utopian world, in which the islands are completely different from the fourth century dystopia of Plato. The philosopher depicts the island of Atlantis, located at a distant point in the Atlantic Ocean, beyond the Pillars of Heracles. It was indeed fertile and contained trees and animals of every kind, as well as warm and cold springs of water. Moreover, its inhabitants, provided with all the necessities of life, were kind and noble, conducting themselves with both gentleness and wisdom. However, because they changed their ways and became arrogant, the island of Atlantis was swallowed up by the sea and the Ocean at that spot became impassable (Pl., *Ti.* 24e–25d; *Critias* 108e–109c, 113c–121c.).

Yet, the sea is not only a significant component of the utopian or dystopian worlds, but it is also a central element in descriptions of imaginary empires. To take one example for the sake of interest, Sesostris, the mythical king of Egypt, made a journey recorded by Diodorus (1.55.1–10). He traveled from Egypt to India, passing through Ethiopia and Arabia. Having sent his fleet into the Red Sea to take control of the islands and the coast of the mainland as far as India, Sesostris himself made his way by land and conquered all Asia. After crossing the River Ganges and arriving at the Ocean, Sesostris turned north, and reached Scythia, Lake Maeotis, and the River Tanais. Sailing in the Black Sea, he crossed into Europe at the Hellespont, and reached the Cycladic islands. Arriving in Thrace, he ended his campaign and went back to Egypt. During his expedition,

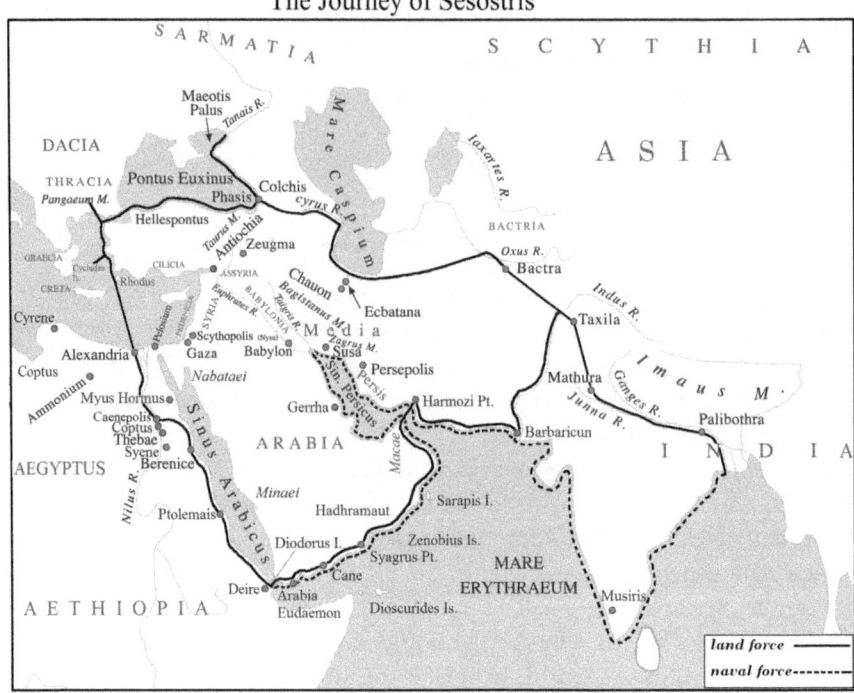

FIGURE 8.5 The journey of Sesostris. © Iris Sulimani (author).

Sesostris annexed lands and settled their affairs, thus creating an empire.[42] The resemblance between Sesostris's expedition and that of Alexander the Great is obvious, and yet the Egyptian king reached places where Alexander never set foot. It is possible, therefore, that Sesostris's imaginary empire was intended to provide a precedent for either existing or future imperialistic expansion,[43] perhaps even to convey the author's own idea in favor of the creation of an empire in the real world.

NOTES

Preface

1 Cindy Starr, "Annual Arctic Sea Ice Minimum 1979–2015, with graph," NASA Scientific Visualization Studio, released on March 10, 2016, https://svs.gsfc.nasa.gov/4786 (accessed 23 October 2020).

Introduction

1 See also Watkins (1985, *s.v.* "*pent-").
2 See the summary in Sacks (1989: 45–7).
3 Unless otherwise indicated, the references to the Latin version of the *Navigatio* follow Selmer's edition.
4 This labor of Heracles is only attested in vase paintings: *LIMC* (*s.v.* "Geras (Shapiro)"). For a comparison between Geras and the Old Man of the Sea, see Détienne ([1967] 1996): 59.
5 See also Honoré of Autun's *Imago Mundi* (I. 35); *Lucidarius* (1.61); Gervase of Tillbury (*Otia Imperialia* 2.11); and the Map of Angelino Dulcert (fl.1339) in Harley and Woodward (1987: 378, 410).
6 The story of Brendan continues to inspire reinterpretations. Most recently, see Holland's poetic reconstruction of the narrative, Holland (2014).
7 See the texts collected in Kohns and Sideri (2009).

Chapter 1

1 Most famously, Pericles' "ship of state" (Plato, *Republic* 488a–d; Thucydides; see also Alcaeus f6, f208 Campbell), but also "reef of justice" (Aeschylus, *Eumenides* 564); sea (of troubles) (Sophocles, *Oedipus at Colonus* 1746).
2 Strabo cites Homer as the "father of geography" (1.1.11).
3 In the 280s BCE, Patrocles erroneously postulated that the Caspian was linked with the Ocean, a mistake that was perpetuated (Eratosthenes f110; Pliny, *NH* 6.58). Only Herodotus (1.202.4) and Aristotle (*Meteorology* 2.1 354a4) recognized the Caspian as land-locked.

4 Beaulieu (2016: 25): *pontus* indicates a path that is difficult to cross, as in Sanskrit *pántāḥ* (a road marked by obstacles). Indeed poets refer to the "paths of the sea": for example, Jason sees on display in Aeëtes' palace tablets that displayed "all the roads and paths of both the wet and the dry for those who travel all about" (Apollonius, *Argonautica* 4.279–81); in the thick of a virulent storm, the talented helmsman Palinurus was unable to remember the path in mid-wave (Vergil, *Aeneid* 3.201–2).

5 For example, the Aegean (πέλαγος Αἰγαῖον: Aeschylus, *Agamemnon* 659); the Sardinian (τὸ Σαρδόνιον καλεόμενον πέλαγος: Herodotus 1.166); the Adriatic and Tyrrhenian seas (ἐκ τοῦ Ἀδρίου καὶ ἐξ ἑτέρου πελάγους ὃ καλεῖται Τυρσηνόν: Pausanias 5.25.3); and the Euxine (ἐν δ' Εὐξείνῳ πελάγει: Pindar, *Nemean Ode* 4.49).

6 The Mediterranean is variously referred to simply as ἡ θάλασσα: the sea (e.g. *Il.* 2.294; *Od.* 5.413); ἡ μεγάλη θάλασσα: the Great Sea (Arrian, *Indika* 2.7); ἡ ἡμέτερα θάλασσα: Our Sea (Plato, *Phaedo* 113a; Aelian, *On Animals* 12.25; Strabo 1.2.29); this sea: ἥδε ἡ θάλασσα (Herodotus 1.1, 185, 4.39); τῆς νῦν ἑλληνικῆς θαλάσσης: the Hellenic Sea (Herodotus 5.54; Thucydides 1.5; Plutarch, *Cimon* 13); ἡ θάλαττα ἡ καθ' ἡμᾶς: the sea around us (Polybius 1.3.9); ἡ παρ' ἡμῖν θάλασσα: the sea near us (Plato, *Phaedo* 113a; Strabo 2.5.18); the deep sea of salt water (πέλαγός τε θαλάσσης: Apollonius, *Argonautica* 4.608). The Romans called that body of water *mare nostrum* (Our Sea). "Mediterranean" does not come into common use until the sixth century CE, recorded as such by Isidore of Seville (*Etymologiarum sive Originum* 9.1.8). This represents a paradigm shift as emphasis is transferred from the sea (*mare*) to the lands (*terrae*).

7 See Beaulieu (2016: 5, 34) on Ocean as a conceptual border between humans and gods, and the living and the dead.

8 The parallels between the *Theogony* and Hurrian/Hittite, Mesopotamian, and Jewish cosmological myths have been discussed at length elsewhere (e.g., Mondi 1990; Naddaf 1986; Solmsen 1982).

9 Anaximander's map may have been intended to respond to the practical concerns of colony founders. The philosopher is believed to have founded a colony perhaps on the Black Sea: Hahn 2001: 202–3.

10 Only one redaction suggests that one "cannot step twice into the same river" (*TEGP* 63).

11 Aristotle, *Meteorology* 3.1 371a15–17; Pliny, *NH* 2.133. See Kahn (1979: 141–2) for an analysis of evidence from Hesiod, Herodotus, Aristophanes, Xenophon, and Aristotle.

12 In Empedocles, fishes are "water-nourished" (*TEGP* 41).

13 The Epicureans, who adapted Democritus's atomic theory, believed in the senescence of the earth, exhaustion of the soil, and the eventual failure of agriculture (Lucretius, *On the Nature of Things* 2.1144–77).

14 Wilson (2013: 179): Aristotle seems to criticize Plato for placing a *katabasis* at the center of the discussion on ocean. We also note that Odysseus reached the underworld by first sailing to Ocean (*Ody.* 11.13–14. Cf. Beaulieu 2016: 10).

15 The figures are strictly theoretical: parts of the Ionian are deeper than the Sardinian Sea, and the Black Sea is deeper than the Aegean (Leier 2001: 230–1; Oleson 2008: 131).

16 Strabo vividly described the Dead Sea (which he mistakenly called "Lake Sirbonis:" 16.2.42); cf. Pliny, *NH* 2.226 on the bitumen-producing lake Asphaltitis in Judea.

17 Manilius's (10–30 CE) theory that the stars also affected tidal amplitude was not embraced (2.89–92).
18 A storm surge may have contributed to swells of such amplitudes (Roller 2006: 76–7). The Jersey Channel Islands have tides up to 12.5 meters (41 feet), and tidal amplitude at the Bay of Fundy in Canada, renowned for its high tides, can reach up to 17 meters (56 feet) (see Waddelove and Waddelove 1990).
19 Seneca correctly noted the effects of coinciding spring and equinoctial tides: *Natural Questions* 3.28.6. In *The Periplus of the Erythraean Sea*, *nocturnal* spring tides seem to have the greatest force (Eckenrode 1975: 279–81, 286).
20 Plutarch, *Platonic Questions* 8.1; Roller 2005: 112–14. In his old age Plato had considered its merits. Seemingly Metrodorus and Crates also promoted heliocentrism (pseudo-Plutarch, *Placita* 2.15), and perhaps Anaximander, though the evidence is contradictory. Athenodorus of Tarsus (fl.60–20 BCE) also composed a work on tides, in which he compared tidal behavior to breathing and explained tidal peaks as enhanced by sub-oceanic springs (f6a).
21 Poseidonius either misunderstood his sources or was misinterpreted by Strabo (Irby 2016: 186).
22 Justin Martyr (*Cohortatio ad graecos* 34b Migne); Procopius (8.6.20); Wilson (2013: 179).
23 *On Floating Bodies* 1 proposition 2; cf. Pliny, *NH* 2.163 with empirical proofs.
24 Petronius also employed the whirlpool to wreck Encolpius' ship (*Satyricon* 114).
25 See further El-Geziry and Bryden (2014) for a model of both surface and deep water Mediterranean currents.
26 Oleson (2008) provides a useful catalog of Greco-Roman sounding weights.
27 Herodotus mentioned the alluvial nature of the Mediterranean waters into which the Nile debouches (2.5.28), and Olympiodorus, and Aristotle (*Meteorology* 1.13.351a,) refers to sand brought up by the weights (*Commentary on Aristotle's Meteorologica* 107.21–5). Aristotle eschewed mention of sediment samples. See further Casson (1995: 245–6n85) and Oleson (2008: 126).
28 Professional divers in premodern societies continue to puncture their eardrums to avoid the lengthy process of equalizing the pressure within the ear (Frost 1969: 182). See also Aristotelian *Problems* 32.2 (sponges prevent water from entering the ears with too much force) and 32.11 (divers put oil into their ears before a dive). Men would also dive with a mouthful of olive oil (Oppian, *On Fishing* 5.638, 646), perhaps to protect their Eustachian tubes from excessive exposure to sea water (Frost 1969).
29 Nearchus took advantage of his excellent swimmers to launch a surprise attack along the Tomerus River in 325 BCE. He ordered the men to fall into a phalanx formation on the sea's bottom, charging once the ranks were three deep (Arrian, *Indika* 24.6–7).
30 Juba II used Onesicritus as a source for his own *Libyka* (Roller 2003: 194, 228, 240n93).
31 Roller (2018: 877). The Nereid seems to be a doublet for Circe.
32 See Casson (1989) for text, translation, and commentary.
33 Frost (1969: 182–3): the average unaided diver can spend two to four minutes underwater.

Chapter 2

1 For example, *Anth. Pal.* (7. 267, 278–9, 283–4, 287, 382, 501, 665, 738–9). Cf. Romero Recio (1998: 39–50).
2 Please refer to Wachsmuth (1967) and Romero Recio (2000), which contain detailed analyses of matters related to religious practices associated to navigation (types of offerings, sanctuaries, venerated deities, and so on). This has been recently summarized in Fenet (2016) and Blakely (2017).
3 On the sea as a point of contact between the imaginary world and the real world, see Beaulieu (2016).
4 See, among others, Bisi, Amadasi Guzzo, and Tusa (1969: 45–6, tav. XIX–XX, 53, fig. 25, tav. XXIV); Coacci Polselli, Amadasi Guzzo, and Tusa (1979: 58–70); Purpura (1979).
5 In addition to the Bibliography cited in this publication, see Bruun (2017: 219–22) and the references made therein.
6 Volume 46 of *The International Journal of Nautical Archaeology* contains several articles on ship graffiti, among others: Demesticha et al. (2017) (examples between the fifteenth and twentieth centuries).
7 On the island of Leuce (White Island) in the Euxine, where the existence of a cult to Achilles has been established in connection to sailor religiousness, devotees needed to embark before sunset to avoid spending the night on land; even if they were unable to set sail due to unfavorable winds, they were to remain moored and wait onboard (Philostr., *Her.* 54. Cf. n66).
8 A collection of sources, coming mainly though not only from *The Natural History* by Pliny the Elder, from the *Nautical Lapidary* and from the *Kerygmata*, in Perea Yébenes (2010).
9 On the ability of the vessel Argo to speak, built by the goddess Athena (A.R. 1.525-527; 4.580–3; cf. Apollod., *Bibl.* 1.9.19). On offerings of ships and ship models see Romero Recio (2000: 2–22).
10 On Herakles as tutelary god for sailors, please see Romero Recio (2000: 30 ss., 84 ss., 93ss). Worship of this deity in relation to the sea was continued in Roman times, as shown, among other testimonies, by an inscription in Greek, found in the old Signia, South or Rome, and dating from between the second and third centuries CE, which indicates that a group of sailors had dedicated an offering to Herakles thanking him for their lives after surviving a shipwreck (Kajava 2002).
11 See, as well, Edlund (1987: 48 ss.). Other connections have been studied between ancient and modern cults in the marine sphere, for instance Palmisano (2010).
12 Hom., *Od.* 3.286–90; 4.512–15; 9.79–81; *Hym. Hom. Ap.* 410; B. 3.72–3; Eur., *Cyc.* 18–24; Hdt. 4.179.2; 7.168.4; D.H. 1.72.3; Str. 8.6.20; Paus. 3.23.2; Alc. 1.10.3; *Orph. Arg.* 1363–5; Procop., *Vand.* 3.13.5; *Anth. Pal.* 7.214, 275, 584; SIG III.1229.
13 On the dangers of Athos: Hdt. 6.44.2–3; 95; 7.22; 23.1. On Caphereus: Eur., *Hel.* 766 ss., 1126 ss.; *IA* 198; *Ag.* 626; Soph., *Aj.* 1295 ss.; 2.826 ss., schol. 4.1901; Lyc. *Alex.* 381 ss., 1093 ss.; Diod. Sic. 4.33; Ov., *Met.* 14.472 ss.; *Tr.* 1.1.83; 5.7.35 ss.; Str. 8.6.2; Plu., *Mor.* 301e; D.Chr., *Eub.* 32; Apollod., *Bibl.* 2.1.5, 7.4; 3.2.2; *Epit.* 6.7–11; Paus. 2.23.1; cf. 4.36.6; Q.S. 14.613–26; Hyg., *Fab.* 116, 117, 169, 249, 277; Schol. *Od.* 4.797; Tzetz., *ad Lyc. Al.* 386, 992, 1093 ss.; Serv., *ad Aen.* 11.260.

14 Serv., *ad Aen.* 3.411, 687. Cf. Diod. Sic. 4.85.5; Str. 6.1.5; Verg., *Aen.* 3.411, 688; Val. Max. 9.8.2; Trogo 4.1; Mela, 2.7; *Anth. Pal.* 6.224.
15 On the festival of the Cybernesia, see Romero Recio (2010: 55–74 with bibliography).
16 On the offering of oars and other riggings, as well as on the importance of the oar as an element symbolizing loss of life at sea, whether voluntarily or caused by the passing of a sailor or fisherman, see Romero Recio (2000: 22–8).
17 *Od.* 10.552–60; 11.51–83; 12.10-15; Ov., *Ibis.* 487; Theophr. 5.8.3; Pseud. Scyl. 8; Plin. *NH* 15.36, 119; Apollod., *Epit.* 7.17; Ivv. 15.19–22; Serv., *ad Aen.* 6.107. Cf. Ampolo (1994: 268–80). Also the enchantress Circe was a goddess connected to Venus on this promontory, where she had a temple (Str. 5.3.6; Cic., *de nat. deor.* 3.19; Quilici 1992: 407–29; Quilici and Gigli 2005: 407–29).
18 Verg., *Aen.* 6.162–74, 212–35; D.H. 1.53.3. On the matter of the perils of this promontory: D.H. 7.5.6; Tac., *Ann.* 15.46. Cf. McKay (1984: 130–7).
19 Verg. *Aen.* 3.200–4, 269, 513–20, 561–3; 5.12–25; D.H. 1.53.2; D.C. 49.1–2; Vell. 2.79.3–4; Oros. 4.9.11; Serv., *ad Aen.* 6.378–9. Cf. McKay (1984: 130–7); Nicoll (1988: 459–72). The name, associated with the wind, *palinouros,* "wind blowing back" or "unfavorable wind," can be connected with the sources that mention the difficult navigation of this cape, see cf. Ambrose (1980: 449–57) and Poccetti (1996: 64).
20 Pinzone (1999: 274–6) solidly defended that the statue was on the Sicilian coast and not on the other side of the strait.
21 *c.* 734 CE the colonizers of Naxos built an altar to Apollo *Archegetes* who was venerated by the rest of Sicilian colonies: Thes. 6.3.1; cf. App. BC 5.454–5; Romero Recio (2000: 85, with bibliography).
22 It is interesting to point out that Diodorus (4.23.1) mentions how, when Herakles arrived in Sicily, he left from Cape Pelorus toward Eryx, another site of great relevance for marine worship in the Mediterranean.
23 Lyc. *Schol.* Lyc. *Alex.* 229–31, 359; Paus. 2.34.8; 15.3, 41.6; Becker, *Anecd.* 299. Romero Recio (2000: 26 ss., 80ss., 118 ss.).
24 On the finding in Ortygia, see Kapitän (1989: 147–8). On the worship to Achilles in the Black Sea, see Arr. *Peripl.M.Eux.* 32 GGM; Hooker (1988); Okhotnikov and Ostroverkhov (1991: 55, 65–70); Hedreen (1991: 315–22); Hind (1996); Kozlovskaya (2017: 29–49).
25 It means, "the one that is marching" and refers to the unfermented grape juice and the figs with which the god stains his face during the grape harvest: Zenob. Vulg. 5.13; Zenob. Ath. 3.68, Phot, μ 652 y *Suda* μ 1343.
26 The links between this deity and the sea have already been indicated, see Romero Recio (2010: 101–6). A famous myth, recreated on the kylix of Exekias, reported that the god was shanghaied by pirates who, upon realizing their mistake when seeing vines sprouting from their mast, threw themselves into the sea and were transformed into dolphins: *Hym. h. Dion.* 7; Apollod., *Bibl.* 3.5.3; Ov., *Met.* 3.581–686; Sen., *Oed.* 449–66; Hyg., *Fab.* 134.2.
27 On the Anthesteria as festivities associated with navigation, see Romero Recio (2010: 101–6). On other funerary gods linked with maritime activity, see Romero Recio (2000: 49–51).
28 See, among others, Rossignoli (2004: 195 ss.) and Fasolo (2013: 103).

29 My gratitude to Dr. Maria Teresa Di Blasi for the information provided on the offerings presented by sailors during contemporary times in Sicily. Cf. Saija and Cervellera (1997) and Leonardi and Rizzo (2011).
30 *Hym. Hom. Diosc.* 33.6–8; *PMG* 998, 1004; Pind., fr. 140c; Eur., *Hel.* 140; Theoc. *Id.* 22.1–22; Str. 1.3.2; Plu., *Mor.* 426 c; *Thes.* 33.3; Lucian. *DDeor.* 26; Arr., *Peripl.M.Eux.* 32 GGM; Artem., *Onir.* 2.37.
31 *Hym. Hom. Diosc.* 33.11–17; Alc. 5.34. According to Arnobius (Arnobius, *Adversus Nationes* VII, 19, 3–4) white victims were offered to gods of the sky and earth, while infernal divinities would receive black animals. See Mantzilas (2016).
32 One of the most recent collective publications that deals with the study of this sanctuary as a place of worship for sailors is Acquaro, Filippi, and Medas (2010).
33 IG X. II, 1, 254; XII.5, 14, 739; Hyg., *Fab.* 277; Cassiod., *Var.* 5.17; Lucian. *DMar.* 7; Apul., *Met.* 11.5.1), Cf. Müller (1961: 41–2, 61–7); Tran Tam Tinh (1964: 98 ss.); Romero Recio (2010: 74–80); Bricault (2006, 2020).
34 Mart. *epigr.* 12.57; Phaedr., *Fab.* 4.23; Ivv., *Sat.* 12.30-83; 14.300–2; Pers., *Sat.* 1.89; Hor., *Ars P.* 20–1.
35 Apul., *Met.* 11.23.7: *nocte media vidi solem candido coruscantem lumine.* Also Plutarch refers to the light that comes to meet the initiates (frg. Stob. 4.52.49).

Chapter 3

1 A system of military allies by which the native communities remained, theoretically, independent but were in practice subjects of the Roman Empire.
2 Roman military roads fortified with towers and forts.
3 *Cheirismos* probably refers to officials and bureaucratic processes rather than a physical place (Adams 2018: 189).
4 Merchant galleys were used for carrying cargo as well as passengers. The name *kerkouros* is the Greek interpretation of the Assyrian *qurqurru*, a type of Mesopotamian riverboat. The Greek papyri from Egypt give a better understanding of the *kerkouros* vessels. They also indicate that this type of vessel was the standard carrier of grain on the Nile (Casson 1971: 164). The *Papyri of Tebtynis* 857 mentions that at Ptolemais, *kerkouroi* were mobilized to transport the annual grain revenue in 171 BCE down the Nile to Alexandria; also in this papyrus it is mentioned that the smallest type carried a load of 225 tons, most carried 250 to 275 tons, and the largest carried 450 tons (*P.Teb.* 167 and n40).
5 The boats for unloading cargo and ferrying it either to harbor warehouses or upriver were known in Greek as *hyperetikai skaphai*/service boats, and in Latin as *scaphae* (Casson 1971: 336).
6 *Stlatta* was a small riverboat (Casson 1971: 333). In the mosaic pavement from Althiburus in Tunisia depicting a "catalog of ships and boats," dated to the third century CE, appear a *stlatta* boat (Casson 1971: fig. 137/15).
7 This kind of machine with many pulleys is called *polyspaston* (a compound pulley). The use of a single pole has the advantage that by inclining it beforehand it can deposit the load sideways to the right or left as desired (Vitruvius 10.2.10). The use of all contrivances described above is available not only for these purposes, but also for loading up and unloading ships.

Chapter 4

1 On the origins of piracy, see de Souza (1999: 14–17).
2 The problem of identifying "proper" piracy is discussed in Ormond (1924: 59–74) and de Souza (1999: 2–12).

3 For a brief overview over the history of modern privateering Stark (1897: 49–136) is still useful.
4 On Cilician piracy, see de Souza (1999: 97–148, particularly 98–101); on Pompey's eventual suppression of the threat, see de Souza (1999: 149–78).
5 See Lloyd (1968) on the involvement of the West African Squadron in the suppression of the slave trade.
6 For a recent experiment in long-distance sailing on the Danube, see Himmler, Konen and Löffl (2009).
7 Pointedly, Julian Corbett puts at the very beginning of his theory of naval war: "The object of naval warfare must always be directly or indirectly either to secure the command of the sea or to prevent the enemy from securing it" (1972: 86).
8 Among the first true amphibious assaults was the capture of the coastal town of Pisagua by a Chilenian force in the War of the Pacific in 1877; see Sater (2007: 172–6).
9 The Gallipolli campaign is usually seen as the starting point for the development of specialized landing craft, see Speller (2004: 137–42).
10 The term is first used by Herodotus describing the rule of the legendary Cretan king Minos, see Herodotus 3.122.3.
11 In two large storms Rome lost possibly well over four hundred warships, see Polybius 1.37.2 and 1.39.6.
12 On Maništušu as Sargon's successor, see Hasselbach (2005: 5); on his campaigns, see Potts (2015: 98) and Magee (2014: 116).
13 Starr (1955) has shown that the idea of a Minoan thalassocracy is unsupportable by any evidence and indeed a "patent falsity" (283); on Minoan ships, see Wachsmann (1998: 83–122); on Mycenaean ships see Wachsmann (1998: 123–62).
14 On the Medinet Habu reliefs, see Redford (2000: 8–20).
15 Radner (2010: 435–40); a royal stele discovered in 1844 on Cyprus is the most impressive witness of the activities of the Assyrian king (429–35).
16 On Sennacherib's Phoenician campaign, see Gallagher (1999: 91–104).
17 For the most recent overview over the evolution of warship design in antiquity, see Rankov (2017: 15–26).
18 An early piece of textual evidence is preserved in Homer (*Iliad* 2.509–10), where a ship with 120 rowers is mentioned.
19 See Rankov (2017: 27–33) for the most recent overview over the development of ramming tactics.
20 For the most recent overview over the history of the trireme, see Rankov (2017: 16–18); for an extensive discussion see Morrison, Coates, and Rankov (2000).
21 On trireme tactics, see Taylor (2012).
22 On Greek shipsheds, see Blackman (2013); on the construction of shipsheds, see Rankov (2013: 91–9).
23 According to Diodorus (14.42.2–3) both the tetreres and the penteres were invented by Dionysius I of Syracuse (r.405–367).
24 Nearchos's cruise gained considerable attention already in antiquity (Wirth (1972: 629–35; see also Badian 1975).
25 For a full discussion of the available evidence, see Wallinga (1956).
26 *FGrHist* 176 F 1 = P.Würzb.Inv. 1; the Würzburg papyrus is the only independently transmitted fragment of the Greek historian Sosylos, see Wilcken (1906) and Schepens (2004).
27 For overviews, see Lazenby (1996: 81–96) and Rankov (2010: 154–6); Polybius was confident the battle would "strike […] even a hearer with amazement at the

magnitude of the struggle and at that lavish outlay and vast power of the two states" (Polybius 1.25.9).

28 The literature on the battle is extensive; for a recent overview based on both the available sources and experimental data, see Schäfer (2006: 222–30).
29 On Ptolemaic activities in the Southern Agean, see Meadows (2013).
30 Livius 29.25.1; Scipio moved a force of around 35,000 men, which will have required hundreds of ships.
31 For the two engagements, see Livius (37.23.4–24.10) and Appian, *Syriaca* (6.27), who mentions the successful use of fire by the Rhodians.
32 The use of naval power in the civil wars at the end of the Roman Republic has so far seen only limited attention; for an overview, see Gray-Fow (1993).
33 For the most recent overview, see Rankov (2017: 33–4).
34 See, for example, Rodgers (1937: 538), who pointedly notes at the very end of his study: "After many centuries of naval warfare, the battle of Actium established the economic unity of the Mediterranean basin and thereafter [...] the peace of Rome prevailed over those waters, during which period the Roman navy shrank to a mere coast guard for the protection of the public against pirates."
35 At times the naval units of Misenum and Ravenna could also serve as an additional manpower reserve from which to recruit land forces, see, for example, Tacitus (*Histories* 1.6.2) for the Year of the Four Emperors (69 BCE).
36 Zosimus 2.23.3–24.3; other examples include the ravaging of the coasts of Southern Gaul in 69 BCE by elements of the *classis* in Misenum, see Tacitus (*Histories* 1.87); on these operations, see also Kienast (1966: 63–4).
37 On the careers of the known commanders of Roman imperial *classes*, see Zyromski (2001).
38 Germanicus in 16 CE had in excess of 1,000 ships at his disposal, while the fleet necessary to carry the Roman invasion force to Britain in 43 CE will have required around 1,000 ships.
39 Admittedly the available evidence is extremely thin on the ground; apart from an episode where Caesar brought crewmen recruited elsewhere into his theatre of operations (Caesar, *Bellum Gallicum* 3.9.1), very little information on the recruitment of crews survive.
40 Historia Augusta, *Gallienus* 13.7; see also de Souza (1999: 222–3).
41 Tacitus, *Agricola* 38.3; see Wolfson (2008: 47–62).
42 Augustus, *Res Gestae* 26.1; Pliny, *Natural History* 2.167.

Chapter 5

1 On insularity in Greek ancient thought, see Ceccarelli (1989); Vilatte (1991); Gabba (1991); Lätsch (2005: 21–47); Constantakopoulou (2007: 1–19); Ampolo (2009b).
2 For the inventory of the primary sources and for an overview of the floating islands issue, see Cook (1940 III.2: 975–1015) and Moret (1997).
3 See also the case of Delos/Ortygia/Asteria, a floating island until the birth of Apollo: Pind., *HZeus* (frr. 33c–33d Race) and *Pae.* 7b.43–52 (= fr. 52h); Call. *HDelos* 4.11–18, 30–54, 191–4, 213; Apollod., *Bibl.* 1.4.1; Cook (1940 III.2: 14–18). The change of the island's name from Asteria ("the star island") to Ortygia, namely, Delos (Δᾶλος "visible from afar," "the island who shines like a star"), to which Ortygia finds itself identified, serves to express the change of its status. Pindar does not specify the name of the divine author of this transformation, he merely qualifies it as "founded by the gods" (fr. 33c.1); other later sources designate Zeus or Poseidon as authors of Delos' foundation.

4   Strab. 1.1.8, 2.5.5–6. See also Maddoli (2009) on Strabo's view on islands/insularity and Cordano (2009) on circumnavigation in relation to the idea of the *oecumene* surrounded by the sea.
5   The encirclement by the sea is highlighted most often by the use of the terms ἀμφίρυτος, περίρρυτος, ἀμφίαλος, or simply περί.
6   Without exception, all these physical features are designated by conventional terms and formulaic expressions.
7   Strab. 3.5.5; Plin. *NH* iii.4; Apollod., *Bibl.* 2.5.10; Diod. Sic. 4.18.5; Sen., *HF* 235–8. See Davies (1992).
8   Pind., *Ol.* 3.43–5; *Nem.* 3.20–3; *Isthm.* 4.29–31; Eur., *Hipp.* 742–50. See Romm (1992: 17–18).
9   For other expeditions through or beyond the Pillars of Heracles, see Beaulieu (2016: 2–5).
10 On *porthmeutike*, see Dilke (1998: 30–3); Malkin (1998: 1–31); Hartog (2001: 88–9); Constantakopoulou (2007: 222–6). For an overview on the theories of island colonization (in the Western and Eastern Mediterranean), see Malkin (1987, 1998); Lätsch (2005: 49–74); Dawson (2016: 42–68).
11 See the example of Ancona, situated on a promontory which forms a remarquable curve or elbow, so as to protect and almost enclose its port, hence the Greek name of the colony, Ἀγκών "the Elbow" (Mela 2.4; Plin. 3.13.18). Its port was the only natural harbor along this line of the Adriatic coast of Italy and its importance was sealed even on the coins of Ancona belonging to the period of the Greek colony: on the reverse, it bears a bent arm or "elbow," in allusion to its name.
12 See, for example, the harbor of the Cyclopes' mythical island (*Od.* 9.125–9, 136–9) or that of the ambivalent island of the Laestrygonians (10.87–97), where "the paths of day and night are close together" (10.86), which both separate and allow the passage between West and East and from one world to another.
13 As if to respect and validate the sanctity of Delos, Datis, and Artaphernes *did not anchor* there, but passed on to Rhenaea (cf. Hdt. 6.97).
14 For example, the "wooded Zacynthus" (Hom., *Od.* 1.246, 9.24, 16.123, 19.131; *HHAp.* 430); the wooded Plakos (*Il.* 6.396 and 425, 22.479); Sunium's jutting plateau (Soph., *Aj.* 1218), the highest summit of timbered Samos, Poseidon's fief in the *Iliad* (13.12); Chios, whose earlier name was Pityusa or Pine Island, from the pine forests (Plin., *NH* 5.31), etc.
15 For example, Mount Aegeum (Hes., *Th.* 484); Phaeacia and its "shadowy mountains" (*Od.* 5.279, 7.268); the small anonymous island located "neither near nor far from the Cyclopes' land" is a rough and wooded one (9.116–18).
16 For example, Ogygia (*Od.* 5.55, 7.244), Thrinacia (12.135), the wide Crete (13.256–7) situated "nearly on the very fringes of Europe" (Eur., *Thes.* fr. 381), etc. On the liminal vs remote status of Crete, see Guizzi (2009).
17 For example, Ancona was founded about 380 BCE by Syracusan exiles who fled hither to avoid the tyranny of the elder Dionysius (cf. Strab. 5.1.3; Solin. 2.10; Juv. 4.40). On islands and their *peraiai* as suitable locations for exiles, see Lätsch (2005: 217–21) and Constantakopoulou (2007: 129–34, 249–53).
18 Historical examples include: in 422 BCE, the Athenians banished all the inhabitants of Delos, their removal being seen by the Athenians as essential to complete the purification of the island, already done in 426 (Thuc. 5.1; Paus. 4.27.90); Donussa, a small island near Naxos, was used as a place of banishment under the Roman Empire, as well as Amorgos, island of the Sporades in the Aegean Sea (Tac., *Ann.* 4.30).

19 Worse, the insular circularity fuses sometimes with the circular symbolism of death: on the testimony of Dionysus, Artemis killed Ariadne on the "sea-girt Dia" (*Od.* 11.325), Herakles killed Geryon on "Erythea surrounded by water" (Hes., *Th.* 983–4) after he stole his round-hoof cattle, etc.
20 See, for example, in the *Odyssey*, the Elysian Fields (4.563–8, see also Luc. *VH* 2.14–16), Ogygia (5.59–74), Scheria (7.110–33); the Isle of the Blessed (Hes., *Op.* 167–73; Pind., *Ol.* 2.68–75 and fr. 129 Mahler; Luc. *VH* 2.5–6, 11–13); Panchaea in Euhemerus (*FGrH* 63F3) and Diod. Sic. 5.42–6 (see also De Vido 2009; Sulimani 2017); the Island of Helixoia in Hecataeus of Abdera (*FGrH* 264F7); the islands of Hespera and Nysa in Dionysius Scytobrachion (*FGrH* 32F7–8); Iambulus' islands (Diod. Sic. 2.57–9); the Isle of Saturn (Plut., *De faciae*, 26); the Island of Leuke (Pind., *Ol.* 2.62–83; *Nem.* 4.49–51; Eur., *Andr.* 1259–62; *IA* 432–8; Arr., *Per.* 21; Paus. 3.19.12–13; Ant., Lib. *Met.* 27; Phlstr., *Her.* 51.7–53.2; Quint. Smyr. *Posthom.* 3.770–87; Plin., *HN* 4.93), etc.
21 For the proximity between Ogygia and Hades, the Elysian Fields, or the Island of the Blessed, see Anderson (1958); Ballabriga (1986: 118–23); Shelmerdine (1986: 55–7); Jaillard (2007: 31–3).
22 West: Hes., *Th.* 275; Eur., *Her.* 395; North: Pherec., *FGrH* 3F17; Apollod. 2.5.11; Libya: Hdt. 4.204; Ap. Rhod., *Argon.* 4.1390–9; Diod. Sic. 4.26; Plin., *NH* 5.3–4 and 31.5–7; Ptol., *Geogr.* 4.4.9–10.
23 On the eschatological connotations of Pindar's Island of the Blessed, see Solmsen (1982); Brown (1998); Cousin (2012, section 4).
24 See Beaulieu (2016: 59–89) for detailed analysis of Perseus's, Theseus's, and Jason's sea voyages (respectively, Pind., *Pyth.* 10; Bacchylides 17; and Pind., *Pyth.* 4).
25 See Lesky (1947: 188–214) on the sea as a constant symbol of danger in archaic Greek lyric.
26 Hes., *Cat.* fr. 53; Pind., *Nem.* 7.82–6, 8.6–8; *Isthm.* 8.16–24; *Pae.* 6.123–83; Apollod. 3.12.6; Hyg., *Fab.* 52; Paus. 2.29.2; Diod. Sic. 4.72.1, etc.
27 Hes., *Cat.* fr. 90; Moschus, *Europa*; *Anacreontea*, fr. 54, etc.
28 Black-figure hydriae from Caere (540–530 BCE), Louvre: E696.
29 See also Hom., *Od.* 2.260–1.
30 See also Homer (*Od.* 3.4–11, 30–66) for the hecatomb to Poseidon, made ἐπὶ θινὶ θαλάσσης in Pylos, in the presence of Nestor, but also that of Athena (disguised in Mentor) and of Telemachus.
31 For example, Pegasus (alone or with Chrysaor) sprang from the springs "that surround the headwaters of Ocean," as fruit of the union between Poseidon and Medusa: Hes., *Th.* 278–83; Pind., *Ol.* 13.63–4; Apollod. 2.4.2; Hyg., *Fab.* 151, etc.
32 See Beaulieu (2016: 90–118) on the girls of marrigeable age cast out to sea; for examples of myths of children's exposure, see Cursaru (2014).

Chapter 7

1 There is extensive bibliography dealing with the end of the Bronze Age civilizations. The recent synthesis by E. H. Cline (2014: 102–38) is on many points very useful.
2 Skyphos (*c.* 800–760 BCE), Eleusis 741 (Boardman 1998: fig. 41.1,2). See also a pedestalled krater (*c.* 800–760 BCE), New York Metropolitan Museum of Art (34.11.2), with a battle scene in and around two ships (Moore 2000).
3 Crater (*c.* 760–730 BCE) Ischia Sp 1/1 (Brunnsaker 1962; Ahlberg-Cornell 1992: 27; Boardman 1995: 202). See also Attic crater fragments (Brussels and Athens) which shows a battle at sea with dead bodies around the ship (Boardman 1998:

fig. 49). Also, *oinochoe* (wine jug), Munich Antikenmuseum 8696. The scene has been interpreted as the shipwreck of Odysseus (Brunnsaker 1962: 227–33; Ahlberg-Cornell 1992: 27–8, fig. 31).

4 Crater from Thebes (*c.* 735 BCE) attributed to the Subdipylon Group. London, British Museum 1899, 0219.1. For iconographical parallels, see bronze stand from the Idean Cave, Crete (eighth century BCE). Herakleion Museum (Langdon 2010: 216–19, figs. 4.14–16).

5 Crater from the Dipylon Cemetery, Athens (*c.* 750 BCE). Paris, Musée du Louvre A517 (Coldstream 1979: 110–13). See also oinochoe (*c.* 750–730 BCE) from the Thapsos Group (from Thebes), Berlin 3143.45; crater (*c.* 750–730 BCE) also from the Thapsos Group (from Thebes), Toronto 919.5.18 (Coldstream 1979: 170; Boardman 1998: figs. 118, 119).

6 Crater fragment (c. 750 BCE), from Argos, Argos Museum inv. C 240 (Coldstream 1979: fig. 45b; Boardman 1983: 18, figs. 2.4a–b; 1998: fig. 129.1,2).

7 Early Protoattic votive plaque (*c.* 700–675 BCE) from Sunium, attributed to the Analatos Painter. Athens, National Museum 14935 (Boardman 1998: fig. 192; Denoyelle 1996).

8 Ivory plaque from the shrine of Artemis Orthia, Sparta, seventh century BCE (Langdon 2010: 229, fig. 4.20).

9 Black-figure crater, signed Aristonothos (*c.* 650 BCE). From Caere (Southern Italy). Rome, Musei Capitolini.

10 Late Corinthian *aryballos*, from Boeotia (*c.* 575–550 BCE). Boston, Museum of Fine Art 01.8100. See also black-figure *oinochoe* (*c.* 500 BCE). New York, Market, Callimanopoulos.

11 Black-figure volute-krater, signed by the painter Kleitias and the potter Ergotimos (*c.* 570 BCE). Florence, Archeological Museum 4209.

12 Black-figure *dinos* (*c.* 530–510 BCE). Boston, Museum of Fine Arts 90.154.1–2. See also black-figure column krater attributed to the Likomedes Painter (*c.* 520–510 BCE). New York, Metropolitan Museum of Art 07.286.76. The painter added leaping dolphins between the ships. Also black-figure dinos attributed to the Antimenes Painter (*c.* 530–510 BCE). Malibu, The J. Paul Getty Museum 92.AE.88; black-figure dinos, Exekias (*c.* 540–530 BCE). Rome, Villa Giulia Museum 50599.

13 Black-figure *hydria*, Leagros Group (*c.* 515–500 BCE). Paris Cabinet des Médailles 255.

14 Black-figure dinos or crater from the sanctuary of the Dioskouroi (*c.* 560–550 BCE). London, British Museum 1888,0601.586.

15 Red-figure *lekythos* (*c.* 404–420 BCE). Berlin Antikensammlungen V.I. 3247. Two erotes, one with lyre, riding a dolphin. Red-figure cup attributed to Apollodoros (*c.* 500 BCE). Malibu, J. Paul Getty Museum 85. AE. 377. A sphinx carries away the body of a dead youth over the sea. The picture also has an erotic meaning. See Vermeule (1979: 145–78).

16 Tomb of the Diver. Paestum-Poseidonia (*c.* 480–470 BCE). Paestum Archeological Museum (Warland 1996; Holloway 2006). Also tomb of "Hunting and Fishing" in Tarquinia (*c.* 520 BCE): in a seascape, a young man dives into the sea.

17 Cup, black and red-figure (*c.* 510–490 BCE). London, British Museum E2. On the exterior of the cup: youth reclining, dancing and holding drinking vessel. Also black-figure band-cup from the "little master" workshop (*c.* 540–530 BCE). Paris, Musée du Louvre F145 (in the center: Poseidon or Nereus on a seahorse).

18 Corinthian amphora (*c.* 575–550 BCE). Berlin Staatliche Museen inv. F1652 (Perseus, Andromeda, and Ketos); column crater (corinthian), *c.* 550 BCE. Boston, Museum of Fine Art 63.420 (Heracles, Hesione, and Ketos).
19 Hydria from Caere (*c.* 530–500 BCE). Eagle Painter. Paris, coll. Niarchos (Boardman 1998: fig. 496).
20 For example, funerary amphora (red-figure, Apulian), connected to the Darius Painter (*c.* 350–330 BCE). Berlin, Antikensammlungen F 3241. Europa riding the bull, on her left, a Nereid riding a Ketos; plate (red-figure, Apulian), Phrixos Group Painter/Underworld Painter (*c.* 340 BCE). Berlin, Antikensammlungen 1984.47 (in the center: Apotheosis of Heracles, conducted on a chariot by Athena; on the edge: Nereids riding sea animals and ketos).
21 Black-figure dinos signed by Sophilos (*c.* 580–570 BCE). London, British Museum 1971,1101.1
22 Bronze shield-band (*c.* 575–550 BCE). Olympia Museum inv. 1881.
23 Black-figure lekythos, Istanbul Painter, *c.* 590–580 BCE. Paris, Musée du Louvre Ca 823.
24 For example, pediment of the Athena Temple on the Acropolis at Athens (c. 550–540 BCE) attributed to the Moscophoros Master. On the left corner: Heracles combating Triton. Athens, Acropolis Museum 35; same: limestone pediment found on the Acropolis, Heracles combating Triton (*c.* 560–550 BCE). Athens, Acropolis Museum 2. Black-figure amphora (*c.* 530 BCE). Toronto, Royal Ontario Museum 919.5.19. Heracles combating Triton. The sea is indicated by five dolphins and an octopus.
25 Red-figure cup signed by Euphronios (potter) and Onesimos (painter) (*c.* 500–490 BCE). Paris, Musée du Louvre G 104. The myth was also pictured on the wall of the Theseion in Athens dated *c.* 475 BCE (Pausanias 1.17.2–4). Compare with red-figure calyx-crater attributed to the Kadmos Painter (*c.* 420–400 BCE). Bologna, Museo Civico 303. The underwater field is indicated by a line from which Helios's chariot is emerging.
26 Pausanias 5.11.5–6.
27 Athena: red-figure lekythos, Brygos Painter (*c.* 480–470 BCE). New York Metropolitan Museum 25.189.1. Nike: red-figure lekythos, Paris Gigantomachy Painter (*c.* 480–470 BCE). Berlin, Antikensammlung F 221.
28 The black-figure technique remains in use until *c.* 475 BCE. It is called "late black-figure"(Boardman 2003: 146–51).
29 Pelike, red-figure, attributed to the Painter Myson (*c.* 500–480 BCE). Munich, Antikensammlungen 8762.
30 Red-figure calyx-crater, Polygnotean Group (*c.* 420 BCE). Bologna, Museo civico Archeologico 288 bis. Compare with volute-krater, red-figure, Apulian (*c.* 340–330 BCE). Geneva, collection Hellas and Roma inv. HR. 44. Helen and Paris arrive at Troy. Lower register, on left: the sea is depicted by the stern of a boat, ripples in added white, and little dots that indicate a pebbly beach.
31 For example, red-figure pelike, Marsysas Painter (*c.* 380–360 BCE). London, British Museum E424. Peleus seizing Thetis. The sea is suggested by a plunging dolphin.
32 Red-figure basin (Apulian) attributed to the Phrixos Painter (*c.* 330 BCE). Berlin, Antikensammlung F 3345. Phrixos: Gantz (1993: 179–80, 183). See also red-figure basin (Apulian), attributed to the Baltimore Painter (*c.* 330–320 BCE). Collection A.C (Aellen, Cambitoglou, and Chamay 1986: 229–31). Nike driving her chariot over the sea (Nereid riding a dolphin, fish, and shell).

33 Red-figure basin (Apulian), attributed to the Phrixos Group (*c.* 340–330 BCE). Private collection.
34 Fish plate, paestan, Asteas Painter workshop (*c.* 340–330 BCE). Collection J.C. The plate is decorated with an octopus, a wrasse, and a smooth-hound and different kind of seashells (Aellen, Cambitoglou, and Chamay 1986: 271–3). Also fish plate, campanian (from Cumae), related the Grassi Group (*c.* 350–330 BCE). London, Brisith Museum 1876,1112.1. A cuttlefish, a perch, and a torpedo. See McPhee and Trendall (1987, 1990).
35 Strabo 14.2.19; Pliny the Elder, *Natural History* 35.91; Suetonius, *Vespasian* 18; *Greek Anthology* 16.182, 178, 180, 179; Cicero, *De divinatio* I. 12.23; *De natura deorum* 27.75; Ovid, Amores, 1.14.31–34; Ovid, Tristia, 2.527–8. I. 14. 31–4; *Trist.* 2.527–8; etc. (See Reinach 1921: 332–9.)
36 Born from the sea foam and the severed testicles of Ouranos (the Sky) (Hesiod, *Theogony* 188–206). See Gantz (1993: 99–100).
37 Marble statuette of Aphrodite rising from the sea. Hellenistic *c.* 150–100 BCE. Boston, Museum of Fine Arts 1986.20. Also: lekythos in the shape of Aphrodite rising from an open shell. Mid-fourth century BCE. Boston, Museum of Fine Arts 00.269.
38 Mosaic, *opus vermiculatum*. Signed by Sophilos (late third century BCE). Alexandria, Greco-Roman Museum.
39 Nike of Samothrace. Marble from Paros (statue) and grey marble from Latros (ship prow) (*c.* 190 BCE). Paris, Musée du Louvre MA2369.
40 Pair of armbands, gold. Greek, Hellenistic *c.* 200 BCE. New York Metropolitan Museum of Art 56.11.5.6. Also silver-gilt lid of a cosmetic box from the Tomba dei Ori at Canosa (Southern Italy) (*c.* 250–200 BCE). A nereid riding a sea monster (ketos), the sea is pictured with spiral waves suggesting movement. Taranto, Museo Nazionale Archeologico (Stewart 2014: fig. 132).
41 Triton, acroterion from the Great Altar in Pergamon. Greek, Hellenistic *c.* 160 BCE. Berlin, Antikensammlung, Staatliche Museen, AvP VII 166–167 (Picón and Hemingway 2016, cat. 118–19).
42 Marble relief, front panel. Altar of Domitius Ahenobarbus (*c.* 150 BCE). Munich, Glyptothek inv. 239.
43 Mosaic of the House of the Dolphins. Delos, *c.* 130–88 BCE. Signed by [Askle]piades d'Arados (Syria). In situ.
44 Black-and-white mosaic. Triumph of Neptune, Baths of Neptune, Ostia (18.10 m × 10.40 m), (*c.* 139 CE).
45 Mosaic. Triumph of Neptune. Baths of the "House of Cato" (from Utica, Tunisia). End of second to early third century CE. Tunis, Bardo museum.
46 Atrium mosaic floor (4.90 m x 4.85 m). Triumph of Neptune. The four seasons. From la Chebba, Tunisia, mid-second century CE. Tunis, Bardo museum inv. 292.
47 For a comprehensive introduction to "Roman art" (with extensive bibliography), see Borg (2015: esp. 11–33) ("Defining Roman Art," C. H. Hallett). Always useful: Bandinelli (1970, 2010).
48 Landscapes with scenes from the *Odyssey* 9–12 (the land of the Laestrygonians, the House of Circe and the Underworld). Fresco, originally divided into eight panels and reassembled in pairs forming four rectangular panels (mid-first century BCE). Rome, Vatican Museum Cat. 41013, 41016, 41024, 41026.
49 For more on landscape painting in Roman art, see Leach (1988); Clarke (1996); Croisille (2005).

50 Perseus and Andromeda. Fresco from Pompeii (the House of the Priest Amandus, I.7.7), c. 40–79 CE. See also in the same house, Daedalus and Icarus, Polyphemos and Galatea.
51 For example, sarcophagus of Aurelius, third century CE. Rome, Thermae Museum 113 227. Sarcophagus from Volterra, third to fourth century CE. Florence, Archeological Musem (Touchefeu-Meynier 1968: cat. 301–17).
52 Also, Floor Mosaic, Basilica of the Bishop Theodoros Aquileia (c. 308–319 CE).
53 Silver plate, from Mildenhall, fourth century CE. Romano-British. London, British Museum 1946, 1007.1.

Chapter 8

1 Herodotus refers to the river Triton and Lake Tritonis also in 4.180.1 (the Machlyes and the Auseans are separated by river Triton, and live on the shores of Lake Tritonis), 4.188.1 (the inhabitants by Lake Tritonis sacrifice mainly to Athena, and then to Triton and Poseidon), and 4.191.1, 3 (the River Triton is mentioned as a land mark of Libya). See Asheri, Lloyd, and Corcella (2007: 701–3, 709, 713).
2 Euphemus accepts the clod of earth from Triton and has a dream, following which he throws the clod into the sea and the clod transformed into an island, Calliste (*Argon.* 4.1551–62, 1731–64). For the link between this myth and the Greek settlement in Libya and the foundation of Cyrene, see, for example, Malkin (1994: 161–4, 169–81, 198–9); Hunter (1993, 1996); and Stephens (2003: 171–237; 2008, 2011). Additionally, Hunter and Stephens maintain that, in writing his *Argonautica*, Apollonius Rhodius had the Ptolemaic context in mind and that he produced a myth for Ptolemaic rule in North Africa.
3 Cf. the version of Pindar (*Pyth.* 4). For Apollonius, see Hunter (2015, esp. 8–14).
4 This is indicated by Diodorus's remark that he saw the *rostra* before the Senate house on which the laws of the Twelve Tables had been engraved (12.26.1). This *rostra* was removed in 45 BCE by Caesar, who set up a new one in the redesigned *forum* (Diod. Sic. 51.19.2, 54.35.5, 56.34.4; Suet., *Aug.* 100.3; Frontin., *Aq.* 129).
5 See further, for example, Sacks (1990: 160–203); Sulimani (2011: 1–3 and passim); Muntz (2017: 1–21).
6 Diodorus's account of the Argonauts and his description of both Lake Tritonis and the river Triton are drawn from Dionysius Scytobrachion. Yet, Diodorus never produced an exact copy of his source, but altered and adapted it. See, for example, Sacks (1990); Sulimani (2011); and Muntz (2017).
7 It is interesting to compare this description with the letter allegedly written by the Amazons to Alexander the Great, incorporated in Pseudo-Callisthenes' history of the Macedonian king (3.25). In this letter, the Amazons attest to their happy life on an island that lies on the river Amazon. It takes a year to travel around this island and the river that surrounds it has no beginnings and only one entrance. The Amazons also attest to their way of life stating, *inter alia*, that they are warrior virgins whose men live on the other side of the river. See now the commentary of Nawotka (2017).
8 See Figure 8.1 for a map showing the location of Lake Tritonis and the river Triton according to Diodorus. This map also demonstrates other sites mentioned in this chapter and is used several times below to illustrate the journeys made by various figures to imaginary places. It thus offers a visual means to follow the progression of the main theme of this chapter.
9 Cf. Apollodorus of Athens (*apud* Strabo, 7.3.6 C 299), stating that a city named Dionysopolis exists in Libya, and that it is impossible for the same man to find it twice. Rusten (1982: 114–6) argues for the identification of this Dionysopolis with

Diodorus's Libyan Nysa. See also Eustathius (*Od.* 1644.59): Dionysopolis was a floating island, and hence it could not be found twice.

10 Athena's epithet Tritogeneia (appearing also in Hom., *Il.* 4.515; *Od.* 3.378; Hes., *Theog.* 924) is variously explained by the ancient authors. Pausanias (9.33.7), for instance, states that it derives from the river named Triton in Boeotia, while Diodorus (1.12.8) suggests that the meaning of Tritogeneia is "thrice-born," since the goddess' nature changes three times a year, in the spring, summer, and winter. See also Schol. Ap. Rhod. 1.109, 4.1311; Tztez., *ad Lycoph.* 519.

11 See also Apollonius Rhodius, *Argonautica* (4.811), where the name Elysian plain reappears, denoting the agreeable home of the dead.

12 But in the next section (5.20.5) Diodorus says that the Carthaginians prevented the Tyrrhenians from establishing a colony on the island, partly because of its excellence, and partly to keep it as a place of refuge in case of Carthage's destruction. Cf. pseudo-Aristotle, *Mirabilia Auscultationes* (84), depicting an island outside the Pillars of Heracles that was found by the Carthaginians, rich with forests and navigable rivers, as well as all kinds of fruit. Owing to its prosperity, the Carthaginians wished to prevent others from reaching it. For a discussion of Diodorus's treatment of this island, see Sulimani (2017: 224–8).

13 I follow the fragment numbers in McGushin (1992). The numbers in Maurenbrecher's 1891 edition are given in parentheses within parentheses. See also McGushin's commentary (1992: 164–7).

14 It is also possible that Plutarch followed other authors, such as Posidonius. See, for example, McGushin (1992: 166); García Moreno (1992: 141–51); and Konrad (1994: 106–8).

15 For Sertorius's episode of the Islands of the Blessed in Sallust, Plutarch, and Horace, see McAlhany (2016). On Horace's Epode 16, see Watson (2003: 479–533, esp. 514–30).

16 See, for example, Sacks (1990); Yarrow (2006: 152–6); Sulimani (2011); and Muntz (2017).

17 For the utopian idea and the "utopian genre," see, for example, Ferguson (1975) and Gabba (1981: esp. 55–60).

18 Cf. Virgil's reference to the golden age in his fourth *Eclogue*, written not long before Horace's *Epode* and affected by the same turbulent period.

19 See Gabba (1981: 59): "Escapism in the face of civil war may have replaced the egalitarian aspirations of the Hellenistic utopias."

20 See, for example, Cary and Warmington (1963: 125); Kidd (1988: 246); Konrad (1994: 106–9); and Roller (2006: 47–8); see also Martínez Hernández (1992: esp. chs. 3–5). For further suggestions, see Martín and Cobo (2004: 224).

21 Most of Euhemerus's account is found in Diodorus's Book 5, but part of it appears in the fragmentary Book 6 and is known to us from Eusebius' summary (*Praep. Evang.* 2.2.59B–61A). Euhemerus's *Hiera Anagraphe* is also preserved in Lactantius's *Institutiones Divinae*, with references to Ennius's now lost translation of Euhemerus's work into Latin. See Winiarczyk (1991, 2013).

22 According to some scholars, Panchaea may be identified with Taprobane (Sri Lanka). For various identifications of Panchaea, see Winiarczyk (2013: 18).

23 For the literary convention of *locus amoenus*, see Curtius (1953: 183–202). For Panchaea as *locus amoenus*, see Winiarczyk (2013: 18–19, 90).

24 See, for example, Schwarz (1982) and Weerakkody (1997: 171–7).

25 Iambulus is an obscure figure, mentioned only in Diodorus and Lucian (who describes him as the author of an enjoyable false story, *Ver. Hist.* 1.3, 22–6). It is assumed that

he wrote in the second or the first century BCE. See, for example, Winston (1976) and Clay and Purvis (1999: 46–8, 107–17).

26 On the role of the sea in funerary rituals and the significant location of the Greek *nekyomanteia* near the sea, see Beaulieu (2016: 26–31). On the connection between water and the oracles of the dead, see also Ogden (2001, 2004).

27 According to Diodorus, the Red Sea usually refers to the modern Persian Gulf and the Arabian Sea, but it may also include the modern Red Sea (the ancient Arabian Gulf), as in 3.18.3.

28 For examples of such expeditions, see Sulimani (2011: 169–70).

29 For example, Ahmad (1972: 126–31) and Nayak (2005: 555–6).

30 The Latin word *clementia* means clemency, tolerance, and their synonyms. The idea and the politics of clemency were inspired by Caesar's conduct. Having defeated his enemies, both Roman and foreign, and having taken captives, the Roman dictator excelled in his leniency toward them. As *clementia* was also a Roman goddess personifying the virtue of clemency, a temple was built in honor of *clementia Caesaris* (Caesar's clemency).

31 See Sulimani (2011: 82–109).

32 For a detailed discussion of the means by which Diodorus presents imaginary islands as part of the real world, see Sulimani (2017: 228–41). For a thorough comparison of Lipara and Panchaea, see de Angelis and Garstad (2006: 225–30).

33 For example, Alcaeus, fr. 307C (quoted in Himer. *Or*. 48.10–11); Hdt. 4.13, 32–3, 35–6; Hecataeus of Abdera, *FGrHist* 264 F12 (quoted in Aelian, *On Animals*, 11.1); Mela, 3.36–7; Pliny *NH* 4. 88. See, for example, Romm (1989); Bridgman (2005); and Beaulieu (2016: 151–3).

34 Pind., *Ol*. 3.43–5; *Isthm*. 4.12–3; *Nem*. 3.20–3, 4.69, and see below.

35 See the thorough discussion in Beaulieu (2016: esp. 60–9, 87–8). See also Romm (1992: 60–7); Brown (1992); and Kyriazopoulos (1993).

36 See Bridgman (2005: 127–40 with further references).

37 Cf. Gabba (1981: 59), maintaining that these islands interested those "who longed to escape from the present to an egalitarian dream-world."

38 See the recurrent references in Sacks (1990); Sulimani (2011); and Muntz (2017).

39 Some of Caesar's deeds accord well with the theory of the unity of mankind. For instance, he allowed men who had been given Roman citizenship into the senate, including half-barbarian Gauls, if Suetonius is to be trusted (Suet., *Iul*. 76, 80; cf. Cic., *Fam*. 9.15.2), and yet he also depicted a certain German king as a barbarian, irascible and thoughtless (Caesar, *Gallic Wars* 1.31).

40 Sulimani (2011: 315–330, 342–343).

41 See Beaulieu (2016: 61): "Pindar declares that mortals must not display *hybris*, an attitude that he compares to a foolhardy sailing expedition beyond the Pillars of Heracles." See also Sulimani (2011: 191–2).

42 For the journeys of Sesostris and other mythical figures, see Sulimani (2011, 2015). It is interesting to note that, unlike Euhemerus (Figure 8.2), Zeus (Figure 8.3), and Iambulus (Figure 8.4), Sesostris made a circular journey. In fact, many of Diodorus's heroes completed a circular expedition: setting out from one point, they returned to it at the end of their journey. Diodorus creates a well-defined perimeter within which his mythical heroes moved, spread their messages, and established their empires. Diodorus reflects the cyclical concept in his geographical descriptions, just as authors such as Plato and Polybius were concerned with this concept when discussing the cycle of governments.

43 For this idea in Hellenistic literature, see Mendels (1997: 81–99, 243–66; 1996: 446–7).

BIBLIOGRAPHY

Abramson, Herbert (1979), "A Hero Shrine for Phrontis at Sounion?," *California Studies in Classical Antiquity*, 12: 1–19.
Acquaro, Enrico, Antonino Filippi, and Stefano Medas, eds. (2010), *La devozione dei naviganti: Il culto di Afrodite Ericina nel Mediterraneo*, Lugano: Athenaion.
Adams, Colin (2018), "Nile River Transport under the Romans," in Andrew Wilson and Alan K. Bowman (eds.), *Trade, Commerce and the State in the Roman World*, 175–208, Oxford: Oxford University Press.
Adams, Winthrop Lindsay (2007), "The Hellenistic Kingdoms," in Glenn R. Bugh (ed.), *The Cambridge Companion to the Hellenistic World*, 28–51, Cambridge: Cambridge University Press.
Aellen, Christian, Alexander Cambitoglou, and Jacques Chamay (1986), *Le peintre de Darius et son milieu: vases grecs d'Italie méridionale*, Geneva: Association Hellas et Roma.
Ahlberg-Cornell, Gudrun (1984), *Herakles and the Sea-Monster in Attic Black-Figure Vase-Painting*. Acta Inst. Athen. Regni Sueciae Ser. in 4°, XXXIII, Sävedalen: Åström.
Ahlberg-Cornell, Gudrun (1992), *Myth and Epos in Early Greek Art: Representation and Interpretation*, Jonsered: Paul Åströms Förlag.
Ahmad, Enayat (1972), *Coastal Geomorphology of India*, New Delhi: Orient Longman.
Allen, John L. (1976), "Lands of Myth, Waters of Wonder: The Place of Imagination in the History of Geographical Exploration," in David Lowenthal and Martyn J. Bowden (eds.), *Geographies of the Mind. Essays in Historical Geosophy*, 41–61, New York: Oxford University Press.
Alvar Nuño, Antón (2017), "Riesgo marítimo, astrología y devoción en Roma," *Klio*, 99 (2): 528–44.
Álvarez Martí-Aguilar, Manuel (2017), "Talismans Against Tsunamis: Apollonius of Tyana and the stelai of the Herakleion in Gades (VA 5.5)," *Greek, Roman, and Byzantine Studies*, 57: 968–93.
Ambrose, Z. Philip (1980), "The Etimology and Genealogy of Palinurus," *American Journal of Philology*, 101: 449–57.

Ampolo, Carmine (1994), "La ricezione dei miti greci nel Lazio: l'esempio di Elpenore ed Ulisse al Circeo," *Parola del Passato*, 49: 268–80.
Ampolo, Carmine, ed. (2009a), *Immagine e immagini della Sicilia e di altre isole del Mediterraneo antico*, 2 vols, Pisa: Edizioni della Normale.
Ampolo, Carmine (2009b), "Isole di storia, storie di isole," in Carmine Ampolo (ed.), *Immagine e immagini della Sicilia e di altre isole del Mediterraneo antico,* vol. 1, 3–11, Pisa: Edizioni della Normale.,
Anderson, William S. (1958), "Calypso and Elysium," *Classical Journal*, 54: 2–11.
Arnaud, Pascal, ed. (2005), *Les routes de la navigation antique: Itineraires en Mediterranée*, Paris: Errance.
Asheri, David, Alan Lloyd, and Aldo Corcella (2007), *A Commentary on Herodotus Books I–IV*, Oxford: Oxford University Press.
Aubet, Maria Eugenia (1982), *El Santuario de Es Cuieram: Trabajos del Museo Arqueológico de Ibiza*, 8, Ibiza: Museo Arqueològic d'Eivissa i Formentera.
Aubet, Maria Eugenia, ed. (2001), *The Phoenicians and the West: Politics, Colonies, and Trade*, Cambridge: Cambridge University Press.
Babcock, W. H. (1919), "Saint Brendan's Explorations and Islands," *Geographical Review*, 8 (1): 37–46.
Badian, Ernst (1975), "Nearchus the Cretan," in Donald Kagan (ed.), *Studies in the Greek Historians*, 147–70, Cambridge: Cambridge University Press.
Ballabriga, Alain (1986), *Le Soleil et le Tartare: L'image mythique du monde en Grèce archaïque*, Paris: Éditions de l'EHESS.
Bandinelli, Ranuccio Bianchi (1970), *Rome, the Centre of Power: Roman Art to AD 200*, London: Thames & Hudson.
Bandinelli, Ranuccio Bianchi (2010), *Rome, la fin de l'art antique: l'art de l'empire romain de Septime Sévère à Théodose Ier*, Paris: Gallimard.
Barchiesi, Alessandro (1994), "Immovable Delos: *Aeneid* 3. 73–98 and the *Hymns* of Callimachus," *Classical Quarterly*, 44: 438–43.
Barringer, Judith M. (1995), *Divine Escorts: Nereids in Archaic and Classical Greek Art*, Ann Arbor: University of Michigan Press.
Barron, John P. (1980), "Bacchylides, Theseus and a Wooly Cloak," *Bulletin of the Institute of Classical Studies*, 27: 1–8.
Barron, W. R. J. and Glyn S. Burgess, eds. (2002), *The Voyage of St. Brendan: Representative Versions of the Legend in English Translation*, Exeter: Exeter University Press.
Basch, Lucien (1978), "Graffiti navals grecs," *Le Petit Perroquet*, 22: 40–54.
Basch, Lucien (1987), *Le musée imaginaire de la marine Antique*, Athens: Institute Hellénique pour la preservation de la tradition nautique.
Beaulieu, Marie-Claire (2015), "Ulysse et l'Hadès brumeux," *Les Études Classiques*, 83: 101–15.
Beaulieu, Marie-Claire (2016), *The Sea in the Greek Imagination*, Philadelphia: University of Pennsylvania Press.
Beaulieu, Marie-Claire (2018), "Θεῶν ἄγνισμα μέγιστον: la mer et la purification en Grèce Ancienne," *Kernos*, 32 (suppl.): 207–24.
Belén, María (2000), "Itinerarios arqueológicos por la geografía sagrada del Extremo Occidente," in Jordi H. Fernández Gómez and Benjamí Costa (eds.), *Santuarios fenício-púnicos en Iberia y su influencia en los cultos indígenas. Actas de las XIV Jornadas de Arqueología Fenicio-púnica*, 57–102, Ibiza: Museo Arqueològic d'Eivissa i Formentera.

Belén, María and Inmaculada Pérez (2000), "Gorham's Cave, un santuario en el Estrecho: Avance del estudio de los materiales cerámicos," in *Actas del IV Congreso Internacional de Estudios Fenícios y Púnicos*, bk 2, 531–42, Cádiz: Universidad de Cádiz.

Ben-Abed, Aïcha (2006), *Tunisian Mosaics: Treasures from Roman Africa*, Los Angeles: The Getti Conservation Institute.

Beresford, James, ed. (2012), *The Ancient Sailing Season: Mnemosyne Suppl. 351*, Leiden: Brill.

Bernard, Marie-Benoît (2007), "L'Odyssée monastique de Saint Brandan," *Collectanea Cisterciensia*, 69: 164–75.

Bierl, Anton F. H. (2004), "'Turn on the light !': Epiphany, the God-Like Hero Odysseus, and the Golden Lamp of Athena in Homer's 'Odyssey' (especially 19, 1–43)," *Illinois Classical Studies*, 29: 43–61.

Bisi, Anna Maria, Maria Giulia Amadasi Guzzo, and Vincenzo Tusa (1969), *Grotta Regina I*, Roma: Consiglio Nazionale delle Ricerche.

Blackman, David (2013), "Classic and Hellenistic Sheds," in David Blackman and Boris Rankov (eds.), *Shipsheds of the Ancient Mediterranean*, 16–29, Cambridge: Cambridge University Press.

Blakely, Sandra (2017), "Maritime Risk and Ritual Responses: Sailing with the Gods in the Ancient Mediterranean," in Philip de Souza and Pascal Arnaud (eds.), *The Sea in History: The Ancient World*, 362–79, Woodbridge: The Boydell Press.

Boardman, John (1983), "Symbol and Story in Geometric Art," in Warren G. Moon (ed.), *Ancient Greek Art and Iconography*, 15–36, Madison: Wisconsin University Press.

Boardman, John (1987), "Very Like a Whale: Classical Sea Monsters," in Ann E. Farkas, Prudence O. Harper, and Evelyn B. Harrison (eds.), *Papers in Honor of E. Porada*, 73–84, Mainz: Phillip von Zabern.

Boardman, John (1989), "Herakles at Sea," in *Festschr. N. Himmelmann*, 191–5.

Boardman, John (1994), *The Diffusion of Classical Art in Antiquity*, Princeton, NJ: Princeton University Press.

Boardman, John (1995), *Les Grecs outre-mer: colonisation et commerce archaïques*, Études (Centre Jean Bérard) 2, Naples: Centre Jean Bérard.

Boardman, John (1997), *Les vases athéniens à figures rouges: la période archaïque*, Univers de l'art, 63, Paris: Thames & Hudson.

Boardman, John (1998), *Early Greek Vase Painting: 11th–6th Centuries BC: A Handbook*, London: Thames & Hudson.

Boardman, John (2000), *Les vases athéniens à figures rouges: la période classique*, Univers de l'art, 85, Paris: Thames & Hudson.

Boardman, John (2003), *Athenian Black-Figure Vases*, London: Thames & Hudson.

Bonnet, Corinne and Laurent Bricault (2016), *Quand les dieux voyagent: Cultes et mythes en mouvement dans l'espace méditerranéen antique*, Geneva: Labor et Fides.

Borg, Barbara, ed. (2015), *A Companion to Roman Art*, Blackwell Companions to the Ancient World, Hoboken, NJ: John Wiley & Sons/Blackwell.

Braudel, Fernand (1972), *The Mediterranean and the Mediterranean World in the Age of Philip II*, London: Harper Collins.

Bravi, Alessandra (2015), "The Art of Late Antiquity," in *A Companion to Roman Art*, 130–49, Wiley-Blackwell.

Bricault, Laurent (2006), *Isis, Dame des flots*, Liège: Université de Liège.

Bricault, Laurent (2020), *Isis Pelagia: Images, Names and Cults of a Goddess of the Seas*, Leiden-Boston: Brill.
Bridgman, Timothy P. (2005), *Hyperboreans: Myth and History in Celtic-Hellenic Contacts*, New York and London: Routledge.
Brommer, Frank (1983), "Herakles und Nereus," in *Image & céramique grecque*, 103–10.
Brown, A. S. (1998), "From the Golden Age to the Isles of the Blest," *Mnemosyne*, 51: 385–410.
Brown, Christopher G. (1992), "The Hyperboreans and Nemesis in Pindar's Tenth Pythian," *Phoenix*, 46 (2): 95–107.
Brunnsaker, Sture (1962), "The Pithecusan Shipwreck: A Study of a Late Geometric Picture and Some Basic Aesthetic Concepts of the Geometric Figure-Style," *Opuscula Romana: Annual of the Swedish Institute in Rome*, 4: 165–242.
Bruun, Krister (2017), "La mentalità marinara di Ostia, città portuale, nella documentazione epigrafica e iconográfica," in Laura Chioffi, Mika Kajava, and Simo Örmä (eds.), *Il Mediterraneo e la Storia: II. Naviganti, popoli e culture ad Ischia e in altri luoghi della costa tirrenica*, 215–27, Rome: Acta Instituti Romani Finlandiae 45.
Bugh, Glenn R. (2006), "Hellenistic Military Developments," in Glenn R. Bugh (ed.), *The Cambridge Companion to the Hellenistic World*, 265–94, Cambridge: Cambridge University Press.
Burgess, Jonathan (1999), "Gilgamesh and Odysseus in the Otherworld," Echos du monde classique, 18 (2): 171–210.
Calame, Claude (1996), *Thésée et l'imaginaire athénien: légende et culte en Grèce antique*, 2nd rev. edn., Sciences humaines (Lausanne, Suisse), Lausanne: Éditions Payot.
Carlson, Deborah N. (2009), "Seeing the Sea: Ships' Eyes in Classical Greece," *Hesperia*, 78 (3): 347–65.
Carpenter, Thomas H., Kathleen M. Lynch, and E.G.D Robinson (2014), *The Italic People of Ancient Apulia. New Evidence from Pottery for Work Shop, Markets, and Customs*, New York: Cambridge University Press.
Caruso, Benedetto and Maria Teresa Di Blasi (2017), *Miracoli al fronte: Ex voto della grande guerra dalla provincia di Catania*, Catania: Regione siciliana, Assessorato dei beni culturali e dell'identità siciliana.
Caruso, Fabio (2012), "Il mare, il miele, il vino: Dioniso Morychos a Siracusa," in Fabio Caruso and Giuseppina Monterosso (eds.), *Dionysos: mito, immagine, teatro (Catalogo della mostra, Museo Archeologico Regionale Paolo Orsi, 10 maggio–30 settembre 2012)*, 19–26, Syracuse: Museo archeologico regionale Paolo Orsi.
Caruso, Fabio (2017), "Zeus *Peloros* e gli altri: un nuovo sguardo ai dipinti del 'sacello pagano' nella catacomba di Santa Lucia a Siracusa," in Elisa Chiara Portale and Giusj Galioto (eds.), *Scienza e archeologia: Un efficace connubio per la divulgazione della cultura scientifica*, 31–45, Pisa: Edizioni ETS.
Cary, Max and Eric Herbert Warmington (1963), *The Ancient Explorers*, 2nd edn., Baltimore: Penguin Books.
Casson, Lionel (1971), *Ships and Seamanship in the Ancient World*, Princeton, NJ: Princeton University Press.
Casson, Lionel (1981), "Maritime Trade in Antiquity," *Archaeology*, 34 (4): 37–43.
Casson, Lionel (1989), *The Periplus Maris Erythraei: Text with Introduction, Translation, and Commentary*, Princeton, NJ: Princeton University Press.

Casson, Lionel (1992), *The Ancient Mariners Seafarers and Sea Fighters of the Mediterranean in Ancient Times*, Princeton, NJ: Princeton University Press.

Casson, Lionel (1994a), *Ships and Seafaring in Ancient Times*, London: British Museum Press.

Casson, Lionel, ed. (1994b), *Travel in the Ancient World*, Baltimore: Johns Hopkins University Press.

Casson, Lionel (1995), *Ships and Seamanship in the Ancient World*, Baltimore: Johns Hopkins University Press.

Castriota, David (1992), *Myth, Ethos, and Actuality: Official Art in Fifth-Century B.C., Athens*, Madison, WI: University of Wisconsin Press.

Ceccarelli, Paola (1989), "Nesiotika," *Annali della Scuola Normale Superiore di Pisa*, 19: 903–35.

Ceccarelli, Paola (2009), "Isole e terraferma: la percezione della terra abitata in Grecia arcaica e classica," in Carmine Ampolo (ed.), *Immagine e immagini della Sicilia e di altre isole del Mediterraneo antico*, vol. 1, 31–50, Pisa: Edizioni della Normale.

Chami, Felix (2017), "Ancient Seafaring in Eastern African Indian Ocean Waters," in Philip de Souza and Pascal Arnaud (eds.), *The Sea in History: The Ancient World/La Mer dans l`Histoire: L`Antiquité*, 523–35, Woodbridge: The Boydell Press.

Chantraine, P. (1968), *Dictionnaire étymologique de la langue grecque: histoire des mots*, Paris: Klincksieck.

Chapouthier, Fernand (1935), *Les Dioscures au service d'une déesse*, Étude d'iconographie religieuse, Paris: De Boccard.

Chazalon, Ludi (1995), "Héraclès, Cerbère et la porte des Enfers dans la céramique attique," in Aline Rousselle (ed.), *Frontières terrestres, frontières célestes dans l'Antiquité*, 165–87, Perpignan: Presses universitaires de Perpignan.

Christian, Mark A. (2013), "Phoenician Maritime Religion: Sailors, Goddess Worship, and the Grotta Regina," *Die Welt des Orients*, 43 (2): 179–205.

Clarke, John R. (1996), "Landscape Paintings in the Villa of Oplontis," *Journal of Roman Archaeology*, 9: 81–107.

Clay, Diskin and Andrea L. Purvis (1999), *Four Island Utopias*, Newburyport: Focus Publishing.

Cline, Eric H. (2014), *1177 B.C.: The Year Civilization Collapsed*, Princeton, NJ: Princeton University Press.

Coacci Polselli, Gianna, Maria Giulia Amadasi Guzzo, and Vincenzo Tusa (1979), *Grotta Regina II*, Rome: Consiglio nazionale delle ricerche.

Coldstream, J. Nicolas (1979), *Geometric Greece*, London: Methuen.

Constantakopoulou, Christy (2007), *The Dance of the Islands: Insularity, Networks, the Athenian Empire, and the Aegean World*, Oxford: Oxford University Press.

Cook, Arthur Bernard (1940), *Zeus: A Study in Ancient Religion*, vol. 3, Parts 1 and 2, Cambridge: Cambridge University Press.

Corbett, Julian (1972), *Some Principles of Maritime Strategy*, London: Conway.

Cordano, Federica (2009), "La circumnavigazione come strumento di conoscenza," in Carmine Ampolo (ed.), *Immagine e immagini della Sicilia e di altre isole del Mediterraneo antico*, vol. 1, 133–40, Pisa: Edizioni della Normale.

Corner, Sean (2010), "Transcendent Drinking: The Symposium at Sea Reconsidered," *Classical Quarterly*, 60 (2): 352–80.

Cousin, Catherine (2012), *Le monde des morts: Espaces et paysages de l'Au-delà dans l'imaginaire grec d'Homère à la fin du Ve s. avant J.-C.*, Paris: L'Harmattan.

Creston, Robert Yves (1957), *Journal de bord de Saint Brendan à la recherche du paradis*, Paris: Éditions de Paris.

Croisille, Jean-Michel (2005), *La peinture romaine*, Paris: Picard.

Crowley, Janice L. (2013), *The Iconography of Aegean Seals*, Liège: Peeters.

Cunliffe, Barry, ed. (2002), *The Extraordinary Voyage of Pytheas the Greek*, rev. edn., New York: Walker & Company.

Cursaru, Gabriela (2014), "Exposition et initiation: enfants mythiques soumis à l'épreuve du coffre et abandonnés aux flots," in Chiara Terranova (ed.), *La presenza dei bambini nelle religioni del Mediterraneo antico*, 361–85, Rome: Aracne.

Curtis, Robert (1988), "Spanish Trade in Salted Fish Products in the 1st and 2nd Centuries AD," *International Journal of Nautical Archaeology*, 17 (3): 205–10.

Curtius, Ernst Robert (1953), *European Literature and the Latin Middle Ages*, trans. Willard R. Trask, New York: Pantheon Books.

D'Arms, J. H. and E. C. Kopff, eds. (1980), *The Seaborne Commerce of Ancient Rome: Studies in Archaeology and History*, Rome: Memoirs of the American Academy in Rome XXXVI.

Darwin, G. H. (1898), *The Tides and Kindred Phenomena in the Solar System: The Substance of Lectures delivered in 1897 at the Lowell Institute, Boston, MA*, Boston: Houghton, Mifflin and Company.

Davies, Malcolm (1992), "Heracles in Narrow Straits," *Prometheus*, 18: 217–26.

Davies, Mark I. (1978), "Sailing, Rowing and, Sporting in One's Cup on the Wine-Dark Sea: ἄλαδε, μύσται," in William A.P. Childs (ed.), *Athens Comes of Age: From Solon to Salamis*, 72–95, Princeton, NJ: Archaeological Institute of America, Princeton Society and the Department of Art and Archaeology, Princeton University.

Dawson, Helen (2016), *Mediterranean Voyages: The Archaeology of Island Colonisation and Abandonment*, London: Routledge.

de Angelis, Franco and Benjamin Garstad, (2006), "Euhemerus in Context," *Classical Antiquity*, 25: 211–42.

de Souza, Philip (1999), *Piracy in the Greco-Roman World*, Cambridge: Cambridge University Press.

de Souza, Philip and Pascal Arnaud, eds. (2017), *The Sea in History: The Ancient World/La Mer dans l' Histoire: L'Antiquité*, Woodbridge: Boydell Press.

De Vido, Stefania (2009), "Insularità, etnografia, utopie: il caso di Diodoro," in Carmine Ampolo (ed.), *Immagine e immagini della Sicilia e di altre isole del Mediterraneo antico*, vol. 1, 113–24, Pisa: Edizioni della Normale.

Delgado, James P. (2001), *Encyclopedia of Underwater and Maritime Archaeology*, London: The British Museum Press.

Demesticha, Stella, Katerina Delouca, Mia Gaia Trentin, Nikolas Bakirtzis, and Andonis Neophytou (2017), "Seamen on Land? A Preliminary Analysis of Medieval Ship Graffiti on Cyprus," *International Journal of Nautical Archaeology*, 46 (2): 346–81.

Demetriou, Denise (2010), "Τῆς πάσης ναυτιλίης φύλαξ: Aphrodite and the Sea," *Kernos*, 23: 67–89.

Denoyelle, Martine (1996), "Le Peintre d'Analatos: Essais de Synthèse et Perspectives Nouvelles," *Antike Kunst*, 39 (2): 71–87.

Depew, Mary (1998), "Delian Hymns and Callimachean Allusion," *Harvard Studies in Classical Philology*, 98: 155–82.

Desborough, Vincent Robin d'Arba (1972), *The Greek Dark Age*, London: Benn.

Détienne, M. ([1967] 1996), *The Masters of Truth in Archaic Greece*, New York: Zone Books.

Dickinson, Oliver (2010), "The Collapse at the End of the Bronze Age," in Erich H. Cline (ed.), *The Oxford Handbook of the Bronze Age Aegean (ca. 3000–1000 BC)*, 483–90, New York: Oxford University Press.

Dicks, D. R. (1960), *The Geographical Fragments of Hipparchus*, London: Athlone.

Dilke, O. A. W. (1998), *Greek and Roman Maps*, Baltimore MD: Johns Hopkins University Press.

Diodorus Siculus (1939), *Library of History*, Volume III: *Books*, trans. C. H. Oldfather, Cambridge, MA: Harvard University Press, from the Loeb Classical Library 340.

Domínguez Monedero, Adolfo (2018), "Las religiones coloniales y su impacto en los cultos indígenas de la Península Ibérica," *Revista de Historiografía*, 28: 13–46.

Dowden, Ken (1989), "Pseudo-Callisthenes, The Alexander Romance," trans. with introduction and notes in B. P. Reardon (ed.), *Collected Ancient Greek Novels*, 650–735, Berkeley, CA: University of California Press.

Duchêne, Hervé (1992), "Initiation et élément marin en Grèce ancienne," in *L'initiation: actes du colloque international de Montpellier, 11–14 avril 1991, II: L'acquisition d'un savoir ou d'un pouvoir, le lieu intiatique, parodies et perspectives*, 119–33, Montpellier: Université Paul Valéry.

Dunbabin, Katherine M. D. (1999), *Mosaics of the Greek and Roman World*, Cambridge: Cambridge University Press.

Eckenrode, T. R. (1975), "The Romans and Their Views on the Tides," *Rivista di cultura classica e medioevale*, 17: 269–92.

Edlund, Ingrid E. M. (1987), *The Gods and the Place: Location and Function of Sanctuaries in the Countryside of Etruria and Magna Graecia (700–400 B.C.)*, Stockholm: Paul Åström.

Edmondson, J. C. (1989), "Mining in the Later Roman Empire and Beyond: Continuity or Disruption?," *Journal of Roman Studies*, 79: 84–102.

Egeler, M. (2017), *Islands in the West: Classical Myth and the Medieval Norse and Irish Geographical Imagination*, Turnhout: Brepols N.V.

El-Geziry, Tarek M. and I. G. Bryden (2014), "The Circulation Pattern in the Mediterranean Sea: Issues for Modeller Consideration," *Journal of Operational Oceanography*, 3 (2): 39–46. https://doi.org/10.1080/1755876X.2010.11020116.

Étienne, Roland (2017), "Introduction: Can One Speak of the Seventh Century BC?" in Xenia Charalambidou and Catherine Morgan (eds.), *Interpreting the Seventh Century BC.*, 9–14, Oxford: Archaeopress Publishing.

Fabre, David, ed. (2004), *Seafaring in Ancient Egypt*, London: Periplus Publishing London.

Fagles, Robert, trans. (2009), *The Odyssey* (Penguin Classics), introduction and notes by Bernard Knox, London: Penguin.

Fasolo, Michele (2013), *Tyndaris e il suo territorio I, Introduzione alla carta archeologica del territorio di Tindari*, Rome: MediaGEO.

Faure, Paul (1964), *Fonctions des cavernes crétoises*, Paris: E. de Boccard.

Faure, Paul (1969), "Sur trois sortes de sanctuaires crétois," *Bulletin de Correspondance Hellénique*, 93: 174–213.

Febvre, Lucien (1932), *A Geographical Introduction to History*, London: Kegan Paul.

Fenet, Annick (2016), *Les dieux olympiens et la mer: Espaces et pratiques cultuelles*, Rome: École Française de Rome.

Ferdi, Sabah (1998), *Mosaïques des Eaux en Algérie: Un langage mythologique des pierres*, Algiers: Regie Sud Mediterranee.

Ferguson, Everett (2012), "Jonah in Early Christian Art," in Aliou Ciss. Niang and Carolyn Osiek (eds.), *Text, Image, and Christians in the Graeco-Roman World: A Festschrift in Honor of David Lee Balch*, XXXVIII –400 P., 342–53, Princeton Theological Monograph Series, 176, Allison Park, Pennsylvania: Pickwick Publ.

Ferguson, John (1975), *Utopias of the Classical World*, London: Thames & Hudson.

Ferrari-Pinney, Gloria and Brunilde Sismondo Ridgway (1981), "Herakles at the Ends of the Earth," *Journal of Hellenic Studies*, 101: 141–4.

Ferrer, Eduardo (2002), "Topografía sagrada del Extremo Occidente: santuarios, templos y lugares de culto de la Iberia púnica," in Eduardo Ferrer (ed.), *Ex oriente lux: las religiones orientales antiguas en la Península Ibérica*, 185–217, Seville: Universidad de Sevilla.

Filgueiras, Octávio Lixa (1995), "Some Vestiges of Old Protective Ritual Practice in Portuguese Local Boats," in Harry Tzalas (ed.), *Tropis III: 3rd International Symposium on Ship Construction in Antiquity, Athens 1989*, 149–66, Athens: Hellenic Institute for the Preservation of Nautical Tradition.

Fischer-Bossert, Wolfgang (2012), "The Coinage of Sicily," in William E. Metcalf (ed.), *The Oxford Handbook of Greek and Roman Coinage*, 142–56, Oxford: Oxford University Press.

Fitzpatrick, Matthew P. (2011), "Provincializing Rome: The Indus Ocean Trade Network and Roman Imperialism," *Journal of World History*, 22 (1): 27–54.

Fowler, Robert L. (2017), "Imaginary Itineraries in the Beyond," in Greta Hawes (ed.), *Myths on the Map: The Storied Landscapes of Ancient Greece*, 243–60, Oxford: Oxford University Press.

Foxhall, Lin (2005), "Village to City: Staples and Luxuries? Exchange Networks and Urbani-zation," in Robin Osborne and Barry Cunliffe (eds.), *Mediterranean Urbanization 800–600 BC*, Proceedings of the British Academy 126, 233–48, Oxford: Oxford University Press.

Friedman, Zaraza (2005/6), "Sea-Trade As Reflected in Mosaics," *SKYLLIS*, 1–2: 126–34.

Friedman, Zaraza (2006), "Kelenderis Ship – Square or Lateen Rig?," *International Journal of Nautical Archaeology*, 35 (1): 108–16.

Friedman, Zaraza (2008), "The Ship Depicted in a Mosaic from Migdal, Israel," *JMR*, 1–2: 45–54.

Friedman, Zaraza (2011), *Ship Iconography in Mosaics: An Aid to Understanding Ancient Ships and Their Construction*, Oxford: BAR International Series 2202.

Frost, F.J. (1968), "Scyllias: Diving in Antiquity," *Greece and Rome*, 2nd ser., 15: 180–5.

Frost, Honor (1969), "The Stone Anchors of Byblos," in *Mélanges offerts à M. Dunand, I, Mélanges de l'Université Saint-Joseph*, 45, fasc. 26, 423–42, Beirut: Dar el-Machreq SARL.

Frost, Honor (1970), "Some Cypriot Stone-Anchors from Land Sites and from the Sea," *Report of the Department of Antiquities Cyprus*: 14–24.

Frost, Honor (1991), "Anchors Sacred and Profane: Ugarit-Ras Shamra, 1986; the Stone Anchors Revised and Compared," in *Ras Shamra-Ougarit VI: Arts et Industries de la Pierre*, 355–410, Paris: ERC.

Gabba, Emilio (1981), "True History and False History in Classical Antiquity," *Journal of Roman Studies*, 71: 50–62.

Gabba, Emilio (1991), "L'insularità nella riflessione antica," in Francesco Prontera (ed.), *Geografia storica della Grecia antica*, 106–9, Rome: Laterza.

Gallagher, William R. (1999), *Sennacherib's Campaign to Judah*, New Studies, Leiden: Brill.
Gantz, Timothy (1993), *Early Greek Myth: A Guide to Literary and Artistic Sources*, Baltimore: Johns Hopkins University Press.
García Moreno, Luis A. (1992), "Paradoxography and Political Ideals in Plutarch's Life of Sertorius," in Philip A. Stadter (ed.), *Plutarch and the Historical Tradition*, 132–58, London: Routledge.
Gianfrotta, Piero A. (1975), "Le ancore votive di Sostrato di Egina e di Faillo di Crotone," *Parola del Passato*, 30: 311–18.
Giangiulio, Maurizio (1996), "Tra mare e terra: L'orizzonte religioso del paesaggio costiero," in Francesco Prontera (ed.), *La Magna Grecia e il mare: Studi di storia maritima*, 251–71, Taranto: Istituto per la storia e l'archeologia della Magna Grecia.
Ginouvès, René (1962), *Balaneutikè: Recherches sur le bain dans l'antiquité grecque*, Paris: E. de Boccard.
Glynn, Ruth (1981), "Herakles, Nereus and Triton: A Study of Iconography in Sixth-Century Athens," *American Journal of Archaeology*, 85 (2): 121–32.
Gomes, Francisco B. (2012), *Aspectos do sagrado na colonizaçâo fenícia*, Cadernos da UNIARQ 8, Lisbon: Centro de Arqueologia da Universidade de Lisboa.
Graham, Daniel W. (2010), *The Texts of Early Greek Philosophy: The Complete Fragments and Selected Testimonies of the Major Presocratics*, 2 vols, Cambridge: Cambridge University Press.
Gray-Fow, Michael J.G. (1993), "Qui mare teneat (Cicentury Att. 10.8): Caesar, Pompey, and the Waves," *Classica & Mediaevalia*, 44: 141–79.
Grottanelli, Cristiano (1981), "Santuari e divinità delle colonie d'Occidente," in *La religione fenicia: matrici orientali e sviluppi occidentali*, 109–133, Rome: CNR.
Guarducci, Margherita (1984), "Le insegne dei Dioscuri," *Archeologia Classica*, 36: 133–54.
Guizzi, Francesco (2009), "Creta nel Mediterraneo: insularità o isolamento?" in Carmine Ampolo (ed.), *Immagine e immagini della Sicilia e di altre isole del Mediterraneo antico*, vol. 1, 347–57, Pisa: Edizioni della Normale.
Hamiaux, Marianne, Jean-Luc Martinez, and Ludovic Laugier (2014), *La Victoire de Samothrace: Redécouvrir Un Chef-d'œuvre*, Paris: Musée du Louvre, Somogy.
Hahn, Robert (2001), *Anaximander and the Architects: The Contributions of Egyptian and Greek Architectural Technologies to the Origins of Greek Philosophy*, Albany: State University of New York Press.
Harley, J.B. and David Woodward, eds. (1987), *The History of Cartography*, vol. 1, Chicago: University of Chicago Press.
Harris, William V. (2018), "The Indispensable Commodity: Notes on the Economy of Wood in the Roman Mediterranean," in Andrew Wilson and Alan Bowman (eds.), *Trade, Commerce and the State in the Roman World*, 211–36, Oxford: Oxford University Press.
Harris, William V. and Kristine Iara, eds. (2011), *Maritime Technology in the Ancient Economy: Ship-design and Navigation*, Portsmouth, RI: JRA Supplementary Series Number 84.
Hartog, François (2001), *Memories of Odysseus: Frontier Tales from Ancient Greece*, trans. Janet Lloyd, Chicago: University of Chicago Press.
Hasselbach, Rebecca (2005), *Sargonic Akkadian: A Historical and Comparative Study of the Syllabic Texts*, Wiebaden: Harrassowitz.
Healy, John F. (1978), *Mining and Metallurgy in the Greek and Roman World*, London: Thames & Hudson.

Hedreen, Guy (1991), "The Cult of Achilles in the Euxine," *Hesperia*, 60: 313–30.
Hesiod (2006), *Theogony, Works and Days, Testimonia*, ed. and trans Glenn W. Most, Cambridge, MA: Harvard University Press, from the Loeb Classical Library 57.
Himmler, Florian, Heinrich Konen, and Josef Löffl (2009), *Exploratio Danubiae: Ein rekonstruiertes spätrömisches Flusskriegsschiff auf den Spuren Kaiser Julian Apostatas*, Berlin: Frank & Timme.
Hind, John G. F. (1996), "Achilles and Helen on White Island in the Euxine Sea: Side B of the Portland Vase," in Gocha R. Tsetskhladze (ed.), *New Studies on the Black Sea Littoral, Colloquia Pontica*, vol. 1, 59–62, Oxford: Oxbow Books.
Holland, Patrick (2014), *Navigatio*, Melbourne: Transit Lounge Australia.
Holloway, R. Ross (2006), "The Tomb of the Diver," *American Journal of Archaeology*, 110 (3): 365–88.
Holt, Philip (1992), "Heracles' apotheosis in lost Greek literature and art," *L'Antiquité classique*, 61: 38–59.
Holum, Kenneth G., A. Raban, and J. Patrich, eds. (1999), *Caesarea Papers 2: Herod's Temple, the Provincial Governor's Praetorium, and Granaries, the Later Harbor, and Other Studies*, Portsmouth, RI: JRA Supplementary Series Number 35.
Hooker, James T. (1988), "The Cults of Achilles," *Rheinisches Museum*, 13: 1–7.
Horden, Peregrine and Nicholas Purcell, eds. (2000), *The Corrupting Sea: A Study of Medi-terranean History*, Oxford: University Press.
Householder, F. and G. Nagy (1972), "Greek," *Current Trends in Linguistics*, 9: 735–816.
Hunter, Richard (1993), *The Argonautica of Apollonius: Literary Studies*, Cambridge: Cambridge University Press.
Hunter, Richard (1996), "The Divine and Human Map of the Argonautica," *Syllecta Classica*, 6: 13–27.
Hunter, Richard (2015), *Apollonius of Rhodes: Argonautica Book IV*, Cambridge: Cambridge University Press.
Iannello, Fausto (2010), "Brendano di Clonfert Homo Religiosus e Homo Viator: Note sull' Identiftà Spirituale di un Santo Asceta e Navigatore," *Fortunatae*, 21: 9–25.
Ibba, Maria Adele, Alfonso Stiglitz, Fabio Nieddu, Francesca Costa, Francesca Collu, Anna Luisa Sanna, and Maria Grazia Arru (2017), "Indagini archeologiche sul Capo Sant'Elia a Cagliari," *Quaderni: Rivista di Archeologia*, 28: 353–86.
Irby, Georgia L. (forthcoming), *Aspects of Hydrology in the ancient Greco-Roman World: Connected by Water*, London.
Jaillard, Dominique (2007), *Configurations d'Hermès. Une "théogonie" hermaïque*, Liège: CIERGA (= *Kernos*, Suppl. 17).
Jourdain-Annequin, Colette (1989), *Héraclès aux portes du soir*, Paris: Les Belles Lettres.
Jung, Reinhard (2010), "End of the Bronze Age," in Erich H. Cline (ed.), *The Oxford Handbook of the Bronze Age Aegean (ca. 3000–1000 BC)*, 171–84, New York: Oxford University Press.
Kahlaoui, Tarek (2018), *Creating the Mediterranean: Maps and Islamic Images*, Leiden: Brill.
Kahn, Charles H. (1979), *Art and Thought of Heraclitus: An Edition of the Fragments with Translation and Commentary*, Cambridge: Cambridge University Press.
Kajava, Mika (2002), "Marinai in tempesta," in Mustapha Khanoussi, Paola Ruggeri, and Cinzia Vismara (eds.), *L'Africa romana: lo spazio marittimo del Mediterraneo occidentale, geografia storica ed economía; Atti del XIV Convegno di studio, Sassari, 7–10 dicembre 2000*, 139–43, Rome: Carocci.

Kapitän, Gerhard (1989), "Archaeological evidence for rituals and customs on Ancient ships," in Harry Tzalas (ed.), *Tropis I: 1st International Symposium on Ship Construction in Antiquity*, Piraeus 1985, 147–62, Athens: Hellenic Institute for the Preservation of Nautical Tradition.

Karakantza, Efimia D. (2004), "Literary Rapes Revisited: A Study in Literary Conventions and Political Ideology," *Mètis*, n.s., 2: 29–45.

Kidd, I. G. (1972), *Poseidonius*, Cambridge: Cambridge University Press.

Kidd, I. G. (1988), *Posidonius: II. The Commentary*, (i) Testimonia and Fragments, 1–149, Cambridge: Cambridge University Press.

Kienast, Dietmar (1966), *Untersuchungen zu den Kriegsflotten der römischen Kaiserzeit*, Bonn: Habelt.

King, Charles (2004), *The Black Sea: A History*, Oxford: Oxford University Press.

Kissel, Theodor (1995), *Untersuchungen zur Logistik des römischen Heeres in den Provinzen des griechischen Ostens 27 v. Chr. – 235 n. Chr.*, St. Katharinen: Scripta-Mercaturae-Verlag.

Kohns, Oliver and Ourania Sideri (2009), *Mythos Atlantis: Texte von Platon bis J.R.R. Tolkien*, Stuttgart: Reclam.

Konrad, Christoph F. (1994), *Plutarch's Sertorius: A Historical Commentary*, Chapel Hill: University of North Carolina Press.

Kozlovskaya, Valeriya (2017), "Ancient Harbors of the Northwestern Black Sea Coast," in Valeriya Kozlovskaya (ed.), *The Northern Black Sea in Antiquity. Networks, Connectivity, and Cultural interaction*, 29–49, Cambridge: Cambridge University Press.

Kraay, Colin (1966), *Greek Coins*, New York: Abrams.

Kugler, H. (2007), *Die Ebstorfer Weltkarte*, Berlin: Oldenbourg Akademieverlag.

Kyriazopoulos, Athanase (1993), "The Land of the Hyperboreans in Greek Religious Thinking," *Parnassos*, 35: 395–98.

Lacroix, Léon (1965), *Monnaies et colonisation dans l'Occident grec*, Brussels: Palais des Académies.

Langdon, Susan (1989), "The Return of the Horse-Leader," *American Journal of Archaeology*, 93: 185–201.

Langdon, Susan (2010), *Art and Identity in Dark Age Greece, 1100–700 BC*, Cambridge: Cambridge University Press.

Larson, Jennifer (2001), *Greek Nymphs: Myth, Cult, Lore*, Oxford: Oxford University Press.

Lätsch, Frauke (2005), *Insularität und Gesellschaft in der Antike: Untersuchungen zur Auswirkung der Insellage auf die Gesellschaftsentwicklung*, Stuttgart: Franz Steiner Verlag.

Laurens, A.-F. (1996), "Héraclès et Hébé dans la céramique grecque ou Les noces entre terre et ciel," in Colette Jourdain-Annequin and Corinne Bonnet (eds.), *IIe rencontre héracléenne: Héraclès, les femmes et le féminin*, 235–58, Turnhout: Brepols N.V.

Laymond, Ramon and Diego Jiménez de Cisneros y Hervás (1906), in Fidel Fita, "Inscripciones griegas, latinas y hebreas," *Boletín de la Real Academia de la Historia*, 48: 157. Available online: http://www.cervantesvirtual.com/obra/inscripciones-griegas-latinas-y-hebreas-litoral-del-cabo-de-palos-mahn-palma-de-mallorca-0/ (accessed May 21, 2019).

Lazenby, John F. (1996), *The First Punic War. A Military History*, Abingdon: Routledge.

Leach, Eleanor Winsor (1988), *The Rhetoric of Space: Literary and Artistic Representations of Landscape in Republican and Augustan Rome*, Princeton, NJ: Princeton University Press.

Leier, Manfred (2001), *World Atlas of the Oceans*, Buffalo, NY: Firefly Books.
Leonardi, Giuseppe and Gerardo Rizzo (2011), *Da Didyme a Salina: Storia dell'isola di Salina dalla preistoria alla prima metà del Niovecento*, Messina: Intilla Editore.
Lesky, Albin (1947), *Thalatta: der Weg der Griechen zum Meer*, Vienna: Rohrer.
Levine, Daniel B. (1985), "Symposium and the Polis," in Thomas J. Figueira and Gregory Nagy (eds.), *Theognis of Megara*, 176–96, Baltimore: Johns Hopkins University Press.
Ling, Roger (2015), "Mosaics," in Barbara E. Borg (ed.), *A Companion to Roman Art*, 268–85, Hoboken, NJ: Wiley-Blackwell.
Lissarrague, François (1987), *Un Flot d'images: Une Esthétique Du Banquet Grec*, Paris: Éditions Adam Biro.
Lloyd, Christopher (1968), *The Navy and the Slave Trade*, London: Frank Cass.
López-Bertrán, Mireia, Agnès García-Ventura, and Michał Krueger (2008), "Could You Take a Picture of My Boat, Please? The Use and Significance of Mediterranean Ship representations," *Oxford Journal of Archaeology*, 27 (4): 341–57.
Lorenz, Katharina (2015), "Wall Painting," in Barbara E. Borg (ed.), *A Companion to Roman Art*, 252–67, Hoboken, NJ: Wiley-Blackwell.
Lovejoy, Jack (1972), "The Tides of New Carthage," *Classical Philology*, 67: 110–11.
Maddoli, Gianfranco (2009), "Le isole in Strabone," in Carmine Ampolo (ed.), *Immagine e immagini della Sicilia e di altre isole del Mediterraneo antico*, vol. 1, 125–32, Pisa: Edizioni della Normale.
Magee, Peter (2014), *The Archaeology of Prehistoric Arabia: Adaptation and Social Formation from the Neolithic to the Iron Age*, Cambridge: Cambridge University Press.
Malkin, Irad (1987), *Religion and Colonisation in Ancient Greece*, Leiden: Brill.
Malkin, Irad (1994), *Myth and Territory in the Spartan Mediterranean*, Cambridge: Cambridge University Press.
Malkin, Irad (1998), *The Returns of Odysseus: Colonization and Ethnicity*, Berkeley: University of California Press.
Malkin, Irad (2001), "The *Odyssey* and the Nymphs," *Gaia*, 5: 11–27.
Mantzilas, Dimitrios (2016), "Sacrificial Animals in Roman Religion: Rules and Exceptions," in Patricia A. Johnson, Attilio Mastrocinque, and Sophia Papaioannou (eds.), *Animals in Greek and Roman Religion and Myth*, 19–38, Newcastle upon Tyne: Cambridge Scholars Publishing.
Marín Ceballos, Maria Cruz, María Belén, and Ana Maria Jiménez (2010), "El proyecto de estudio de los materiales de la Cueva de Es Culleram," *Mainake*, 32: 133–57.
Marinatos, Nannó (1993), *Minoan Religion: Ritual, Image, and Symbol*, Columbia: University of South Carolina Press.
Marinatos, Nann. (2010), "Light and Darkness and Archaic Greek Cosmography," in Menelaos Christopoulos, Efimia Karakantza, and Olga Levaniouk (eds.), *Light and Darkness in Ancient Greek Myth and Religion*, 193–200, Lanham, MD: Lexington Books.
Markoe, Glenn (1996), "The Emergence of Orientalizing in Greek Art: Some Observations on the Interchange between Greeks and Phoenicians in the Eighth and Seventh Centuries B.C.," *Bulletin of the American Schools of Oriental Research*, 301: 47–67. https://doi.org/10.2307/1357295.
Marsden, Eric W. (1969), *Greek and Roman Artillery. Historical Development*, Cambridge: Cambridge University Press.
Martín, Alfredo Mederos and Gabriel Escribano Cobo (2004), "Los periplos de Eudoxo de Cízico en la Mauretania Atlántica," *Gerión*, 22: 215–33.

Martínez Hernández, Marcos (1992), *Canarias en la Mitología: Historia mítica del Archipiélago*, Santa Cruz de Tenerife: Centro de la Cultura Popular Canaria.
Maurenbrecher, Bertoldus (1891), *C. Sallusti Crispi Historiarum Reliquiae*, Leipzig: Teubner.
McAlhany, Joseph (2016), "Sertorius between Myth and History: The Isles of the Blessed Episode in Sallust, Plutarch &Horace," *Classical Journal*, 112 (1): 57–76.
McGrail, Seán (2001), *Boats of the World: From the Stone Age to Medieval Times*, Oxford: Oxford University Press.
McGushin, Patrick (1992), *Sallust: The Histories,* vol. 1, Oxford: Oxford University Press.
McKay, Alexander G. (1984), "Vergilian Heroes and Toponymy: Palinurus and Misenus," in Harold D. Evjen (ed.), *Mnemai, Classical Studies in Memory of K.K. Hulley*, 130–7, Chico, CA: Scholars Press.
McKechnie, R. (2002), "Islands of Indifference," in W. H. Waldren and J. A. Ensenyat (eds.), *World Islands in Prehistory: International Insular Investigations*, 127–34, Oxford: Archaeopress.
McPhee, Ian and Arthur Dale Trendall (1987), *Greek Red-Figured Fish-Plates*, Basel: Vereinigung der Freunde antiker Kunst.
McPhee, Ian and Arthur Dale Trendall (1990), "Addenda to Greek Red-Figured Fish-Plates," *Antike Kunst*, 33 (1): 31–51.
Meadows, Andrew (2013), "The Ptolemaic League of Islanders," in Kostas Buraselis, Mary Stefanou, and Dorothy J. Thompson (eds.), *The Ptolemies, the Sea and the Nile: Studies in Waterborne Power*, 19–38, Cambridge: Cambridge University Press.
Medas, Stefano (2004), *De rebus nauticis: L'arte della navigazione nel mondo antico*, Rome: "L'Erma" di Bretschneider.
Medas, Stefano (2010), "Gli occhi e l'anima propia delle barche: religiosità e credenze popolari tra antichità e tradizione," in Enrico Acquaro, Antonino Filippi, and Stefano Medas (eds.), *La devozione dei naviganti. Il culto di Afrodite Ericina nel Mediterraneo*, 11–23, Lugano: Athenaion.
Mederos, Alfredo (2009), "La fundación de la ciudad de Gadir y su primer santuario urbano de Astarté-Afrodita," *ISIMU*, 13: 183–207.
Meiggs, Russell (1980), "Sea-borne Timber Supply to Rome," in John H. D'Arms and E. Christian Kopff (eds.), *The Seaborne Commerce of Ancient Rome: Studies in Archaeology and History*, 185–96, Rome: Memoirs of the American Academy in Rome XXXVI.
Mendels, Doron (1996), "Pagan or Jewish? The Presentation of Paul's Mission in the Book of Acts," in Peter Schafer (ed.), *Geschichte – Tradition – Reflexion,* Vol. 1, *Judentum*, 431–52, Tübingen: Mohr Siebeck.
Mendels, Doron (1997), *The Rise and Fall of Jewish Nationalism: Jewish and Christian Ethnicity in Ancient Palestine*, 2nd edn., Grand Rapids, MI: Eerdmans.
Mili, Maria (2015), *Religion and Society in Ancient Thessaly*, Oxford: Oxford University Press.
Mohler, S. L. (1944–1945), "Caesar and the Channel Tides," *Classical Weekly*, 38: 189–91.
Mondi, Robert (1990), "Greek Mythic Thought in the Light of the Near East," in Lowell Edmunds (ed.), *Approaches to Greek Myth*, 141–98, Baltimore: Johns Hopkins University Press.
Moore, Mary B. (2000), "Ships on a 'Wine-Dark Sea' in the Age of Homer," *Metropolitan Museum Journal*, 35: 13–38.
Moreau, A. (1994), "Le voyage initiatique d'Ulysse," *Uranie*, 4: 25–66.
Moreno, Alfonso (2008), "HIERON: The Ancient Sanctuary at the Mouth of the Black Sea," *Hesperia*, 77: 655–709.

Moret, Pierre (1997), "*Planesiai*, îles erratiques de l'Occident grec," *Revue des Études Grecques*, 110: 25–56.

Morris, Ian (2009), "The Eighth-Century Revolution," in Kurt A. Raaflaub Hans van Wees (eds.), *A Companion to Archaic Greece*, 64–80, Malden, MA: Wiley-Blackwell. https://doi.org/10.1002/9781444308761.ch4.

Morrison, John S., John F. Coates, and Boris Rankov (2000), *The Athenian Trireme*, 2nd edn., Cambridge: Cambridge University Press.

Motte, André (1973), *Prairies et jardins de la Grèce antique: De la religion à la philosophie*, Brussels: Académie Royale de Belgique.

Mountjoy, P. A. (1984), "The Marine Style Pottery of LMIB/LH IIA: Towards a Corpus," *Annual of the British School at Athens*, 79: 161–219.

Mountjoy, P. A. (1985), "Ritual Associations for Marine Style Vases," in Pascal Darcque and Jean-Claude Poursat (eds.), *L'iconographie Minoenne*, 231–42, Athens: École Française d'Athènes.

Mountjoy, P. A. (1993), *Mycenaean Pottery: An Introduction*, Oxford: Oxford University Committee for Archaeology, 36.

Mourelatos, Alexander P.D. (2008), "The Cloud-Astrophysics of Xenophanes and Ionian Material Monism," in Patricia Curd and Daniel W. Graham (eds.), *The Oxford Handbook of Presocratic Philosophy*, 134–68, Oxford: Oxford University Press.

Muckelroy, Keith (1980), *Archaeology Under Water: An Atlas of the World's Submerged Sites*, New York: McGraw-Hill Book Company.

Müller, Dieter (1961), *Aegypten und die Griechischen Isis-Aretalogien*, ASAW, vol. 53.1, Berlin: Akademie-Verlag.

Mund-Dophcie, Monique (1998), "'Heureux qui comme Ulysse a fait un beau voyage ... ' Problèmes de géographie odysséenne à l'époque des Grandes Découvertes," in Acta colloquia Namurcansis habitis diebus 7–9 mensis Septembris anni 1995, Louvain, 213–29.

Muntz, Charles E. (2017), *Diodorus Siculus and the World of the Late Roman Republic*, Oxford: Oxford University Press.

Murray, Oswyn (2009), "The Culture of Symposion," in Kurt A. Raaflaub and Hans van Wees (eds.), *A Companion to Archaic Greece*, 508–23, Malden, MA: Wiley-Blackwell.

Naddaf, Gérard (1986), "Hésiode, précurseur des cosmogonies grecques de type « évolutionniste »," *Revue de l'histoire des religions*, 203–4: 339–64.

Nagy, Gregory (1973), "Phaethon, Sappho's Phaon, and the White Rock of Leukas," *HSPh*, 77: 137–77.

Nawotka, Krzysztof (2017), *The Alexander Romance by Ps.-Callisthenes: A Historical Commentary*, Leiden: Brill.

Nayak, Ganapati N. (2005), "Indian Ocean Coasts, Coastal Geomorphology," in Maurice L. Schwarz (ed.), *Encyclopedia of Coastal Science*, 554–7, Dordrecht: Springer.

Nenci, Giuseppe (1973), "Leucopetrai Tarentinorum (Cic., Att., 16, 6, 1) e l'itinerario di un progettato viaggio ciceroniano en Grecia," *Annali della Scuola Normale Superiore di Pisa. Classe di Lettere e Filosofia*, s. III, 3 (2): 387–96.

Nesselrath, Heinz-Günther (2005), "Where the Lord of the Sea Grants Passage to Sailors through the Deep-Blue Mere No More: The Greeks and the Western Seas," *Greece and Rome*, 52 (2): 154–71.

Nicoll, W. S. M. (1988), "The Sacrifice of Palinurus," *Classical Quarterly*, 38: 459–72.

Nigro, Lorenzo (2010), "L'orientamento astrale del Tempio del Kothon di Mozia," in Elio Antonello (ed.), *Il cielo e l'uomo: problema e metodi di astronomia culturale*;

Atti del VII Convegno Nazionale della Società Italiana di Archeoastronomia, Roma 2007, 15–24, Rome: Società Italiana di Archeoastronomia.
Nigro, Lorenzo and Federica Spagnoli (2012), *Alle sorgenti del Kothon: Il rito a Mozia nell'Area sacra di Baal 'Addir–Poseidon. Lo scavo dei pozzi sacri nel Settore Sud–Ovest (2006–2011), Quaderni di archeologia fenicio–punica/CM 02*, Rome: Università di Roma "La Sapienza."
Nigro, Lorenzo (2013), "Before the Greeks: The Earliest Phoenician Settlement in Motya. Recent Discoveries by Rome «La Sapienza» Expedition," *Vicino Oriente*, 17: 39–74.
Nigro, Lorenzo (2014), *The So-called "Kothon" at Motya: The sacred pool of Baal 'Addir/Poseidon in the light of recent archaeological investigations by Rome "La Sapienza" University – 2005–2013; Stratigraphy, architecture, and finds*, with the contribution of Federica Spagnoli, *Quaderni di archeologia fenicio-punica/CM 03*, Rome: Università di Roma "La Sapienza."
Nilsson, Martin Persson ([1921] 1967), *Geschichte der griechischen Religion*, vol. 1, Munich: Beck.
Nishimura-Jensen, Julie (2000), "Unstable Geographies: The Moving Landscape in Apollonius' *Argonautica* and Callimachus' *Hymn to Delos*," *Transactions of the American Philological Association*, 130: 287–317.
Ogden, Daniel (2001), "The Ancient Greek Oracle of the Dead," *Acta Classica*, 44: 167–95.
Ogden, Daniel (2004), *Greek and Roman Necromancy*, 2nd edn., Princeton, NJ: Princeton University Press.
Okhotnikov, S. B. and A. S. Ostroverkhov (1991), "L'île de Leuke et le culte d'Achille," *Pontica*, 24: 53–74.
Ormond, Henry A. (1924), *Piracy in the Ancient World*, Liverpool: Liverpool University Press.
Orselli, Alba Maria (2010), "Santi che navigano, santi dei naviganti," in Enrico Acquaro, Antonino Filippi, Stefano Medas (eds.), *La devozione dei naviganti: Il culto di Afrodite Ericina nel Mediterraneo*, 173–85, Lugano: Athenaion.
Ovtcharov, Nikolaj (1995), "Legendes et rites maritimes refletés dans les dessins graffiti des églises de Nessebar (XIV–XVIII s.)," in Harry Tzalas (ed.), *Tropis III: 3rd International Symposium on Ship Construction in Antiquity, Athens 1989*, 327–33, Athens: Hellenic Institute for the Preservation of Nautical Tradition.
Oleson, John Peter (2008), "Testing the Waters: the role of Sounding Weights in Ancient Mediterranean Navigation," *Memoirs of the American Academy in Rome*, Supplementary Vols, vol. 6, *The Maritime World of Ancient Rome*, 119–76.
Palmisano, Emanuela (2010), "La Dea e la Vergine. La festa di Santa Maria di Ognina," in Enrico Acquaro, Antonino Filippi, Stefano Medas (eds.), *La devozione dei naviganti. Il culto di Afrodite Ericina nel Mediterraneo*, 187–202, Lugano: Athenaion.
Parker, R. (1983), *Miasma: Pollution and Purification in Early Greek Religion*, Oxford: Clarendon Press.
Pearson, Lionel (1960), *The Lost Histories of Alexander the Great*, New York: American Philological Association.
Perea Yébenes, Sabino (2010), "Magic at Sea: Amulets for Navigation," in Richard Gordon and Francisco Marco (eds.), *Magical Practice in the Latin West*, RGRW 168, 457–86, Leiden: Brill.
Péron, Jacques (1974), *Les images maritimes de Pindare*, Paris: Librairie C. Klincksieck.

Philostratus ([1912] 1989), *The Life of Apollonius of Tyana (Books 1–4), The Epistles of Apollonius and the Teatrise of Eusebius*, with an English trans. F. C. Conybeare, vol. 1, Cambridge, MA: Harvard University Press, from the Loeb Classical Library.

Piccirillo, Michele (1993), *The Mosaics of Jordan*, Amman: ACOR.

Picón, Carlos A. and Seán Hemingway (2016), *Pergamon and the Hellenistic Kingdoms of the Ancient World*, Metropolitan Museum of Art, New Haven, CT: Yale University Press

Pinzone, Antonino (1999), "La fallita invasione alariciana della Sicilia tra visione provvidenzialistica cristiana e miracolistica pagana," in *Provincia Sicilia. Ricerche di storia della Sicilia romana da Gaio Flaminio a Gregorio Magno*, 271–9, Catania: Edizioni del Prisma.

Poccetti (1996), "Aspetti linguistici e toponomastici della storia maritima dell'Italia antica," in Francesco Prontera (ed.), *La Magna Grecia e il mare. Studi di storia maritima*, 35–73, Taranto: Istituto per la storia e l'archeologia della Magna Grecia.

Pocock, L. G. (1962), "The Nature of Ocean in the Early Epic," *Extrait de Proceedings of the African Classical Association*, 5: 1–17.

Pollitt, Jerome Jordan (1986), *Art in the Hellenistic Age*, Cambridge: Cambridge University Press.

Potter, Lawrence G. (2009), *The Persian Gulf in History*, Basingstoke: Palgrave MacMillan.

Potts, Daniel T. (2015), *The Archaeology of Elam: Formation and Transformation of an Ancient Iranian State*, Cambridge: Cambridge University Press.

Potts, Timothy F. (1989), "Foreign Stone Vessels of the Late Third Millennium BC from Southern Mesopotamia: Their Origins and Mechanisms of Exchange," *Iraq*, 51: 123–64.

Potts, Timothy F. (1993), "Patterns of Trade in Third-Millennium BC Mesopotamia and Iran," *World Archaeology*, 24: 379–402.

Pritchard, James (1969), *Ancient Near Eastern Texts Relating to the Old Testament*, 3rd edn. with Supplement, Princeton, NJ: Princeton University Press.

Prontera, Francesco, ed. (1996), *La Magna Grecia e il mare: Studi di storia maritima*, Taranto: Istituto per la storia e l'archeologia della Magna Grecia.

Purpura, Gianfranco (1979), "Raffigurazioni di navi in alcune grotte dei dintorni di Palermo," *Sicilia Archeologica*, 12: 58–70.

Quilici, Lorenzo (1992), "L'iscrizione del prumunturium Veneris al Circeo," in Lidio Gasperini, *Rupes loquentes: Atti Convegno Roma-Bomarzo 1989*, 407–29, Rome: Istituto italiano per la storia antica.

Quilici, Lorenzo and Stefania Quilici Gigli (2005), "La cosiddetta acropoli del Circeo: Per una lettura nel contesto topográfico," in Lorenzo Quilici and Stefania Quilici Gigli (eds.), *La forma della città e del territorio*, vol. 2, 91–146, Rome: "L'Erma" di Bretschneider.

Raaflaub, Kurt A. and Richard J. A. Talbert (2009), *Geography and Ethnography: Perceptions of the World in Pre-Modern Societies*, New York: Wiley-Blackwell.

Raaflaub, Kurt A. and Hans van Wees (2009), *A Companion to Archaic Greece*, Malden, MA: Wiley-Blackwell.

Raban Avner (1988), "The Boat from Migdal Nunia and the Anchorages of the Sea of Galilee from the Time of Jesus," *International Journal of Nautical Archaeology*, 17 (4): 311–29.

Raban, Avner (1999), "The Lead Ingots from the Wreck Site (area K8)," in Kenneth G. Holum, Avner Raban and J. Patrich (eds.), *Caesarea Papers 2: Herod's Temple, the Provincial Governor's Praetorium, and Granaries, the Later Harbor, and Other Studies*, 179–88, Portsmouth, RI: JRA Supplementary Series Number 35.

Radner, Karin (2010), "The Stele of Sargon II of Assyria at Kition: A Focus for an Emerging Cypriot Identity?," in Robert Rollinger, Birgit Gufler, and Martin Lang (eds.), *Interkulturalität in der Alten Welt: Vorderasien, Hellas, Ägypten und die vielfältigen Ebenen des Kontakts*, 429–51, Wiesbaden: Harrassowitz.

Rankov, Boris (2007), "The Olympias Trireme Reconstruction: A 'floating hypothesis' and Its Successor Projects," in *Historic Ships*, Royal Institution of Naval Architects International Conference February 21–22, 2007, 49–59, London: Royal Institution of Naval Architects Corporation.

Rankov, Boris (2010), "A War of Phases: Strategies and Stalemates 264–241," in Dexter Hoyos (ed.), *A Companion to the Punic Wars*, 149–66, Oxford: Wiley-Blackwell.

Rankov, Boris (2013), "Ships and Shipsheds," in David Blackman and Boris Rankov (eds.), *Shipsheds of the Ancient Mediterranean*, 76–101, Cambridge: Cambridge University Press.

Rankov, Boris (2017), "Ancient Naval Warfare, 700 BC – AD 600," in Michael Whitby and Harry Sidebottom (eds.), *The Encyclopedia of Ancient Battles*, vol. 1, 3–41, Malden, MA: Wiley Blackwell.

Redford, Donald B. (2000), "Egypt and Western Asia in the Late New Kingdom: An Overview," in Eliezer D. Oren (ed.), *The Sea Peoples and Their World: A Reassessment*, 1–20, Philadelphia: University of Pennsylvania Press.

Reece, Richard (1983), "Art in Late Antiquity," in Martin Henig (ed.), *A Handbook to Roman Art*, 234–48, Ithaca, NY: Cornell University Press.

Rehm, Rush (1994), *Marriage to Death: The Conflation of Wedding and Funeral Rituals in Greek Tragedy*, Princeton, NJ: Princeton University Press.

Reinach, Adolphe (1921), *Textes grecs et latins relatifs à l'histoire de la peinture ancienne*, Klincksieck.

Rice, E. E., ed. (1996), *The Sea and History*, Phoenix Mill: Sutton Publishing.

Rickman, Geoffrey (1996), "Mare Nostrum," in E. E. Rice (ed.), *The Sea and History*, 1–14, Phoenix Mill: Sutton Publishing.

Ridgway, David (1992), *The First Western Greeks*, Cambridge: Cambridge University Press.

Robertson, Noel (1984), "Poseidon's Festival at the Winter Solstice," *Classical Quarterly*, n.s., 34: 1–16.

Rochberg, Francesca (2012), "The Expression of Terrestrial and Celestial Order in Ancient Mesopotamia," in Richard J. A. Talbert (ed.), *Ancient Perspectives: Maps and Their Place in Mesopotamia, Egypt, Greece, and Rome*, 9–46, Chicago: University of Chicago Press.

Rodgers, William L. (1937), *Greek and Roman Naval Warfare*, Annapolis, MD: Naval Institute Press.

Roller, Duane W. (2003), *The World of Juba II and Kleopatra Selene: Royal Scholarship on Rome's African Frontier*, London: Routledge.

Roller, Duane W. (2005), "Seleukos of Seleukia," *Antiquite Classique*, 74: 111–18.

Roller, Duane W. (2006), *Through the Pillars of Herakles: Greco–Roman Exploration of the Atlantic*, New York: Routledge.

Roller, Duane W. (2010), *Eratosthenes' Geography: Fragments Collected and Translated with Additional Material*, Princeton, NJ: Princeton University Press.

Roller, Duane W. (2014), *The Geography of Strabo: An English Translation, with Introduction and Notes*, Cambridge: Cambridge University Press.

Roller, Duane W. (2018), *A Historical and Topographical Guide to the Geography of Strabo*, Cambridge: Cambridge University Press.

Romero Recio, Mirella (1998), "Conflictos entre la religiosidad familiar y la experiencia sacra de los navegantes griegos," *ARYS: Antigüedad: religionesy sociedades*, 1: 39–50.

Romero Recio, Mirella (1999), "El rito de las piedras volteadas (Str. 3.1.4)," *ARYS: Antigüedad: religionesy sociedades*, 2: 69–82.

Romero Recio, Mirella (2000), *Cultos marítimos y religiosidad de navegantes en el mundo griego antiguo*, BAR International Series 897, Oxford: John and Erica Hedges and Archaeopress.

Romero Recio, Mirella (2008), "Rituales y prácticas de navegación de fenicios y griegos en la Península Ibérica durante la Antigüedad," *Mainake*, 30: 75–89.

Romero Recio, Mirella (2010), "Extrañas ausencias. Las fiestas marítimas en el calendario litúrgico griego," *Dialogues d'Histoire Ancienne*, 36 (1): 51–117.

Romm, James S. (1989), "Herodotus and Mythic Geography: The Case of the Hyperboreans," *Transactions of the American Philological Association*, 119: 97–113.

Romm, James S. (1992), *The Edges of the Earth in Ancient Thought: Geography, Exploration, and Fiction*, Princeton, NJ: Princeton University Press.

Roseman, Christina Horst (1994), *Pytheas of Massilia: On the Ocean; Text, Translation and Commentary*, Chicago: Ares.

Rossignoli, Benedetta (2004), *L'Adriatico Greco: Culti e miti minori*, Rome: "L'Erma" di Bretschneider.

Rusten, Jeffrey S. (1982), *Dionysius Scytobrachion*, Opladen: Westdeutscher Verlag.

Rutter, N. K. (2012), "The Coinage of Italy," in William E. Metcalf (ed.), *The Oxford Handbook of Greek and Roman Coinage*, 128–41, Oxford: Oxford University Press.

Sabin, Philip and Philip De Souza (2007), "Battle," in Philip Sabin, Hans van Wees, and Michael Whitby (eds.), *The Cambridge History of Greek and Roman Warfare*, 399–460, Cambridge: Cambridge University Press.

Sacks, Kenneth S. (1990), *Diodorus Siculus and the First Century*, Princeton, NJ: Princeton University Press.

Sacks, Richard (1989), *The Traditional Phrase in Homer: Two Studies in Form, Meaning and Interpretation*, Leiden: Brill.

Saija, Marcello and Alberto Cervellera (1997), *Mercanti di mare: Salina 1800–1953*, Messina: Trisform.

Sater, William F. (2007), *Andean Tragedy: Fighting the War of the Pacific, 1879–1884*, Lincoln: University of Nebraska Press.

Savoldi, E. (1996), "Ieros Ichtus. Sacralita e proibizione nell' epica greca arcaica," *ASNP*, 1 ser. 4: 61–91.

Scarpi, P. (1988), "Il ritorno di Odysseus e la metafora del viaggio iniziatico," in Marie-Madeleine Mactoux and Évelyne Geny (eds.), *Mélanges Pierre Lévêque*, vol. 1, *Religion*, 245–59, Paris: Université de Besançon.

Schäfer, Christoph (2006), *Kleopatra*, Darmstadt: Wissenschaftliche Buchgesellschaft.

Schaps, David (2010), *Handbook for Classical Research*, London: Routledge.

Scheidel, Walter (2011), "A Comparative Perspective on the Determinants of Scale and Productivity of Roman Maritime Trade in the Mediterranean," in William V. Harris and Kristine Iara (eds.), *Maritime Technology in the Ancient Economy: Ship-design and Navigation*, 21–37, Portsmouth, RI: JRA Supplementary Series Number 84.

Schepens, Guido (2004), "Die Westgriechen in antiker und moderner Universalgeschichte: Kritische Überlegungen zum Sosylos-Papyrus," in Rüdiger

Kinsky (ed.), *Diorthoseis: Beiträge zur Geschichte des Hellenismus und zum Nachleben Alexander des Großen*, 73–107, Leipzig: K. G. Saur.

Schnapp-Gourbeillon, Annie (2002), *Aux Origines de la Grèce (XIIIe–VIIIe siècles avant notre ère): La genèse du politique*, Histoire, Paris: Les Belles Lettres.

Schulz, Raimund (2016), *Abenteurer der Ferne: Die großen Entdeckungsfahrten und das Weltwissen der Antike*, 2nd edn. Stuttgart: Klett-Cotta.

Schwarz, Franz F. (1982), "The Itinerary of Iambulus: Utopianism and History," in Günther Dietz Sontheimer and Parameswara Kota Aithal (eds.), *Indology and Law: Studies in Honour of J. Duncan M. Derrett*, 18–55, Wiesbaden: Franz Steiner Verlag.

Segal, Charles P. (1965), "The Tragedy of the Hippolytus: the Waters of Ocean and the Untouched Meadow," *Harvard Studies in Classical Philology*, 70: 117–69.

Semple, Ellen Churchill (1927), "The Templed Promontories of the Ancient Mediterranean," *Geographical Review*, 17 (3): 353–86.

Semple, Ellen Churchill (1931), *The Geography of the Mediterranean Region: Its Relation to Ancient History*, New York: Henry Holt and Company.

Severin, Timothy (1978), *The Brendan Voyage*, New York: McGraw-Hill.

Shapiro, Harvey Alan (1994), *Myth Into Art: Poet and Painter in Classical Greece*, Abingdon: Routledge.

Shelmerdine, Susan C. (1986), "Odyssean Allusions to the Fourth Homeric Hymn," *Transactions of the American Philological Association*, 116: 49–63.

Smith, D. J. (1983), "Mosaics," in Martin Henig (ed.), *A Handbook of Roman Art*, 116–38, Ithaca, NY: Cornell University Press.

Snodgrass, Anthony M. (1980), *Archaic Greece, the Age of Experiment*, London: J. M. Dent & Sons.

Snodgrass, Anthony M. (2000), *The Dark Age of Greece: An Archaeological Survey of the Eleventh to the Eighth Centuries BC*, Oxfordshire: Taylor & Francis.

Snodgrass, Anthony M. (2011), *Homer and the Artists: Text and Picture in Early Greek Art*, Cambridge: Cambridge University Press.

Solmsen, Friedrich W. (1982), "Achilles on the Islands of the Blessed: Pindar *vs.* Homer and Hesiod," *American Journal of Philology*, 103: 19–24.

Solmsen, Friedrich (1989), "The Two Near Eastern Sources of Hesiod," *Hermes*, 117: 413–22.

Sourvinou-Inwood, Christiane (1995), *"Reading" Greek Death: To the End of the Classical Period*, Oxford: Oxford University Press.

Sourvinou-Inwood, Christiane (2011), *Athenian Myths and Festivals: Aglauros, Erechtheus, Plynteria, Panathenaia, Dionysia*, Oxford: Oxford University Press.

Spagnoli, Federica (2013), "Demetra a Mozia: Evidenze dall'area sacra del Kothon nel V secolo a.C.," *Vicino Oriente*, 17: 153–64.

Speidel, Michael (2007), "Außerhalb des Reiches? Zu neuen römischen Inschriften aus Saudi Arabien und zur Ausdehnung der römischen Herrschaft am Roten Meer," *Zeitschrift für Papyrologie und Epigraphik*, 163: 296–306.

Speller, Ian (2004), "In the Shadow of Gallipoli? Amphibious Warfare in the Inter-War Period," in Jenny Macleod (ed.), *Gallipoli: Making History*, 136–81, London: Frank Cass.

Stark, Francis R. (1897), *The Abolition of Privateering and the Declaration of Paris*, New York: Columbia University Press.

Starr, Chester G. (1955), "The Myth of the Minoan Thalassocracy," *Historia*, 3: 282–91.

Starr, Cindy (2016), "Annual Arctic Sea Ice Minimum 1979–2015, with graph," NASA Scientific Visualization Studio, March 10. Available online: https://svs.gsfc.nasa.gov/4435 (accessed October 9, 2020).

Stephens, Susan A. (2003), *Seeing Double: Intercultural Poetics in Ptolemaic Alexandria*, Berkeley: University of California Press.

Stephens, Susan A. (2008), "Ptolemaic Epic," in Theodore D. Papanghelis and Antonios Rengakos (eds.), *Brill's Companion to Apollonius Rhodius*, 2nd edn., 95–114, Leiden: Brill.

Stephens, Susan A. (2011), "Remapping the Mediterranean: The Argo Adventure in Apollonius and Callimachus," in Dirk Obbink and Richard Rutherford (eds.), *Culture in Pieces: Essays on Ancient Texts in Honour of Peter Parsons*, 188–207, Oxford: Oxford University Press.

Stewart, Andrew (2014), *Art in the Hellenistic World: An Introduction*, Cambridge: Cambridge University Press.

Stiglitz, Alfonso (2014), "'parva Cynosura. Hac fidunt duce nocturna Phoenices in alto': Archeologia e astronomia, una navigazione oltre l'orizzonte," in *La misura del tempo: Atti del 3° Congresso Internazionale di Archeoastronomia in Sardegna. 13° Convegno Società Italiana di Archeoastronomia. Cronache di Archeologia*, 11: 35–45.

Suárez Otero, José (2017), "Dioses del Mar Exterior. Punta do Muiño y la religión púnica en el Atlántico," in *X Coloquio Internacional del CEFYP. Mare sacrum. religión, cultos y rituales fenicios en el mediterráneo Homenaje al Profesor D. José María Blázquez Martínez*. Available online: https://www.academia.edu/35476018/Dioses_del_Mar_Exterior (accessed May 14, 2018).

Sulimani, Iris (2011), *Diodorus' Mythistory and the Pagan Mission: Historiography and Culture-Bringers in the First Pentad of the Bibliotheke*, Leiden: Brill.

Sulimani, Iris (2015), "Egyptian Heroes Travelling in Hellenistic Road Networks: The Representation of the Journeys of Osiris and Sesostris in Diodorus," *ARAM Periodical*, 27 (1–2): 81–96.

Sulimani, Iris (2017), "Imaginary Islands in the Hellenistic Era: Utopia on the Geographical Map," in Greta Hawes (ed.), *Myths on the Map: The Storied Landscapes of Ancient Greece*, 221–42, Oxford: Oxford University Press.

Tallet, Pierre (2012), "Ayn Sukhna and Wadi el-Jarf: Two Newly Discovered Pharaonic Harbours on the Suez Gulf," *British Museum Studies in Ancient Egypt and Sudan*, 18: 147–68.

Taub, Liba (2003), *Ancient Meteorology*, London: Routledge.

Taylor, Andrew (2012), "Battle Manoeuvers for Fast Triremes," in Boris Rankov (ed.), *Trireme Olympias: The Final Report*, 231–43, Oxford: Oxbow.

Tchernia, André, P. Pomey, Antoinette Hesnard (1978), *L'Épave Romaine de la Madrague de Giens* (Var); Campagnes 1972–1975, XXXIV supplément à Gallia, Paris: Éditions du Centre National de la Recherche Scientifique.

Topper, Kathryn (2012), *The Imagery of the Athenian Symposium*, Cambridge: Cambridge University Press.

Torr, Cecile (1964), *Ancient Ships*, Chicago: Argonaut.

Touchefeu-Meynier, Odette (1968), *Thèmes odysséens dans l'art antique*, Paris: de Boccard.

Tracy, Robert (1996), "Sailing Strange Seas of Thought: Imrama, Máel Duin to Muldoon," in Kathryn Klas, Eve E. Sweetser, and Claire Thomas (eds.), *A Celtic Florilegium: Studies in Memory of Brendan Ó Hehir*, 169–86, Lawrence, MA: Celtic Studies Publications.

Tran Tam Tinh, Vincent (1964), *Le culte d'Isis a Pompéi*, Paris: de Boccard.

Treuil, René, Pascal Darcque, Jean-Claude Poursat, and Gilles Touchais (2008), *Les Civilisations Égéennes Du Néolithique et de l'âge Du Bronze*, 2nd edn., Nouvelle Clio, L'histoire et Ses Problèmes, Paris: Presses Universitaires de France.
Tripputi, Anna Maria (1995), *Bibliografia degli ex voto*, Bari: Paolo Malagrinò.
Tsangari, Dimitra I. (2015), "Images of the Sea on the Coins of Ancient Greek Colonies," in *Greek Colonisation*, 183–91.
Twede, Diana (2002), "The Packing Technology and Science of Ancient Transport Amphoras," *Packaging Technology and Science*, 15: 181–95.
Tzalas, Harry, ed. (1995), *Tropis III: 3rd International Symposium on Ship Construction in Antiquity, Athens 1989*, Athens: Hellenic Institute for the Preservation of Nautical Tradition.
Van Berchem, Denis (1985), "Le port de Séleucie Pièrie et l'infrastructure logistique des guerres parthiques," *Bonner Jahrbücher*, 185: 47–87.
Vermeule, Emily (1979), *Aspects of Death in Early Greek Art and Poetry*, Berkeley: University of California Press.
Vian, Francis (1952), "Génies des passes et des défilés," *Revue archéologique*, 39: 129–55.
Viera y Clavijo, J. de ([1772] 1991), *Historia de Canarias*, vol. 1, Madrid: Viceconsejeria de Cultura y Deportes Gobierno de Canarias.
Vilate, Sylvie (1991), *L'insularité dans la pensée grecque*, Paris: Les Belles Lettres.
Vinson, Steve (1994), *Egyptian Boats and Ships*, Oxford: Shire.
Vitruvius (1962), *On Architecture*, Volume II, trans. F. Granger, Cambridge, MA: Harvard University Press, from the Loeb Classical Library.
Völcker-Janssen, Wilhelm (1987), "Klassische Paradeigmata: Die Gemälde des Panainos im Zeus-Tempel zu Olympia," *Boreas: Münstersche Beiträge zur Archäologie*, 10: 11–31.
Wachsmann, Shelley (1998), *Seagoing Ships and Seamanship in the Bronze Age Levant*, College Station: Texas A&M University Press.
Wachsmann, Shelley (2000), "To the Sea of the Philistines," in Eliezer D. Oren (ed.), *The Sea Peoples and Their World: A Reassessment*, 103–44, Philadelphia: University of Pennsylvania Press.
Wachsmuth, Dietrich (1967), Pompimos ho Daimon: Untersuchung zu den antiken Sakralhandlungen bei Seereisen, PhD diss., Freien Universität Berlin.
Waddelove, E. and A.C. Waddelove (1990), "Archaeology and Research into Sea-level during the Roman Era: Towards a Methodology based on Highest Astronomical Tide," *Britannia*, 21: 253–66.
Walcott, Derek (2017), "The Sea Is History." Available online: https://poets.org/poem/sea-history (accessed 23 October 2020).
Wallinga, Herman T. (1956), *The Boarding Bridge of the Romans*, Groningen: J. B. Wolters.
Wallinga, Herman T., ed. (1993), *Ships and Sea-Power before the Great Persian War. The Ancestry of the Ancient Trireme*, Leiden: Brill.
Watkins, Calvert (1985), *The American Heritage Dictionary of Indo-European Roots*, Boston: Houghton Mifflin.
Warland, Daisy (1996), "La Tombe 'du Plongeur'," *Revue de l'histoire Des Religions*, 213 (2): 143–60.
Watson, Lindsay C. (2003), *A Commentary on Horace's Epodes*, Oxford: Oxford University Press.
Weerakkody, D. P. M. (1997), *Taprobane: Ancient Sri Lanka as Known to the Greeks and Romans*, Turnhout: Brepols.

West, M. L. (1966), *Hesiod: Theogony*, Oxford: Oxford University Press.
Westrem, Scott D. (2001), *The Hereford Map: Transcription and Translation of the Legends*, Turnhout: Brepols.
White, K. D. (1984), *Greek and Roman Technology*, London: Thames & Hudson.
Whitewright, Julian (2016), "Sails, Sailing and Seamanship in the Ancient Mediterranean," in Christoph Schäfer (ed.), *Connecting the Ancient World. Mediterranean Shipping, Mari-time Networks and their Impact (Pharos 38)*, 1–26, Rahden: Verlag Marie Leidorff GmbH.
Wilcken, Ulrich (1906), "Ein Sosylos-Fragment in der Würzburger Papyrussammlung," *Hermes*, 41: 103–41.
Wilson, Andrew and Alan Bowman, eds. (2018), *Trade, Commerce and the State in the Roman World*, Oxford: Oxford University Press.
Wilson, Malcolm (2013), *Structure and Method in Aristotle's Meteorologica*, Cambridge: Cambridge University Press.
Winiarczyk, Marcus (1991), *Euhemeri Messenii Reliquiae*, Stuttgart: Teubner.
Winiarczyk, Marcus (2000), "La mort et l'apothéose d'Héraclès," *Wiener Studien*, 113: 13–29.
Winiarczyk, Marcus (2013), *The "Sacred History" of Euhemerus of Messene*, Berlin: De Gruyter.
Winston, David (1976), "Iambulus' Islands of the Sun and Hellenistic Literary Utopias," *Science Fiction Studies*, 3: 219–27.
Wirth, Gerhard (1972), "Nearchos. Der Flottenchef," *Acta Conventus XI "Eirene" diebus XXI–XXV mensis octobris anni MCMLXVIII*: 615–39.
Wolfson, Stan (2008), *Tacitus, Thule and Caledonia: The Achievements of Agricola's Navy in Their True Perspective*, Oxford: Oxbow.
Yarrow, Liv Mariah (2006), *Historiography at the End of the Republic: Provincial Perspectives on Roman Rule*, Oxford: Oxford University Press.
Young, Gary K., ed. (2001), *Rome's Eastern Trade: International Commerce and Imperial Policy 31 BC–AD 305*, London: Routledge.
Younger, John G. (2010), "Mycenaeans Seals and Sealings," in Erich. H Cline (ed.), *The Oxford Handbook of the Bronze Age Aegean (ca. 3000–1000 BC)*, 329–39, Oxford: Oxford University Press.
Zamora López, José Ángel, José M. Gutiérrez López, M. Cristina Reinoso del Río, Antonio M. Sáez Romero, Francisco Giles Pacheco, J. Clive Finlayson, and Geraldine Finlayson (2013), "Culto y culturas en la cueva de Gorham (Gibraltar): La historia del santuario y sus materiales inscritos," *Complutum*, 24 (1): 113–30.
Żyromski, Marek (2001), *Praefectus Classis: the Commanders of Roman Imperial Navy during the Principate*, Poznań: Adam Mickiewicz University Press.

CONTRIBUTORS

Gabriela Cursaru is Research Associate at the University of Montréal. Her main areas of expertise are Greek Religion, Ancient Greek literature, philosophy, and cultural history in general, and her research is focused on topics related to spatiality, sacred space, and time representations in Ancient Greek religious thought. She is the author of *Parcourir l'invisible: Les espaces insondables à travers les mouvements des dieux dans la pensée religieuse grecque de l'époque archaïque* (2019), a book which investigates the ways in which archaic Greek thought symbolically came to grips with three elements of physical reality which can never be thoroughly accessed by humans: the ether, the air, and the marine abyss. Another topic of her research is devoted to the bodily or noetic ascent of mortals across the ether or through the air and she is equally interested by the mortals' descent to the Underworld and their fascination with the faraway/beyond and has published numerous articles on this topic, including editing "Katábasis, *the descent to the Underworld in Ancient Greek Tradition and Religious Thought*" (2 volumes, 2015, coedited with Pierre Bonnechère). She is currently involved in an extensive research project on the motif of the whirlpool in Greek religious thought.

Zaraza Friedman received her PhD in 2005 from the Department of Maritime Civilizations, at the University of Haifa, Israel. She is a marine archaeologist and an independent scholar. Her main area of expertise is the iconography of ships, mainly in mosaics, which she developed while carrying out research on mosaics that depict ships in the Eastern Mediterranean (Israel and Jordan) for her MA thesis. This research immediately developed into a PhD dissertation on mosaics with depictions of ships for the entire Mediterranean. Since then, she has published many articles. Her PhD dissertation was published in an extensive volume *Ship Iconography in Mosaics – An Aid to Understanding Ancient Ships and Their Construction*, BAR International Series 2202 (2011).

Georgia L. Irby is Professor of Classical Studies at William and Mary, in Williamsburg, Virginia. She studied Mathematics and Latin at the University of Georgia, Athens, and she holds a PhD in Classical Philology from the University of Colorado at Boulder. She is the author of several articles on cartography in the ancient world, the interstices of science and culture, Greco-Roman medicine, astrology, and Greek pedagogy. Her books include *The Encyclopedia of Ancient Natural Scientists: The Greek Tradition and Its Many Heirs* (2008, with Paul T. Keyser); *Greek Science of the Hellenistic Era: A Sourcebook* (London, 2002, with Paul T. Keyser); *A New Latin Primer* (2015, with Mary C. English); a *Little Latin Reader* (2017; second edition, with Mary C. English). Her two volumes on water in the Greco-Roman world are forthcoming from Bloomsbury.

Mirella Romero Recio is Professor of Ancient History at the Universidad Carlos III, Madrid. She holds a Bachelor's degree in Geography and History from the Universidad Complutense, where she obtained her PhD in 1999. She furthered her studies in different international research centres, namely England, Italy and France. She is the author of several books, including *Ecos de un descubrimiento: Viajeros españoles en Pompeya* (2012), *Pompeya. Vida, muerte y resurrección de la ciudad sepultada por el Vesubio* (2010), and *Cultos marítimos y religiosidad de navegantes en el mundo griego antiguo* (2000), and has published a number of papers in prestigious scientific journals and publishers. She is an *Academica correspondiente* of the Real Academia de la Historia, and codirects the *Revista de Historiografía*.

Raimund J. Schulz is Professor of Ancient History in the Department of History at Bielefeld University in Germany. He studied History, Latin and Science of Education at the University of Göttingen. He received his PhD in Ancient History from the Technical University at Berlin, where he earned his Habilitation and was Assistant Professor before being appointed full professor at Bielefeld. His main research interests are nautical history, empire-building, discovery, and world history of antiquity. Among his books are *Abenteurer der Ferne: Die großen Entdeckungsfahrten und das Weltwissen der Antike* (2016, second edition; Italian and Polish translations forthcoming), *Feldherren, Krieger und Strategen. Krieg in der Antike von Achill bis Attila* (2018, third edition), *Kleine Geschichte des antiken Griechenland* (2010, second edition), and *Die Antike und das Meer* (2005). He is currently working on a new world history of antiquity.

Iris Sulimani is Senior Lecturer at the Open University of Israel. She is the author of *Diodorus' Mythistory and the Pagan Mission: Historiography and Culture-heroes in the First Pentad of the Bibliotheke* (2011) and has published other works on historiography, mythography, and geography of the Hellenistic period. She is currently working on Diodorus's mythography as well as Plutarch's biographies of mythical figures.

Valérie Toillon is currently a visiting researcher in the Department of Art history and Cinematographic studies at the University of Montreal, Canada. She received her PhD in 2014 in Art History. Her fields of research are the iconography and iconology of Ancient Greek Art, especially in archaic and classical times. Since 2015 she has been working on the digitization of a corpus of Greek and Latin texts connected to Ancient Greek and Roman painting, the Digital Milliet Project, based on the so-called *Recueil Milliet* sourcebook of texts on Greek and Roman painting, originally published in 1921 by A. Reinach. The project is hosted at Tufts University.

Jorit Wintjes is tenured Senior Lecturer in Ancient History and Digital Humanities at the Julius-Maximilians-Universität in Würzburg, Germany. His research interests include ancient Lydia, ancient Greek rhetoric in late antiquity, and ancient military history. He also works on the history of nineteenth-century military technology and on the history of wargaming. He has authored multiple scientific articles on these topics. His most recent book is *Die römische Armee auf dem Oceanus* (2020). He is also the author of *Lords of Asia Minor: An Introduction to the Lydians* (2016, with A. Payne), *Die ecloga des Theodulus* (2012, with K. Goehl), and *Das Leben des Libanius* (2005).

INDEX

2001: A Space Odyssey (film) 18

acanthus leaves 166
Achilles 123
Aegina 121
Aelius Aristides 60, 62
Aelius Gallus 108
Agathocles 96
Alexander of Macedon 31, 39, 101, 144
Alexander Romance, The 19
Amazons 175–6
amphorae 66, 68–71
amulets 49
Anaximander of Miletus 23, 141
anchors 48, 49
Aphrodite 55–6, 165
Apollo 121
Apollonius Rhodius 174, 177
Argonauts 44, 174–5
Aristotle 28–30, 33, 34, 36
armbands 166
Arrian 40
art 153–72
artillery 97–8
Astarte 47, 51, 55–6
Athena 54, 137, 176
Athenaeus 52
Atlantis 17
Augustus 108
Avalon 17

Baal 'Addir 47
Battle of the Delta 90–1
Berenike II 166
black diorite 89
black-figure technique 158–9, 161
blockade 85, 86
boarding bridges 98
Brendan, Saint 7–13

Caesar, Julius 31, 105–6
Callimachus (*Hymn to Delos*) 110–11
Calypso 14, 114, 116, 118, 119, 123–4
Canaries 16–17
Cape Malea 120
capstan 74
cargo records 72–3
carreras 131
Carthage 135–6
caves 45–6, 124–5
Chalkidean Strait 33–4
Charybdis 33, 34
Chloris 121
Christianity
  arts 170–1
  shrines 51
Cinaethus 52
Circe 14, 33, 116, 118, 124–5
classes 102
coastal travel 131
coinage 163

INDEX

communication, sea-borne 85, 86
Constantinus 104
corvus 98
cranes 73
craters 157, 158
currents 33–5, 131
Cybernesia festival 52

Darius 143–4
Delta, Battle of 90–1
Demetrios I Poliorketes 97
Democritus of Abdera 26–7
depth of sea 35–6
destruction horizons 154
Diagoras 56–7
Diodorus Siculus 52–3, 175–7, 178, 179–80, 181–2, 183–7, 188–91
Diomede 129
Dionysius of Halicarnassus 64
Dionysos *Morychos* 55
Dionysus 176
Dioscuri 55, 57
diving 36–7
dystopias 118–19

Eidothea 126
Elpenor 52
Empedocles of Acragas 26
Eratosthenes 34
Es Culleram caves 45–6
Eudoxus 146, 178–9
Euhemerus 181
Euripides 1, 3
Europa 121
exile 118
eyes, prow of ships 49–50

female ritual initiations 120–2
fire pots 98–9
fish consumption 2
floating islands 110
Flora 121
Fortuna Redux mosaic 68
funerary iconography 170
funerary vessels 156, 158

garum 60–1
Germanicus 106
Gilgamesh 14

gold mining 64–5
Gorham's cave 46
graffiti 46
grain trade 60, 61, 62
Grotta Regina 46
Gyrae 120

Hades 121
Halios Geron 9
Hanno 136
harbor activities 71–2
Hecataeus 23
Hell 12
Heracles 2, 9, 15–16, 163
Heracles-Melqart 48–9
Heraclitus of Ephesus 25–6
Herodotus 35, 92, 134, 137, 138, 174, 177
Hesiod 1–2, 20–1, 43
Hesperides 119
Hieron 45
Hiram, King 133–4
Homer 21, 31, 33, 34, 35
Horace 179, 180
Hymn to Delos (Callimachus) 110–11
Hyperboreans 187–91

Iambulus 183–6, 187
initiation rituals 119–22
Isis 57
islands 109–27
    floating 110
    Island of the Sun 183–6, 187
    Islands of the Blessed 177–80

Jasconius 12
Jason and the Argonauts 44, 174–5
jewelry 166
Jonah 170
Josephus 75
Judas 13
Justinian 105

Kaleb 106
Kelenderis mosaic 72
Kothon of Motya 47, 58
Kreousa 121
Kubrick, Stanley 18
Kyrene 121
Kyrenia wreck 70

lead trade 64, 65
light 55–7
Lipara 187
lookouts 87

Madrague de Giens 70–1
Malea, Cape 120
male ritual initiations 119–20
Maništušu 89
maps 16–17, 23
Melqart 51
Menelaus 9, 118, 126, 129
mercenaries 137
merchantmen 71, 73, 74–5
mermaids 10–11
Messina Strait 33, 52–4
metal trade 64–6
Midakritos 139
Miletus 23
mining for metal 64–5
Misenus 52
mosaic-work 63, 65–6, 68–9, 71–2, 73, 167–8

Naram-Sîn 89
Nausithous 51–2
naval siege 101
naval warfare 79–108, 143
Navigatio Sancti Brendani Abbatis 7–13
Nearchus 39–40, 98
Necho II 134
Nereus 9, 161–2
Nestor 129

oared ships 74, 75, 93, 94, 97, 133
octopus stirrup jars 154
Odysseus 1, 2, 10, 14, 118, 119, 123, 124, 129, 136–7
Ogygia 119
Okeanos 161
olive oil trade 60
Olympias 83
Onesicritus 39–40
Oppian 36
Orion 52, 54

paintings 164–5
    on vases 156, 159, 160–1, 163–4
    on walls 164, 168–70

Palinurus 52
Panchaea 181–3, 186, 187
passenger ships 74–5, 141
Paul the Hermit 13
Peloria 52
Pelorus 51
Pepi I 88
Periplus of the Erythraean Sea 40–1
Persephone 121
Phaeax 51–2
Phaedo (Plato) 27–8
Phaon 163
Philoctetes 125
Phoenicians 48–9, 51, 92, 93–4, 133–6, 137–9, 178
phosphoric deities 56
Phrixos Group 164
Phrontis 52
Pillars of Heracles 8, 51, 115, 190
pilots
    festival 52
    sanctuaries dedicated to 51
Pindar 187–9, 190–1
piracy 104, 137
Plato 27–8
Pliny the Elder 114, 179
Pomponius Mela 34
Poseidon 52, 54, 110–12
Poseidonius of Apamea 19–20, 30, 32–3, 36, 178–9
pottery 154, 156–9, 160–1, 163–4
Proteus 9, 126
Psammetichus 36
Punic Wars 100, 101
purification 3, 124
Puteoli 62
Pytheas of Massilia 19–20, 31, 139

raiders 86
ram 93, 94
Ramesses III 90
reconstructions, warships 83–4
red-figure technique 163–4
reefs 35
religion 43–58, 170–1
Rimini harbor mosaic 71
ritual 3, 44–9, 119–22, 124, 126

INDEX

sacrifice 16, 35, 44, 47, 49, 51, 52, 55, 57, 124
saints 51
    Brendan 7–13
Sallust 179, 180
saltwater 3, 25, 26, 29–30
sanctuaries 47–9, 51–2, 54
Sargon II 92
Sargon the Great 89
Scipio Africanus 31
sculpture 165, 166
Scylla 33
sea control 85–6
sea denial 85
sea monsters 161–2
seawater 3, 25, 26, 29–30
Seleucus of Seleucia 31–2
self-exile 118
Sennacherib 92
Sertorius 179
Sesostris 191–2
Severin, Tim 8
sexual initiations 120–2
ships
    attributing human qualities to 49–50
    graffiti 46
    merchantmen 71, 73, 74–5
    oared 74, 75, 93, 94, 97, 133
    passenger ships 74–5, 141
    warships 83–4, 92–7, 143
shipwrecks 56–7, 70, 156–7
shores 115–16, 122–7
shrines 51
siege of Tyre 101
silk roads 148
silver mining 64
Skylax 144
Skyllias 37
Skyllus 37
Socrates 27–8, 124
Sophocles 130
soundings 35–6
spice trade 60–1
stars 57–8
Statius Sebosus 179
Strabo 31, 34, 46–7, 179, 180
symposion 160

tabularius 72–3
Tartessos 134–5
tetreres 97
thalassocracy 85
Thales of Miletus 21–3, 141
Theogony (Hesiod) 1–2, 20–1
Theseus 162
throwing objects into the sea 54–5
Thucydides 59
tides 30–3
timber trade 62–4
"Tomb of the Diver" 159–60
torsion artillery 97–8
trade 59–76, 89, 135–6, 137, 138–9, 141, 145, 146–7, 148
trireme 83, 94–5
Triton 162, 174, 175, 176–7
Tyre, siege 101

Uni 88
utopias 118–19

vase-painting 156, 159, 160–1, 163–4
Vello, Pedro 17
Venerianus 104
Victory of Samothrace 166
votive offerings 46, 56–7, 165

wall paintings 164, 168–70
warfare 79–108, 143
warships 83–4, 92–7, 143
whirlpools 33, 34–5
white rocks 45
winds 35, 40, 131
wine drinking 160–1
wine trade 60, 70
women, ritual initiations 120–2
wood trade 62–4

Xenophanes of Colophon 24–5
Xerxes 96

Zephyrus 121
Zeus 121, 181
Zeus *Peloros* 52, 54